Horror
Film
READER

Also by Alain Silver

David Lean and His Films

The Vampire Film

The Samurai Film

Film Noir: An Encyclopedic Reference to the American Style, Editor

Robert Aldrich: a guide to references and resources

The Film Director's Team

Raymond Chandler's Los Angeles

More Things Than Are Dreamt Of

What Ever Happened to Robert Aldrich?

Roger Corman: Metaphysics on a Shoestring

The Noir Style

Film Noir Reader, Editor

Film Noir Reader 2, Editor

Also by James Ursini

David Lean and His Films

The Life and Times of Preston Sturges, An American Dreamer

The Vampire Film

Film Noir: An Encyclopedic Reference to the American Style, Editor, 3rd Edition

More Things Than Are Dreamt Of

What Ever Happened to Robert Aldrich?

Roger Corman: Metaphysics on a Shoestring

The Noir Style

Film Noir Reader, Editor

Film Noir Reader 2, Editor

Horror Film
READER

Edited by
ALAIN SILVER &
JAMES URSINI

LIMELIGHT EDITIONS
NEW YORK

Limelight Editions
512 Newark Pompton Turnpike
Pompton Plains, New Jersey 07444

First published in 2000 by Limelight Editions
Reprinted in 2006

Printed in the United States of America

Library of Congress Cataloging-in-Publication Data

The horror film reader / edited by Alain Silver & James Ursini.—1st
    Limelight ed.
        p. cm.
    ISBN 0-87910-297-7
        1. Horror films—History and criticism. I. Silver, Alain, 1947-
    II. Ursini, James.

PN1995.9.H6 H68 2000
791,43'6164—dc21

00-044366

The editors are grateful for permission to reprint copyrighted material as detailed in the Acknowledgments.

www.limelighteditions.com

Contents

Acknowledgments

In spirit, at least, this anthology is closely tied to several previous collaborations: our study of the genre, *More Things Than Are Dreamt Of*, and our two readers on *film noir*. The popularity of the *Film Noir Readers* validates the belief that the anthology format is ideal for the introductory study of any genre, as it affords the reader not only varied critical perspectives on the subject but also reveals the evolution of the critical thought itself. As with previous readers, our process in selecting essays begins with seminal articles and spreads outward from there. When the first *Film Noir Reader* appeared in 1996, it had been preceded by three other anthologies (and another was published concurrently). Its emergence as the preeminent anthology on the subject derives primarily from its first part, "Seminal Essays." While there is obviously room for disagreement over what pieces are the foundation critical texts on any subject (and usually too many to fit into one book, as evidenced by *Film Noir Reader 2*), the history of *film noir* made it hard to go wrong. As regards this *Horror Film Reader*, however, we must acknowledge the existence of many previous studies of the subject, more than one or two previous anthologies (though mostly out of print), and a somewhat broader subject area in terms of total filmography. As a consequence, it became clear from our researches that, as with the *Film Noir Readers*, the seminal essays herein would be restricted to the post-World War II era, when most of those pieces were written. We have also tried to maintain a balance between overview pieces and studies of individual films or series, between a genre perspective and an auteurist analysis. Also we have limited ourselves to articles or book excerpts which are not easily accessible and not classics such as Lotte Eisner's *The Haunted Screen* or Carlos Clarens' *Illustrated History of the Horror Film* which are generally available.

As before, we were gratified by the enthusiasm of all the authors whom we contacted personally about reprints or new pieces. As usual other research was done at the Academy of Motion Picture Arts and Sciences Library in Beverly Hills. Permissions editors were Peter Cowie at The Tantivy Press; Brian Whittaker at *Sight and Sound*; Roy Frumkes at *Films in Review*; and Jeff Moen at the University of Minnesota Press.

Stills and frame enlargements not from the editors' personal collections were loaned by David Chierichetti, Glenn Erickson, David Fiore, and Timothy Otto and are reproduced courtesy of American-International, Astor Pictures, Columbia, Hammer, MGM, New Line, Paramount, RKO, 20th Century-Fox, TriStar, Turner Pictures, United Artists, Universal, and Warner Bros. The reprints have been reformatted to various extents for stylistic consistency. Except for this, the text is that of the original authors. With regard to the illustrations, we have tried when possible to find images identical to or from the same films as those used with the original article. As usual we have taken the liberty of occasionally injecting our own viewpoint in the captions.

"Maria Bava: the Illusion of Reality" by Alain Silver and James Ursini originally appeared in *Photon* (No. 26, 1975). Copyright © 1975 by *Photon* and the authors and was previously reprinted in the internet magazine *Images*. New material copyright © 1997 and 1999 by Alain Silver and James Ursini. Reprinted by permission of the authors.

"Neglected Nightmares" by Robin Wood originally appeared in *Film Comment* (March-April, 1980). Copyright © 1980 by *Film Comment*, the Film Society of Lincoln Center and the author. Reprinted by permission of the author.

"Is the Devil American? William Dieterle's *The Devil and Daniel Webster*" by Tony Williams. Copyright © 1999 by the author. Printed by permission.

"Violence, Women, and Disability in Tod Browning's *Freaks* and *The Devil Doll*" by Madeleine Cahill and Martin F. Norden originally appeared in *The Journal of Popular Film and Television* (Summer, 1998). Copyright © 1998 by the authors. Revisions copyright © 1999. Reprinted by permission.

"Monsters as (Uncanny) Metaphors: Freud, Lakoff, and the Representation of Monstrosity in Cinematic Horror" by Steven Schneider orginally appeared in *Paradoxa* (November, 1997). Copyright © 1997 by the author. Revisions copyright © 1999. Reprinted by permission.

"The Anxiety of Influence: Georges Franju and the Medical Horror shows of Jess Franco" by Joan Hawkins is excerpted from her forthcoming book for the University of Minnesota Press, *Cutting Edge Art: Art-Horror and the Horrific Avant Garde*. Copyright © 1999 by the author. Printed by permission.

"Seducing the Subject: Freddy Krueger" by Ian Conrich originally appeared in the book **Trash Aesthetics: Popular Culture and Its Audience** edited by Deborah Cartnell, I.Q. Hunter, Heidi Kaye, and Imelda Whelehan, London: Pluto Books, 1997. Copyright © 1997 by the author. Revisions copyright © 1999. Reprinted by permission.

"What Rough Beast? Insect Politics and *The Fly*" by Linda Brookover and Alain Silver. Copyright © 1999 by the authors. Printed by permission.

"Demon Daddies: Gender, Ecstasy and Terror in the Possession film" by Tanya Krzywinska. Copyright © 1999 by the author. Printed by permission.

Horror
Film
READER

Above, Im-ho-tep posing as Ardath Bey (Boris Karloff) holds up a mirror with an ancient hand for a mesmerized Helen Grosvenor (Zita Johann) now "transformed" into
the Princess whom he loved in the original Universal production of **The Mummy**
(directed by Karl Freund, 1932).

Introduction

James Ursini

The horror film is not only the most fecund of movie genres but the most resilient. If there is any doubt of the validity of this proposition, one only has to page through *Horror*, Phil Hardy's encyclopedic survey of the genre through the decades, for evidence. From its earliest roots in German Expressionism (so brilliantly analyzed by Lotte Eisner in *The Haunted Screen* and Siegfried Kracuaer in *From Caligar to Hitler*, both still in print) through the cycles produced at Universal and RKO (under Val Lewton) in the thirties and forties, the Hammer revival in England, the blossoming of "Euro-horror" in the seventies and eighties, and the concurrent American "renaissance" during the last twenty-five years —the horror film genre has outstripped all the other major genres in its ability to rise from the grave after being pronounced dead by countless critics in generation after generation. In fact, the only period in which the horror film has seen a decline is the post-World War II era when it was pushed aside by what was originally a sub-genre, the emerging science fiction film, which was given a tremendous boost in popularity by the anxiety of the atomic-bomb and the rapid development of new technologies. While genres like the Western, the musical, or the gangster film have limped into the 21st Century with occasional, mildly successful attempts at resuscitation (e.g. *Unforgiven, Evita, Hoodlum*), the horror genre thrives on the enthusiasm of each new generation. As evidence, witness most recent box-office successes such as the *Scream* series or the ultra low-budget *The Blair Witch Project*. In reality, the horror film's only real competitors as a genre in current cinema are science fiction and neo-*noir*.

If the horror film's amazing vitality is a given, then the question becomes "why?" What is there in this genre that speaks to audiences across generations and cultures? Horror was, of course, an established literary genre long before Edison first turned the crank of his kinetoscope which soon engendered the earliest incarnation of Frankenstein's monster. The horror film genre traces its roots back to E.T.A. Hoffmann's dark, dream-like tales as well as to those of his more perverse German descendant Hanns Heinz Ewers (*Alraune*); to British

3

Gothics like Mary Shelley (*Frankenstein*), Matthew Lewis (*The Monk*), Horace Walpole (*Castle of Otranto*), Bram Stoker (*Dracula*), and Robert Louis Stevenson (*The Strange Case of Dr. Jekyll and Mr. Hyde*); to the Americans—the ironic Washington Irving ("The Legend of Sleepy Hollow"), the arcane Nathaniel Hawthorne ("Young Goodman Brown") and the tormented tales of Edgar Allan Poe; and returning to Europe for such French fin-de-siecle decadents as Theophile Gautier ("La Morte Amoureuse").

The most insightful early analysis of the power and appeal of horror came relatively early in its history, from the febrile brain of Sigmund Freud. In his essay "The Uncanny," Freud pinpoints the appeal of the horror story. He begins by discussing the etymological root of the word "uncanny" in German, a word long associated with the horror genre, demonstrating how both the word and its opposite are very close in definition and usage. He then applies this discovery to an analysis of literary works like E.T.A. Hoffmann's "The Sand Man" and ends with this conclusion, "It may be true that the uncanny [unheimlich] is something which is secretly familiar [heimlich-heimisch], which has undergone repression and returned from it, and that everything that is uncanny fulfills this condition." In this short but very influential essay, Freud has hit upon the key to understanding the core of the horror genre. Horror is dissimilar from much of science fiction genre in which the threatening "monster" (often created because of the interference of science or technology)—whether it be an alien, atomic mutant, or cyborg—is portrayed as the Other which must be destroyed or controlled by science, often in conjunction with the military/industrial complex, in order to save humanity. Horror tends rather to concentrate on another type of "Other," an "Other" which is very familiar and because of that much more frightening, an "Other" which is rooted in our psyche, in our fears and obsessions. There are, of course, crossover films like *Frankenstein, Dr. Jekyll and Mr. Hyde, Invasion of the Body Snatchers* or both versions of *The Fly* which contain elements of both science fiction and the uncanny horror movie.

Julia Kristeva in her book *Powers of Horror* elaborates on Freud's thesis in a typically poetic passage on the first page:

> There looms, within abjection, one of those violent, dark revolts of being directed against a threat that seems to emanate from an exorbitant outside or inside, ejected beyond the scope of the possible, the tolerable, the thinkable. It lies there, quite close, but it cannot be assimilated. It beseeches, worries, and fascinates desire, which, nevertheless, does not let itself be seduced. Apprehensive,

desire turns aside, sickened, it rejects. A certainty protects it from the shameful—a certainty of which it is proud holds on to it. But simultaneously, just the same, that impetus, that spasm, that leap is drawn towards an elsewhere as tempting as it is condemned. Unflaggingly, like an inescapable boomerang, a vortex of summons and repulsion places the one haunted by it literally beside himself.

Horror is based on recognizing in the unfamiliar something familiar, something attractive even as it is repulsive. It may be a seductive vampire who exploits erotic longing; a mummy who evokes nostalgia through an almost forgotten piece of racial memory; an alienated and abused child-like Creature (*Frankenstein*); a serial killer (*Psycho*) who reflects the oedipal guilt buried in our psyche; a "demon-daddy" (*The Exorcist*) who tests our faith and fears; a doppelganger who seems to shadow us (*The Student of Prague*); an animal incarnation or totem which frees us of our sexual inhibitions (*Cat People*); an all too familiar ghost who torments us (*The Innocents*); or an avatar from our dark side who does what we dare not (*Dr. Jekyll and Mr. Hyde*). A motto for the entire genre might be taken from the ancient Indian **Upanishads**, "Thou art That," for in the finest of horror films there is no separation. Fear explodes from inside our psyche when encountering a vision which touches our deepest emotions, an image which forces the spectator to examine, even if momentarily, the territory of what Kristeva calls "the abject," that which is unpleasant and repressed. The best horror films are those that evoke that feeling of the uncanny in us most strongly.

Like our *Film Noir Reader I* and *II* before, this book is divided into sections: "Seminal Essays" and "New Persectives." The first section of essays begins with two of the earliest articles which attempted to analyze and catalogue the burgeoning horror genre: "Ghoulies and Ghosties" by screenwriter-director/critic Curtis Harrington and "Horror Films" by the formidable William K. Everson. Also included is an excerpt from the out-of-print book *The Horror Film* by Ivan Butler. It, along with Carlos Clarens' influential *An Illustrated History of the Horror Film* (still in print), is one of the earliest full-length treatments of the genre. Another early analysis of the genre is exemplified in this excerpt from Raymond Durgnat's ground-breaking Freudian dissections of the subconscious in movies. Here, in "From Pleasure Castle to Libido Motel," he concentrates on the horror film itself. In "The Face of Horror" by Derek Hill and "Horror Is My Business" by Hammer *auteur* Terence Fisher we have both sides of an argument which is still raging today, namely, the effect of movie violence on society. Also included in this section are two pieces ("A Bloody New Wave in the United States" and

Two forms of menace: above, the classic style in the Val Lewton production of **The Curse of the Cat People** (directed by Robert Wise, 1944); and below, a more recent variant, Leatherface in Tobe Hooper's 1972 **The Texas Chainsaw Massacre,** which for Robin Wood exemplifies "seeing the victims as mere objects."

"From Voyeurism to Infinity") from the French cult magazine *Midi-Minuit Fantastique,* one of the first periodicals to discuss with seriousness the Euro-horror of the Sixties and Seventies (called derogatorily by some and lovingly by others, "Euro-trash"), as well as American low-budget horror of the same period. The analysis of Euro-horror is carried on in several more articles: "Mario Bava: The Illusion of Reality," by the editors of the volume, in the first section; and in the second section: "Women on the Verge of a Nervous Breakdown: Sex, Drugs and Corpses in *The Horrible Dr. Hichcock"* by Glenn Erickson and "The Anxiety of Influence: Georges Franju and the Medical Horror shows of Jess Franco" by Joan Hawkins.

In the second section, "New Perspectives," the always controversial and perspicacious Robin Wood analyzes several nearly forgotten horror films of the Seventies, most notably Wes Craven's *Last House on the Left* and George Romero's *Jack's Wife,* and such staples as *Texas Chainsaw Massacre* in "Neglected Nightmares." Tony Williams digs back into the genre's history for an in-depth case study of a horror film maudit, *The Devil and Daniel Webster,* in "Is the Devil American? William Dieterle's *The Devil and Daniel Webster."* Linda Brookover and Alain Silver develop their own case study of the hybrid science fiction/horror film *The Fly* (David Cronenberg) in "What Rough Beast? Insect Politics and *The Fly,"* as does Pam Keesey in her astute formalist analysis of Robert Wise's *The Haunting* in "*The Haunting* and the Power of Suggestion: Why Robert Wise's Film Continues to 'Deliver the Goods' to Modern Audiences."

Two topics rarely covered before are also considered within this section: disability and the horror film in "Violence, Women, and Disability in Tod Browning's *Freaks* and *The Devil-Doll"* by Madeleine Cahill and Martin F. Norden and race politics in "Candyman: Urban Space, Fear, and Entitlement" by Aviva Briefel and Sianne Ngai. In "Monsters as (Uncanny) Metaphors: Freud, Lakoff and the Representation of Monstrosity in Cinematic Horror" Steven Schneider refines and reworks Freud's theory of the uncanny in the context of more contemporary semiological thought. In "Seducing the Subject: Freddy Krueger" Ian Conrich discusses media manipulation in relation to the incredibly successful *Nightmare on Elm Street* series. Finally Tanya Krzywinska in "Demon Daddies: Gender, Ecstasy and Terror in the Possession Film" argues that possession films like *The Exorcist* and *Lost Highway,* rather than being "feminine" directed (the traditional critical perspective), are examples of a contemporary crisis in male identity, a subject much discussed recently in both film (*Fight Club*) and literature (*Stiffed*).

Ghoulies and Ghosties

Curtis Harrington (1952)

The ability of the camera to present hallucinatory or supernatural phenomena was one of the first discoveries made by the earliest creators of cinema; indeed, the most outstanding of the early innovators, Melies, presented a great variety of supernatural visions in his "magically arranged scenes." His films abounded in fairies and ghosts and powerful magicians. But because of the camera's more obvious talent for objective recording, the cinema, as it subsequently grew and as it still is made use of today, has largely served to reconstruct a very earthbound reality. In the United States the financial failure of a "fantasy" is considered almost certain, and so they are rarely attempted. The few successes (the *Topper* series, *Here Comes Mr. Jordan*) have been mostly whimsical, using the tricks made possible by the varied mechanical resources of the camera for laughter rather than mystery or awe; while films that started out seriously, like *The Uninvited*, usually lost their supernatural convictions halfway through and dwindled away into obvious comedy. In Europe, ghosts have been the subject of more genuine wit, as Rene Clair's *The Ghost Goes West* and, more notably, Max Ophuls' *La Tendre Ennemie*, in which three ghosts–of a woman's husband and her two lovers–sit on a chandelier during a dinner party given to celebrate the engagement of the woman's daughter to an old man she does not love. They finally alter the course of her life by persuading her to elope with someone else.

The fact of the matter is the camera "magic," despite its slickness and theoretically real and solid appearance, is a fairly obvious thing: a man double-exposed so that he can be seen through looks not so much as we imagine a ghost might, but rather as a man double-exposed. The latter effect used today is really only a formal device; we say, "there is a figure double-exposed, which means he is supposed to be a ghost." But we are not convinced; there is not truly a "suspension of disbelief," so we can hardly be captured even momentarily by the illusion, as we may so often be by the dramatic pull of a situation, or the dramatic reality of a character. The mechanical fact stares us in the face, and that is all.

Opposite, Max Schreck in **Nosferatu**.

9

During the 'teens and 'twenties the supernatural was treated in many ways, perhaps most often by the Germans, whose love of mysticism is reflected strongly in their cinema. There were supernatural elements in all of the early German legend films, such as Galeen's *The Golem*, von Gerlach's *Chronicle of the Grieshuus*, and Lang's *Siegfried*. The first contained a remarkably well handled sequence of the summoning of a demon according to the kabbala; the second—about the ghosts of two tormented lovers who rescue a child from scheming relatives in a Gothic castle—had Lil Dagover appearing in double exposure rather often as a warning spirit; and the third showed Siegfried's borrowed cloak of invisibility in all its practicality. The Germans also produced the first film version of Bram Stoker's classic vampire story, **Dracula**, although it was considerably rewritten by its scenarist, Henrik Galeen, made into a kind of old German legend and retitled *Nosferatu*. In this the director, F.W. Murnau, used with, to contemporary eyes, rather crude but charming effect, the device of speeded action to show the supernatural strength of the master of the castle. A genuine sense of the macabre was conveyed by this, in combination with a general air of mystery and the frightening make-up of Max Schreck as the bloodthirsty count. Here double exposure, that obvious and so dangerous device for showing the supernatural, was used toward the end of the film to convey the death of the latter; and as a commentary rather than sustained image (the figure dissolves into the air, disappearing altogether) its use was, even, effective.

About this same time in Hollywood the French director Maurice Tourneur, who had established a reputation for his pictorial style (not, one suspects, without considerable help from his art directors) during the late 'teens, produced Maeterlink's *The Blue Bird* (1921) and a fantasy called *Prunella* (1922), about a strange little girl brought up in a strange house by three grim aunts and two prim maids, who kept her from the outside world, but could not prevent her falling in love with a pierrot. In these the fantastic effects were achieved as they are on the stage (both were originally plays), mechanically rather than by trickery of the camera. After *The Four Horsemen of the Apocalypse* and its misty apocalyptic visions, Rex Ingram included a fantastic and terrifying dream sequence in *The Conquering Power* (1921), and the morality tale within his *Trifling Women* (1923) was an elaborate and macabre vampiric love story in the tradition of Huysman's *A Rebours*. There were fantastic episodes also in Ingram's *Mare Nostrum* (1926), and in his version of Maugham's novel *The Magician* (1927), with its central figure drawn from the late Aleister Crowley, which contained an orgiastic dream sequence concerning Pan. Other American directors during the 'twenties dealt with the fantastic but Tourneur and Ingram were perhaps the two most consistently interested in using films to present fantasy rather than reality.

It is difficult to place where the fantastic "horror" film, as a genre, became established; but in America certainly the actor Lon Chaney, in a series of alarming make-ups, helped to establish the tradition. However, it was not until the coming of sound, and, incidentally, the stock market crash, that the fantastic horror film became a staple Hollywood commodity. With *Dracula* (1930) directed by Tod Browning (he had earlier directed Lon Chaney in *The Unholy Three*), and James Whale's *Frankenstein* (1931), the genre was definitely launched. These were followed by, to name a few of the most outstanding: *The Werewolf of London* (1933), *The White Zombie* (1933); *The Mark of the Vampire* (Browning, 1933), with Professor Zalen, an expert on vampire lore, solving the mystery of vampiric attacks on a young girl in a derelict castle; *The Mummy* (1934) and *The Black Cat* (1934), based on the Edgar Allan Poe story; *The Devil Doll* (Browning, 1934), about a French scientist who could reduce living creatures to a sixth of their normal size; and *The Bride of Frankenstein* (James Whale, 1935), with its splendid climax of a bride being created for the monster during a raging thunderstorm at night, the bride (Elsa Lanchester) being brought to life inside a bottle [Editors' note: the bride is actually brought to life, like her potential mate, full size, by revivifying a dead corpse] but horrified, upon emerging, at her intended mate. James Whale, a British stage director imported to America, brought to his films a fine sense of Gothic terror in the English tradition, as well as an irascible though perhaps less evident sense of humour. Tod Browning's work was less distinguished, though *The Mark of the Vampire* has its following. Its illusion, however, is quite destroyed when the ending of the film reveals the whole story to have been a carefully staged hoax.

Edmund Wilson has remarked how the popularity of the ghost and horror story in literature rises during times of outward stress in society, and certainly the vogue for this genre of film follows the same pattern. By 1939 the horror film had almost ceased to be produced, and it was only during the subsequent war that it was revived by the late Val Lewton, a producer then at R.K.O. studios. During the time the popularity of the horror film had declined in inverse proportion to the gradual revival of economic strength and prosperity, it had not only been produced less often but became exclusively "B," or low-udget, second feature work. Thus, when Val Lewton produced his first film of this type, *The Cat People* (1943), it was at the customary low cost. To everyone's surprise, it had an amazing success as a first-class feature and took in a great deal of money. It was, however, something slightly new.

The story of *Cat People* is of Irena (Simone Simon), descendant of a race who, at times of emotional crisis, could turn into cats. Her psychiatrist is skeptical, but a few days later his body, bloody and clawed, is found in her apartment. Lewton had observed that the power of the camera as an instrument to generate suspense in an audience lies not in its power to reveal, but its power to suggest; that what takes place just off-screen in the audience's imagination, the terror of waiting for the final revelation, not the seeing of it, is the most powerful dramatic stimulus toward tension and fright. Moreover, where a fantastic subject is concerned, in order to obtain the modern audience's "suspension of disbelief," they must be kept in suspense as to the exact nature of whatever phenomenon they are to be frightened by—and this centre of suggested terror must be surrounded by human, understandable people in realistic though possibly exotic surroundings. Thus the predicament of the girl in *The Cat People*, her growing realisation of her impulses, was made direct and real. Upon this formula Lewton produced a number of horror fantasies, made by directors now well-known: Jacques Tourneur (*The Cat People*), the son of Maurice Tourneur, Mark Robson and Robert Wise. The films dealt with zombies in Haiti (*I Walked with a Zombie*), devil worship (*The Seventh Victim*), a child's imagination (*The Curse of the Cat People*),

Below, **The Cat People**, prototype of the low-budget atmospheric horror film, starring Simone Simon as Irene and Kent Smith as Oliver Reed.

the living dead (*Isle of the Dead*), and an especially macabre murderer (*The Leopard Man*). Robert Louis Stevenson's *The Body Snatchers* was also imaginatively filmed with Lewton as producer and Wise as director, as was a story based on Hogarth's drawing of *Bedlam* (Mark Robson).

Though made independently on a very low budget, a film that deserves mention along with the Lewton product is Frank Wisbar's *The Strangler of the Swamp*. Wisbar, who directed *Anna und Elizabeth* and *Fahrmann Maria* during the early 'thirties in Germany, came to Hollywood as a refugee during the war, and made several rather curious low-budget films. *The Strangler of the Swamp*, the only fantasy among them, dealt with the malign ghost of a man unjustly hung in a southern swampland. Although the treatment was on the whole realistic, it contained suggestions of German expressionism, and succeeded in evoking with considerable effect the mist-laden, spirit-haunted country in which the strange story takes place.

These have been the most interesting horror fantasies produced in Hollywood; one must record, for other reasons, the films made by Universal Studios during the war years. Whereas Val Lewton attempted within commercial restrictions to do something new and imaginative, all the films produced at Universal (a studio famous as the home of "horror" films, though in the early 'thirties both Paramount and MGM probably produced an equal share) were lifeless repetitions of ancient penny-dreadful formulas. A whole series of crudely ridiculous films were made, exploiting some famous originals–*House of Frankenstein, Son of Dracula, The Wolf Man, The Spider Woman, The Mummy's Ghost*–and the final death agony of James Whale's originally marvelous creation, *Abbott and Costello Meet Frankenstein*. Columbia Studios' product of this type was only very occasionally better: Edward Dmytryk's *The Devil Commands* (1942) built to a genuinely frightening climax, but it was weighted by a dully concocted story–a grief-stricken husband tries to contact the spirit of his dead wife through a brain machine, with the aid of a weird medium.

With the end of the war the popularity of horror films quickly diminished, so that since 1947 there have been few, if any produced. Even Universal gave them up. Recently, a new type of fantasy has come to the screen in the form of "science-fiction" films, which "explain" the supernatural in terms of science and in which mysterious happenings are generated by machines rather than human beings. At least one of these, however, proves to be simply a modern version of Mary Shelley's old morality thriller, **Frankenstein; or a Modern Prometheus**. In *The Thing*, horror and suspense are produced during the first part by only suggesting verbally the nature of "The Thing," a monstrous vegetable-man from

another planet but as soon as he is seen, fully clothed and looking altogether like Karloff's creation of "The Monster" in *Frankenstein,* the illusion of horror that been built up is quickly dispelled. By now we have
seen this creature too often; we produced him on this earth, and we expect another planet to be able to think up something different.

This brief outline of, primarily, the supernatural horror film may
serve to indicate what has, in the main, been done with the genre; now
this varied, sometimes remarkable, but relatively unimaginative output
must be contrasted with one truly serious and brilliant creation, Carl-
Theodor Dreyer's *Vampyr.* Dreyer's work, besides, is particularly interesting in this respect, since he is the only outstanding film director to
have used the supernatural more than once to express a personal out-
look on life. Produced in France during 1930 and 1931, about the same
time as *Dracula* and *Frankenstein,* Dreyer's *Vampyr* was released in 1932,
at the time the vogue for horror films, at least in America, was mounting
quickly. The film was premiered in Berlin, and although it was dubbed
(easily and effectively, for there was very little dialogue) in both French
and English it had little success outside of Germany, where its mystic
quality seems to have been appreciated.

Inspiration for the story of *Vampyr* is credited to Sheridan Le Fanu's
In a Glass Darkly. A reading of this collection shows that only one story
bears any relationship to the film, and that only vaguely, the tale of a
vampire, *Carmilla.* Rather than from any particular literary basis, the
film seems more to have developed from its settings (it was shot entirely
on location in various deserted buildings), in which were placed a certain number of rather extraordinary characters living out their destiny in
the shadow of a human vampire. Briefly, the continuity reveals the arrival of a young man at an inn beside a lake, where, during the night, a
man enters his room and leaves with him a sealed package, with instructions that it is to be opened upon his death. The next morning the
young man investigates a strange building where shadows dance eter-
nally, and visits an odd little doctor at his office where he meets an old
lady (who is the vampire). Presently he arrives at a chateau whose master is the man who had come to his room at the inn. The man has two
daughters, Gisele and Leone, and two servants. Leone is ill, having been
attacked by the vampire. Suddenly and mysteriously the girls' father is
shot, and the young man opens the package he had been given earlier.
In it is *The Book of Vampires,* which relates the vampire legend, and
tells how the vampire can be destroyed. Leone leaves her bed and is discovered in the woods surrounding the chateau, attacked once again by
the vampire. The doctor is called to administer a transfusion, and the
young man gives his blood. Later the young man's doppelganger, in a

dream, experiences his enclosure in a coffin by the doctor and the vampire, and he is carried toward the cemetery. Then, awakening, he goes to the cemetery, where the old servant opens the tomb of the vampire and drives a stake through her heart; she turns to a skeleton, and Leone sits up in bed, released. With the power of the vampire no longer sustaining him the doctor runs away in panic, and is trapped by the old servant in a mill where the machines bury him slowly in a shower of white flour. The young man and Gisele, meanwhile, ride in a boat through the misty lake and at last, arriving on the other side, walk into a forest illumined by the sun.

As with any film of style and value, a bare recounting of the plot (I prefer in this the word "continuity," since it sounds more sequential, in a filmic sense, than constructed, in a literary sense) does not give one any idea of what the film is actually like; the structure of Vampyr is based more upon imagery than idea. Ebbe Neergaard, in his *Carl Dreyer*, one of the British Film Institute Index Series, tells how the script called for the doctor to die by sinking into a bog of mud. Yet when Dreyer came by chance upon a plaster-works where everything was covered with a fine white dust, he realised the image-requirement for the film was the doctor die in whiteness, and so an old flour mill, where the doctor could be trapped in the cage where the bags are filled, was chosen for the film. The earlier sequences, then, were carefully photographed by Mate to match, in style, the final image material. The first arrival of the young man at the inn is suffused in a later afternoon greyness. The sequence of his discovery of the building filled with mysterious shadows is in tones of white and grey. The succeeding exteriors—the young man's arrival at the chateau, his walk to the cemetery, and Leone's encounter with the vampire, are all extremely diffused so as to give a kind of preternatural mist-effect. There is no sun in the film until the final moment.

What is especially striking about *Vampyr* is that light and shadow become more than just contributors to a consistent style; they serve as dynamic participants in the story unfolded. Dreyer recognised immediately the principle that Val Lewton applied to his series of films dealing with the supernatural twelve years later, that you must only suggest horror; you cannot show it, or at least, if you do, it must only be momentarily, for you cannot sustain it. It is the audience's own imagination, skillfully probed, that provides, out of its well of unconscious fear, all the horror necessary.

In what are perhaps the most uncanny and terrifying moments of *Vampyr*, only a wild inexplicable play of light and shadows is seen; but the terror of the malevolent supernatural force is brilliantly conveyed.

Icons of early horror: Boris Karloff (above) as Frankenstein's monster; a vampiric Bela Lugosi confronts a wolfman (Matt Willis in **Return of the Vampire** [1943], opposite top); and the Doctor (Jan Hieronimko) drowned in flour in **Vampyr** (1930)

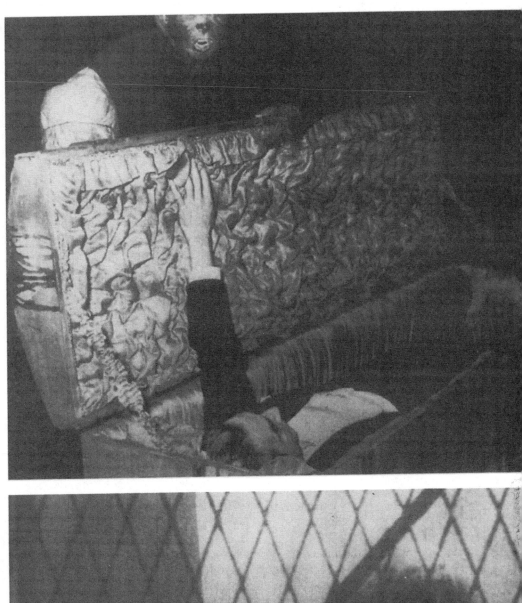

One of the most effective of these moments is when the doctor, after having given the blood transfusion, leaves Leone's room and the young man runs after him, only to reach the head of the stairs and find them quite empty; then we hear an abrupt crash and see the shadows cast by the staircase railings jerking crazily around on the walls of the stairwell. Throughout the film all such moments, actions communicated by purely filmic means, are left an unexplained part of the general uncanny atmosphere. We are transported to the heart of a battle between ancient evil and the young, the pure in heart, taking place in a land convincingly haunted, where anything may at any moment happen and does.

One cannot properly divorce *Vampyr* from Dreyer's other work, as it must be considered partly, along with these, as an expression of his personality. Certainly Dreyer is one of the very few directors of whom this may be fairly and safely said; no major studio chose the script of *Vampyr*, and there was no "front office" to interfere in any way with the execution. This seems to be fairly true also of *Jeanne d'Arc* and *Day of Wrath*–the former made immediately before *Vampyr*, the other twelve years after it. Seen in perspective the three films make up a kind of trilogy; they all bear definite affinities of theme, style and content. Each presents a struggle between good and evil, age and youth, and in each there is an intense concern, almost amounting to obsession with the act of death; in *Jeanne d'Arc* the progress toward death by fire; in *Vampyr* the death of the head of the manor, then the true death of the living dead and of the doctor and his assistant and, during the whole of the film, the delicate suspension near death of Leone; and finally, in *Day of Wrath*, the death, again by fire, of the old lady declared a witch, the death of the parson, and Anne's acceptance, at the end of the film, of her identity as a witch, indicating surely the death to follow. In all three of the films the conquering of this miasma of death and old age is shown as only a temporary thing–a gesture of St. Joan's; the young lovers' idyll in *Day of Wrath*; and although in *Vampyr* the young man and Gisele escape, at the end, they never really seem to emerge from the land of phantoms. Another recurrent figure that one notices in many of Dreyer's films is the powerful, often malevolent old lady. She was not, of course, seen in *Jeanne d'Arc* (where certain of the older priests might be said to have taken her place), but she was protrayed with humour very early in Dreyer's career as *The Parson's Widow* (1920) and she mastered the tyrant in *Thou Shalt Honour Thy Wife* (1925). In *Vampyr* she becomes the ancient, powerful living dead creature of the title, and in *Day of Wrath* she is two forces–the narrow, suspicious old mother of the parson, and Marte, the old Lady accused as a witch who goes to her death uttering dire curses against those who have condemned her.

As remarkable as the photographic treatment of *Vampyr* is the sound. Wolfgang Zeller composed a score that for suggestivity has seldom been equalled, perhaps because there have been no other films since then requiring quite such imaginative work. It is not, of course, music that could be divorced from the film. The dialogue is very sparse and effectively pointed, as when, after giving the blood transfusion to Leone, the young man complains (he is resting in an adjoining room) to the doctor; who peeks out at him from behind the door of Leone's room, that he is losing blood, "Don't be silly," the doctor replies very slowly, "your blood is in here." Sound effects are also used with the utmost suggestivity. One remembers the inexplicable noises heard in the doctor's office, distant barkings and cryings, which make the young man ask the doctor if there are children or dogs on the premises. "There are no children or dogs here," the doctor replies. When from a subjective point of view, we experience with the young man our enclosure in a coffin, there is unique horror as we hear the close grinding of the screws into the coffin-lid, and experience the splutter of a match struck to light a candle placed on the coffin-lid by the vampire who, in doing so, peers at us intently.

The last sequence of the film is very formally constructed and gives us, I believe, insight into Dreyer's creative method, one which always tends toward formal control, especially when he is dealing with incident and outward movement rather than people. Here we have the escape of the young couple counter-pointed with the death of the doctor in the flour mill. The sequence is cross-cut, so that at one moment we see and hear the machinery rhythmically grinding out its white death, and the next we see the young couple gliding slowly on the mist-covered lake, the image being accompanied by a slow sustained note of music. The combination of shots is repeated in alternation until the couple get out of the boat and go into the sunlit forest. The very final shot is a close-up of the white turning gears of the flour mill machinery; their movement slows, and at last stops. Fade out; we have reached the end of the adventure. The construction and the image-material here employed is perfectly cinematographic; the meaning communicated is melodramatic incident abstracted into a pattern of time, space and sound. The sum of this design toward a conclusion becomes greater than the actions of its parts; it brings to an end not only the adventure we have had (for it has been our adventure as much as the protagonist's), but encloses the film perfectly in its own uniqueness as the sole cinematic work that shakes us with its revelations of the terrors that still haunt us in the deep and unknown place of the human psyche.

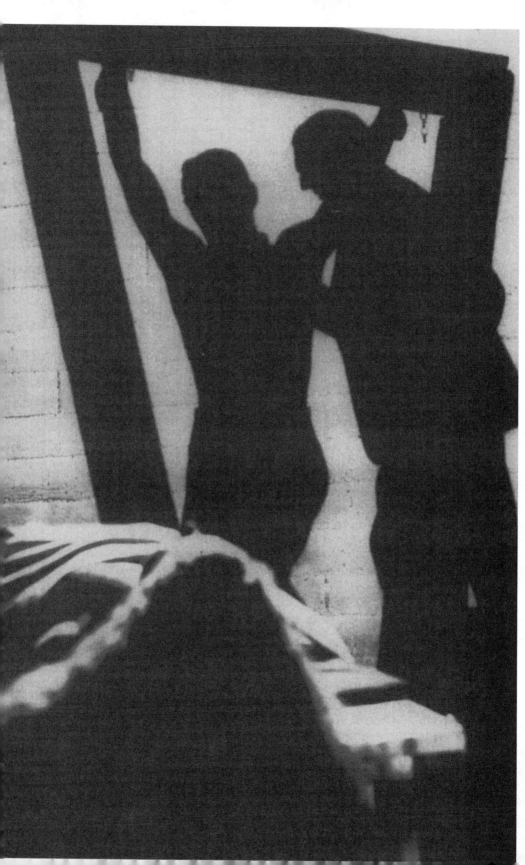

Horror Films

William K. Everson (1954)

Horror stories are as old as the human race and have frightened, controlled and beguiled men and women for longer than anyone knows. Even a literature as sophisticated as that of the Greeks is full of stories of ghosts and the supernatural, and includes at least one tale about a werewolf. The description in *The Odyssey* of Erebus, the misty land of blood-drinking phantoms, is one of the grimmest horror stories ever told. And what is "Little Red Riding Hood" but a werewolf story?

Since men and women like to scare themselves silly with horror stories, it is only natural that movie-makers, always avid for "pre-sold audiences," should spend time, talent and money on scaring the daylights out of movie audiences the world over.

Frankenstein and *Dracula* (both 1931) are the two most familiar titles of screen horror-lore, and certainly no two films did more to influence the genre. They introduced stars who still head the roster of "menace" performers. Boris Karloff, the monster of Frankenstein, continued to inspire a certain amount of pity and understanding, along with horror, whether he was monster or mad scientist. Bela Lugosi, however, emulating Dracula, continued to project evil for its own sake, with sympathy neither warranted nor desired. True, there have been occasional exceptions to these generalizations. In their co-starring films (five at Universal, two at RKO) unexpected switches in their types occurred once or twice, and in later years they were frequently used as "red herrings" to divert attention from more sophisticated villains.

Frankenstein and *Dracula* were notable for much more than merely Karloff and Lugosi. Their respective directors, James Whale and Tod Browning, remained the outstanding masters of horror until the advent, much later, of Val Lewton. The two films also created a sort of stock company for subsequent horror films. Players like Dwight Frye, Edward Van Sloan and Lionel Barrymore found themselves continuing to be cast as hunchbacks, doctors and burgomasters. And finally, *Frankenstein* and *Dracula* were endlessly imitated. There have been five *Frankenstein* films, three *Dracula* films, and three others in which both of those menaces were part of the plot.

Opposite, Hjalmar Poelzig (Boris Karloff) is flayed by Vitus Verdegast (Bela Lugosi) over the latter's wife (foreground) in Edgar Ulmer's stylish *The Black Cat*.

It should not be forgotten that, between them, *Frankenstein* and *Dracula* presented a monster, a bemused scientist, a ghost, four vampires, a (offscreen) werewolf, and a transplanted brain–six little eye-poppers that have hopped up the plot-lines of scores of subsequent horror pictures.

All horror films fall into one of seven categories. In the order of most frequent usage these are: scientific experiments; monsters; vampirism and lycanthropy; voodoo; "old house"; necromancy and diabolism; ghosts and apparitions; and an unclassifiable group that includes "stunt" thrillers and such infrequent near-spectacles as *The Phantom of the Opera.*

Let's look at the outstanding characteristics of each group.

In later horror films it seemed to have become a necessity for any doctor involved in scientific experiments to be insane, but this was not a staple requirement initially. All of the Frankensteins were perfectly sane, although, they were cursed with unusually mad assistants bent upon putting the wrong brains into the wrong skulls and similar pleasantries. But the Frankensteins (four different members of the family were experimenters in horror films) were all men of reason and integrity. That illustrious family apart, however, it can generally be said that most horror film scientists are insane. However, one must differentiate. Most of Karloff's mad scientists were basically sympathetic: accident or injustice was usually offered as the cause of their unbalanced condition (*The Man They Couldn't Hang, The Devil Commands*). Lugosi and Lionel Atwill were always mad without stated cause. Karloff's experiments aimed at the good of mankind but Lugosi and Atwill's were for selfish ends.

The mad doctors of the horror films usually strived to create "eternal life," although transplanting the heroine's brain into the head of a gorilla occupies of fair number of them. Sometimes, when a heroine denounced the scientist with "Why, you're mad!" the scientist would reply by reciting the names of great scientists who were thought by their contemporaries to be unbalanced. And his punch-line, "Think of it, my dear, I offer you eternal life," became as much of a cliché in horror films as the timeless "Let's get outta here" is in Westerns.

Two films made in the same year (1932-1933) are the best examples of the category of horror films based on scientific experimentation.

We need devote no space to the story-line of *The Mystery of the Wax Museum*, since the current re-make (*House of Wax*) repeats it almost intact. The original had a grim power and some subtlety in contrasting the wise-cracking Broadway of the thirties and the unreality of the museum, an unreality heightened by intelligent use of two-color Technicolor. It had none of the street chases and fisticuffs of the re-make, and its menace was concentrated in the museum itself. It permitted only fleeting glimpses of the monster, who wasn't seen at all until long after the establishment of the character of the maimed sculptor, superbly played by Atwill. Thus, it was not too certain that sculptor and monster were one and the same, and the climactic face-smashing scene had genuine surprise, as well as physical shock. That scene, much longer and better handled than in the 3-D re-make, remains one of the most gripping sequences of any horror film.

Murders in the Rue Morgue, though a wild and hoked-up version of the Poe story, was influenced by the German classic of 1919, *The Cabinet of Dr. Caligari*. It was directed by Robert Florey (who also wrote the script, in collaboration with John Huston) and was photographed by Karl Freund, both recruits from Europe. The plot vaguely paralleled that of *Caligari*, with a giant ape substituted for the somnambulist. Also, an amusement park was the background. Further parallels can be found in the character of the hero (a medical student); in the abundance of odd, distorted roof-tops; and in the composition of many individual scenes. Lugosi's first appearance, and his subsequent lecture in the tent, follows rather closely the similar sequence with Krauss and Veidt in the German film. Few horror films before or since have contained such unrestrained savagery as does *Murders in the Rue Morgue*. The laboratory scenes are surprisingly grim, and the hero's discovery of his mother's corpse stuffed head down in a chimney has sometimes been cut.

Movie monsters follow no set pattern, except that their malevolence (or their very existence) is due to the interference of some scientist, usually mad. In this respect films about monsters are an offshoot of the above group.

The monsters in horror films are almost always presented as the misunderstood victims of social complexity. E.g.: Lon Chaney, Jr. as an electrical monstrosity in *Man Made Monster*; Karloff as Frankenstein's creation; the familiar ape-man of *The Monster and the Girl* and many lesser shockers. These creatures are usually two-thirds human. The really genuine monsters of the King Kong family are so few and far between that they comprise a different category.

To me, the most impressive of all the monster films is *The Mummy*, directed by Karl Freund in 1932. It was as much a photographer's film as *Waxworks* had been an art director's and had a slow, brooding pace, little physical horror in spite of Karloff's fearsome make-up, and a wonderful feeling of vague, impending disaster. Its simple plot was handled in the style of a well controlled nightmare and concerned an Egyptian mummy restored to life when his tomb is defiled by archaeologists and his belief that a young American girl is a reincarnated princess. This plot-line, and one long flashback sequence laid in ancient Egypt, provided the basis for a series of Mummy shockers produced by Universal some ten years later. The first, *The Mummy's Hand*, retained much of the spirit of Freund's original, but the three subsequent ones were mediocre. In retrospect, *The Mummy* appears as the forerunner of Val Lewton's series for RKO in the forties.

Vampirism and werewolfism are inter-related and in horror films have much in common. They are concepts of ancient mythology and, to make them at all credible now, set rules have to be followed. Age-old rituals–the use of garlic, wolf-bane, coffins of native earth, and other standard necessities–cannot be tampered with, and because of this rigidity there have been only one or two really worthwhile vampire and werewolf films, and a small group of standardized unimportant "B" shockers of the calibre of *Dead Men Walk*.

The two best films utilizing vampirism are Murnau's *Nosferatu* and, more especially, Dreyer's *Vampyr*, one of the eeriest films ever made (both are European). Tod Browning's *Dracula* is the obvious leader of the American vampire product, though it was far from the classic of terror it might have been. A too literal adaptation of the play (not the book) resulted in a plodding, talkative development, with much of the vital action taking place off-screen.

However, it did have some superb moments–and the opening two reels contain some of the best horror of the American cinema. Perhaps the credit for this should go to the cameraman (Freund) rather than to Browning, for the atmosphere of obscure, mystic terror of these scenes is reminiscent of the earlier German fantasies. Particularly memorable are the first scenes in the crypt of Dracula's castle. The camera seems to float around the misty walls, almost like a phantom, and Dracula's emergence from his coffin is recorded casually, without any attempt to shock. The gliding movements of Dracula's three wraith-like sisters as they pass among the last rays of light of the dying day, and the bloated rats scampering in and out of the coffins, are also devoid of sensationalism.

There has not yet been a movie with a werewolf theme that compares with the three great vampire thrillers just described, but two werewolf films have some interest and merit.

The Werewolf of London (1935) did not evoke much actual terror, but it did suggest the immanence of an occult curse. More superficial, but perhaps more successful was *The Wolf Man*, made six years later. It was far from subtle and relied for its horror solely on unexpected physical shock and violence, fog-swept moors and the repellent make-up of Lon

Chaney, Jr. However, it was neatly written, faithfully followed the standard laws of lycanthropy, featured some unusual trick photography (involving the werewolf's change-overs), and was ambitiously cast (Claude Rains, Warren William, Lugosi, Ralph Bellamy and others).

In horror films the werewolf motif inevitably culminates with the monster changing slowly back into human form in his dying moments, and with the suggestion, supplied by the incidental music, of the attainment of a long sought peace. The vampire motif, of course, poses no such plot problem–the vampire being disposed of as quickly as possible via the reliable stake-through-the-heart treatment, before he can induce the heroine to join him in the realm of the undead. The vampire must never be so depicted as to elicit sympathy, but the werewolf is a basically pitiful creature who, though he has to be destroyed, is yet entitled to understanding. On the screen werewolves and vampires have been both male and female.

Voodoo has been neglected by Hollywood's horror men–rather surprisingly, in view of its exotic quality and the fact that its mysticism is not entirely fantasy. For the most part it has been wasted in "B" chillers, but one of the Lewton group, I Walked with a Zombie, has considerable interest. It had two particularly powerful sequences: an uneasy opening scene of an entire village disturbed by sounds of a child sobbing in the night, and later, a wonderful, terrifying journey through open fields to a voodoo ceremony.

However, the most interesting example of film voodoo was the independently produced White Zombie of the early thirties. Like so many of the independently made shockers of that period, it tried too hard to outdo its predecessors in thrill and shock, and the result was often near farce. But White Zombie was more fortunate than most, and the advantages of a good cast, exotic settings and imaginative photography, almost offset an outrageous script and direction. Like Dracula, it was best in the purely visual, predominantly silent, scenes of the zombies silhouetted against the sky, parading silently through a hillside graveyard, and the burial sequence with its stately march to a forbidding crypt, and the sudden, unexpectedly harsh sound of the coffin-wood scraping against flagstones. When it tried to horrify, as in close-ups of the hideous zombies, ridden with bullet-holes, and the shot of the native worker falling to his death in a sugar-cane crusher, it became ridiculous. Nevertheless, White Zombie remains the most interesting filmic essay in voodooism to date.

The category we have loosely described as "old house" is essentially a product of the silent films. Because the action is restricted and effect is dependent more upon atmosphere than sensationalism, "old house" films were more suited to the slower-paced, more methodical silent cinema.

Leni's *The Cat and the Canary* (1927), with its brilliant opening scenes (perhaps the most distinctive establishing sequence of any horror film), is still one of the best "old house" films, and was certainly superior to its two talkie remakes. Naturally, it contained many traces of the best elements of German fantasy. The make-up of the fake psychiatrist (Lucien Littlefield) was based on that of Werner Krauss as Caligari. *The Cat and the Canary* was not the first of the "old house" chillers, having been preceded by *The Bat* and others, but it had an influence that was particularly apparent in the early thirties. *The Thirteenth Guest*, and more notably, *The Old Dark House* (one of the best of the several fine horror films made by James Whale) were much indebted to it.

In recent years "old house" films have tended more and more to comedy-thrill and away from out-and-out melodrama, although there has been a refreshingly straightforward revival of the former style in the current 3-D *The Maze* (which also has a monster).

Necromancy and diabolism, which include black magic and witchcraft, have, like voodooism, been neglected on the screen. Exuberant devil-worshipping and the like run up against censorship, in all parts of the world.

The Black Cat (1934)–recently revived under the title *The Vanishing Body*–was directed by Edgar Ulmer and though it had nothing whatever in common with the Poe story, it nevertheless created real Poe atmosphere by its glorification of evil and devil worship. Long silent sequences and wonderful sets and modernistic décor abetted the unreality. Karloff and Lugosi, bearing the delightful names of Hjalmar Poelzig and Vitus Verdegast respectively, had roles that reversed their usual ones. Karloff, as the head of the devil-worshipping cult in a fort built over a still mined ex-battlefield, was opposed by the sinister–but completely sympathetic–Lugosi, returning from a pest-hole imprisonment, brought about by Karloffian betrayal. Karloff, who had married Lugosi's wife, and keeps her corpse in a temple that is lined with glass coffins, subsequently married Lugosi's daughter. The natural antagonism between Karloff and Lugosi, however, is kept on a high level of cultured, intellectual dignity, typical of which is their chess game for possession of a girl stranded at the fort. Then, suddenly, all pretences are dropped and the film finishes with wholly unrestrained savagery. Following a black mass ceremony, Lugosi skins Karloff alive prior to blowing up the entire fortress.

Two lesser films in the this category, though both disappointing, are not without interest. *The 7ᵗʰ Victim,* another of the Lewton series, was a much later essay on devil-worship that misfired but did capture the oppressive atmosphere of death and decay which pervaded *The Black Cat.* And Republic's *The Woman Who Came Back* (1945), with a story of a witch in contemporary New England, also achieved atmosphere of eerie terror. But trite scripting weakened the climax with a "logical explanation."

The few film attempts at serious ghost stories have usually been outside the field of horror films. *The Uninvited, Peter Ibbetson* and *A Christmas Carol,* e.g., are considered drama or romanticism, rather than Grand Guignol. Ghosts in horror films have tended to be disguised as vampires, or as creatures brought back to life by mad scientists.

The one really outstanding horror film involving ghosts and apparitions was the British-made *Dead of Night,* which, after *Vampyr,* is probably the most effective and genuinely horrifying film ever made.

It consisted of five separate stories, dealing with possession, premonitions, and ghostly manifestations, bound together in a sixth story that had the design of a nightmare. The visually gruesome was avoided, save for a quick shot of a hearse waiting in the cold dawn, and a sustained feeling of something intangible and invisible hovering over all, was achieved by skillful suggestion only. This atmosphere of the power of the unseen was particularly strong in a macabre story about a mirror in which its new owner sees reflected a ghastly murder committed a century before and thereupon repeats the crime. In another story about a children's Christmas party, the horrified realization of Sally Ann Howes that a sobbing little boy she comforted in a deserted room was actually the ghost of a child murdered by his sister fifty years before, convinces all kinds of audiences. Unfortunately this and one other story (totalling some 4,000 feet) were omitted from the version of *Dead of Night* released in the US.

In recent years only one American horror film has dealt seriously with a ghost–an overlooked minor budget film, *The Strangler of the Swamp* (1945). It was a moody and unconventional little piece, directed by Frank Wisbar, and dealt with the haunting of a lonely swampland ferry by the ghost of a wrongly hanged man (played by Charles Middleton). Its climax paralled that of *Nosferatu,* in that the spirit was defeated by the true love of a girl who offered her life for that of her fiance.

Our last category is without pattern and classifies together the miscellaneous "stunt" and off-beat thrillers that do not come under any other heading.

The silent *The Phantom of the Opera* contains some of the screen's finest examples of terror–the phantom guiding his gondola through the misty canal beneath the opera house; his hand suddenly emerging from beneath the waters to drag an intruder to his death; the searchers wandering through the dark catacombs with hands raised above their heads to ward off the unseen noose of the madman. And the sudden close-up of the phantom's face as his mask is ripped away by Mary Philbin is a scene that has been duplicated countless times since, but equalled only once in *The Mystery of the Wax Museum.*

Without question, *King Kong* is a giant among spectacular "stunt" shockers. It did not rely only on brilliant trick photography and sheer spectacle. Tension was built steadily via a deliberate, precise formula. Neither *Kong* nor any of the other monsters appeared during the first three reels, which started out in the wise-cracking manner typical of the thirties. Gradually the humor lessened, the dismal fog rolled in, and the mystery deepened. We knew only that a daredevil film producer (Robert Armstrong) was approaching a mysterious island where he hoped to photograph something horrifying. His star (Fay Wray) was put through a series of tests which included her screaming at some unseen, nameless terror presumably on the island. Just as the tension reached

Below, the silent ***The Phantom of the Opera***: a costumed Lon Chaney descends the grand staircase during a masquerade.

breaking point, the forbidding uncharted island was revealed and still there was no explanation. Merely more mystery, incessant drumming, and hysterically screaming natives, living in fear of some unknown terror. Then, as the drumming reaches fever pitch, ominous grunts were heard from afar, and suddenly Kong burst on to the screen in all his glory.

Then the film's whole pattern changed: the slow, deliberate pace became hysterical, shock piled upon shock without time for recovery, and the chase was maintained until the final frame.

It was formula that worked admirably and was repeated with equal success in another off-beat thriller, *The Most Dangerous Game*, and in a sequel to *King Kong*. A current equivalent shocker, *The Beast from 20,000 Fathoms*, proves the value of the formula by repudiating it. It introduces its monster too casually and too soon; and when the monster is off-screen the writing is so trite there is no tension-building. One is impressed by the technical wizardry of the rhedosarus, but the film itself fails to thrill.

Perhaps there is an eighth category of horror films—the horror satire. Most of the categories already described have inspired at least one allegedly humorous takeoff, and the "old house" has been mocked most of all.

The best take-offs were the two Bob Hope films, *The Cat and the Canary* and *The Ghost Breakers*. Subsequent satire fell rather flat, for their formula consisted of a couple of comics going through their standard routines with a horror plot-line merely providing additional pegs for gags (*The Gorilla, You'll Find Out, Zombies on Broadway*). In 1948, Universal (which by then had abandoned horror films, after shamelessly degrading in cheap thrillers some of their wonderful original creations) produced *Abbott and Costello Meet Frankenstein*. It was far from first-rate satire, but it was a good deal better than one expected. Some of the gags built around the monsters were quite inventive. The horror content was well to the fore, and when not being played straight, was pleasingly satirized rather than ridiculed.

The introduction of sound did not create the horror film but it did give it an enormous boost. MGM's *The Mysterious Island*, made in 1929 by Maurice Tourneur, that French specialist of the macabre, was a definite portent of the future in that it used sound to increase the melodramatic thrills of its science-fiction scenes. Those early days of sound offered an unprecedented opportunity for stunts—weirdly whirring machines, screams of terror, howling wolves, wind, thunderstorms, crashing orchestrations for unexpected close-ups of the monster.

Candles alone might illuminate dark passages more brightly than flashlights: Dr. Edelman (Onslow Stevens) encounters Dracula (John Carradine) in **House of Dracula** (above). Opposite top, Bob Hope and Willie Best in **Ghost Breakers**.

Some protagonists are more horrific than others: Fredric March as Mr. Hyde (opposite below) strikes a less dashing figure than Gary Cooper (below, holding Ann Harding) in **Peter Ibbetson**. But aspects of the well-coiffed Cooper combine with Hyde's wardrobe in Carradine's Dracula.

The great period of American horror films was between 1931 and 1935. The major companies, as well as the independents, went at them full-throttle with star casts and lavish bankrolls. Scripts and production values were of a high order and the films contained a more intelligent use of the moving camera than did any other single type of motion picture. Very often there were dramatic emphases that recalled the images of *Destiny* and *Siegfried*. The plots were not standard formula ones, since, for the most part, these were the films that created the formulae.

In addition to the films already discussed, there was produced in this "golden period":

By Universal: Whale's *The Invisible Man;* Stuart Walker's version of Dickens' *The Mystery of Edwin Drood*, and two field days for Karloff and Lugosi, *The Invisible Ray* and *The Raven* (which more resembled Chaney's silent *The Monster* than the Poe story), Warners made *Dr. X* and *The Walking Dead*, Majestic did *The Vampire Bat.*

MGM produced some beauties–*The Mask of Fu Manchu, Mark of the Vampire, The 13th Chair* and *The Devil Doll*. The last, a story of a French scientist who reduced humans to homunculi and covered his activities by posing as an elderly lady toyshop keeper, had distasteful elements which were doubtless due to Erich von Stroheim's script. Paramount's *Island of Lost Souls* (Laughton and Lugosi, and an H.G. Wells story), and the title-explaining *Murders in the Zoo* (Atwill), were followed by the Fredric March *Dr. Jekyll and Mr. Hyde,* considerably more gruesome than the silent versions and the subsequent re-make with Tracy. Independent output, on the whole, was lurid and crudely sensational. *The Monster Walked* was almost farce.

During this period certain patterns for horror films were evolved that have endured to today. One of the most interesting is that the villain seldom meets his end at the hands of the hero. Usually one of his own creations or a double-crossing henchman turns on him in the final reel (*Bride of Frankenstein*). Or, if the villain is a basically sympathetic character whose misdeeds are the result of scientific zeal he may die in a laboratory mishap, quite happily, regretting his mistakes (*The Devil Commands*).

The hero, in fact, has always been unimportant in horror films. His usual role is that of casual observer (often a newspaper reporter) and prospective husband for the heroine at the fadeout. David Manners, the stock hero in most of Universal's early melodramas, was a typically useless leading man, and was knocked out, locked up, or shut out, after only the most passive kind of resistance. This trend can be seen in the silents too. In *The Phantom of the Opera*, Norman Kerry faints at a moment when his aid is sorely needed.

Another interesting pattern is the use of ancient proverbs at the beginning and end of horror films. The connection between the words of wisdom and the events portrayed n the screen is often none too obvious, but they help the audience to the willing suspension of disbelief.

For the most part, the really worthwhile, off-beat horror films (those which follow none of the standardized paths described above) disappeared in the mid-thirties. One of the last was MGM's *Mad Love* (1935). Directed by Karl Freund and starring Colin Clive and Peter Lorre, it was an interesting re-make of the old Wiene-Veidt German thriller, *Hands of Orlac*.

By 1936 the horror film had settled down into the popular-programmer niche. Karloff, Lugosi and Atwill had expended their best. Fay Wray, who screamed her way through three encounters with Atwill, and one each with King Kong and Leslie Banks, left shockers for more sedate roles, as did Valerie Hobson. Aside from Whale's second Frankenstein film (silly script, wonderful material), and such odd items as Roy William Neill's *The Black Room*, nothing very much happened.

Then, in 1939, Rowland V. Lee returned to chillers for the first time since his *Mysterious Dr. Fu Manchu* of ten years before. He gathered together Karloff and Lugosi (who had been busy in British shockers) and Rathbone and Atwill, and let them loose in *Son of Frankenstein*. Liberally budgeted, and with a running time in excess of 90 minutes (rare in horror films) its very size and meticulous construction were impressive. Once more the poor villagers were roused by the burgomaster to go through the countryside with flaming torches (each Frankenstein film— all eight of them—has such a sequence).

The success of Rowland Lee's *Frankenstein* opus helped revive Grand Guignol in Hollywood. Lee followed it with another Karloff-Rathbone blood-bath, *Tower of London*, and chillers appeared on the schedules of both major and independent companies.

The enthusiasm didn't last, and by 1942 the horror film had become mass-produced "B" commodity for the action houses. When Universal finally abandoned horror films, one picture was considered so inferior they sold it to a lesser company to release.

The only really bright spots of the early forties were the modestly budgeted horror films Val Lewton produced for RKO with a team of upcoming untried directors that included Jacques Tourneur, Mark Robson and Robert Wise. These films preferred studies in fear, superstition and the supernatural to physical action, employed suggestion, rather than

Some of the many other faces of Boris Karloff (clockwise from above); the arcane Asian (with Myrna Loy and Charles Starrett) in **The Mask of Fu Manchu** (1932); the Val Lewton-produced **Bedlam** (1946); the butler in James Whale's **Old Dark House** (1932); and mirrored menace in **The Raven** (1935).

outright statement, and contained some of the best horror the American horror school has achieved. The first of Lewton's series, e.g *Cat People*, was something of a minor masterpiece. A macabre variation on the werewolf theme, it contained one episode of authentic nightmare in which the heroine, alone in a darkened swimming pool, is menaced on all sides by unseen and barely audible terror.

By the mid-forties the horror film was in eclipse. Only an occasional mediocre independent quickie, of the calibre of *Scared to Death*, kept the genre alive. But now science fiction—and the new wide-screen processes—have brought the horror film back once more.

The science fiction cycle started out with expeditions to the Moon and Mars. The objectives were exploratory and constructive, the dangers limited to small groups of men ready and willing to face them. It was soon obvious that it would be much more fun to subject Earth to invasion and onslaughts from other planets. This was a far cry from the well-intentioned, albeit unfortunate, scientists of the thirties, who had at least been interested in such useful projects as prolonging human life or creating artificial hearts.

Science itself, instead of the mad scientist, has become the heavy in the new order of things. In *The Beast from 20,000 Fathoms*, a scientific atomic test blast was responsible for setting the huge monster at liberty. In *The Thing* the efforts of one of the scientists to study the creature caused most of the trouble. And in *War of the Worlds* the advanced scientific technics of another planet all but demolish the earth. With *The House of Wax* and *The Maze*, the nerve-shattering possibilities of the added visual depth of 3-D and the volume possibilities of stereophonic sound offer the horror film new ways to scare audiences.

Universal's 3-D *It Came from Outer Space* shows that these new technics can change the face of the horror film but not its form. All the stock characters are there, all the familiar situations. The scientist (Richard Carlson) explains early in the proceedings that he is compelled to work alone in the desert because the townspeople distrust him—later they also believe him mad. The sudden close-up of the "thing" with the huge eye isn't much different from the shock close-up in *The Most Dangerous Game* of a pickled human head floating in a jar of alcohol. Like the Frankenstein monster the "thing" is basically sympathetic, for all its hideous appearance, for, let alone, it will harm nobody. The old-time interfering and bumbling burgomaster of Lionel Barrymore or E.E. Clive is reincarnated in the hot-headed and unreasonable sheriff of Charles Drake. And when, in the final reel, the townspeople riot through the countryside bent on destroying the invaders, one can't help but recall

the mobs of villagers with flaming torches raging to kill the Frankenstein monster.

Science fiction, however, may not dominate the 3-D, wide-screen future. *The Neanderthal Man*, a combination of Jekyll and Hyde and werewolf themes, directed by our old friend E.A. Dupont, has just been
released. Warners have remade *Murders in the Rue Morgue* and another
version of *The Raven* is under way in England. Who knows—today's
tendency toward big-screen shock and sensation may mean the future of
the horror film is bright.

Below, Boris Karloff as the Monster bends over the fallen Igor (Bela Lugosi) in Rowland
V. Lee's **Son of Frankenstein**.

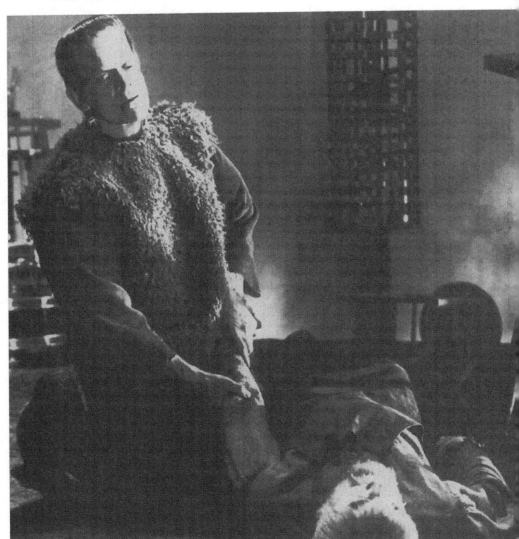

The Subconscious: From Pleasure Castle to Libido Motel

Raymond Durgnat (1958)

The only films whose erotic content is as open as that of musicals are horror films—again, fantasy allows the film-makers to cock a snoot at logic. We expect horror films to be "bad" or enjoyable in an "illegitimate" way. Like poets, directors of horror films tend to be specialists. Their non-horror films are generally brutal or disturbing; and if a film company is ever foolish enough to give a horror director a free hand, what comes out is not infrequently horror made twice as horrible because it is not even fantasy (*Le Sang des Betes, Freaks*).

Ernest Schoedsack's pioneering documentary *Grass* pales into insignificance beside *King Kong*. You may think the film is naïve and artless (I think you'd be very wrong) but it's one of those films which nobody who's seen forgets, which makes strong men want to cry, is one of the all-time box-office heavyweights and as the self-chosen name of a champion boxer has provided a folk-symbol for the oppressed South African, "That's me. I'm him, King Kong!"

As in James Whale's *Frankenstein* (far superior to the Hammer remake though one shouldn't despise Hammer's *Dracula*), it doesn't take much to make us sympathize (i.e. identify with the monster and say, "Well, he's only a monster, poor thing—you can't expect him to understand civilized behaviour—you shouldn't have created or kidnapped him in the first place, and he's absolutely in the right to defend himself in any way he can."). It's a charming irony that the cinema audience who have come to see King Kong on the screen chuckle and cheer as King Kong terrorises the audience in the film who have come to see him in captivity on the stage. It's a good job they never re-made *King Kong* in 3-D; that would have been tempting providence.

The kingpin of the horror film is the rendezvous of eroticism and violence. When, at the beginning of James Whale's film, Frankenstein cries, "I have always longed to create human life" and his fiancee (Valerie Hobson) inquires, "How?", even the yokellest yokel will, in the long pause obligingly provided for him, grasp the double meaning (in the se-

Opposite, Fay Wray about to be sacrificed to the beast in **King Kong**.

quel, *Bride of Frankenstein*, the scientist cries, "Nothing is so enthralling as the act of creation"). To the religious impiety of creating human life in a crudely physiological way (taking this criminal's trunk off the gibbet and stitching it to another criminal's brain taken out of pickle), the script-writers add the psychological perversity of creating human life without the aid of sex. Frankenstein's laboratory is a stone tower set on a hilltop, and the scene where the "embryonic" compendium of carcasses hoisted to the top of a tower while a storm rages is a crude but by no means unimpressive image for tumescence.

Despite his unfavourable heredity, the Monster (Boris Karloff) is pathetic as well as evil—after all, he awoke from the tomb to find himself chained up in a dreadful tower; he was fairly peaceful and even slightly happy while he lived with the blind old hermit who played tunes on his violin; and he didn't mean to drown the little girl, he just saw her throwing flowers on to the lake and played the same game with her—he wasn't to know she wouldn't float.

Later, when her father carries his daughter's corpse through the village festivities, music and raucous laughter echo on the soundtrack, while the girl's dangling limbs swing in a grotesque parody of dancing, and, emphasising a strip of thigh, sexualises the corpse of an underage girl. Enough to make Humbert Humbert turn in his grave. After all this it's not surprising that the Monster times its last breakout at the wedding ceremony and attacks his creator's bride. In the sequel, Frankenstein and Dr. Praetorius (Ernest Thesiger) put their heads together and concoct a female monster (Elsa Lanchester)—pity she's an improved model and screams in a paroxysm of callous snobbery as the obsolescent old Mark I lumbers amorously towards her. James Whale may use a naïve idiom, but he uses it with a very sophisticated expertise. None of the humour is unintentional; every joke is a sick joke, and the film has immense brio.

The old-fashioned ghost story is so rare now that even the "haunted house" burlesques have become dim memories. Perhaps it's time to conjure up a few spooks again.

The more exotic forms of the supernatural—*Dracula, The Mummy, The Night of the Demon*—retain their popularity, but, usually, it is scientists whose spiritual pride, heartless logic and will to conquer nature are convenient "logical bridges" to the next world. These days, the diabolical or mad scientist is rarer than the dedicated seeker after truth whose obsession and incautious caring arouses our sympathy as well as our misgivings.

Even The Devil is quite an amiable, reasonable gentleman—Yves Montand or Claude Rains, whose pedantry about signing on the dotted line recalls the showmen of *Expresso Bongo*. The real menace to mankind these days is the inhuman creature with biological tendency to eat human beings, to take over their minds to feed on their radio-activity, or tear them to pieces.

Horror has two aspects. In the obvious "Monster" type, humans unleash, meet, or periodically become a werewolf, a gorilla, a vampire, a beast from 20,000 fathoms, anything suggesting the wild animal in man (ripping, ravishing, biting and bloodsucking, and so on). In a more sophisticated variety, the source of horror is altogether subtler, consisting in coming up against something whose feelings are completely inhuman. It may be expressed physically, as in *The Quatermass Experiment* where Richard Wordsworth slowly turns into a vegetable lump. But it is usually accompanied by mental derangement or alienation. There is a horror of impersonality. In *Quatermass II* "they" from Outer Space take over the less unfriendly "they" of Whitehall, and it's only after you've blurted out your suspicions to the attentive Scotland Yard chief that you see the tell-tale scar.

In *Village of the Damned* the women of the ordinary Home Counties village all give birth, simultaneously, to children with strange, piercing, contemptuous eyes. In *Invasion of the Body Snatchers*, mysterious pods burst open to produce vague humanoid shapes which gradually become exact duplicates of your best friends. They betray themselves only by a slightly unfeeling response in everything; they are very correct; only children are sensitive enough to shriek that "Grandad" isn't really Grandad, and the real human beings won't believe them. While your best friend sleeps you watch the Shape in the corner of the room gradually becoming him and find your own pod waiting for you to fall asleep. Suddenly you and your fiancee are the only humans in town, and "they" are politely but implacably offering you rest and freedom from those degrading, irrational human emotions, if only you will come over. And later, as you kiss your fiancee, her lack of response, her wide-open, slaty eyes reveals that she too...

The erotic perversity of all this is hard to pinpoint because it is a perversity of non-eroticism, a perversity of spiritual hunger without love (without even love-hate), implacable yet impersonal, a vast collectivity from Outer Space, an abstraction with a normal, neighborly face. Its erotic perversity is precisely a death of feeling, a renunciation of all erotic relationships in favour of a totalitarian—what? Something inconceivable, a Nothing. Perhaps it's significant that the only criticism (or at least, so far as I know) which begins to explore the undertones of this weird and memorable film appeared in a French theological monthly, *Les Cahiers Protestants*. Yet the film's exploitation of a quiet, reasonable, unobtrusive madness, a madness of a passionless collectivity, is arguably, as "central" an image of our time as the metamorphosis of Dr. Jekyll into Mr. Hyde was for the Victorian era.

Although *Invasion of the Body Snatchers* is an intellectual film, it still derives its emotional strength from a nightmare situation—the sort of nightmare which a child tearfully explains as "It was like you, only you were horrible." Most of Roger Corman's remake of *The Fall of the House of Usher* may have been unusually dull, but it used its traditional horrors to great effect—coffins crashing to the floor so that skeletons leap out as if alive; a pale young girl acquiring superhuman strength after burial alive and strangling her lover [brother]; and brothel-coloured dream-sequence where the friendly but evil dead grin seductively and invite us to join them. The screen is packed tight with their garish and gruesome faces and their gestures don't just mean "Come into the tomb" but "Mingle with us, let us touch you all over."

The dead, when frightening, are apt to be very erotic—I have it on the authority of one intelligent 'teenager that Christopher Lee in *Dracula* was the sexiest male in English pictures since James Mason in *The Seventh Veil*. And it isn't very far from the dead in the *House of Usher* to Mummy's mummy in *Psycho*, which, with *King Kong*, the James Whale films and Dreyer's *Vampyr* is surely one of the most erotic horror films.

But don't read any further if you haven't seen *Psycho* yet. The reason is that this article is partly about people's reactions to "overtones."

On a hot day during the lunch-hour, in an impersonal hotel bedroom Marion Crane (Janet Leigh) and Sam Loomis (John Gavin) are half-naked and necking. The nightmare begins on a hot midday during a dissatisfying hour of necking. The heat, the bleached feel of the visuals, the half-nakedness, evoke an atmosphere of unsatiated sensuality—indeed the prolonged necking in so many of Hitchcock's American films, from *Notorious* to *North by Northwest,* has a furtive resemblance to sexual intercourse without orgasm or emotional relaxation. With American matter-of-factness the lovers are talking about divorce and the money they need if they are to marry. The general situation (stripping at lunchtime) is crudely sensual—enjoyable but vaguely offensive. This ambiguity permeates their whole relationship.

She wants to end these degrading situations, is tempted to break off the affair. She returns to the sane, shallow, superficial people of the office where she works. A client makes a rather coarse and vulgar attempt to flirt with her, by brandishing a fat bankroll in her face. The client brags that he wouldn't miss the money if it were stolen and her boss absolutely insists on trusting Marion with it. Such smug, false, imperceptive responses all round reinforce our feeling that Marion has a right to the money. These pinpricks accumulate into a kind of obsession and reinforce the confusion between her respectability (which may be mainly pride) and her love (which may be mainly sensuality). The money seems to offer a solution to all these "raw edges" of feeling. Her theft is (so to speak) an impulse born of converging obsessions. It is a tribute to her daring, her strength of passion; she is challenging society, for the sake of her own happiness.

Soon she is driving hard away from the town, tormented not so much by conscience as by fear. We can't believe she'll go away with it but we hope she will.

The rain forces her into a motel, run by Norman Bates (Anthony Perkins), an engagingly naïve country youth, very honest, unconcerned with making money, almost a symbol of rustic virtue and country and contentment. The whole film hinges on his sensitivity and charm—we tend to like him whatever his faults. His friendliness is all the more reassuring in contrast with the sinister atmosphere (the stuffed birds, the Victorian house with the petulant, tyrannical old mother), though he

Below, *Psycho*: "...heat, the bleached feel of the visuals, the half-nakedness, evoke an atmosphere of unsatiated sensuality..."

seems tainted by it. The over-obvious horror cliches shift our suspicions from Norman to the atmosphere; they camouflage the inevitable stilted-ness of his relationship with Mrs. Bates; they contrast with the previous slick, modern, informal style of the film. Mrs. Bates comes from Nor-man's childhood and she exists in an aesthetic idiom now considered childish—she would have felt at home in James Whale's *The Old Dark House*. But Hitchcock does not simply put us off the scent. Marion calls Norman's bird-stuffing a rather morbid hobby and says Norman resem-bles a bird—he does.

Gradually Marion realises that she is his superior, that, if unhappy, she is self-possessed, whereas his "contented" acquiescence in staying with his mother is something weak, childish, abject.

We would like her to help him free himself from his horrible mother, whom we blame for the eccentricities of this likable chap. There is some-thing slightly brusque, indifferent in Marion's attitude to him: he needs help which she doesn't offer. She simply decides to return alone, to the dissatisfying everyday, with its petty concealments, degradations, choices. A sort of bewilderment percolates through the audience: the film is continuing, yet there seems nothing in the offing. The film elabo-rately establishes Marion trying to find a hiding-place for the cash—a rather cynical act, since Norman isn't the sort of lad to steal it, really. As she undresses, Norman is watching through a peephole with an avid sexuality which we laugh at uneasily but which does not quite put him in our bad books—for he has been lonely and dominated by his puri-tanical mother, his spying on Marion represents a movement towards her, normality and freedom. This is almost a dissatisfying love-scene (like necking at lunchtime) because (whatever our sex) the erotic over-tones are pleasantly juicy, and we can feel the story moving again.

The "movement towards" Marion is intensified with a vengeance when Mrs. Bates with knife upraised charges in and stabs her to death in the bath. The murder is too erotic not to enjoy, but too grisly to enjoy; its ferocity and pornography are opposed. They force on the spectator a rapid, hysteric oscillation between outraged shock and enjoyment. There is a sort of Hays Code moral in the air—"Look what sexy, immoral, thieving girls get"—but it is also extremely unjust (for she had just re-pented). If the Peeping Tom episode is a "weak" yet eerie version of the hotel scene, the assault is a sarcastic exaggeration of it—her sensuality's satisfied now, all right. We feel guilty at enjoying the film, but, as shock subsides, we have to admit we're having our money's worth of fun and fear.

Mom would be a convenient scapegoat, but we are confused by the tolerant distress and concern for her of Norman, who, in the next scene, begins mopping up operations, the action of an extremely dutiful son. The presence of Marion's naked corpse is both erotic and very, very uncomfortable. The film offers us a "first-person" experience answering the question which so often occurs to crime fans: "Would I be able to bear the practical details of clearing up the corpse and the blood?"—for many people a more frightening prospect than the actual killing. They turn out to be more bearable—this is disquieting to the better side of our nature, but gratifies the other.

The audience's moral purity is being outflanked at both ends—by morbid, slightly pornographic fascination, and by pity for the charming Norman. Not that indignation and disgust are lulled asleep. For example there is a very precise mix between a C.U. of the plughole down which our saintly Peeping Tom is washing the blood, and a C.U. of Marion's eye staring at us as if to say, "What about my feelings?" She's peeping back at us from beyond the grave, from down the drain, with protest and indignation—or surprise and fear—or just nothing. This visual rhyme is not simple a piece of sadistic wit but a little essay in metaphor, e.g. the plughole is like an eye-socket, the eye ("window of the soul" as they say) is just a mushroom out of a black hole. There is a sense of total nothingness and if the "joke" provides a little hysteria which relieves the horror a little it insinuates a subtler unease: we must be mad to be laughing at a joke like this.

Norman is chewing candy as he watches the white car sink beneath the very black surface of the swamp; and when he tosses in the cash, which he nearly overlooked, a cry of shock and regret runs through the audience—that valuable money, what a waste! His saintliness hurts us. We wanted to forget Marion, probably because her murder shook us up so much; but the money has become "what she died for," almost a substitute identity. Its derisive disappearance creates hysteria as again the narrative seems to "end."

Sam Loomis discusses Marion's disappearance with her sister Lila (Vera Miles). A detective, Arbogast (Martin Balsam), insists on offering his services. In the battle of wits between him and Norman we sympathise with them both; he wants to get at the truth, for Norman only wants to save his mother (and perhaps Arbogast). But as Arbogast climbs the stairs towards the old lady's room, we realise clearly that his pushful cynicism, hitherto his strength, is now his weakness. He is formidable, and might just prove to be Mom's match, but he hasn't the mental "set" to be prepared when she comes tearing out of her room with the superstrength of the insane and with repeated jabs sends him tumbling backwards down the stairs, just like that. Is Mom invincible?

Another car sinks into the swamp, the narrative "ends" at another nihil-
istic moment.

The whole "plot," which has twice ended so disastrously, starts up
again as the young couple comes to investigate the disappearance of the
investigator who came to investigate the disappearance of...

Probably most of the audience have guessed by now that Mom is
Norman. But we can't be sure in so twisty a film. The only certain thing
is the imminence of violent death. What matters is not whether we
know, but whether Lila and Loomis find out—or get killed.

Loomis keeps Norman talking while Lila sneaks into the house to explore—clearly a very dangerous thing to do, with or without Mom. As
we can't make up our mind whether the danger's coming from in front
(Mom) or behind (Norman) we're no longer thinking very coherently,
but yield to the atmosphere. Norman grows more anxious and angry as
Loomis brutally presses him.

Lila explores the house. Amidst the tension there is an unexpected intellectual interest and pathos—the rooms are a picture of Norman's
mind, his everyday life. There is the record-player with the classical record (so out-of-key in this Gothic house), there are the fluffy childhood
toys, which are obviously still played with. Norman is weaker-minded
than we thought, which makes him both more dangerous and more pathetic. Norman, mad with suspicion, rushes from the motel to the house
as Lila takes refuge in the cellar. And Mom does exist, there she is, horri-
bly old, evil and withered—a closer look she's dead and withered, but
still grinning malevolently, she's a ghost, death in the abstract, and
when Lila turns, there's another Mom, grinning malevolently, very
much alive with knife upraised. There aren't *no* Moms, there are two—
then the second disintegrates, the wig slides off, it's Norman.

It's not simply the surprise that shocks; it's the intensity of terror and
the obscenity of the disintegration. (In rather the same way, when Mom
came tearing out of her room at Arbogast, she had the terrible strength
of the insane, and a visible virility quite obscene in an old lady; and the
explanation doesn't explain that away, it intensifies its impact because
illusion and explanation co-exist.)

We are relieved to hear that everything is going to be comfortably explained for us by the police psychologist. As soon as we see him we begin to dislike his brash, callous, know-all manner, he puts our back up
as Arbogast did. We expect the cliches: poor mixed-up kid, it was all the
fault of the stern, possessive, puritanical Mom. Gradually we realise he's
not saying this at all. It was the son who was jealous, who imagined his
(probably) normal Mom was a promiscuous Mom and then imagined

she was a jealous puritanical Mom and then lived out two false characters—Normal Norman and nasty Mom. For all this, he seemed nearly normal—rustic contentment, in fact. Norman was never entirely Norman (i.e. even when he was being charming and we felt sorry for him, he knew, deep down, what he was doing).

The psychologist's explanation takes away our explanation; what we thought was "deep," the "solution," is merely the topmost level of horror, he restores terror, guilt and injustice. Up till now the gruesome appearance of Mom has been in accord with her character: "Well, if she's dead, she asked for it, look how she messed up her tender and devoted son"; suddenly, all this is reversed, we realise the coconut-faced corpse may once have been an apple-cheeked mother. The boy has turned her (literally) into his illusion of her. There are several cellars beneath the cellar.

But if the psychologist, brutal and cynical, is the most intimate of private eyes, the joke is still to come. All we've had has been an intellectual, rational explanation, designed to lead up to the following scene. Norman sits against a blank, white, hygienic wall. He is in full-face close-up, his madness is rammed into the cinema. Briefly our entire world is his face, and the thoughts behind it. We have little else with which to identify. An utter flatness, whiteness, simplicity, in short, eternity. He is cackling to himself, in Mummy's mummy's voice. She is jubilant because she will outwit them all by pretending to be a sweet old lady who won't even hurt a fly. Mom has just killed Norman, and disguised herself as him. He has become the mummy of a Mummy who never existed outside his own imagination. The Chinese sage wrote: "Now I do not know whether I was then a man dreaming I was a butterfly or whether I am now a butterfly dreaming I am a man." Norman's self-punishment is so total that— we don't pity him, for there's no one there left to pity, and he seems to think he's escaping punishment, but a nausea like compassion makes itself felt. We are too thoroughly disturbed to hate him. The appearance of Mom's face under the madman's, and of a skull under Mom's, has a climactic brutality, but also simplifies, liberates us from the baffling maze of malevolent Nothings which our sensitive boy has become. But it is followed by a shot of the police lifting Marion's car, wrapped in chains, from the swamp. There is no "decent obscurity." And "nothing" to the nth degree has killed real people, whom we sympathised with—But we hoped that car would sink (just as we hoped Marion would get away with the theft). We too have been accomplices after the acts—futile acts.

People leave the cinema, chuckling incredulously, groggy, exhilarated yet hysterical, half ready to believe that everybody is slightly as mad as

Norman. A cathartic indulgence in erotic murder is succeeded by an embarrassed humility, an unsentimental compassion towards insanity. The entire film is a prolonged practical joke in the worst of taste—if it weren't in bad taste, it would be neither cathartic, embarrassing, nor compassionate.

It is not just a sick joke, it is also a very sad joke. Because it is outrageous, it is exhilarating, but is a very depressed film as well. The by-play with the money is strange and disturbing. It is produced as a weapon of seduction by a repulsive but normal male; Marion, resenting the implied insult, yields to the money (i.e. respectability becomes mere money); at last it becomes a last clue, a substitute-identity, a soul. Marion is reduced to a nude body, a car and a wad of notes: and all that piles up in the swamp.

The film is not just a sick and a sad joke, it is a derisive misuse of the key-images of the American way of life—Momism (but it blames son), cash (and rural virtue), necking (and respectability), plumbing and smart cars. The reality to which Lila and Loomis return is not a joyous one, but a drab shop of insecticides, pitchforks and a memory of horror. Only Norman has defied society and superficially found "rest." What was Marion's sin—not the illegal theft, but the crime for which "fate" killed her? Wasn't it that she refused to choose between self-respect (or just respectability, or cold pride) and love (or just sensuality). She hoped to avoid having to choose between happiness and respectability. Only Norman has found himself, and lost himself.

Psycho works not by providing enlightening information about the experiences of the characters—it provides just enough to confuse us—it works by luring the audience into becoming the characters, sharing and living out their experiences with them.

Its creation of atmosphere is brilliant enough to overwhelm our common sense. In describing the sort of feelings which the film evokes, I have used the editorial "we" but no two critics, no two spectators would respond in the same way (not that critics habitually agree on the meanings and contents of works of art anyway). A comparison of any two accounts shows how complicated the film is, not in what it says, but in what it makes one feel.

In the film nothing that isn't disturbing or tainted ever happens, and to enjoy or feel exhilarated by it (as most people do, of course) is to stand convicted of an unconscious nostalgia for evil, i.e. of enjoying it, at least in fantasy. Norman's only mistake is that he let fantasy enjoy him.

Most of us don't get very emotional about original sin, are apt to duck the issue of being guilty about sins we never consciously wanted to commit. But this film is a demonstration of it. One does not watch it, one participates as one might in a religious ritual involving the confession of guilt, and a final absolution (which we deserve, because we pity the victims). I don't think it's a Christian film, though; it has a Dionysiac force and ruthlessness, one might call it a Greek tragi-comedy (giving both terms their full meaning). From Pleasure Castle to Libido Motel is only a short walk.

All these films used aesthetic idioms which by "academic" standards are "illegitimate." None has much value as "drama." They are more interested in the frivolous, the supernatural, the brutal. Instead of giving us familiar points to cling to, they evoke and explore the "zone" of indeterminate, elusive feelings between common sense and the erotic wish. For passionate love they substitute the erotic fiesta (42nd Street), the erotic obsession (Psycho), the death of love (Invasion of the Body Snatchers), and an ordered luxe, calme and volupte (L'Eau a la Bouche). They depict the strength of erotic impulses and their disjunction from the "sensible" layers of our minds. Their fresh gaiety or terror evokes not so much contemporary ideas of "art" as themes derived from classical antiquity—the pastoral, the Broadway idyll, the madness of incest or of indifference to instincts. They touch on what Nietschze called the Dionysiac spirit.

Below, Norman Bates and Marion Crane outside the motel office in **Psycho**.

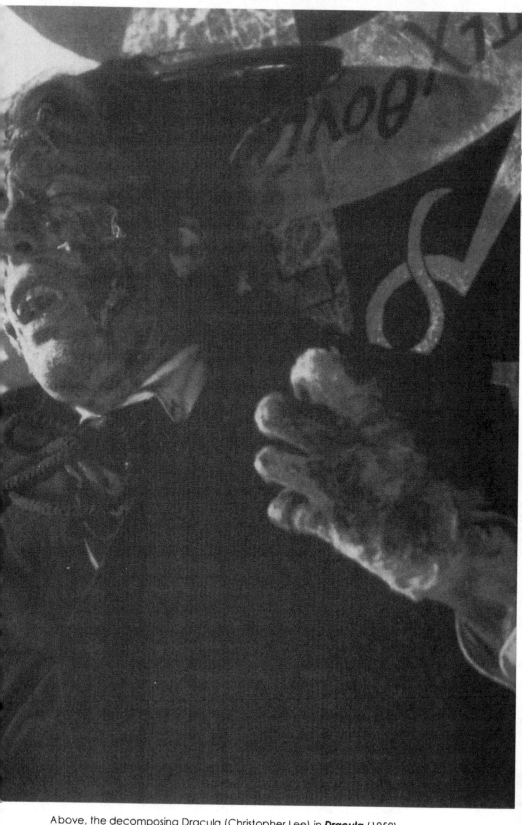

Above, the decomposing Dracula (Christopher Lee) in **Dracula** (1958).

The Face of Horror

Derek Hill (1958)

> Latest teenage idol showing at cinemas in Washington is an endearing character billed as 'The Blob, a blood-bloated mass of man-eating slime.' His supporting feature: 'I married a monster from outer space–shuddering things from beyond the stars here to breed with human women!'
>
> *Daily Express*

Only a sick society could bear the hoardings, let alone the films. Yet the displays, the posters and the slogans have become an accepted part of the West End scene. So, too, have the queues. The horror boom, despite occasional trade rumors, is still prospering. Why?

Scratch a psychiatrist and, it seems, you'll find a horror film advocate. Dr. Martin Grotjahn, a professor of psychiatry at the University of Southern California, is quoted in *Films and Filming* under the headline "Horror–Yes, It Can Do You Good": "There is perhaps a healthy function in horror. It keeps us on the task to face our anxieties and to work on them." And later, on the influence of horror on children: "It is a neurotic child, a frightened child, which takes horror from the screen and the book and worries about it in everyday life, and at night. Altogether it is a tendency of our time to be too concerned, to be too anxious to do it right. We are always in danger to feel like guilty parents who have failed their children. In other words, we are inclined to become over-protective."

An anonymous British psychiatrist declares in *Picturegoer:* "Horror films are a kind of dare to teenagers, a challenge that they just have to take up. And it provides a kind of outlet for them at a time–adolescence–when their feelings and their minds are occupied with sex and violence...I would say that this type of film was generally harmless. It presents a kind of fairy-tale for adolescents that's far removed from real life."

Production companies and distributors have been equally prompt in finding psychiatrists to applaud the horror cult, and publicity departments have defensively dug up some unusually classy references. The

51

following hand-out from Columbia for *The Revenge of Frankenstein* is typical: "Certain psychiatrists and anthropologists have long maintained that the emotional shock experienced by people reading thrillers, watching horror films, can have a salutary effect. In primitive cultures, monstrous, hideous masks were used in festivals, processions, etc.; in the ancient Greek drama, macabre events and vision were an essential ingredient; Aristotle asserted that the essential function of drama was to fill the audience with terror so as to purge their emotions...and how about Shakespeare's *Titus Andronicus*? Even today, in such places as exotic Bali, terrifying monsters and demons predominate in the people's festivals.... On every pleasure beach this summer, children are watching the traditional Punch and Judy show—which has a vicious crocodile that brings screams of fright and then squeals of delight, when Mr. Punch knocks it down to depths again.... Everyone harbours a host of weird and wonderful images in the subconscious—images that intangibly take part in his or her private mental dreams of anxiety. Maybe the uncanny, intriguing power of horror films helps exorcise what William Blake called 'these spectres around us, night and day.'"

Famous Monsters of Filmland puts the same argument in another way: "The day may not be so far distant when vitamins will be replaced by vita-monsters, anti-histamines by haunty-histamines, and the common aspirin by a chill-pill called GASPirin. Un-tranquillisers! Chilltowns instead of Milltowns. That emotional health and mental stability may be improved by subjecting oneself to safe shocks is the conclusion shared by a number of psychiatrists and anthropologists..." Then come the usual references—Greek drama, the invaluable Aristotle, Shakespeare ("Shades of Shakespeare!" exclaims the magazine, pointing out that if he had lived today, he would be writing Frankenstein screenplays), Bali, Faust and Poe. Famous Monsters, incidentally, is in no doubt about the compulsion of horror: "Welcome monster lovers," says the editorial, "You're stuck! The stuff this magazine is printed on, which looks so much like ordinary printer's ink, is actually glue. You cannot put this magazine down! Try as you may to struggle, it is impossible: like a zombie, you have no will of your own."

One of the more bizarre theories about the popularity of horror films has been quoted by John Trevelyan, secretary of the British Board of Film Censors: "It has been suggested to me that young people are unconsciously using these films as a sort of test of courage. Not having been in the last war, they wonder how they would stand up to another. This would seem to be one way they can expose themselves to fear and find out their reactions."

The one thing to be said for this, and for the beguiling rumour that Western governments are encouraging the production of these films in an attempt to blunt people's sensibilities sufficiently for them to face the horrors of atomic warfare, is that the contemporary scene is taken into account. No one has suggested that the individual's "need" for horror occurs in regular cycles. At the moment, admittedly, the horror film seems always to have been around in some degree. But in 1952 Curtis Harrington wrote in *Sight and Sound*: "With the end of the war, the popularity of horror films quickly diminished, so that since 1947 there have been few, if any, produced."

This lull lasted just long enough to give the horror film curiosity value for an enormous number of new young cinemagoers. Until recently, Frankenstein and Dracula were for them only people who Abbott and Costello met. For older filmgoers, the names were undoubtedly nostalgic. They meant excitement, suspense and shock, all valid attributes of any entertainment or art. This double appeal probably brought in the crowds. What brought them back for more was the discovery that they were getting something quite new. Unlike wide screen novelties, the curiosity value of the new kind of horror film is not diminished after the one has been seen. Just as with nudist productions, there is always the chance, rapidly becoming a near certainty, that the next film will go further—a point carefully fostered by the publicity departments.

This aspect, I suspect, accounts for a majority of the queues. What it does not explain is the reaction of audiences to the films. "Whatever the psychologists may make of it, most of the Rialto's patrons had sparkling eyes and ready grins when they proclaimed that they just loved a 'scarey film,'" reported *The Observer* after questioning people coming away from *The Fly*: and this is the general attitude. It is an unavoidable fact that audiences do laugh at the most repugnant details of the new horror films. As a release from suspense and nervous tension, this would hardly be disturbing; but it is often the same kind of laughter that accompanies a successful comedy sequence—laughter not to relieve tension, but express amusement or satisfaction.

Dr. Frederic Wiseman's book *Seduction of the Innocent* is concerned primarily with the influence of horror comics on the child. But, quite apart from his unanswerable refutation of the justifications put up by the horror comic industry—defences which closely parallel the film industry's current arguments—his points are frequently exactly relevant to the current horror film cycle and the adult. "It has been claimed, " he writes, "that if a child identifies himself with a violent character in a comic book it shows the individual child's psychological need to express his own aggression. But this reasoning is far too mechanical. Comic books are not a mirror of the individual child's mind; they are a mirror of the child's environment. They are a part of social reality. They not only have an effect, they also have a cause."

To attempt to understand the reasons for the immediate public response to horror films, it is worth looking briefly back at past cycles. Until the coming of sound, Germany dominated the horror field–a country suffering from post-war depression and the malaise of defeat. The first American cycle ran throughout the 'thirties–the depression years–but the films became less popular as the economy gained strength. By the time America entered the war, virtually no horror films were being made. In 1943 a new boom began; and then, after the war, there was another recession.

Horror literature, it has often been noted, becomes increasingly popular when a society is undergoing outward stress. The cinema, which provides a more accurate reflection of a nation's mood, confirms this. Kracauer has shown, in *From Caligari to Hitler*, how accurately the macabre German film reflected national uneasiness. Every horror film cycle has coincided with economic depression or war. Now we have the biggest, ugliest threat of them all, and a bigger, uglier horror boom than ever before.

This may seem a glib over-simplification. The Bomb has obviously not caused the horror glut. But its existence has fostered an atmosphere in which the horror films has been able to develop in disturbing directions and on an unprecedented scale. The final analysis will find us a nation, probably a world, of quiet, controlled, largely unconscious hysterics, driven to that condition by submerged impotence and fear. The links between insecurity, hidden hysteria, and the current appetite for aggressive violence are not going to be easily broken.

Most of the psychiatrical, psychological and sociological explanations offered for the horror boom suggest that few of the films' defenders–or for that matter their critics–have seen many of the productions in the current cycle. Comparison of the new horror film with anything produced in the past shows that a fresh, profoundly disquieting element has been added to, and often substituted for, recognised ingredients of every previous boom in horror.

Film from past peak periods differed considerably in style. The German productions derived from legend, the supernatural and national mysticism. The first American cycle of Frankensteins and Draculas had strong literary origins and relied on stylised fantasy, with often remarkable qualities of atmosphere and suspense. The second cycle, coming at a time when the most inept productions of any genre were making substantial profits, resulted in a series of unimaginative rehashes of earlier themes.

The beginnings of the new boom can be found in the science fiction film of the early 'fifties. At first most of these concerned outward-bound rocket passengers, and any horror ingredients were disclosed en route or on arrival. Soon, though, the direction switched. The earth became subjected to attacks and visitations from outer space or beneath the sea (*War of the Worlds, The Thing, The Beast from 20,000 Fathoms, Them,* etc.). Economically this was a wise move. It is obviously cheaper to build one monster than a series of planet landscapes and props. Many of the visitors proved unintentionally comic rather than grim. Audiences laughed, but kept going back for more.

It is impossible to pin-point precisely the beginning of the change. But as the monsters lost their initial novelty, the need for new sensationalism became recognised. Instead of using more imagination and invention in the presentation of the invaders, studios endeavoured to make each monster slimier and more repellent than its predecessor. The power of suggestion, the greatest tool of the vintage horror film, was abandoned. Instead, the screen began to concentrate on revolting close-ups. The obligatory last-reel death of the monsters provided plenty of opportunities. It was discovered, too, that details of damage done to human victims could be shown without disturbing the censor.

Soon almost every science fiction production included a few deliberately nauseating details of physical mutilation, which a few years ago the director would more effectively have suggested beyond the frame's borders. And this became as true of British as of American productions. Even the competent and not unimaginative *Quatermass* films had their quota of closely observed melting heads and diseased flesh.

In 1953 only nine releases bore any relation to the horror film, and most of these were naïve, innocuous science fiction productions. In 1954 there were twelve, in 1955 nine, and in 1956 nineteen. In 1957, the year in which *The Curse of Frankenstein* firmly established the trend, there were thirty-five, and a further thirty were released during the first ten months of 1958. Very few of these have the innocence of the films of five years ago. It is interesting to compare these figures with the number of films which fell into the "H" category during the horror boom of the 'thirties: 1933, five films; 1935, six films; 1936, two films; 1937, one film; 1938, one film; 1939, eleven films. Between June, 1942, and November, 1945, the B.B.F.C. banned the import of all "H" films. The accumulation during this second peak period totalled twenty-three.

Hammer Films' revival of the Frankenstein legend was marked by a total disregard for the qualities of the original James Whale films of the 'thirties. Instead of attempting mood, tension, or shock, the new Frankenstein productions rely almost entirely on a percentage of shots of repugnant clinical detail. There is little to frighten in *The Curse of Frankenstein* or *The Revenge of Frankenstein*, but plenty to disgust. "Horror," in fact, is the wrong term for the majority of films that Hammer's successes have inspired. Most are so ineptly written and directed that every chance of genuine suspense is botched in a way that suggests ignorance of cinematic possibilities. In *The Revenge of Frankenstein*, for example, an unknown intruder sits in the shadows of the Doctor's room. There is no build-up, suspense, or climax. Fumbling cross-cutting introduces the stranger's presence quite casually, and only the Doctor is startled when he speaks. Among high spots of the same film, marked by audience laughter, and in the case of the midnight premier audience, occasional applause, are an end-on view of an amputated arm, the transference of a living brain from one body to another, and a smouldering human foot fallen from an oven in which the rest of the body has been burned.

Details immediately reminiscent of concentration camp atrocities are common. *Blood of the Vampire* shows chained humans suffering laboratory experiments. Lunatic asylums, where patients are tortured or flogged, are favourite settings (*Blood of the Vampire, Grip of the Strangler*). But the main obsession is a clinical one. The amputated limbs and floating eyeballs of the British Frankenstein films have led to the detailed surgical operations of the American *Frankenstein 1970*, the crawling brains and spines of *Fiend Without a Face*, the human head torn from its body in *The Trollenberg Terror*. The imaginative treatment of physical horror is one thing; but most of these new films merely attempt to outdo each other in the flat presentation of revolting details which are clearly regarded as their principal box-office assets. *The Fly*, which was genuinely intriguing for its first reel or two, contrived to repeat its sequence of a living body crushed in a hydraulic press by opening with it and then building up to it again in flashback. The first time blood was shown streaming down the sides of the press; the second time we saw the writhing body as the press actually descended on to it. The reluctant last second cut to the victim's wife seemed more the result of practical difficulties in showing the actual crushing than any regard for the feelings of the audience.

These sequences apart, the films have little raison d'etre. Nothing could be duller, for instance, than the "plot" sequences which bridge the sensational sections of the Frankenstein films. The only other element which most of the films can boast is an obsessive concentration on violence. The savage beating-up followed by the close-up strangling in *The Revenge of Frankenstein* is typical.

I concentrate on the Hammer productions because the extraordinary success of *The Curse of Frankenstein* has undoubtedly encouraged other companies to follow the same pattern. Hammer, incidentally, makes three versions of all their horror films–the mildest for Britain, a stronger version for America, and the strongest of all for Japan. In the version of *Dracula* distributed in Japan, I understand that the principal addition was a series of long-held close-ups of the stake being hammered into the vampire's heart.

Playing simultaneously in two Tokyo theatres, *Dracula* broke both house records. In Britain it has set new house records in many Rank circuit cinemas. *The Curse of Frankenstein* took over 300,000 pounds in Britain, 500,000 pounds in Japan, and more than 1,000,000 pounds in America.

The success of British horror films has had some curious incidental results. Peter Cushing and Christopher Lee have now, apparently, joined Alec Guinness to become the only three British stars whose names attract American cinemagoers. Lee, who played Count Dracula and also the monster in *The Curse of Frankenstein*, receives enormous fan-mail, much of it said to be remarkably romantic in tone.

Both *Films and Filming* and *Picturegoer* have recently brought out horror issues. The latter featured a short story by Jimmy Sangster (writer of many of the British horror scripts) which concerned a woman who had eaten her male companions after preventing their escape by amputating their feet. A publicity representative of Universal-International recently told me, with some pride, "We were the first to use a blood-dripping machine in a foyer display. We spent 200 pounds experimenting before we found a satisfactory way of pumping blood up through the model's feet so that it dripped convincingly from her neck. We used it for *Dracula* and everybody's copied it since. But we were the first."

All these developments are a long way from the Punch-and-Judy, fairy tale and therapy through fear defences. Nor is much good done by such modishly gay dismissals as that typified in a recent letter from Beverly Nichols to the *New Statesman*: "When I see a beetle the size of a bison inserting its plastic claws into the buttocks of some tedious Hollywood blonde, I heave a sigh of delight because this is just what I have been wanting to do for years and years...." With the kind of film that now confronts us, such a comment becomes irrelevant as well as irresponsible.

Recognising the clinical cult and tracing its origins is not difficult. The gap between the mutilation of monsters and the mutilations of men has been surprisingly quickly bridged, but it was never large. What is more to the point is the question of the new horror films' influence. Is this merely an unpleasant phase? Or are these films seriously capable of damage?

Again almost all the assurances so far produced answer the wrong questions. Christopher Lee, quoted in *Picturegoer*, summed up the most popular of the defensive arguments: "A couple of realistic films such as *On the Waterfront* and *Blackboard Jungle* can do more to incite hooliganism than a dozen horror films." Immediate incitement to violence may be rare; and it is true that any adolescent anxious to imitate a screen hero would find the majority of monsters frustrating models. But the harmfulness of these films is not to be judged by isolated incidents which they may have directly inspired, nor by the alarming parade of the perverted and the cranky which Associated-Rediffusion's *This Week* discovered in the queues and foyers. The real test is their influence on public taste, and their long-range effect on public morality. And this is where the new viciousness must be utterly condemned: during the past five years, there has been a steadily accelerating corruption of the public's appetite.

In *Seduction of the Innocent*, Dr. Wertham recalls a strikingly relevant conversation: "A ten-year-old girl from a cultivated and literate home asked me why I thought it was harmful to read "Wonder Woman" (a horror comic)...'Supposing,' I told her, 'You get used to eating sandwiches made with very strong seasonings, with onions and peppers and highly spiced mustard. You will lose your taste for simple bread and butter and for finer food. The same is true of reading strong comic books. If later on you want to read a good novel it may describe how a young boy and girl sit together and watch the rain falling. They talk about what their innermost little thoughts are. This is what is called literature. But you will never be able to appreciate that if in comic-book fashion you expect that at any minute someone will appear and pitch both of them out of the window.' In this case the girl understood, and the advice worked."

Perhaps adult cinemagoers should be more resistant than children. But the corruption of taste is, after all, a pretty insidious business. Given the Bomb, given the insecurity, producers have relentlessly used the fallacious old argument about giving the public what it wants. (And, inevitably, the bigger and more reputable companies, who at first held aloof, are finding it difficult to resist when they see the profits made by the smaller concerns.) Cinemagoers' appetites harden on what they are fed. The new horror gimmick is repulsive physical detail: so the next horror film, if it is to compete with the last, must always be that much bloodier, that much closer in its concentration on nauseating matter. Some producers have been happy to follow this trail; and no "give them what they want" formula can excuse their irresponsibility. This wasn't what anyone wanted–until they were given it.

Nor was this what anyone would have laughed at until they were trained to do so. The first science fiction monsters were undoubtedly funny. Their destruction by flame-thrower or disintegrator was less amusing but the switch often passed unnoticed. Laughing at a monster being burned alive or jabbed in the eye was still considered a healthy reaction to impossible fantasy; but when the dismembering of humans brought the same laughs, the joke, it should have been realised, was over. Even now critics who ought to know better treat the genre lightheartedly. Paul Dehn gleefully lists the number of lopped-off limbs in the latest Hammer production, insisting that there is nothing to offend because the film is not realistic in setting or mood. But, whatever the background, surgery and slaughter-house details don't easily lose their vividness; nor, when exploited for their own sake, can they be anything but disgusting. It was notable that the only Hammer film which purported to use similar ingredients for a purpose–*Camp on Blood Island*– was infinitely more acceptable, despite its suspect motives.

Already, this new viciousness has invaded other spheres. *The Fiend Who Walked the West* was adopted as a title at the last minute for a film previously known as *The Hell-Bent Kid*. It was astutely billed as the first horror Western by someone who recognised that it shared the same sadistic love of violent detail as the other "horror" films. Even a recent revival of *Battleship Potemkin* was advertised as "the bloodiest massacre on record."

All the obvious horror films have received "X" certificates. *The Vikings*, with moments equal to these productions, mysteriously got an "A." Its boisterous air presumably led the B.B.F.C. to accept it as a harmless adventure story. I gather that it was trimmed a little before the "A" certificate was granted, but its highlights still included the tearing out of Kirk Douglas's eye by a falcon, the amputation of Tony Curtis's hand, Curtis being eaten alive by crabs, and a sequence in which Douglas, about to rape Janet Leigh, pleads, "Go on, scratch me, bite me, fight me." The first two incidents at least were treated in a way typical of the new horror cycle.

As far as censorship goes, it is an open secret that any producer anxious to get a script okayed which contains, say, eight dubious sequences will add three or four more before submitting it to the Board. Then, when the protests begin, he will politely concede the sequences he has added. (It is not rare, I understand, to end up one or two sequences to the good.) The censorship of completed horror films has clearly become a matter of frame snipping, computing the blood as if it were cleavage. The basic intentions of a film, or even of a sequence, scarcely seem to enter into consideration. The corruption of taste has as yet produced no public comment or reaction from the Board's representatives; and there is little point in counting on censorship to check the downward trend. Any attempt to tighten control here would probably do more harm than good.

The public temper, allied to the irresponsibility of some producers, distributors and critics, hardly tempts one to forecast either the end of the horror cycle or the limits it will reach. At present there are about twenty new horror films in production in this country and America.

One logical extension of the surgical obsession of these films is already with us–the hospital drama featuring lengthy operation close-ups. "I'm glad to hear," wrote Josh Billings in *Kine Weekly*, "that the stark operation sequences of *Behind the Mask*...have been toned down. The exploitation of the human 'interior' should be left to the horrific boys and other purveyors of offal." *Emergency Ward Ten*, produced by Ted Lloyd (*The Giant Behemoth*), directed by Robert Day (*Grip of the Strangler*) for Eros (*Jack the Ripper*) will include two heart operations, the second lasting ten minutes. The exhibitor who was attacked for billing *The Birth of a Baby* with two new horror films and calling it an all-horror programme was more perceptive than his critics realised.

It is a generally accepted, but untrue, theory that a society gets the films it deserves. The end of the clinical cult, however, must depend on cinemagoers themselves. This may sound like a trite and woolly conclusion, if there were not already signs that attempts have made been made to debase standards more quickly than a substantial proportion of the public will allow. John Davis, managing director of the Rank Organisation, states that an analysis of "thousands of letters" received shows that more than ninety per cent of the correspondents are disturbed about current horror and sex trends. The British Film Producers Association, at Mr. Davis's request, added the subject of horror films to their next council meeting, which was subsequently postponed. The Federation of British Film Makers, according to *Kine Weekly*, "has had the question of the problems created by over-exploitation of the horror theme under consideration for some time...."

The joint censorship committee of the poster advertising industry has recently declared that unless showmen ban the more vicious horror posters themselves, the committee will enforce its own ban. Any drop in revenue, they state, "will be more than offset by the knowledge that the

Above, a preliminary moment to "close-ups of the stake being hammered into the vampire's heart"--longer, of course, in Japan.

evil influence of such posters will be withheld from the eyes of impressionable youth." The film industry's own concern with this problem is shown by the setting up of a special committee to exercise control over sensational poster advertising.

Receipts of the latest horror films have apparently provided some surprises. *Blood of the Vampire*, said to have been scheduled for a six-week run at the London Pavilion, was taken off after four weeks. *The Revenge of Frankenstein's* taking fell far below those of its predecessor. When the novelty of a horror picture is publicised, however, the takings can still be huge. *The Fly*, which cost only 155,000 pounds, grossed more than 1,000,000 pounds in America and Canada; and at the Rialto it took 100 pounds a day more than any previous Fox film shown at the cinema, including such box-office successes as *Carmen Jones*, *The Seven Year Itch* and *Anastasia*.

With profits like these to be made from comparatively inexpensive productions, it is pointless to expect the sections of the industry concerned to make more than a show of self-control. Outside control of any kind could be not merely undesirable but dangerous. No matter how you look at it, the answer, every time, is in the hands of the same people who are being conditioned to accept the worst that the industry has ever offered.

Above, low-budget atmosphere: the funeral in **The Curse of the Living Corpse**.

A Bloody New Wave in the United States

Jean-Claude Romer (1964)

After directing *Blood Feast* in 1963–"the horror film to end all horror films," according to the advertisements–Herschel G. Lewis was not satisfied with this accomplishment. He has just surpassed it, which was not an easy thing to do after *Blood Feast*, with a second film made on a larger budget (but still in "Blood Color") and evocatively titled *2,000 Maniacs*. It recounts the story of a small town in the American South, Pleasant Valley, whose two thousand inhabitants are staging a centennial celebration. But it's a bloody centennial.... In 1865, during the Civil War, a roving band of Union soldiers massacred six of the townspeople. The town has waited a century to take its revenge. Six Northerners, young men and women en route to Florida for spring break, will be captured by the townspeople and made to suffer a terrible fate: murdered by hacking, quartering, and crushing. Four of them will perish. One man and one woman alone will manage to escape from their tormentors and report their horrible experience to the authorities; but their story seems so insane that no one will believe them. Returning to the scene of the events, they discover that Pleasant Valley and its two thousand inhabitants has completely disappeared.

The main actors are Shelby Livingston, Ben Moore, Jeffrey Allen, Yvonne Gilbert, Mark Douglas, Jerome Eden, Linda Cochran, etc... The escapees are portrayed by Thomas Wood and Connie Mason, a ravishing blonde who fortunately had already survived in one piece the gory sacrifices of *Blood Feast*. It was with the enthusiastic participation of the entire population of St. Cloud (in Florida) that the exteriors of *2,000 Maniacs* were filmed (in 15 days in the first part of 1964).

Indefatigably David F. Friedman also produced a third motion picture, again for Box Office Spectaculars, Inc., *Color Me Blood Red*. In this instance, the story revolves around an artist gone mad who uses the blood of young women to mix his paints.... Although there has been talk of a fourth film which would have been entitled *Suburban Roulette*, *Color Me Blood Red* will undoubtedly be the last of the series, because, as David F. Friedman himself has affirmed, "I think that for now we're going to abandon making any more 'super blood and gore' movies, since

63

so many of our contemporaries are launching similar productions, causing a risk that the market will quickly reach a saturation point..."

Concurrent with the trend of "super horror" films, the U.S. has also
seen a distracting rise in "super sex" productions. The simpler "nudies"
have given way to films in which complaisant young people, while still
displaying their prodigious charms, are now part of incredibly realistic
images of violence, sadism, and eroticism. Sample titles, "strictly for
adults": *The Orgy at Lil's Place*, in "blushing color"; *The Seducers*; *Many
Ways to Sin...*; *Wild is My Love*; *The Unsatisfied Sex*; *The Moral and the Immoral*; *The Sadistic*; etc. etc. Some of them even make incursions, more or
less parodies, into horror through Frankenstein-style laboratories: *How
to Succeed with Girls*. And most recently a new twist, "the first Horror
Monster Musical"–or so the tag-line affirms–*The Horror of Party Beach*,
which was released in the U.S. coupled with *The Curse of the Living
Corpse*, another movie which the posters modestly claim is "more terrifying than Frankenstein, more deadly than Dracula." The theater manag-
ers where this double bill is showing must also warn their clientele that
they are "not responsible in case of death by fright during the showing
of these two films."

The Horror of Party Beach opens with shots of care-free teenagers party-
ing and dancing at the beach. Nearby, in the ocean depths, an unformed
living mass slumbers. It is precisely at this spot that a passing ship is
part of an unfortunate plan to dump a container of radioactive waste. As
it hits the rocky bottom, the container ruptures and discharges a dark
liquid which transforms the inert mass into a monstrous being. The
"horror" of party beach has been born....

Soon not just one but a plethora of creatures are rising from the sea in
search of human blood, the only food on which they can subsist. The
creatures begin their assault with the happy group on the beach, killing
a young woman, Tina. Hank Green, college football hero, and Elaine Gavin rush to seek the help of her father, Dr. Gavin, a science professor.
They vainly try to find the progenitors of this bloodthirsty killer.

In the meantime, the creatures continue their rampage. They attack
another band of teenages and slaughter three more girls. In the course of
this onslaught, one of the monsters loses an arm. In examining it Dr. Gavin discovers that only sodium is capable of destroying these horrific
beasts, whose organisms are composed primarily of water.

While Hank gathers up all the nearby sodium for their defense, Dr.
Gavin, Elaine, and the police check the radioactive levels of all the lakes
and ponds in the environs. Eventually Elaine finds the monsters' den;
but, in her haste to inform the others, she stumbles and injures her leg.

Night falls and one can hear the sinister sounds of the creatures, thirsting for blood, emerging from their submerged lair. Frozen in terror, unable to make the slightest movement, Elaine watches the monsters approach.... At this point, we'll let the reader imagine how this film ends (it's inevitable), and tackle *The Curse of the Living Corpse*.

A wealthy old tyrant, Rufus Sinclair, dies and leaves his descendants a heavy heritage of hate and peril. The old man knows better than anyone the weaknesses and petty hatreds of each of his heirs. Through a bizarre testament, he predicts that he will return from the grave to wreak his revenge if certain conditions surrounding his death and burial are not respected. To his widow Abigail, Rufus foretells a death by fire; his eldest son Bruce will be disfigured; Philip, his other son will be asphyxiated; and this last's wife will perish by drowning....

A few days after the reading of this disquieting will by James Benson, the family lawyer, the corpse of Rufus Sinclair mysteriously disappears from its crypt, thus putting the string of prophecies into motion. Each family member meets a horrible fate identical in every particular to that specified by Rufus. Reanimated, his corpse wanders the night crying out for vengeance. This demoniac apparition is finally apprehended by Robert Harrington, a nephew of Rufus who is engaged to Benson's daughter Deborah. After a fierce fight to the death in a marshland full of quicksand, the apparent zombie is unmasked; and it is, of course, the character in this story one would least suspect.

While American International Pictures is marking this year the 10th anniversary of its founding with the release of Roger Corman's latest Vincent Price-starring Poe-adaptation, *The Masque of Red Death*, one must take note of "Iselin-Tinney Productions" born in America with similar ambitions. In fact, after the resounding box-office success of *The Horror of Party Beach* and *The Curse of the Living Corpse*, Iselin-Tinney has announced a slate of upcoming horror productions: *Frankenstein Meets the Space Monster* and *Voodoo Blood Death*. Happy Americans!

Translated from the French by Alain Silver

Above, trade advertisement for Terence Fisher's **Curse of the Werewolf**.

Horror Is My Business

Terence Fisher (1964)

The moment you put out the light, man reverts to the primitive. What is the cinema? It's the place where the lights are put out. Enjoyment of horror is one of the deepest things. Electric light can't kill horror any more than it can kill nightmare. And do you know what the worst horror is? It's when you switch on the electric light and the ghost is still there.

In our world, of Hiroshima and Belsen, there are plenty of waking horrors. If you dig into people's minds, you'll find belief in ghosts, in vampires, in a great many things they don't know they believe in. We're not as materialistic and income-tax conscious as we think. At the moment our superstitions are tucked away, but they come out sometimes in strange ways–sex crimes, black masses. Sometimes they're the results of genuine lunacy but usually they're an attempt to escape from society which is too well-ordered. So well ordered that as soon as somebody like Hitler rebels against it, out come all the hidden hatreds and fears.

Continental film critics acknowledge the English as the world experts in horror. It's because we're timid. Shyness breeds shadows and shadows breed vampires. The American are different, they're brash; and their audiences don't like ghosts, they like monsters.

The written word is the basis of everything. Most important, the idea, and after, the dialogue. You can rehash the dialogue as you go along–it's disgraceful to have to do this but now and again you have no choice. Basically I say: "All right, this is, within its formula, a picture I can probably make something of." I've never accepted anything I couldn't believe in. I favour a rather slow pattern to the story. [Curse of the] Were-wolf goes through three generations.

One ought to plan a film with costume and set designers before shooting; but I've never had the time or the money. There is the danger of over-preparation, of loss of spontaneity; over-rehearsal is the most terrible thing you can imagine. We do have a very close association between costume and set designer, though. And the cameraman is very important, of course. The cameraman of Phantom [of the Opera] prefers what he calls natural, neutral colour, whereas Jack Asher likes to go for strong colour effects. And then you really have to stylise and discipline the colour; and the closer you move your camera in, the more you have to bunch your colour. One blob of red in the wrong place and the audience isn't looking at the hero, they're looking at a patch of curtain (or something similar) and your whole effect is lost.

A director has a very loose control in low-budget pictures, and Hammer's are comparatively low budget. Bernard Robinson is a genius at revamping sets; colour brings the price up a little, not much. We shoot in from six to eight weeks, say 30 days. Robert Aldrich quoted 28 days for [What Ever Happened to] Baby Jane? and they had a week of rehearsals before that. We had a one-day reading of [Two Faces of Dr.] Jekyll when it so happened that the artists were available and Michael Carreras wanted one. Otherwise one character may kill another, but the actors never meet...

I must work with the make-up artist on the monster's faces. It's one sketch after another. He does any additional experiments on the face and we test on that. The werewolf make-up is based on the traditional conception. But the Frankenstein Monster with his do-it-yourself Monster stitches is very different from Karloff's nuts and bolts. We refused to have anything to do with anything mechanical. We wanted the Monster to fit Chris Lee's melancholy personality. We wanted a thing which looked like some wandering, forlorn minstrel of monstrosity, a thing of shreds and patches, but in flesh and blood and organs—eyes and brains and arms and so on. The one case where I was afraid we'd gone too far was in Werewolf with the syphilistic old man who gets stabbed over his chessboard. It's horrid when you see those warts with the hairs growing out of them, isn't it? But his face had to be an image for his soul. He was evil, rotting away.

The censor allowed everything about the man's appearance, but for one little detail. On the set the actor was fiddling about, just getting into the part, and I saw him scratch a flake of skin off his nose, and I said, "That's it—do that when we shoot" and he lifted a flake of skin off his nose and flicked it away with his fingers. And this one detail was not allowed to stand. Our other censor problem here was with the script. The censor wouldn't allow us to say definitely that the monster raped the hero's mother: we had to imply it.

Film-making is quite unlike the stage. There things can be ironed out during your period of rehearsal. But on the screen you can't sit down and predict exactly what you are going to do. I know Hitchcock says he does, but I don't believe him for a moment. Even your actors go in "cold." In Revenge of Frankenstein there's a man in a hospital bed, with no

Above, Peter Cushing as Dr. Frankenstein in Fisher's first "re-make," **Curse of Frankenstein**.

legs because the Baron has cut them off to put them on the creature. So the man sits with his arms coiled round just where his legs were, as if he would have liked to rest his elbow on his knee but couldn't any more. We only "saw" this on the floor. And did you notice the scene where Frankenstein lights the bunsen burner in front of the eyeballs in the tank? He wants to demonstrate the movement of the dismembered arm in the adjoining tank. The reflection of the flame in the glass seems to be touching the hand. And you feel the helpless fear of these dismembered parts. This sort of thing can hardly be visualized at the script stage.

I start from the basis of the master-scene. First there's a rehearsal and before I'm halfway through I know roughly what we're going to do, because the physical movements of the actor determine the camera position. I don't think pre-planning is any good except for certain very fixed effects. First see how people react and move to the décor and to each other, and then before you know what's happening the thing is beginning to mould itself. After all, you've talked to the actors beforehand, and let them know what you're out to do. But after they've brought their personalities to it, then you control and break the scene into dramatic set-ups and start punching and punctuating where you want to. I find personality so important; I like a more theatrical style than this realism. I like the Victorian period especially.

Dracula: "...we had to show the face and the fangs. And we did"

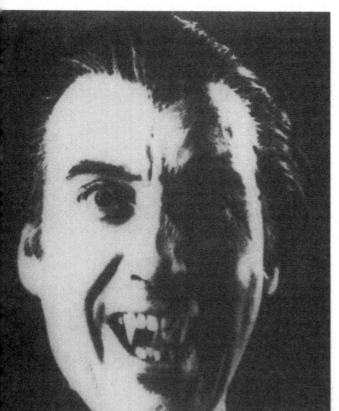

Most of what I learned filmwise was in the cutting rooms. That gives you a great sense of the pattern of a film, the overall rhythm. This dramatic rhythm is the basis of technique, of style. For example I've always involved the monster in the frame, planted him in the décor. I've never used the conventional style, where you keep harping on reaction shots and cutting away from him. I believe in building things up, naturally, but I've never isolated the monster from the world around, or tried to avoid showing him. The exception is *Phantom*; there was no reason to show his face there; you'd seen the acid go into his face, you knew how pitifully he was in agony all the time. But in *Dracula* of course we had to show the face and the fangs. And we did. But most of my films aren't horror films, you know. They're macabre, which is a little different.

Stranglers of Bombay went wrong. It was too crude. The basic idea was the absolutely true story of thugee. The producers felt it was better in black-and-white because it was a documentary story rather than a myth. But in the written word there was too much Frankenstein and Dracula and I was still with the previous approach.

I saw most of the original versions of my monster films when they originally came out; but I no longer had any clear recollection of them. They were re-shown at the studio but I wouldn't see them. I did see about three reels of the Claude Rains *Phantom*, which I loathed. There are certain key scenes in *The Mummy* which you can't get away from, but the similarities are in the script only. I think Carol Reed once said that he doesn't see any films because he's terrified of being influenced, which I can understand. I'm even terrified of seeing my own films, or I have been.

Chris Lee and Peter Cushing–I can't speak too highly of them. In fact to my mind the best films were those in the early days, with Cushing and Lee. Lee is a mime expert; he studied ballet at one time, and he can express emotions eloquently in the simplest physical movements, just in his walk. This is the se-

Phantom: "...no reason to show his face"

cret of his Mummy and his Frankenstein Monster. The Mummy is swathed for the best part of the film, and yet, when he recognises the girl whom he thinks is a reincarnation of the Princess he once loved, you can feel with him even though he's dumb and his face is swathed. He never menaces her at all; he's saying, "Come to me..."

I like working with Miles Malleson. Give him two lines and he'll work throughout the scene. With real actors like him you sometimes have to say, "Oh for God's sake you're overdoing it a bit"--but still; an amazing number of film actors really do think that if they're not speaking they can just go dead on you until their next line.

In some ways though I like those spacious days–the film in a period frame–when people had more time than they do now...and the era was damn good, because it was so full of hypocrisy. You can't make a modern Frankenstein because it's all happening anyway. They're making Frankensteins out of those blighters whom they're sending up in rockets and space capsules–they're the modern Frankensteins.

I go for basic things in drama. Fire is a pictorially very exciting thing, isn't it? And it's a very complete form of destruction. It has a certain spiritual sense. People talk about the purifying theme. And physical destruction makes a nice contrast with supernatural things. They're destroyed by the basic elements—earth, fire, water. The Mummy slips into a bog. Dracula is killed by a stake being hammered through his heart, or burned up by the sun. And after all, mental destruction makes physical destruction look mild, doesn't it?

Baron Frankenstein wants to create something. He has a great ideal, to create a perfect human being with a perfect brain and perfect physique. He was after perfection—the tragic pursuit of perfection. He's ruthless only because of his ideals. Unfortunately, he doesn't succeed. The thing fails and gets out of hand and takes charge of him.

Idealism is the only excuse he could have and it's a great excuse. Maybe I didn't plug his idealism enough. But he had only one aim in life, and he didn't care whether he lopped somebody's arm off or took a couple of eyeballs out, because he considered the end justified the means.

Below, *Dracula*: Michael Gough (left) as Arthur, Melissa Stribling as Mina, and Peter Cushing as Van Helsing.

Jekyll is indeed an idealist but Hyde is a complete brute from beginning to end. There's no redeeming feature in him. He loved every second of his crimes, and when he finally had an excuse to kill Jekyll's wife, he was delighted. Personally I would have written it differently...made him more horrible *and* given him some redeeming features. But that was the written word.

The monsters must outrage innocents or semi-innocents because it wouldn't mean so much if they wronged hardboiled people. Or maybe it could...actually that might be interesting.

Cushing was very conscious of all this. Cushing and Lee are very intelligent men, Cushing particularly is a very deep thinker. In *Curse of Frankenstein*, which started out as a bit of a giggle almost, the great temptation was for the actors to try and send it up, to overdo things. That's always the danger with these films. But once I'd told them to take it straight, they knew exactly what I was after.

Below **Brides of Dracula**: "...We tried to make the vampires a bit more human than they usually are." David Peel as Baron Meinster.

Sex? Certainly Dracula did bring a hell of a lot of joy to a hell of a lot of women. And if this erotic quality hadn't come out we'd have been very disappointed. We tried to make the vampires a bit more human than they usually are. In *Brides of Dracula* they have the possibility of repenting even after death, or undeath. The process is very gradual, you see. At first there's the tainted stage; they know what will eventually happen to them if they go on but they say, "Oh God, don't do it to me, do it again, please, please." Actually the French titles are better, *Mistresses of Dracula* or *Fiancees of Dracula* because they're not actually married to him, they can still break off the engagement. Cushing is the rationalist, the moralist who is trying to break an unholy pleasure. But a pleasure.

There is a redeeming feature in the Frankenstein Monster. His brain is damaged; he can't control himself. Christopher Lee didn't want to kill the old blind man. He was pleased with him, quite friendly. Then the silly old man got frightened and poked at him with his stick. Suddenly the Monster's mind went wrong and he killed the old fellow. But he wasn't evil in any way at all.

Do I believe in the supernatural? Oh yes, certainly. I can't believe, I can't accept that you die and that's the end. Physically maybe it is a fact. It probably is. But there's something about the mind that's more than that. It goes on, it must go on, in some other form perhaps.

Immortality isn't a particularly Christian thing. I wouldn't claim to be very much of a Christian.

Some people criticise the morality of my work. I've never been worried that my daughter's seen my films, although she was only 13 or 14 when *Revenge of Frankenstein* appeared. I'd rather she saw mine than some others. Films are still frightening when you know your father made them. You don't connect the two.

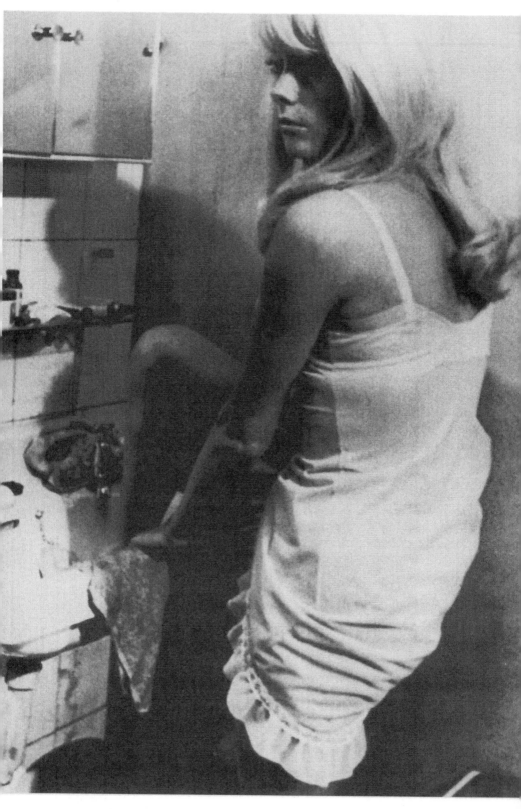

Above, Catherine Deneuve as the demented Carol in **Repulsion**.

The Horror Film: Polanski and *Repulsion*

Ivan Butler (1967)

Monsters and vampires, man-made creatures and ghosts, mob cruelty and murderers, these are the stock ingredients of horror, and most of them have been handled on occasion with sufficient imagination to lift the result above the category of mere sensationalism. All such terrors, however, are seen from a distance, approaching us from outside ourselves. Our own feet rest on firm ground. Even the psychopathic killer of *Psycho* is treated from the viewpoint of his victims or pursuers, and his deeds are framed in the conventions of a mystery-killer. But when the mind is the actual stuff of horror, when madness and collapse are presented from inside, rather than viewed from without, then the solid ground itself shifts and crumbles, and we do indeed find ourselves looking into a bottomless pit. This is the fearful theme of *Repulsion*, described by one critic as the most terrifying film ever made. In a most perceptive article, Kenneth Tynan states that Carol, the girl in *Repulsion*, "has much in common with Tony Perkins in *Psycho*, but he [Polanski] goes deeper than *Psycho* by presenting a double murder from the killer's instead of the victim's point of view." Nor is there any attempt at a glib pyschoanalytical explanation at the end. The film has been criticised for this (although in actual fact a broad hint is provided in the very last shot), but it is just the irrationality of much mental breakdown such as Carol's which gives an added "turn of the screw."

Roman Polanski, the director, was born in Paris of Polish parents in 1933. Both parents were put into a concentration camp by the Nazis—his father survived. After making two prize-winning shorts, and achieving wide recognition with his first feature, *The Knife in the Water*, he met Gene Gutowski in 1964. The result of this collaboration was *Repulsion*. Polanski has stated: "What interested me in making it is the study of a girl's disintegration; withdrawal turning to violence. I'm concerned with showing something—exposing a little bit of human behavior that society likes to keep hidden because then everyone can pretend it doesn't exist. But it does exist, and by lifting the curtain on the forbidden subject, I think one liberates it from this secrecy and shame." Thus pity is allied to terror and, as another critic has put it: "Polanski makes his fair murderess seem authentically tragic, herself the most pitiable victim of the evil she does."

Carol is a Belgian girl living in a somewhat dreary South Kensington flat with her sister Helen. Both girls are working, though Helen's job seems uncertain, and most her time is taken up by an affair with a married man, Michael. Carol herself works in a beauty salon as a manicurist. Although apparently capable enough at her job, she is strangely withdrawn and moody. She treats with cool indifference her pleasant boyfriend, an extremely patient young man named Colin. She obviously resents Michael's presence in the flat, particularly his carelessness in leaving such things as his razor and toothbrush around in the bathroom. In all this, however, her attitude is in no way aggressive or deliberate—it is more a sort of helpless unhappiness. In the middle of an oppressive heatwave Helen and Michael, despite a plea from Carol not to be left alone, go off for a holiday in Italy. In her loneliness (through the film Carol's essential loneliness is marvelously suggested) her mind starts to disintegrate. She begins to have hallucinations—of crumbling walls and strangers in the flat. After an incident at her work she is sent home. She shuts herself up finally in the flat, wandering aimlessly around in her nightgown. An abusive phone call (from Michael's wife, meant for Helen) further upsets her balance. The hallucinations become more terrifying. When Colin comes to see what is wrong and, worried and exasperated beyond bearing, breaks open the front door, she kills him with the utmost violence and hides the body in the bath. Later the landlord, a coarse boor, also forces his way into the flat, which she has feebly barricaded, and, misled by her appearance and manner, starts to make approaches to her. In wild panic and revulsion she slashes him to death with Michael's razor, and attempts to hide his body also. Rapidly the last shreds of sanity give way, and when Helen and Michael come back they find the flat a horrifying shambles, and Carol lying motionless and silent under a bed.

On the bare framework of this horror story Polanski has constructed a film of such complexity and subtlety that an entire book could be written about it. Here we must be content with a brief glance at some of the salient points. The film opens in darkness. We are, in fact, in Carol's mind almost literally, for as the camera draws back the darkness reveals itself as the pupil of her eye. On this enormous close-up the titles are imposed, accompanied by a single long-held note of music and monotonously alternating drumbeats. As the titles finish the camera withdraws further to frame her face, sad, still, and abstracted. Dressed in a white overall, she sits holding the hand of a woman who is lying, a bulky mound, on a raised couch. In the background are trolleys of instruments. It could be a

Above, Carol with her sister; below, teased by her sister's boyfriend.

hospital—but it is in fact the beauty salon where Carol works, with the other girls, like vestal virgins in a temple devoted to the sacred rites of artificial youth. A sharp protest from the inert, mud-masked woman jerks Carol out of her reverie. Later we accompany her, for the first of several important occasions, as she wanders absently through the South Kensington streets on her way to lunch. She passes a group of street workmen. One of them calls out some mild impertinence, which she ignores. The incident is not dwelt on, the words barely distinguishable, but the camera turns back for a brief moment to his face and his sweaty, vest-clad torso. Her boy-friend joins her and finds her aloof, shrinking back from his touch on her hair. After an odd conversation about rabbit for supper they part—he lingering to watch, a little wistfully, her colleague Bridget's affectionate leave-taking of her own boy-friend. Arrived home after work, Carol watches, equally wistfully, young nuns playing some childish game in an adjacent convent. The convent bell tolls. She carefully washes her feet, and removes with fastidious distaste the razor and toothbrush from her glass. She wanders to the kitchen and, after a short exchange with Helen, remarks that a crack in the kitchen wall needs mending. Michael unexpectedly takes Helen out to dinner, leaving Carol alone in the flat, and the rabbit, prepared but uncooked, in the refrigerator. She wanders idly around the place, passing a family group on the sideboard, on which the camera momentarily pauses. It starts to approach it, but before the details become very clear the scene fades. Later that night, lying wakeful in the heat of her schoolgirlish bed, Carol gazes up at the wardrobe set against an unused door and strangely foreboding shapes of suitcases and tennis rackets piled on top. An old-fashioned fireplace yawns blackly. The window curtains move gently and her bedside clock ticks. The convent bell tolls at midnight. Attracted and repelled, she listens to the chuckles and moans of physical enjoyment from her sister's room. As it reaches a climax and dies away, she buries her head in her pillows. Slowly the camera moves back from the quiet room.

This opening section has been described in some detail because every incident has its place in the development of Carol's breakdown. The rabbit, removed from storage and decaying in the heat, resembles a monstrous embryo, the bell triggers off her most violent hallucinations and heralds the second murder, the workman becomes her imaginary rapist, the unused door behind the dark wardrobe lights up, and opens to admit horror, the tiny crack in the kitchen develops into the breaking up of the flat's walls, the family group contains the hint as to Carol's secret, and becomes the last shot of the film, the little clock ticks thunderously in the otherwise dead silence of her nightmares.

Early in the film there is a long-held motionless shot of the full extent of the flat. Nothing happens, except an occasional glimpse of Helen making breakfast through the half-open kitchen door. This lengthy contemplation is very important, for seldom has an ordinary setting been given such significance. It is, indeed, a central character, and by the end we feel we have lived in it ourselves. Though by no means uncomfortable, it is as depressing as any living place which is not a home. Through it we can visualize the whole house full of solitary, rootless flat-dwellers—personalized in the glimpses of the woman opposite taking her dog down in the lift for "walkies"; and keeping the door on the chain to refuse use of the telephone at the time of the tragedy, which, incidentally, she precipitates by causing Colin to shut Carol's front door behind him to prevent her from watching them. The flat, shut-off and solitary, reflects Carol's own withdrawn and lonely state, and eventually shares, literally, in her disintegration. By an inspired use of the distorting lens the sitting-room is made to become a vast cavern, the white-tiled bathroom a huge, dim, grey space with a tiny distant washbasin. All sense of proportion is lost. Huge cracks suddenly split the walls of the rooms, and those in the passage grow soft so that her hands sink into them—and later other hands reach through them to grab at her. A pendant in its plaster decoration swoops down at her as she lies in her bed. Finally the ceiling itself crumbles and dissolves into the pouring rain through which Helen and Michael drive up on their return from holiday.

All the hallucinations are handled with terrifying power. The first one of all, a momentary glimpse of man's figure seen in a swinging wardrobe mirror, takes the breath away. The first time the light appears above the unused door Carol by a tremendous effort controls her imagination and when she looks up again, restful darkness has returned. The next time, however, there is no escape, and our horror equals hers as the door is pushed against the wardrobe. It is not happening to the heroine of the film; it is happening to us.

Throughout Polanski invites us to share, and thus to understand, Carol's repulsion. Even the clients in the beauty salon are gross, greedy, useless women, waited on by young girls with the ugly appurtenances of artificial beautification, their talk of either food, themselves or—scathingly—of men.

Polanski also comments ironically on our own attitude towards horror. Michael shrinks back from the dreadful sight of Colin's body in the bath—but then leans forward for a further slow look. Carol picks up Michael's soiled vest in utter disgust, but cannot resist holding it to her face. She flings it away from her, but later it is in her room, and later still, as her mind goes, she is seen pathetically ironing it—with an unconnected iron. There is also an extraordinary moment towards the close of the film as Michael, refusing to wait for the ambulance, insists on carrying Carol out of the flat. On his way, he pauses, gazing down at her face with its open, unseeing eyes. It is a quite unfathomable look, and one of the most disquieting moments of the whole film.

Some of the symbolism is fairly obvious—such as the postcard of Leaning Tower of Pisa, and the playing nuns—but much of it is subtle and apt. There are two neat cuts from the flat to the beauty salon: one from the crumpled sheets of Helen's and Michael's bed to the girl's smooth white overall; the second from the wrinkled, aging potatoes to the equally raddled face of Madame Denise. In the second the effect is increased by Madame's voice momentarily anticipating the visual cut. Left in the flat alone, Carol sees her reflection in a polished kettle, leaning forward so that her face is distorted by the curve. Returned from work, she slowly peels a glove off her hot fingers, as if removing not only the gross outer world, but a layer of her consciousness. After unexpectedly coming across Michael stripped to the waist as he shaves, she is seen crouched on the bed, absently wiping one hand across her nightgown. Lying alone in bed, just after Helen and Michael go, she moves her finger idly over the wall by her side, encounters a tiny crevice in the wallpaper and draws back sharply.

The scene with the landlord, which could so easily have been heavily melodramatic, is full of subtle touches. Having forced his way in, he comes across her standing just inside the sitting-room doorway, looking upwards and sideways at him rather like a child who is anxious to conceal a broken ornament. "Where is Miss Ledoux?" he asks her. She replies, "I am Miss Ledoux." But her tone is ambiguous, ending almost as a query. Is she, indeed, Miss Ledoux any longer? At what stage of mental collapse does personality cease to exist? Having handed him the money he has come to collect (and refused to allow him to let in the light to see it), she speaks only one word more: "Brussels," in answer to a question

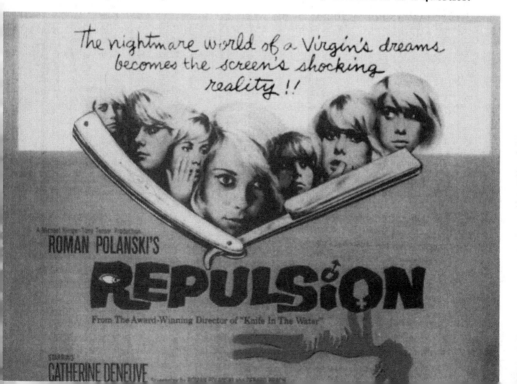

about where the family photograph was taken. Slouching listlessly on the sofa she watches, not his face, but his hands as they move in front of her—as a cat looks at a pointing finger rather than the object indicated. Only once does she look up at his face, raising her own in a most pathetic gesture when he asks if she is ill. Otherwise her abstraction is apparently complete—even his horrified exclamations at the general mess leave her unmoved—but when she is momentarily out of the room, she picks up the razor from the floor.

The actual murders, gruesome enough though they are, give no impression of being committed in a frenzy of blood-lust. Carol is not, to her, killing human beings at all, but rather destroying some threatening obscenity as one might stamp repeatedly on a loathsome insect. In the second, that of the landlord, she uses no violence until the last possible moment, even after he has made one attempt to assault her. Only when he comes at her again (after the sound of the convent bell) does she destroy him.

Very important are the various wanderings round the South Kensington and neighboring streets on which we accompany her. Starting with the reasonably normal walk to lunch already noticed, each subsequent journey reflects her growing withdrawal until on her final one, before shutting herself up for ever, not even the most attention-drawing of all events, a car accident, has the power to rouse her. It is difficult to account for the powerful influence these wanderings, often photographed in large close-up, have in drawing us closer to her, in helping us, so to speak, to "know" her.

Sound is brilliantly used. It is hard to imagine a more apt musical accompaniment, from the sad, touching little tune which might be called Carol's "theme" (resolving most beautifully into the closing chord at the end), to the sinister arpeggios as she moves down the darkened passage, and the drum-beats or clashing cymbals of her hallucinations. Natural noises heighten the atmosphere—dripping taps, distant piano scales, clanking lift doors, a group of musicians playing "Waltzing Matilda" on a guitar accompanied by spoon-castanets (a weird trio, with its crab-like spoon-player), the convent bell. Note how subtly the last stroke is emphasized and cut off just before the landlord's murder. Then there are distortions—the loud clock-tick during the silent hallucinations, the apparent cries and grunts during the murders, the ever more piercing phone and door bells, the ghastly travesty of sexual ecstasy in the final nightmare of rape. Note, too, how Helen's hysterical sobs at the end are made a grotesque echo of her own earlier cries of pleasure.

Catherine Deneuve is superb as Carol—it is quite unnerving to see her in some other film shortly afterwards. Yvonne Furneaux could not be bettered as her sister lacking understanding rather than sympathy, yet cleverly hinting at some secret knowledge of Carol, in a little scene in the lift with Michael. Ian Hendry as Michael, conventional enough in earlier scenes, has some impressive moments on the return from the holiday. His indecision, shock, bewilderment, realisation that the publicity resulting from all this must break up his affair, if not his home—none of this mentioned in words—his mingled horror and fascination, above all that final enigmatic look at Carol

At the very end of the film, after her inert form has been carried out of the flat and the neighbours (a cleverly selected group) have taken away the collapsing Helen, the camera slowly travels right round the sitting-room, passing over the strangely pathetic debris of that dreadful fortnight—a broken biscuit, the crumpled Pisa postcard, some half-finished sewing. Then it moves up to the family photograph. This time it does not stop at the frame. It moves, inexorably, right into the group, past the smiling elder daughter, the cheerful mother, the complacent father and others, to the small girl in the background. Standing behind her mother's chair, out of the enclosed little circle, her eyes fixed on the man—her father. The expression on the child's face is terrifying, and the more so for being inscrutable. Loathing, fear, resentment, a longing for affection turned sour—it coud be any of these, and it is unforgettable. The camera advances further—to the girl's eye, to the pupil—until nothing is left but the darkness of the mind from which, at the opening of the film, it slowly withdrew.

Inevitably, so controversial a film aroused criticism as well as high praise. Polanski was accused of generating no sympathy for his heroine. This is incomprehensible. Anyone who could hear unmoved (to take only two face examples) Carol's last, hopeless plea to her sister, "Oh please—don't go!" or her broken voice as she sits in the flat after the first murder crooning a monotonous little chant such as children sing to comfort themselves in the dark, must indeed be devoid of understanding.

The two public house scenes, in which Carol is not involved, have been condemned as irrelevant. On the contrary, they are vital. One of the few moments where credulity might be slightly strained is when so harmless and gentle a young man as Colin takes a running jump at Carol's door and smashes it down. As it is, we can understand how his frustration and worry are fanned to the necessary heat by the chaffing and petty obscenities of his pub companions in the second scene—and the first is necessary preparation for this.

One or two shots through a lensed Judas window in the front door have been described as affectation. In actual fact, Carol's last view of

Colin is through this distorting medium (she does not look at him once he is in the hall), and this adds to her panic, leading to the murder.

Only two false notes are struck, and both are minor ones. The first is a very obviously posed shot of Carol lying on the floor the morning after one of her nightmares—apparently nude, with the bed coverlet draped discreetly over her. It is far too pretty to be natural, and seems to have been inserted for the sake of obtaining a box-office still. The second concerns the topography of South Kensington as Carol wanders. To anyone with any knowledge of the district she appears to be constantly doubling back on herself as shot succeeds shot, and the result is to make the watcher feel dizzy. A small point—but in so realistic a film (there has never been a more convincing set than the flat, and the beauty salon is easily discoverable a few minutes away from the Museums), this seems a pity.

The truth is that, like any worthwhile film, *Repulsion* demands more than a single viewing. There is hardly a frame which has not a dual purpose—simultaneously developing and commenting on the story. A shot of the sprouting potatoes, for instance serve (a) to mark the passage of time, (b) to reflect the growing distortion of Carol's mind, and (c) to make a parallel cut to Madame Denise's wrinkled face. To take one simple instance of the film's complexity—the crack in the kitchen wall. Some time in her wanderings Carol becomes fascinated by a crack in some paving on a traffic island—actually sitting down to gaze at it and forgetting a date with Colin. The next time we see the kitchen crack, it has taken on the exact shape of the flaw in the paving. There is no close-up, the crack is seen from a different angle; it is probable that not one viewer in a hundred would notice this subtlety on a first visit, and it is only one of many.

Opinions will differ as to the most "shocking" moment in this film so crowded with shocks—the man in the mirror, perhaps, the opening of the unused door, or the last sudden thrust of a pair of hands through a patch in the wall. It may well be, however, that the most unnerving moment of all is a quieter one. Carol is sitting alone in the little basement of the beauty salon after listening to Bridget's tearful complaints of her boyfriend's "beastliness." She is staring idly in front of her, abstracted and withdrawn. Suddenly a shaft of sunlight comes through the dusty little window and falls on a chair beside her. For a moment she gazes at it blankly, then slowly leans forward and tries to brush the ray off the seat. On the quiet sound of her hand against the wood the scene fades. This intimation of the failing of reason, the remorseless approach of madness, is more fearful than any screaming shock cut would be. The dark door is opening, for Carol—and for us.

Above, Mark Lewis (Carl Boehm) with his camera in **Peeping Tom**.

From Voyeurism to Infinity

Raymond Lefevre (1968)

The film lover is the supreme voyeur. Hidden in darkness, he watches...
There is no shame in this, because the screen is not a keyhole and, above
all, he is not watching alone. A totally sane complicity joins him to the
other spectators. He is far removed from the guilty conscience of those
who leer alone.

One must recognize that this sort of gluttony for spectacle affects all
of us. In our voyeur's paradise, the loveliest of women may ignore all
modesty. The visual temptations are varied and renewable: our favorite
actresses rising from the bath; the paroxysms of lovers; murderous liber-
tines; sadistic relief. Radiant nakedness: Brigitte Bardot, Catherine
Deneuve, Marika Green, Mireille Darc or Joanna Shimkus. And don't
forget those curious Swedish girls. And so much more.... Now for us voyeurs, here is the story of another voyeur, also a film lover and, in addition, a filmmaker.

This gives us *Peeping Tom*, a film without precedent, entirely remarkable in its wide-ranging portrayal of a voyeuristic obsession. To make a
film about an obsessive, a vision of the obsessive world is required, the
vision of Michael Powell, whose directing has never been so inspired.

All of this revolves around a singular concept: the eye. The details of
set decoration, staging, and casting, lines of dialogue, color, plot line, editing, all come together to express a world captured by a gaze. In fact,
the first shots clearly define the metaphor, a peremptory association of
the eye and a target. One glance and the world is possessed.

No character can escape this obsession: Mark Lewis, the voyeuristic
killer; Helen, the insignificant little neighbor whose curiosity compels
her to flip the start switch on a 16mm projector; the old aficionado of artful nudes; the doddering psychiatrist; the locals and their various enthu-
siasms; and above all the blind woman. In fact, this is one of the film's
most extraordinary conceits: the blind voyeur. The blind person always
on the lookout for the slightest trace of another presence, senses distorted by the secondary influence of alcohol, the unexpected realization
that the blind person can also take a snapshot by running hands over

Mark's face. The hand becomes the eye and develops an image of reality, just as the multiple cameras which populate the film.

The decor also reinforces the focus on obsessive voyeurism. We are in London, the recognized capital of the voyeur. The prostitutes are referred to by the euphemism of "models," who are in theory women who permit their bodies to be leered at. London is the capital as well of specialty book stores which stock "sexy" books and magazines, which patrons can leaf through which much more ease than in French drug stores. Movie houses are just as permissive, and the nudist film rounding a double bill will guarantee good box office to Godard's *A Married Woman*. Harrison Marks is one of the most celebrated "nude" artists, whose photographs, picture series ("Kamera"), calendars, and 8mm films feed the cravings of the image gluttons. His models are as well known as TV stars, among them being the voluptuous Pamela Green, leading lady of the naturist film, *Naked as Nature Intended*.

Director Michael Powell strove for additional authenticity in conferring the role of cover girl to this same Pamela Green. As a result *Peeping Tom* became a more realistic portrayal of this sort of voyeurism. To unmask that remarkable British sanctimoniousness, one creates a scene of an elderly gentlemen about to purchase *The Times* but leaving the store with a large envelope labeled "Educational Books" which contains a variety of "art" magazines. He is so intent of getting home with his package that he almost forgets his newspaper. "There's another one who won't be doing crosswords this evening," concludes the blasé sales clerk.

Behind this particular bookstore is a photo studio, equipped with some rudimentary backdrops and lighting. The store sells sensationalistic tabloids also, and it is through one of these that Mark Lewis gazes at his first victim as a stack of papers is spread out for display and the photo of the prostitute Dora is multiplied before his eyes. The association of sex-crime is evoked, and we are clearly in the presence of mental disturbance, disturbance which has taken hold of Mark Lewis. Even in a sub-culture built around looking, this man is distinctive.

This context quickly distinguishes him from wastrel voyeurs: the man with binoculars in *Fleur d'Oseille* (watching as Mireille Darc sun-bathes), another balancing a pair of field glasses in one hand and a telephone in the other as he contemplates the charms of Marika Green in *La Fille en Face*. We are far removed as well from the use of home movies as visual mementos as with {Michel] Piccoli in *All About Loving* [*De l'Amour*]. His true fellows would be Mabuse with a thousand eyes or the preacher in *The Night of the Hunter* flicking open his switchblade as a phallic substitute while watching a strip tease.

But Mark Lewis stands out from this rogue's gallery. His slightest gesture reaffirms his voyeurism, marks him as a uniquely disturbed protagonist and, in this sense, Michael Powell's film is a complete success. Powell never needs to fall back on plot contrivances, no expository dialogue, no voice-over narration, no didactic psychiatry, no subjective camera. The psychological consultation in the film, shot in a sound stage, is calculated rather to deride and destroy all didacticism. The only explications depend on the manner in which the character is observed, in the minute details of his behavior. Because of this context, the voyeur had to be a cinephile and cineaste.

He is a professional photographer, an amateur documentarian (and early exponent of cinema verité), a collector of movies in various formats, a creator of artful nudes, and a sound recordist. He's a regular at the revival movie house on Dean Street and a reader of *Sight and Sound*. In the novel concept of Powell, associating the voyeur with motion pictures themselves, also irrevocably links the academic artifice of 35mm, the spontaneity of 16mm, the clumsiness of the amateur formats and the art photography so cherished by the British.

Every detail of the script and the staging becomes an element of obsession. Even Mark's flip remarks are emblematic of his neuroses. While he films Dora's corpse being taken from the crime scene he is surprised by an onlooker who asks, "What paper do you work for?" He coolly replies, "*The Observer.*"

The presence (or absence) of keys is of literal and symbolic significance in the universe of the voyeur. It's easy to get into Mark Lewis' apartment, since he leaves it unlocked (which certainly has a direct Freudian implication for a man to whom keys and lock present obstacles). Whenever the voyeur touches a key, he is dumbstruck. A notable moment occurs at the birthday party for his neighbor Helen who, among her gifts, receives a large golden key.

It is also thus that his first declaration of love involves giving himself over to a woman spectator in the course of a private screening of a film featuring himself and revealing his secret. To love, for him, means offering one's own image for inspection and refusing to photograph the beloved. This is the discovery he makes when he ventures out without his camera, for as often as his apparatus is left at home, the more often the prospect of love liberates his mind. There are, of course, the inevitable lost opportunities which draw his attention, which tempt him to stop by a window, which trigger a reflex to seize the camera when he spots a couple wrapped in an embrace. But this lover's promise is the resolve to never gaze at the object of his affection through the viewfinder.

Mark offers her a dragon fly broach because his father used to frighten him with small animals. For her part, his ideal companion is interested in childish things and is preparing a book on the history of the magic lantern. But his obsession will not recede, not even from the young woman's dreams. We understand that he can love Helen, although she is physically and intellectually ordinary. Perhaps Helen reminds him of his mother. In any case, she lives where his mother used to live. And, after quitting Helen's company, Mark takes solitary pleasure in a long kiss of his camera lens, a demented and inspired image.

Below, Carl Boehm as Mark Lewis and Anna Massey as Helen.

A striking image is what fascinates him most. The lithe and naked body, seen in profile, of the model Lorraine, leaves him cold. But once he sees her face, marred by an ugly hair-lip, his response changes abruptly. "It seems that you don't want to shoot my face," the young woman remarks timidly; and Mark discovers in that remark the pain of being scrutinized. Here is his inspiration. He takes out his camera, approaches, and films her face. Nothing else exists for him. But Lorraine is not the sort of woman who impels his murderous impulses. The wicked voyeurism of Mark Lewis is aimed at women who like to be looked at, those whose profession brings them to offer their faces and bodies up for examination: a prostitute, an immodest starlet, a nude model. The art of the crime consists in transforming the ease of accepting the stares of strangers into a terrified panic. And this requires a method, a modus operandi, almost a ritual. The satisfactory accomplishment of the crime relies first and foremost on the staging, on difficult camera placement (most notably in the impossible traveling shot up the stairs to the prostitute's room), on establishing shots, on the cutting, on the associations of the editing scheme. To frame the art of the murder scenes, Mark films the removal of Dora's corpse, the discovery of Vivian's body, the inquest at headquarters, and the police investigation itself. His crimes are conceived with a spectator in mind; and his films are his legacy. It is a dissociative art, filming in order to film.

This permits the extraordinary title sequence, seen in black-and-white on a small screen, composed of the images of the pre-title killing. There is the instantaneous reality of the film, and the images which replay on demand these transitory moments. The voyeur films his victim, then he watches his film. We, the audience, watch the voyeur watching, in our own second-hand voyeurism.

Sadism is also a factor in the staging. The preparation for Vivian's murder is a model of technical planning complete with rehearsals, chalk-marked references, sound effects, and attention to lighting. Mark's violent aggression expresses itself in the raw, undiffused light which tracks his prospective victim, like a cat toying with a mouse, like the mad scientist of *Metropolis* who terrorizes the inhabitants of the depths with his spotlights. Mark lingers over the scene at Vivian's, his eye glued to his viewfinder. The camera as weapon becomes the camera as accomplice. This is an orgasmic moment as the would-be murderer allows himself the pleasure of being seen by his imminent victim. Magnified by this sadistic preparation (or artistic refinement), the fear of the victims is exacerbated by the use of a distorting mirror which reveals the face of death to the dying, the reactions to which he will see on his screen, the perfect intercourse just before the traveling shot which rips out the victim's throat.

In the end, Mark Lewis' suicide is equally a staged scene. Realizing that he has been unmasked, he shoots the arrival of the police through a cracked window glass. It's the ultimate documentary. With a tape recorder, he records a deranged soundtrack: cries of fright, police car sirens, the crackling of flash bulbs, the ideal sound effects for one commemorating his own suicide with the camera as recording instrument.

And all this happened because...? The question provokes the film's most inspired moment, as the answer comes from a fragment of experimental film, from images shot by Mark's father, a well-known authority and author of several studies on paranoia and scopophilia, the obsession with watching. Mark was the guinea pig. And the images, the silent record of those experiments, provide a much more eloquent explanation than any prolonged discourse:

Below, U.S. display art for **Peeping Tom**, "an adventure in terror."

...An anxious infant in a spotlight...

...Perched from a high vantage, a youth watches a pair of lovers...awkward panoramas tilt back and forth going from the child to the couple...

...Another shot of the child in a spotlight

...The youngster on a bed onto which is thrown a lizard which slithers towards him...

...The child wipes tears of fright from his eyes...

...He stands in front of his mother's open coffin...

...A young girl in a bikini...

...The father hands his son a camera...

...The son films the father filming him...

But what exactly does this child see in the viewfinder of his small camera? In all likelihood, standing next to his father is the woman who took his mother's place, a woman he wishes would disappear, a feeling he has for the first time as he uses a camera. The associations are clear: woman, rival, death, camera. It is the birth and the germination of a psychosis.

Peeping Tom is a rigidly constructed and richly illustrated expression of emotions which range from voyeuristic to the universal, a masterpiece of the horror genre, a brilliant depiction of delirium, cold lucidity, sadism, of the anomalous lives concealed in the everyday. It shows us that no one is safe from the disturbing hidden fantasies of seemingly normal individuals.

And you probably never realized that just going to the movies might be living dangerously.

Translated from the French by Alain Silver

Above, Barbara Steele and her mastiffs in **Black Sunday**.

Mario Bava: the Illusion of Reality

Alain Silver and James Ursini (1975)

> What Man that see the ever-whirling wheel
> Of Change, the which all mortall things doth sway
> But that hereby doth find, and plainly feele,
> How MUTABILITY on them doth play
> Her cruell sports, to many mens decay?
>
> Edmund Spenser, *The Faerie Queene*, VII, I, 1-5

A carved sarcophagus reposes in a high-arched, tenebrous crypt. After a montage in which the corpse-woman within it has undergone a metamorphosis from the bony remains of necrosis to newly-moving flesh, the camera has pulled back to view the entire chamber. From this vantage, the viewer familiar with the vampire genre might anticipate a hand stretching out painfully from the enclosure in the manner of *Dracula, Prince of Darkness*. Instead the virulent energy which has re-formed the ashes is suffused into the cinerary stone itself. There is a crack. Then an explosion. The granite fragments break away and crumble into heaps on the floor of the vault. The cloud of dust, disturbed after hundreds of years, settles again and reveals the body lying still unmoved on the catafalque.

This sequence from Mario Bava's *Black Sunday* (*La Maschera del Demonio*, 1960) illustrates the expressive power of his directoral style. The scope and invention of his visual scheme create a Baroque atmosphere which is both evocative in its own right and entirely appropriate to the characters and subjects of the horror genre. Coleridge described stylistic invention in *Biographia Literaria* as a process which "dissolves, diffuses, and dissipates...is essentially vital, even as all objects [as objects] are essentially fixed and dead." For many filmmakers the "fixed and dead" objects are the conventions of the genre. In a vampire film, the cobwebs, the creaking doors, the rubber bats flapping their wings at the end of all-too-visible strings can be suffocating restrictions and overused to the point of becoming laughable clichés. Bava's tactic was a reliance on fresh rendering or novel manipulation of traditional images. The intricate series of dissolves in *Black Sunday* through which a skull re-acquires flesh implies an unseen energy. Details are added to help externalize the metaphysical reality of the moment. As each layer of skin reappears, the punctures in the face left by the demon's mask close into fine circles then recede altogether. The black, empty sockets slowly refill to disclose the whites of eyes enraged by centuries of death. Finally the nostrils flare, the neck constricts, and the whole body arches up under the sting of renewed life. This new vitality--and the simultaneous apprehension which the sequence engenders in the viewer--builds to a point at which it can no longer be contained and the stone itself must rupture to release it.

The unusual and disquieting visuals of Bava's films seem rooted in a conception of life as an uncomfortable union of illusion and reality. The dramatic conflict for his characters lies in confronting the dilemma of distinguishing between the two perceptions. In the black-and-white *Black Sunday* Bava captured the apprehension of a figure moving down a corridor by a device as simple as a shifting sidelight. As this light strikes first one half of the face and then the other, it is easy to equate this technique with the mixture of fear and curiosity that drives the character forward. In his later color films, Bava frequently compounded this equation by changing the light from blue to red with their respective connotations of cold and warmth.

While the plot lines of Bava's movies often contain the presence of an extraordinary being or object in an otherwise natural environment, that is seldom the narrative focus. Instead Bava leads his central figures out of their normal lives into a world of lurking phantoms or psychopaths. Bava situated his protagonists in a mutable world, composed of opposing spheres of influence, of shifting colors and times, of complements and atonalities. This world moves,like Spenser's ever-whirling wheel from reality to illusion and back again, from life to death *and* death to life through a landscape littered with phantasmagorical sights and sounds. On both symbolic and sensory levels, Bava's dramatic personae are thrust into the unstable middle ground between these two existential extremities, where figures glide through misty, opulently decorated but ultimately illusory and insubstantial settings. This spectral passageway linking the natural and supernatural worlds was, for Bava, a world of semi-darkness in which shadows and hallucinations can be real and, more importantly, in which the path forward or back, the way out, is unmarked. The oracle Medea in *Hercules and the Haunted World* (*Ercole al Centro della Terra*, 1961) typifies one strand in this limbo. The masked form of the woman is combined with an eerie, labored voice, modulated as if she were calling from a chamber deep below ground. She is separated from the camera, or real world, plane of view by a curtain of glimmering beads. While she sits swaying between two worlds, a series of green, blue, and gold lights successively cut through the frame, alternately striking her body and falling behind her to throw her into silhouette.

Although Bava developed this photographic style of high contrast and/or saturated primary colors early in his career as a cinematographer, the application of such mood and texture becomes ever more vigorous in his films as a director. Even if the dramatic conflicts are primarily psychological, when characters confront the dilemma of distinguishing between reality and illusion, Bava's emphatic style externalizes the experience for the viewer. In *Black Sunday* the protagonist is faced with the choice between a seductive vampiress and a virginal young woman who happen to be identical in appearance. At the conclusion of *What!* (*La Frustra e il Corpo*, 1963), the heroine dies without resolving the ambiguity: has she been haunted by an actual phantom of her murdered lover or conjured up his vindictive shade out of her guilt-ridden subconscious. In *Hercules and the Haunted World* the travelers to Hades are explicitly warned about the illusory nature of the underworld by the Hesperides ("Do not believe what you think you see.") and armed with this knowledge Hercules and Theseus can dare to dive into a sea of flames which they suspect is only water.

Below, Bava's Gothic architecture: the ruined church in **Black Sunday**.

The paradoxes of Bava's films are not all as metaphysical as these. Some confusions of identity are deliberate deceptions. Others are simply murder-mystery conventions. Some are staged for suspense; others to render a sense of the supernatural. For example, the plot device of physical doubles in *Black Sunday* reappears in *Erik the Conqueror* (*Gli Invasori*, 1961), where there is nothing supernatural about the twins. One, Rama, rescues Erik after a shipwreck and inspires his love. The other, Daja, is the wife of Erik's lost brother, Iron. The confusion is purely mechanical and the irony is purely dramatic, when the two rivals, Erik and Iron, discover they are brothers. In *Black Sunday* both the hero and the audience are unable to differentiate between the vampire sorceress Asa and her descendant Katia (both portrayed by Barbara Steele). In this instance the introduction of physical doubles is central to the film's supernaturalism. The individual viewer, in order to suspend disbelief and to participate in the hero's point of view, is compelled to accept the "reality" of *Black Sunday*'s unnatural twins.

Kill, Baby, Kill (*Operazione Paura*, 1966) contains an even more disorienting doppelganger. Bava isolated his protagonist, a young man like the one in *Black Sunday*, in a manor house which is reputedly haunted by the ghost of a young girl (who strikingly anticipates the child-de-

Below, **Hercules in the Haunted World**: even this "illusory" setting contains massive stonework.

mon created the following year in Fellini's episode of *Spirits of the Dead*). The initial confusion caused when the young man encounters the child's still-living mother, who has surrounded herself with the toys, clothing and other physical remnants of her daughter's life, is compounded by the appearance of what may be the child herself or her specter or another child altogether. In a climactic scene, the young man pursues an assailant through a series of identical doorways and rooms; but when he finally catches him, he discovers that he has been chasing himself or, at least, an apparition that resembles him. After having played with the viewer's genre awareness repeatedly throughout the film and having characters discuss the nature of the haunting, Bava inserted this event without an explanation. In the fantasy sequence which follows, a dream image reveals a man entangled in a huge web in front of a painting of a cathedral. This shot fades, and the man awakens, now free of the web but standing before the actual building. Is this a dream or not? As with Roger Corman's ending to the *Tomb of Ligeia*, Bava exploited the dream context to freely intercut between real and hallucinatory events and compel the viewer to create the distinction between the two.

A similar manipulation occurs in *What!* Not only does Nevenka, a young woman with sado-masochistic proclivities, claim that she is being tormented by a dead lover, but the audience sees several visits to her bedchamber by a dark figure who alternately whips and caresses her. Of course, the audience is free to assume that these visitations are merely projections of her disturbed mind; but there are certain external, physical manifestations. The lover's footsteps are heard in one scene; his laugh, in another. In a third, the footprints of his wet boot soles are left behind. As in *Black Sunday*, the reality of the apparition is reinforced when the spectator is compelled to assume Nevenka's point of view at key moments through the use of subjective camera. In the final scene, Nevenka is scene kissing her ghostly lover from one, quasi-subjective perspective. A cut to another, more objective angle reveals her embracing the empty air.

With *Shock (Beyond the Door II*, 1974) Bava reworks the story of *What!* in a modern setting. The protagonist Dora, like her "sister" in the former film, is haunted by the "ghost" of her dead loved one, in this case her husband. Like Nevenka she has killed her loved one after he exposes her dark side: in Nevenka's case her masochistic proclivities; in Dora's her predilection for drugs. Most of the film focuses in on the heroine's efforts to separate the real from the unreal (ghostly music in the night, sexual visitations to her bed by her dead husband in a state of decay, sounds of slashing razors—all variations of similar scenes in *What!*).

Bava, however, is not satisfied with a simple remake. Instead he adds yet another wrinkle to this tale of the reality of illusions. Dora has a son who identifies with his dead father to the point of sleeping with his mother and stealing her panties from her dresser. His oedipal desire even drives him to take on the personality and desires of his father, watching her nude in the shower or angrily calling her a "pig" for making love to her new husband. Again ambiguity reigns supreme. Is the son actually possessed by the spirit of his father as both he and his mother come to believe? In one shot from the boy's POV the viewer sees a decaying hand caressing Dora and later from the mother's POV the boy changes into the father as he runs towards her. The final shots are of the boy having tea and playing on the swing with his "father," visible to him as Kurt was to Nevenka, but invisible to the viewer. Even the final shot of the swing which seems to move of its own volition does nothing to clear up the intentional ambiguity of the film.

In most of Bava's work this manipulation of reality and illusion was character driven. The visceral impact of particular and peculiar techniques, such as the snap zooms and over-rotated pans, stand alone as part of an overall horror/suspense style but may also be keyed dramatically to the emotions of a character. Bava could quickly evoke his genre on a formal level with stylistic resonances to precedent films of his own and others, that is, through standard genre indicators and expectations. What sets Bava's work apart from most other genre filmmakers is the creation of metaphor and dramatic irony through the interplay of subjective and objective viewpoints and the linking of visual disorientation to character emotion. In the first episode of *Black Sabbath* (*I Tre Volti della Paura*, 1963), a nurse steals a ring from the corpse of a woman over whom she has kept a death watch. In the same manner as Poe's "Tell Tale Heart," her guilt distorts her perceptions, and she is driven mad by the amplified awareness of everyday objects in the house around her. First, she is assaulted by the crashing sound of a drop of water. Then, as she shivers in wordless apprehension, that emotion is objectified by the intermittent glare of a cold blue shop light blinking on and off outside her window.

In the third episode of *Black Sabbath*, a similar blue light envelops a figure returning from killing a vampire. The light, which grips him like an aura of death, makes it clear to his apprehensive family that he has become one of the undead himself. In *Black Sunday*'s colorless world, the simple fear of a character who moves down a corridor without knowing where it leads is underscored by an alternating side light that strikes first one side of the face then the other even as the impulse of

fear on the one hand and curiosity on the other drive the figure hesitat-
ingly forward. As noted before, Bava reused this staging: in *What!* the
added element of color. As Nevenka walks towards a room where she
thinks her dead lover awaits, the sound of a whip and her sensual gasps
are overlaid on the soundtrack. As she continues, uncertain between
what is real and what is illusion, in anticipation of pleasure and pain,
the alternating side lights are blue and red, cold and hot.

Bava's explorations of minds on the edge of nervous breakdown,
done so effectively in *What!* and *Shock*, resemble similar descents into
the psychic maelstrom by classic horror writer Edgar Allan Poe. As Poe
did in stories like "The Fall of the House of Usher," Bava over and over
again blurs the fine line between reality and hallucination in order to
subjectify the experience of the protagonist. In *Lisa and the Devil* (re-ed-
ited and released with added scenes not shot by Bava as *House of Exorcism*, 1974) Bava delineates the protagonist's psychic descent from the
first shots of the movie as Lisa wanders through a maze of cobblestone
streets, lost in an ancient Spanish city, where characters appear and disappear like figures in a living surrealist landscape, including an ominous ventriloquist who bears an uncanny resemblance to a fresco of the
devil on one of the ancient walls and who reappears in different incar-
nations throughout the film. Her hallucinations, if that is what they are,
continue as she finds herself on the grounds of an isolated mansion surrounded by moonlight and fog, much like Poe's house of Usher. Here
she is again tormented by the ventriloquist who is now the servant of
the house and who carries a dummy which resembles a man whose
death she caused earlier. To heighten the oneiric quality of the film the
son of the mansion is convinced that Lisa is the reincarnation of his lost
love Elena whose decaying body he keeps in an upstairs bedroom. In
flashback or in fantasy (the viewer is not given a clue as to which), Lisa
remembers or imagines a back story as Elena which even includes the
figure of the dummy come to life.

Is the son's obsession influencing Lisa or is Lisa really the reincarnation of Elena? Is the dummy nothing but a wooden figure or is he the
husband of the blind Contessa? And, most importantly, is the ventriloquist really the devil or only a prankster? Subjective realities and unanswered questions clash in a particularly rich manner. In the final scenes,
Lisa finds no clear-cut answer to her dilemma. Waking nude in a garden, covered by flowers, she tries to make her escape, only to be stopped
by children who call her a "ghost" and the ventriloquist who now carries an effigy of her. Bava plays with the spectator's mind even in the fi-

nal shots, as Lisa boards a "death plane," empty except for the bodies of the characters murdered in the film.

In his final film *Venus of Ille (La Venere d'Ille*, 1978) Bava reworks his life-long meditation on the ambiguity of reality for one last time. Using a story by Prosper Merimée as his basis, Bava recreates the milieu of a lusty 19th Century village and its manor, replete with orgies of food, lavish wedding celebrations, tennis matches, and sexual dalliances. Into this idyllic setting rises from the ground, literally, a bronze statue of a Greek Venus, discovered by workmen while digging up a tree root. Gradually the statue takes on a life of its own in the minds of the peasants as well as the upper class main characters: the obsessive and melancholy art historian Mathew; the philandering Alfonzo; and his fiancée Claire, the statue's doppelganger. In order to visually reify the perspective of the characters, Bava photographs the Galatea-like statue as if it were a real woman: close-ups of her face covered in rain which resemble tears; low-angle tracking shoots around the figure giving it the illusion of movement; shots of its delicate hand on which Alfonzo had carelessly placed his fiancee's wedding ring; and cross-cutting between Claire's face, with its marble paleness and antique hairdo, and the statue's bronze haughtiness.

This "ferocious Venus," as it is called by the villagers, seems to bring ill fortune to all who come in contact with her. A workman is crushed under her weight, a small boy is hit on the head with a stone which ricochets off its body, and climactically Alfonzo dies mysteriously on his wedding night after "wedding the statue" with his fiancee's ring. Even the detached artist Mathew becomes lost in the enigma of the Venus and her double Claire, sketching both of them as one. Reality, in classic Bava style, shifts unpredictably. As an example, during the wedding night sequence, Claire sees a figure enter her room. The room itself is lit alternately blue, from the night, and red, from the fire, creating a visual tension within the mise-en-scene. As the camera tracks around her bed, she cringes in fear. Is this tracking shot the POV of the Venus come to claim her "husband"? The resolution refuses to answer the question as Bava remains faithful to his vision and the statue itself is melted down to supply a bell for the local church.

Even as he gives the audience additional information about the characters through light and color, Bava could also manipulate mythic and social codes. Even if the plots are predictable, the staging of individual events compels a sense of anxiety in the viewer; and sometimes the events themselves are unexpected. To this end, Bava's mise-en-scene encouraged misreading. For instance, the two formidable leashed mastiffs which accompany Katia when she is first seen in *Black Sunday* suggest, incorrectly, that she might be the sorceress resurrected with two bestial familiars. Inversely, there is the plot twist at the conclusion of *Planet of the Vampires* (*Terrore nello Spazio*, 1965). When the astronauts seen throughout the film are revealed to be aliens and not human as the audience must have assumed by their speech and appearance, the effect is inescapable but not very profound. There is a more complex use of misreading in *Hatchet for a Honeymoon* (*Il Rosso Segno della Folia*, 1969). The character psychology of the film seems obvious enough from the first glimpse of the protagonist's secret room, full of mannequins in bridal gowns, toys, and other artifacts through which he attempts to recapture the innocence of his childhood. The overt "key" to his psychopathology is the elaborate ritual by which he lures fashion models to their deaths. Unlike the serial murders of models in Bava's earlier *Blood and Black Lace* (*Sei Donne per l'Assassino*, 1964), the designer/killer in *Hatchet for a Honeymoon* is revealed in the introductory scenes. His "motifs," the childish music box theme which he plays while seducing his victims or his Oedipal dreams of his own mother's murder on her wedding night, initially suggest a "classic" disturbance of emotional trauma and repressed sexuality redirected into uncontrollable outbursts of violence. However, Bava altered the expressive meaning of these clichéd motifs by disclosing from the first the extent to which the central figure is aware of the symbolic nature of his behavior. As he remarks in voice-over after the title sequence killings, while he examines his face in a train compartment mirror, "No one would think to look at me that I am completely insane."

This awareness at least partially deconstructs the traditional symbols and the false, social assumptions that underlie them. The perversely Freudian touches--such as the burnt bread popping out of the toaster when the protagonist argues with his wife over his sexual disinterest in her--set a tone that is satirical at first. But as the killer is overpowered by his own aberration, they also suggest the breakdown of his control. He violates the criminal pattern he has set for himself, the pattern in which he feels insanely secure, by attacking his wife. The immediate result is that he is almost caught in the act. The long-term effect is that he is now plagued by his wife's vindictive ghost. As in earlier pictures, Bava did not choose to clarify whether this haunting is genuine or imaginary. The schizophrenia of the protagonist is established in the opening scenes, in which the character as a young boy lurks outside a train compartment while his adult self enacts the English-language title and attacks some newlyweds with an ax. As the movie progresses, his disturbance overwhelms both his rational self and the film's imagery.

A single cut from the murderer's subjective viewpoint to an objective angle in *Hatchet for the Honeymoon* may express the same dichotomy between reality and illusion as an entire, elaborate set piece such as the visit to the oracle in *Hercules and the Haunted World*. On some occasions Bava might insert a ritualistic archetype merely to serve the mechanics of plot: for example the black helmet worn by Rurik in *Knives of the Avenger* (*Raffica di Coltelli*, 1967), which conceals his face when he rapes his enemy's bride. But most often these devices have an expressive as well as narrative value. The mask of the oracle Medea or the sorceress Asa may, like that of Rurik, conceal their identities. But masks are also larger-than-life, and the characters who wear them take on a protean aspect that is both figurative and melodramatic outside the context of the story line.

The extent to which Bava's mise-en-scene is calculated to use genre expectations and elicit particular viewer responses is most easily analyzed in his mysteries and costume films. In the former, there are no detective heroes methodically stripping away the layers of deception created by the criminals, as either the criminals themselves or the potential victims are the main characters. Neither the methods of the police nor the intricacies of the plot are as significant as the underworld of deviant behavior, like the ambiance of *film noir*, which criminals and victims cohabit. The long pursuit through the rural streets and alleyways in *Baron Blood* and the opening murder in the night mists of a city park in *Blood and Black Lace* are typical. Figures are forced to flee from obscure assailants, past isolated street lamps or lighted windows offering no safety, across dim nightmarish landscapes which would, in daylight, seem perfectly ordinary and unfrightening. Even inside a locked apartment, as in the second episode of *Black Sabbath* ("The Telephone"), a woman may be so unnerved by a voice coming through a receiver that the sound of telephone ringing is suddenly louder and more menacing than a gun shot.

Such visual and aural statements can have a multiplicity of keys. First, they are direct stagings of suspense sequences, using lighting, opticals, and cuts to enhance viewer apprehension. Second, they externalize the disturbed interior states of the characters. Finally, they are non-specific metaphors for either a *noir*-style underworld as in *The Evil Eye* or *Blood and Black Lace* or, in the supernatural films, a chaotic, almost formless universe somewhere beyond the boundaries of normal, material reality in which ordinary persons may inadvertently stumble as in *Black Sunday* or *Kill, Baby, Kill.* Even in the costume films, which antedate the "sword and sorcery" genre, Bava worked against a type which relies on a hero of preternatural strength or special martial ability. The title figure of *Hercules in the Haunted World* is strong but by no means indomitable and requires the assistance of legendary companions to complete his mission in the underworld. The Viking heroes of *Erik the Conqueror* and *Knives of the Avenger* are strong warriors but their mythic aspect is understated. Just like the non-criminal figures of the modern films, these heroes may be placed in fateful situations by some exterior power, or as Rurik ruefully observes in *Knives of the Avenger*, "Odin decides what our destinies are."

Bava's modern day *giallo* thrillers conform to a somewhat sexist mythology of their own, which can be more rigid than the pre-established context of the costume pictures. The beautiful young models in *Blood and Black Lace,* episode two of *Black Sabbath, Hatchet for the Honeymoon,* and *Five Dolls for the August Moon* (*Cinque Bambole per La Luna d'Agosto,* 1969) are all ostensibly normal people. Yet their very profession suggests a commitment to surface values and appearances. They are perfect victims for Bava's patriarchal narratives because they epitomize the complacency and superficiality of the modern world. Confronted with a paranormal threat, be it a ghost or a psychopath, these human mannequins are ill-equipped to save themselves.

In the 70's Bava continues his idiosyncratic exploration of the violent, often sexist *giallo* genre with films like *Twitch of the Death Nerve (Ecologia del Delitto,* 1971), where the body count anticipates the American gore films of the 80's, and in the recently restored *Rabid Dogs (Cani Arrabati,* 1974). *Rabid Dogs* is unique in that it is Bava's only serious exploration of "reality" as "reality," rather than the interplay of reality and illusion. Shot in a documentary style in real time, it follows three "rabid" criminals as they pull a heist, then carjack a vehicle with a child, a man, and a woman in it. A majority of the film takes place in the claustrophobic confines of the car as it races to freedom. Using wide-angle lenses and hand-held camera, Bava presents for the viewer a vision of the "real world" more horrific and brutal than any of his stylized *giallo* films. Graphic violence, rape, profanity, physical and psychological brutalization, much of it directed against the female hostage Maria, pervade the film. Its music score aggravates the nervous energy with repetitive notes and atonal jazz as the criminals try desperately to avoid capture. In the final scenes of the film the kidnapped man kills the two remaining criminals, only to reveal that he is also a criminal—a kidnapper who has taken the drugged child in the car as a hostage. As in Bava's fantasy world, people are not always what they seem.

In *Baron Blood*, Bava also added another layer of ambiguity and contrast, here between the modern characters and objects and the architecture, antiques, and icons of the past. The "haunted" castle of *Baron Blood* is a maze of stone and iron. Through Gothic arches and down spiral staircases into dungeons decked with iron maidens and racks, characters descend from a modern world into the chambers of the past where ancient horrors still lurk. Bava reinforced the disequilibrium with his usual off-angled shots, spinning pans, and cross-zooms, sometimes dizzyingly repeated as many as four times, and straight cuts from tight long lens close-ups to distorted wide angles of the old castle's expanses. Sustained sequences such as the reanimated Baron's pursuit of Eva through the fog-enshrouded passageways and courtyards at night is vintage Bava, but so are subtler visualizations.

When the child Gretchen flees from an unseen presence in the woods, the camera assumes the pursuer's point of view. Then at a pivotal moment, a low angle captures Gretchen clambering up a gully and over a ridge just before the Baron's black cape cuts across the foreground and blots out the frame. Decor, costuming, and optical effects work with camera movement in the seance to invoke Elizabeth Holly. A tight shot on an amulet in the medium's hand slowly focuses. Then a zoom and dolly shot are combined to pull back to a wide angle, revealing the other characters around a pyre by the monolith where Holly was burned as a witch by the Baron. Finally, her spirit appears, superimposed over the flames at frame right and speaking through the medium at frame left.

Ironically, Bava could also portray those characters whose distrust of every shadow and stray sound helps them survive as semi-comic and slightly paranoid. The heroine of *The Evil Eye* becomes such a figure in self defense. After witnessing the death of a stabbing victim, she faints and comes to her senses in a hospital where she has been admitted for chronic alcoholism. Her story is dismissed as a case of *delirium tremens*. This sets in motion a central series of scenes in which the significant details are designed to be misread. On a visit to a rural locale and an antique Roman site, ominous low angles and traveling shots follow her while she tries to evade a suspicious-looking man. He catches up and reveals that he merely wants to pick her up. In a later sequence, she constructs a maze of thread and talcum powder in a living room to trip up the knife-wielding killer she believes is stalking her. She succeeds in almost breaking the neck of a smitten young doctor trying to cure her delusions. In a final scene, after the killer has been caught, she and the doctor are riding a funicular railway and witness a jealous husband shoot his wife and her lover. He is aghast; but, because she has promised him to forget all about murders, she refuses to admit seeing anything. It is simultaneously one of the most humorous and the one of the darkest endings in Bava's work.

Seriously or satirically, as in his only sex comedy the Rashomon-like *Quante Volte Quella Notte* (*Four Times That Night*, 1972), all of Bava's films question the permanence of commonplace reality. Given this recurrent theme, there are no restrictions on the figurative potential of his visual usage. The catalogue of Bava's style is as broad and eclectic as the genres in which he worked. He may use a long take to build dramatic tension, as in the fashion show which is a prelude to the first murder in *Blood and Black Lace*. He may use a low angle on a figure to suggest dominance, as in the initial encounter between Rurik and the villainous Augen in *Knives of the Avenger*. He may use montage for a "traditional" symbolic rendering, as in the third episode of *Black Sabbath*, cutting from a vampire embracing her lover, to her undead family, to the victim's frenzied horse, whinnying, rearing up, and breaking his tether to flee. An isolated detail which is used for suspense in one film, such as the killer peering through a curtain in *Baron Blood*, may be transmuted for comic effect in another, as in the eyes of her uncle's portrait which seem

Below, astronauts in plastic shrouds in **Planet of the Vampires**.

to leer at the heroine of *The Evil Eye* as she undresses. The make-up and special effects which give a photographic reality to the revivification of the vampire in *Black Sunday,* are reapplied sardonically in *Danger Diabolik* (1968), where exaggerated costuming and matte shots make the characters stand out in relief like comic-book figures. Even the most bizarre images may be used to evoke a *frisson,* as when the dead astronauts stand up in their shallow graves and tear out of their plastic shrouds in *Planet of the Vampires,* or laughter, as in the close shot of the supposedly dead Diabolik encased in translucent gold and winking at his female accomplice.

In many instances, Bava had to rely on visual invention to conceal his limited budgets. To create a raid on a Viking village without scores of extras, he assembles a montage of individual spear thrusts, death blows, figures falling back towards camera, and hurled firebrands, all moving in the same direction and ending with a panning long shot as the last of the raiders rides out of the smoldering remains of the village. In other instances, he could expend a considerable amount of production value merely to add a novel touch to a mythic form as he did in his Western *Roy Colt and Winchester Jack* (1971) as well as his viking films. For the duel in a huge, torch-lit cave in *Erik the Conqueror,* Bava used an establishing long shot and a prologue in which the participants must forge their own weapons, delaying and enhancing the action of the combat itself. In moments of narrative terror the montage, zooms, cross-traveling, acute angles et al. are typically supported by equally unusual sounds.

If the image is the nexus of metaphor for Bava, the soundtrack is reserved for the literal discord. The noises that counterpoint music and dialogue are part of any Italian foley artist's bag of tricks, but Bava's positioning gives them an edge. The underscores may be as insistent as Bava's accelerated zooms, forcing the spectator into a fixed perspective. In the Les Baxter re-scores for Bava's *Black Sunday* and *Baron Blood,* the drums, cymbals, and brass constantly assault the circular measures of the strings with dissonant chords. An eerie plaintive flute or a few piano keys find their voice for a few bars then are displaced by insistent timpani. In the original Stelvio Cipriani score for *Baron Blood,* a pre-disco main title theme gave a pop/travelogue feel to the shots of a jumbo jet flying and setting down. The irony of jingle-like melodies with a lilting chorale back-up opening a horror film was an aural equivalent to some of Bava's visual jokes. The mutable and animated reality of Bava's films may even extend to props, as in the claw-like knife shaped like the fingers of a skeletal hand in *Hercules in the Haunted World,* the marble hand or the floating razor in *Shock,* or the whip in *What!* which writhes in the surf when Nevenka is raped by her ghost lover. That same whip curls and chars like a living thing writhing in agony when the lover's corpse is consumed by flames to create metaphor, personification, and pathetic fallacy all in one.

Although the visual style of his motion pictures may be unmistakable or even unique (and on those several productions where he receives credit under pseudonyms that style is Bava's real and only signature), no director can completely transcend his narrative material. For Bava, who labored exclusively in a system where even A-budgets were small, where multiple cameras and post-synchronization of the dialogue were not options but standard operating procedures, where shooting schedules were short, and post schedules even shorter, the odds against excellent results were always even greater. That the sea battle in *Erik the Conqueror*, staged in a studio tank with two prows, a fog machine, and a speed-rail for the camera should be much more convincing than the clash of custom-made miniatures in *Ben Hur* is a tribute to Bava the technician. That one man working against such limitations could become one of the most striking of genre stylists may seem hard to believe. The proof, beyond the often stilted, dubbed performances, creaky sound effects, and tinny music, beyond the panned and scanned, retimed and sometimes reedited videos, is in the images themselves. No matter how feeble the character development may be or how far-fetched the plot, Bava's visual style is the cornerstone of a sensory package that envelops the audience and sends them on a journey into the undiscovered country.

Below, another enmeshed figure in *Kill, Baby, Kill*.

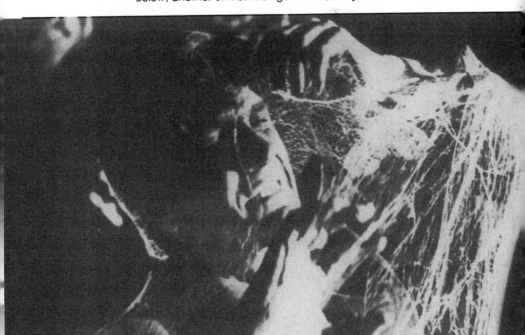

Above, "the road leads to nowhere": the graphic rape scene from *Last House on the Left*.

Neglected Nightmares

Robin Wood

Last year for the Toronto Film Festival Richard Lippe and I organized a sixty-film retrospective of the American horror film called "The American Nightmare," and brought out a book of essays under the same title. The aim of both the retrospective and the book was to further the responsible reading of the horror film as an important phenomenon within our culture, since the genre, and particularly its finest specimens, offer (it seems to us) the material for a radical and diagnostic reading of the culture itself. One of the by-products of the venture was the discovery of a number of remarkable works hitherto unknown to us and generally denied either critical or popular recognition. The present article offers a survey of these discoveries, and should be regarded as an addendum to the book: many of its ideas and valuations have developed out of discussions between Richard Lippe and me, and I would not want his contribution to go unacknowledged.

I want to glance (somewhat perfunctorily–some of the films I was able to see only once, none more than twice) at the work of Wes Craven and Stephanie Rothman; at Bob Clark's *The Night Walk*; and at the lesser-known films of George Romero. Craven, Rothman and Romero all appeared at the retrospective (as did Brian De Palma and David Cronenberg), and all three were extremely articulate about their work. The usual gulf that separates the artist's perception of her/his work from the critic's was on these occasions almost non-existent (though it was wider than ever with De Palma).

Wes Craven

If I begin with *Last House on the Left* it is partly because it has achieved at least a certain underground notoriety (unlike, say, *The Night Walk* or *Jack's Wife*) and surfaced briefly in the pages of *Film Comment* as one of Roger Ebert's Guilty Pleasures. I had better say that the Guilty Pleasures feature seems to me an entirely deplorable institution. If one feels guilt for a pleasure, isn't one bound to renounce either one or the other? Preferably, in most cases, the guilt, which is merely the product of that bourgeois elitism that continues to vitiate so much of criticism. The attitude

111

fostered is essentially evasive (including self-evasive) and anti-critical: "Isn't this muck–to which, of course, I'm really so superior–delicious?"

Ebert's Guilty Pleasure (which may be *Last House's* only recognition so far by a professedly serious critic) is brief enough to quote in full:

"The original Keep Repeating–It's Only a Movie!! Movie. The plot may sound strangely familiar. Two young virgins go for a walk in the woods. One is set upon by vagabonds who rape and kill her. The other escapes. The vagabonds take their young victim's clothes and set on through the wood, coming at last, without realizing it, to the house of victim's parents. The father finds his daughter's bloodstained garments, realizes that he houses the murderers, and kills them by electrifying the screen door and taunting them to run at it, whereupon they slip on the shaving cream he's spread on the floor, fall into the screen, and are electrocuted.

"Change a few trifling details (like shaving cream) and you've got Bergman's *Virgin Spring*. The movie's an almost scene-by-scene ripoff of Bergman's plot. It's also a neglected American horror exploitation masterpiece on a par with *Night of the Living Dead*. As a plastic Hollywood movie, the remake would almost certainly have failed. But its very artlessness, its blunt force, makes it work."

Pleasure or not. Ebert has plenty here to feel guilty about.

1. The virginity of one of the girls (Phyllis) is very much in question. The relationship between them is built on the experienced/innocent opposition (as in Bergman's original, the plot of which, by the way, was also a "scene-by-scene ripoff" of a medieval ballad), though the innocence of Mary (the nice bourgeois family's daughter) is also questioned: she is a flower-child with an ambiguous attraction to violence.

2. The girls meet the "vagabonds" in the latter's apartment in the city; they are on their way to a concert by a rock group noted for its onstage violence, and pause to try to buy some dope from the youngest of the gang, who is lounging about on the front steps.

3. Ebert is decently reticent about the "vagabonds" (their background, relationships, sex, and even their number); his association of them with "the wood" deprives them of the very specific social context that Craven in fact gave them. There are four: an escaped killer, his sadistic friend Weasel, their girl Sadie, and the killer's illegitimate teenage son Junior.

4. I am not clear which girl Ebert thinks "escapes." Phyllis gets away briefly but is soon recaptured, tormented, repeatedly stabbed and (in the original, though Craven himself wonders if a print survives anywhere with this in it) virtually disemboweled. (The abridged version

leaves no doubt that she is dead.) Mary staggers into the water to cleanse herself after she is raped, and is repeatedly shot; her parents later find her on the bank, and she dies in their arms.

5. The "vagabonds" do not take Mary's clothes. Her body, which they presume dead, is drifting out in the middle of a large pond. The mother (as in Bergman), searching the men's luggage after overhearing some semi-incriminating dialogue and one of the gang calling out in his sleep, finds the "peace pendant" her husband gave Mary at the start of the film, and blood on the men's clothes.

6. No one in the film dies from electrocution; the father spreads shaving cream outside the upstairs bedroom door to slow his victims down, and electrifies the screen door to prevent their escaping by it. The gang are disposed of as follows: the nice bourgeois mother seduces Weasel out in the dark pond where Mary was raped, fellates him, and bites off his cock as he comes; the killer contemptuously persuades his son Junior to blow out his own brains; the mother cuts Sadie's throat outside in an ornamental pond while her husband dispatches Junior's father with a chain saw–presumably decapitating him, and thereby completing the parallel between the simultaneous actions (though this is only thing that Craven doesn't show).

That Ebert's plot synopsis sets a new record in critical inaccuracy (combined with characteristic critic-as-superstar complacency) says less about him personally than about a general ambience that encourages opinion mongering, gossip, Guilty Pleasures, and similar smart-assery —and, as an inevitable corollary, actively discourages criticism and scholarship. What does it matter whether he gets the plot right or not? Hell, it's only a movie, and exploitation movie at that, albeit an "American horror exploitation masterpiece on a par with *Night of the Living Dead*"–which Ebert mercilessly slammed when it came out. (Is this supposed to be his public retraction?)

What I mean by bourgeois elitism could as well be illustrated from the writings of John Simon or even Pauline Kael. What the critic demands, as at least a precondition to accord a film serious attention, is not so much evidence of a genuine creative impulse (which can be individual or collective, and can manifest itself through any format) as a set of external signifiers that advertise the film as a Work of Art. No one feels guilty about seriously discussing *The Virgin Spring*, though the nature of Bergman's creative involvement there seems rather more suspect than is the case with *Last House*. What is at stake, then, is not merely the evaluation of one movie but quite fundamental critical (hence cultural, social, political) principles–issues that involve the relationship between critic and reader as well as that between film and spectator.

The relationship *of Last House* to *The Virgin Spring* is not, in fact, close enough to repay any detailed scrutiny–though one might remark that, if the term "ripoff" is appropriate here, it is equally appropriate to the whole of Shakespeare, the debt being one of plot outline and no more. The major narrative alterations–the transformation of Ingeri into Phyllis and of the child goatherd into the teenage Junior, the killing of both girls, the addition of Sadie, the mother's active participation in the revenge, the destruction of Junior by his own father–are all thoroughly motivated and in themselves indicate the creative intelligence at work.

The most important narrative change is that of overall direction and final outcome. Bergman's virgin is on her way to church, and the film leads to the somewhat willed catharsis of her father's promise to build a new church, and "answer" of a spurious and perfunctory miracle. Craven's virgin is on her way to a rock concert by a group that kills chickens on stage and, as the recurrent pop song on the soundtrack informs us, "the road leads to nowhere." The last image is of the parents, collapsed together in empty victory, drenched in blood.

But the crucial difference is in the film-spectator relationship, especially with reference to the presentation of violence. Joseph Losey saw Bergman's film as "Brechtian," but I think its character is determined more by personal temperament than aesthetic theory: the ability to describe coldly and accurately, without empathy–or, perhaps more precisely, with an empathy that has been repressed and disowned. If there is something distasteful in the film's detailing of rape and carnage, it is because Bergman seems to deny his involvement without annihilating it, and to communicate that position to the spectator.

The Virgin Spring is Art; *Last House* is Exploitation. One must return to that dichotomy because the difference between the two films in terms of the relationship set up between audience and action is inevitably bound up with it. I use the terms Art and Exploitation here not evaluatively, but to indicate two sets of signifiers–operating both within the films as "style" and outside them as publicity, distribution, etc.–that define the audience-film relationship in general terms. As media for communication, both Art and Exploitation have their limitations, defined in both cases (though in very different ways) by their inscriptions within the class system. Both permit the spectator a form of insulation from the work and its implications: Art by defining seriousness in aesthetic terms implying class superiority (only the person of education and refinement can appreciate Art, i.e., respond to that particular set of signifiers); Exploitation by denying seriousness altogether. It is the work of the best movies in either medium to transcend, or transgress, these limitations– to break through the spectator's insulation.

In organizing the horror film retrospective, Richard Lippe and I also set out to transgress. We wanted (through the book and the seminar, which only a very small proportion of our audience attended) to cut through the barriers bourgeois society erects as projection against genre's implications–defenses against the genre's implications–defenses that take many forms: laughter, contemptuous dismissal, the term "schlock," the phenomenon of the late-night horror show, the treatment of the horror film as Camp.

In a way, *Last House* succeeded where we failed. A number of our customers–even in the context of a horror retrospective, even confronted by a somewhat bowdlerized print–gathered in the foyer after the screening to complain to the theater management that film had been shown at all. Clearly, the film offers a very disturbing experience, its distinction lying in both the degree and nature of the disturbance. It is essential to this that its creation was a disturbing experience for Craven himself, a gentle, troubled, quiet-spoken ex-professor of English literature. The exploitation format, the request from the producer to "do a really violent film

Below, **Last House on the Left**: "...the crucial difference is in the film-spectator relationship, especially with reference to the presentation of violence."

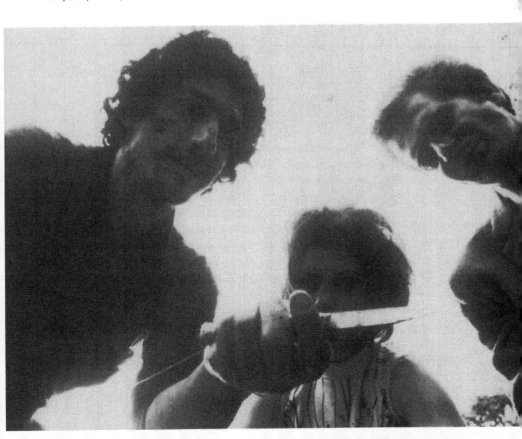

for $50,000," seems to have led him to discover things in himself he scarcely knew were there–which is also the effect it has on audiences.

"I found that I had never written anything like this," Craven said, "and I'd been writing for ten to twelve years already. I'd always written artistic, poetic things. Suddenly, I was working in an area I had never really confronted before. It was almost like doing a pornographic film if you'd been a fundamentalist. And I found that I was writing about things that I had very strong feelings about. I was drawing on things from very early in my own childhood, things that I was feeling about the war, and they were pouring into this very simple B-movie plot."

That extraordinary linking of "things from very early childhood" to "things that I was feeling about the war" is the kind of central perception about a film that criticism strives for and often misses. The connection between Vietnam and the fundamental structures of patriarchal culture is one I shall return to in discussing *The Night Walk*.

The reason people find the violence of *Last House* so disturbing is not simply that there is so much of it, nor even that it is so relentlessly close and immediate in presentation. (Many, myself included, have come to praise films for being "Brechtian," but it should also be acknowledged that distanciation is not the only valid aesthetic method.) I want to draw here on ideas derived from an admirable book, *Violence in the Arts* (Cambridge University Press), whose author John Fraser, was a valuable contributing participant in our seminars. The book is one of the rare treatments of this subject that manages to be intelligent and responsible without ever lapsing into puritanism, hypocrisy or complacency. Its weakness is, I think, a failure to argue clearly as to whether violence is innate in "the human condition," or a product of the specific social structures, or a combination of the two–to speculate, that is, as to the degree to which violence would disappear within a truly liberated society.

Violence, whether actual or implicit, is so powerfully and obstinately inherent in human relationships as we know them (structured as they are on dominance and inequality) that the right to a "pure" denunciation of it must be a hard-won and precarious achievement. It is difficult to point to such an achievement in the cinema: perhaps Mizoguchi (the brandings and cutting of the tendon in *Sansho the Bailiff*), perhaps Fritz Lang (the scalding of Gloria Grahame in *The Big Heat*–but even there, what feelings are aroused by eventual retaliation?). As for myself, I am a committed pacifist who has experienced very strong desires to smash people's faces in, and who can remember incidents when I joined in the persecution of those in an inferior position and took pleasure from it; I have also, not infrequently, been a victim, and my greatest dread is of total helplessness at the mercy of tormenters. It is these three positions–

the position of a victim, the position of a violator, the position of right-eous avenger–and the interconnections among them that *Last House on the Left* dramatizes. Its distinction lies in the complex pattern of empa-thies that it creates.

To empathize exclusively with the victims is to see the violators as strictly Other, non-human, to erect a clear-cut boundary between one's own humanity and the inhumanness of someone "out there"; it is the grave error Michael Cimino makes in the Vietnam sequences of that nonetheless great movie *The Deer Hunter*. On the other hand, to empa-thize exclusively with the violators is to adopt the position of the sadist, seeing the victims as mere objects; it is a position to which Tobe Hooper's *The Texas Chainsaw Massacre* comes perilously close, in its fail-ure to endow its victims with any vivid, personalized aliveness. *Last House* involves the spectator, simultaneously and inescapably, in the ex-perience of both violator and victim.

How does one recognize the aliveness of characters in a movie? What I am pointing to is not merely a matter of subjective impression; nor is it a matter of those "rounded," "complex" characters beloved of critics whose aesthetic criteria are derived from the psychological novel. What is crucial is the suggestion of common intimate experience shared be-tween character and spectator, particularly the suggestion of vulnerabil-ity. It is there in the nervous, darting glances of the Viet Cong tormenter in *The Deer Hunter*–though not sufficiently to offset the film's horrified repudiation of him. It is there much more strongly in *The Texas Chainsaw Massacre*, especially in the little scene (echoed in *Eaten Alive* with Neville Brand) where Leatherface is seen alone and appears at a loss what do next, but also in his curiously endearing dressing-up for the family din-ner, complete with curly wig. In Hooper's films, however, such mo-ments are reserved for monstrous figures. The young people are scarcely more than objects, capable of nothing beyond a completely gen-eralized and stereotypical display of pain and terror.

In *Last House*, all the major characters are allowed these moments of particularized vulnerability (except perhaps the father, the center of Bergman's film, relatively peripheral in Craven's). As the two girls rest in the woods on their way to the concert, Mary talks shyly and hesi-tantly to Phyllis about her sense of awakening womanhood, her devel-oping breasts, her awareness of her own sexuality. The moment involves the spectator in an intimate relationship with her that makes objectification impossible. Yet her counterpart Sadie is equally alive, al-ways groping toward an awareness that is beyond her grasp; she is ac-quainted with "Frood," and knows a telegraph pole is "not just a telegraph pole but a giant p-hyalus"; she has also been brushed by feminism, to the extent that she can sum up one of the men who pushes her around as a "male chauvinist dog."

The men, corrupt and brutalized, never cease to be recognizably human: Weasel's horrendous castration nightmare, wherein the father, as dentist, prepares to knock out his front teeth, with hammer and chisel, attests to a continuing capacity for Oedipal guilt. As for Junior, we have his embarrassed, puzzled, troubled reaction to the extraordinary moment where Mary, in a desperate attempt to seduce him into a relationship with her and break through the gang's objectification of her, confers upon him the name Willow and proceeds to offer to steal him a fix from her father's house.

One incident in Craven's original version clearly dramatized the breakdown of objectification; it must have been the most disturbing moment in this most disturbing of films, bringing home the common humiliation of violators and victims. It may have been cut from all prints, but we have Craven's account of it. "The killing of Phyllis is very sexual in feeling, and ended with her being stabbed not only by the men but by the women repeatedly. Then she fell to the ground and Sadie bent down and pulled out a loop of her intestines. They looked at it and that's where it all stopped. That's when they realized what they had done, and they looked at each other and walked away. They were disgusted at what they had done. It was as if they had been playing with a doll, and it had broken and come apart and they did not know how to put it back together again. Again, there were parallels with what I was seeing in our culture, where we were breaking things that we did not know how to put back together."

The film offers no easily identifiable parallels to Vietnam (in the somewhat opportunistic, though eminently well-intentioned, manner of *Little Big Man*). Instead, it analyzes the nature and conditions of violence and sees them as inherent in the American situation. Craven sees to it that the audience cannot escape the implications. We are spared nothing in the protracted tormenting of the two girls—our having to share the length of their ordeal is part of the point—and we cannot possibly enjoy it. They are us. Yet we also cannot disengage ourselves from their tormenters: They are us, too. We can share the emotional and moral outrage of the parents, yet they take hideous revenge on characters we have entered into an intimate relationship with, and we are kept very much aware that it is the revenge of the "haves" on the "have nots"—that the gang's monstrousness is the product of the inequalities and power structures of a class system into which all the characters are bound. No act of violence in the film condoned, yet we are led to understand every act as the realization of potentials that exist within us all, that are intrinsic to our social and personal relationships.

The domination of the family by the father, the domination of the nation by the bourgeois class and its norms, the domination of other nations and other ideologies, more precisely, attempts at domination that inevitably fail and turn to mutual destruction–the structures interlock, are basically a single structure. My Lai was not an unfortunate occurrence out there; it was created within the American home. No film is more expressive than *Last House* of a (n) (inter) national social sickness, and no film is richer in Oedipal references–an extension, in its widest implications, of the minutiae of human relations under patriarchal capitalist culture. Craven is fully aware of this macrocosm-microcosm relationship; I leave the last word to him, adding merely that these concerns are taken up (with great intelligence, a higher budget, more polish, but less disturbing intensity) in *The Hills Have Eyes*, a work that, while it has not to my knowledge received serious critical treatment, is scarcely unknown.

"The family is the best microcosm to work with. If you go much beyond that you're getting away from a lot of the roots of our own primeval feelings. Let's face it, most of the basic stories and the basic feelings involve very few people: Mommy, Daddy, me, siblings and the people in the other room. I like to stay within that circle. It's very much where most our strong emotions or gut feelings come from. It's from those very early experiences and how they are worked out. I grew up in a white working-class family that was very religious, and there was an enormous amount of secrecy in the general commerce of our getting along with each other. Certain things were not mentioned. A lot of things were not spoken of or talked about. If there was an argument it was immediately denied. If there was a feeling it was repressed. As I got older I began to see that as a nation we were doing the same thing."

Stephanie Rothman

Throughout the series of directors' seminars that formed part of "The American Nightmare," one question recurred: What was the filmmaker's attitude to the possibility of social change, and did s/he feel a responsibility in that direction? The responses of the five directors we interviewed seem closely relevant to their work–indeed, almost deducible from it, though such correspondences are not as common as one might logically expect.

For Brian De Palma, the cultural situation is beyond any hope, social change impossible, and all one has left is to enjoy the fascinating spectacle of corruption and disintegration as best one can; generally, he wanted to discuss his films as formal exercises (invoking Hitchcock as precedent), disclaiming much interest in what they were about. David Cronenberg's attitude was, roughly, that as we all die in the end anyway, what does it matter? He resisted any social analysis of his films in favor of a metaphysical reading (they are about "mortality"). George Romero gave what was at once the most equivocal, guarded, and complex answer. He by no means rejected notions of social engagement, but didn't think of his work primarily in such terms; the desire to change society might be present but was not a primary, conscious motivation. Only Stephanie Rothman and Wes Craven gave unequivocal affirmative answers on the subject of the artist's responsibility; both wished to make films that engaged directly and progressively with social issues.

I certainly don't wish to attribute any absolute authority to an artist's view of her/his own work; but my growing distrust of De Palma's work, my hatred of Cronenberg's, and my increasing interest in and respect for that of the other three directors, all received support from their statements. Equally, of course, one must resist any simplistic equation between conscious social engagement and artistic merit: it is the work that confers significance on the artist's statement, not vice versa.

The interest in Stephanie Rothman's films has been signaled in a number of places–in the work of feminist critics, and in a *Film Comment*

Below, a parade of prisonors led by the scantily clad females in **Terminal Island**.

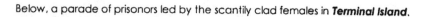

article by Terry Curtis Fox (November-December 1976). Only one of her films (*The Velvet Vampire*) belongs within the horror genre, though we also screened *Terminal Island* for its treatment of violence as a response to oppression.

Rothman's work embodies a vitality, inventiveness and general likability that suggest a potential far beyond the films' actual achievement. I have not seen a Rothman film for which I would stick out my neck, as I would for Larry Cohen's *Demon* [aka *God Told Me To*], De Palma's *Sisters*, Romero's *Dawn of the Dead*, or *Last House on the Left*. But perhaps the absence from her work to date of the fully convincing, fully realized film should not be seen in personal terms or even in terms of the specific production set-ups (with obvious deficiencies of budget, casting and shooting schedules) of each film.

Rothman's films–and particularly *The Velvet Vampire*–raise the question of whether a feminist intervention in heavily male-dominated and traditionally sexist genres can be more than disruptive, can produce more than sketchy, fragmented and self-contradictory texts. De Palma's *Sisters* (co-written by Louisa Rose) suggests that a coherent feminist horror movie is possible, though only in negative terms: the systematic analysis of the oppression of women, the annihilation of any movement of revolt. It is Rothman's desire to offer more positive statements that makes her films at once so sympathetic and so problematic. *Group Marriage*, for example, is one of the only American films actually to propose alternatives to the battered ideological tradition of monogamous relationships, but it evades most of the problems it raises under the alibi of being a light comedy.

The inclusion of *Terminal Island* in the retrospective foregrounded, among other things, the perennial quandary of genre movies with ulterior motives. For me, the film, though invigorating and effective (unlike Terry Curtis Fox, I don't sense any inhibitions whatever in Rothman's treatment of violence), is too clear-cut, too pared down to the bare lines of a thesis; a message-movie is a message-movie, even if one likes the message. Yet, to judge from the reactions of the audience, most people respond only to the generic signifier and miss the message altogether. Despite all the work on genre and "entertainment" that has been done in film education, reactions to films remain largely determined by the spectator's cultural position. To recognize a film as Exploitation, etc., is instantly to know how to respond to it, and all local particularities and inflections become obliterated.

As a "fable for our time," *Terminal Island* works beautifully. To save the taxpayers' money, convicts who would otherwise be subject to the death penalty or life imprisonment are released to fend for themselves on a small island off the coast of California. The action begins and ends with the arrival of the boat that periodically deposits new islanders. The woman who arrives at the start finds a state not without parallels in the real world: on the one hand, a primitive quasi-Fascist dictatorship based on force and terrorization, in which women are prostitutes, ignominiously servicing the men; on the other, a band of guerrillas, disruptive and violent, ultimately impotent and disorganized. The women escape to the guerrillas, help overthrow the dictatorship, and exert their new power to create a free democracy based on true equality (including of course full sexual equality). When the boat arrives at the end, it brings a new murderess and a pardon for the doctor convicted of euthanasia. The doctor decides not to leave–not, as in the traditional genre movies, because he has fallen in love, but because he recognized the superiority of the new order to the "civilized" world that awaits him; and the new woman is welcomed into the order by her sisters.

The film works partly because the action-movie format permits the simplification of the issues and problems arising from the contemporary crisis in male and female roles. But the film's limitations are not, I think, solely explicable in terms of generic determinants. Rothman's work suggests that she is more a liberal feminist than a radical feminist; the key issue of bisexuality is repeatedly evaded, or refused recognition as an issue. The statement that *Terminal Island* seems to be making is that men and women should collaborate and accept each other on equal terms. Fine, of course, as far as it goes; but it leaves undisturbed the fact that the terms "men" and "women" are themselves culturally defined, and defined in terms of specific roles.

The group in *Group Marriage* explicitly rejects bisexuality; on the periphery of the group hovers a gay couple conceived in terms of the most blatant sexual stereotyping. The film does not treat them unkindly; they are permitted to join the group wedding ceremony at the film's climax, but as a couple who tag along, not as full members. Rothman's feminism never wants to acknowledge that male and female roles of our culture are built upon the repression of bisexuality and the resultant separation and reinforcing of masculinity and femininity. She wants men and women to be equal–but without ceasing to be men and women as our culture defines and conditions them.

Bisexuality is allowed far greater freedom in *The Velvet Vampire*, but is treated very equivocally. Both the release and the equivocation are characteristic of the horror genre. I find the film very difficult to come to terms with: it is imaginative and audacious, gaining a strong impetus from Rothman's interest in Surrealism (in her seminar she expressed a debt to and great admiration for Jean Cocteau and Georges Franju), but riven by contradictory impulses and confusions.

The feminist inflection actually intensifies the genre's unresolvable quandary–a problem developed in various way by Andrew Britton, Richard Lippe, and me in our essays in *The American Nightmare*. To wit: if one accepts that the "monster" of the horror films is the embodiment of all that our culture represses, and that (as a direct consequence of this) the monster of almost every "progressive" horror film is necessarily the most sympathetic character, isn't any attempt to find a positive resolution to the conflicts doomed to failure by the inescapable connotations of evil inherent in the genre's basic premises? Larry Cohen's *It's Alive* and *It Lives Again* drive the notion of the "positive" monsters as far as it can be driven; George Romero's *Night of the Living Dead* and *Dawn of the Dead* sidestep the problem by removing all positive connotations from the monsters and restoring them to the human beings. Both directors reach the point where, logically, the genre would have to be abandoned altogether. *The Velvet Vampire* never progresses beyond confusion, but its internal contradictions are very interesting.

They are centered, of course, in the vampire Diane herself. The plot concerns her shifting relationship with a "normal" young couple (quasi-liberated, i.e., bourgeois-trendy) whom she picks up at an art exhibition and invites to her desert retreat, where she seduces both (thereby anticipating *The Rocky Horror Picture Show* by several years). Logically, she should represent a deeper level of sexual liberation than the young couple have hitherto experienced, and this meaning does seem to be intermittently present. This reading is undermined, however, by the fact that Diane's most obvious connotations link her to decadence and perversity. Rothman, in other words, equivocates with her very much as Bernardo Bertolucci equivocates with the Dominique Sanda character in *The Conformist*.

The issue is obfuscated further by the fact that Diane is obsessively tied to a husband (apparently one of those "real men" who, once bedded, is never forgotten), to whom she is faithful, in her fashion; the husband is long dead, so necrophilia enters in as well. By the end of the film the character, in terms of the values she is meant to embody, seems quite unreadable. Rothman produces a splendid climax, with Diane destroyed in the Los Angeles sunshine by an impromptu lynch-mob of young people mindlessly waving at her crosses snatched from a souvenir stall: repression restored by the permissive young having a ball. But the kind of liberation Diane embodies–if indeed she can be said to embody any at all (but if she doesn't, then what is the film about?)–is by this time so unclear that the spectator scarcely knows how to react.

Bob Clark

The great period of the American horror film was the period of Watergate and Vietnam: the genre required a moment of ideological crisis for its full significance to emerge, the immediate cultural breakdown calling into question far more than a temporary political situation. It is scarcely a coincidence that both Wes Craven and George Romero see certain of their films–*The Hills Have Eyes* and *The Crazies*, respectively–as deliberate, if oblique, commentaries on Vietnam and its impact on the structures of American society. The reference of Bob Clark's *The Night Walk* (also known, in the manner of commercially dubious propositions, by several aliases: *Deathdream* and *Dead of Night*) is more direct. The film, made in 1972, seems to have been almost entirely buried; it is certainly worth digging up again. It shares with Bob Clark's subsequent films (*Black Christmas, Murder by Decree*) a certain laboriousness at the level of mise en scene, an over anxiety that points be clearly made. But the concept is remarkable and rigorously worked out; the film accumulates tremendous force by the time its climactic sequences are reached.

Its premise is that a young man, killed in Vietnam, is willed home by his mother (Lynn Carlin). He returns as a zombie, able to sustain himself only on human blood, and driven by a desire for revenge on the society that sent him to war. The film's resonances develop out of the three-way connection set up among the raw materials of the horror film, the family, and Vietnam. Its anticipations are very striking: not just the basic concept (the monster as product of the family) but whole sequences evoke *It's Alive* and Romero's *Martin*. The coincidental proximity of these three distinguished films, without any direct connecting links or influence, greatly strengthens the argument that to study the evolution of a genre is to study the evolution of a national (un)consciousness.

Few horror films have been so explicit about the monstrousness of patriarchal family structures. Within the home, the mother rules–the reward for exclusion from the world of money, power, and politics. She devotes her frustrated energies entirely to the perpetuation of patriarchy, in the shape of her obsessively adored son, relegating her daughter to unconsidered subordination and an impotent and furtive complicity with the ineffectual father (John Marley). The family is seen as a structure of relationships based on hate masquerading as love; everything is to be sacrificed for the son, the future patriarch, the most "loved," hence most resented, of the family group. Of Andy the son the film offers (by presentation and implication) a double image: nice, unremarkable boy and devouring ghoul–a figure quite inadequate to sustain the ideological burden he is meant to carry. The film never falls into the simplistic trap of innocent-boy-corrupted-by-horrors-of-war. It was not Vietnam alone that produced Andy's monstrousness.

The dinner scene near the start of the film, before Andy's return, establishes the theme succinctly. The roast is brought in, and the mother insists that the father carve it; she loves to watch the head of the family carve. Andy has already learned to carve beautifully, as befits a future head of a future family. It is the symbol of his position and the duties that go with it—duties which clearly extend to "serving his country," killing and being killed. Imperialism begins at home. So the father carves, very awkwardly and badly, as his wife watches admiringly.

The film builds logically from that moment to a climax of sustained hysteria: the mother frantically driving her vampire son to the grave he has prepared for himself, before he can wreak further destruction on the community and the family. The film's ultimate insight is remarkable: that, under patriarchy, the patriarch suffers as much as anyone, and from the very assumptions that enthrone him as an ideologically privileged figure. The film is also a useful reminder that a radical statement about Vietnam must be a statement about much more.

George Romero

Anyone happening today upon articles I wrote for *Film Comment* (July-August and September-October 1978) on the horror film must be aware of an absence so glaring as to appear a major critical aberration: aside from a few casual references to *Night of the Living Dead*, George Romero was ignored, and neither the nature nor the scope of his achievement was given recognition. In my defense I must therefore point out that, at that time, *Dawn of the Dead* had not been completed, *Martin* had not been released in Canada, and both *Jack's Wife* and *The Crazies* appeared entirely inaccessible. What reputation they had did nothing to suggest they might be worth the effort of tracing. I assumed, then, that *Night of the Living Dead* represented a one-shot success that its director had feebly tried (with *The Crazies*) to repeat. The news that Romero was currently "remaking" it provoked little beyond a raised eyebrow.

I have some amends in *The American Nightmare*. Clearly, Romero's work demands extended treatment, and in the space available here I can do no more than indicate the lines that exploration might take. To remedy at once, however, the deficiencies of those earlier articles: Romero has already produced a rich, coherent and substantial oeuvre, an achievement matched, in the Seventies horror genre, only by Larry Cohen; none of the films merely repeats or "remakes" of others; the neglected works, far from being negligible, add important dimensions to our knowledge of Romero as an artist and deserve a general rediscovery; *Dawn of the Dead* seems to me among the half-dozen best American movies of the Seventies.

The five Romero films I have now seen (his comedy, *There's Always Vanilla*, remains inaccessible) divide clearly into two groups: on one hand, *Night*, *Dawn*, and *The Crazies*; on the other, *Jack's Wife* and *Martin*. Within each group the films can be seen as complex variations on one another; what I want consider briefly here is the relationship between the two groups. But both groups also stand in an interestingly eccentric relationship to the mainstream horror film (Cohen's work, while not superior, is much more central), and this needs to be defined first.

Romero's zombies carry none of the positive connotations of a "return of the repressed." Their most obvious antecedent is the pod-people of *Invasion of the Body Snatchers*, though they lack the unresolved and unprofitable ambiguity (Commies or Capitalists?) of Don Siegel's film. The zombies can be read as representing the heritage of the past from which the protagonists must struggle to free themselves. Their most obvious characteristic is their need–apparently their sole need–to consume. They represent, that is, the logical end-result, the reductio ad absurdum and ad nauseam, of Capitalism; the fact that they consume flesh is but a literal enactment of the notion that under Capitalism we all live off other people. *Dawn* makes this meaning explicit in the zombies' gravitation, from force of habit, to the shopping mall, and also spells out the relationship of the zombies to the surviving humans ("They are us") whose behavior patterns they reflect and parody.

All three films relate this theme of consumerism to the major relationship-structures of Capitalist society, but with significantly different emphases. The main focus of *Night* (the most "traditional" of the three) is on the family, with the zombies acting out the repressed aggressions between brother and sister, child and parents. *The Crazies*, thematically as well as chronologically, occupies a midway position between the two *Dead* films, reflecting the earlier film's concern with the family (though the pre-credit sequence is the only close recapitulation) and anticipating elements of *Dawn of the Dead*.

Dawn abandons the family to juxtapose the two dominant "couple" relationships of our culture and our cinema: heterosexual marriage, in a society where the sexes are not equal, and the male buddy relationship, where the price of equality is the repression of sexuality. The tentative, provisional optimism of the end–the (temporary) escape by helicopter of the surviving partners of the two relationships, between whom there is never any question of any kind of coupling–is given added point by the presence of a third passenger, the woman's unborn baby, and by the final use the film makes of its two emblems of male authority: the man relinquishes his rifle to the zombies, and the woman is piloting the helicopter.

Jack's Wife and *Martin* counterpoint the progression represented by these three films. Certain oppositions between the two groups help define their relationship. The three films in the first group are built on events, the two in the second (as their titles indicate) on the development and fate of individual protagonists. The first group are about the disintegration of the established order, the second are about people trying to define themselves within it and ultimately defeated or destroyed by it. The implications of Romero's work are that the total disintegration of society is the necessary prerequisite for new growth. For Jack's wife and for Martin, even the heavily qualified optimism of *Dawn of the Dead* is impossible.

The society symbolized in fable or parody form by the zombies is realistically dramatized in *Jack's Wife* and *Martin;* the structures and values of high and low bourgeoisie (respectively) are presented as equally constricting and demoralizing. The two films are perfect companion pieces; the feminist concern with the oppression of women that counterpoints the main plot of *Martin* is the dominant issue of the earlier work. Central to both films is the protagonist's sense of ignominy, of having no respect or recognition as a person. Jack's wife is simply that; she is defined exclusively in relation to the male. Martin's sensitivity and particularity are accorded no value: he is treated as a mental defective, pushed around, reduced to the status of errand boy. So Joan becomes a witch and Martin becomes a vampire (in his case, a ready-made identity, an aspect of his ethnic inheritance). Being a witch gives Joan the illusion of power; Martin's fantasies present him to himself as a charismatic, doomed romantic hero desired by women, hunted down by the society whose codes he transgresses.

But, as Martin himself realizes, "there is no magic.' He is not a romantic vampire but a sexually disturbed boy who cuts the veins of his drugged victims with razor-blades. Joan isn't a witch but an isolated woman moving from one servitude to another; her opening dream of being her husband's dog is echoed at the end when, as part of her initiation into the coven, she is led on a leash.

Romero must be perfectly aware the only answer, within the world he creates, is revolution–and the problem is how a revolutionary filmmaker continues to work within a commercial entertainment medium is likely to become more and more pressing. Meanwhile, he is the producer of an impressive body of work within which no individual film is superfluous. Each throws light on all the others, and it is important that *The Crazies* and *Jack's Wife* be rescued from oblivion.

Above, Walter Huston as "Mr. Scratch" throws multiple shadows in **The Devil and Daniel Webster**.

Is the Devil an American? William Dieterle's *The Devil and Daniel Webster*

Tony Williams

MR. SCRATCH: Who are you calling a foreigner?

WEBSTER: I've never heard you claim American citizenship?

MR. SCRATCH: Who has a better claim?

Although *The Devil and Daniel Webster* (1941, originally released as *All That Money Can Buy*) appears an unusual candidate for consideration as a horror film, this claim has many justifications in terms of authorship, studio, and stylistic choice. Leaving Warner Brothers after a successful series of bio-pics, the film's director William Dieterle (1893-1972) accepted a tempting offer from RKO studios allowing him the creative freedom he lacked as a contract director and the possibility of forming his own production company. Like many European exiles, Dieterle was fascinated by American culture. After considering film versions of national legends such as Washington Irving's "The Legend of Sleepy Hollow" and "Rip Van Winkle," Dieterle decided to adapt a short story by Stephen Vincent Benet for his first RKO production. The combination looked exciting on paper. As actor and director Dieterle had vast experience in German expressionism, literary adaptation, and successful studio bio-pics. *Waxworks* (1924, co-directed with Paul Leni), *A Midsummer Night's Dream* (1935, co-directed with Max Reinhart) and Paul Muni Warner Brothers bio-pics such as *The Story of Louis Pasteur* (1936), *The Life of Emile Zola* (1937), and *Juarez* (1939) represent a few examples of this talented director's artistic accomplishments. Though never politically involved with organizations attacked during the McCarthyite era, Dieterle shared the cultural sophistication and political sympathies of many of his fellow exiles who looked with dismay at the developing European situation which would erupt in 1939. A year prior to the declaration of war by the European Allies on Nazi Germany, Dieterle directed a diluted, but still controversial, version of the Spanish Civil War, *Blockade*, scripted by future Hollywood Ten member John

Howard Lawson. Dieterle also added expressionistic touches to *The Hunchback of Notre Dame* (1939), regarded by a later critic as a commentary upon contemporary European authoritarianism and brutality as well as one of the best Victor Hugo screen adaptations ever made.[1]

Dieterle's background and sympathies provided one of many exciting ingredients leading to *The Devil and Daniel Webster*. Benet's short story had already been performed as a one-act opera in 1939. Now virtually forgotten today, author-poet Stephen Vincent Benet (1889-1943) had received the Pulitzer Prize in 1928 for *John Brown's Body*. He belonged to that group of literary activists who would fall under suspicion a decade later for supposedly "premature anti-Fascist" sympathies. In 1940, Benet wrote a poetic work, **Nightmare at Noon**, warning Americans about the imminent Fascist challenge. Benet also served on the editorial board of a radical literary journal, *Decision*, to which Dieterle contributed in 1941.[2] Benet also wrote a posthumous history about his homeland, *America* (1944), designed for overseas distribution by the Office of War Information. He was the natural choice for co-scenarist by Dieterle who would naturally share the sympathies of *Decision* editor Klaus Mann as the following statement in the first issue reveals. "The most distinguished representatives of European literature in America are bound to perish unless they have contact with the vigor and youth of American literature."[3]

Dieterle's *The Devil and Daniel Webster* is a cinematic variant of this statement. In adapting Benet's story for the screen Dieterle applies European techniques to an American *milieu* in the same manner as other exiles such as Fritz Lang, Douglas Sirk, and Billy Wilder who worked in *film noir* and melodrama. The result is an interesting fusion of European and Hollywood techniques leading to a film combining expressionism with a story having associations with the horror genre.

But Dieterle's involvement must also be seen within the context of the RKO studio system at a particular historical moment. RKO was the studio which invited Orson Welles to become a director on a contract having close parallels to the offer which tempted Dieterle away from Warner Brothers. 1941 was also RKO's monumental year of *Citizen Kane* as well as *The Devil and Daniel Webster*. Welles's first film was also a collaborative effort owing much to the alliance of creative talents such as Bernard Herrmann and Robert Wise who also worked on *The Devil and Daniel Webster*. Ironically, both *Citizen Kane* and *The Devil and Daniel Webster* failed at the box-office. The latter film also suffered the ignominious fate of *The Magnificent Ambersons* by loosing footage. However, *The Devil and Daniel Webster*'s missing footage survived and is now available on restored laser and video versions. Both *Citizen Kane* and *The Devil and Daniel Webster* contain elements of that German expressionist tradition which contributed to American *film noir*. As Thomas Schatz has shown, *Citizen Kane* may also be regarded as a *film noir* as well as a great classical Hollywood masterpiece.[4] Like *Citizen Kane*, *The Devil and Daniel Webster* contains elements with parallels to the American horror film.[5] These films by Welles and Dieterle also exemplify that particular "genius of the system" noted by Andre Bazin, in which individuals often benefitted from a formative cultural and industrial framework allowing for the production of creative works.[6] A year later, RKO would begin the first of its series of low-budget horror films produced by Val Lewton with Jacques Tourneur's *The Cat People* (1942). It featured Simone Simon, an actress who also appeared in Dieterle's film, as well as employing the talents of Robert Wise who had also worked as editor on both *Citizen Kane* and *The Devil and Daniel Webster*.

Despite its supposedly quaint nature, *The Devil and Daniel Webster* is not just a neglected work by a director whose cinematic status still needs re-evaluation. Combining elements of the supernatural, German expressionism, and an American version of the Faust legend, *The Devil and Daniel Webster* has claims for inclusion within the horror film genre. As well as being artistically rich in visual style and acting performances, it combines past, present, and future traditions of the American horror film. The film uses the tradition of supernatural forces as a supposedly external threat to Americans as seen in Universal horror films of the 30s. Its satanic figure is first seen outside the community in the opening scene. But it also begins a tradition initiated by *The Cat People* (1942) and extending to *Psycho* (1960) viewing the threat as an internal one affecting American characters and institutions.[7] Mr. Scratch (Walter Huston) responds to tensions already present within the American psyche. *The Devil and Daniel Webster* also foreshadows themes which appear in the horror cycle of the 60s and 70s begun by *Rosemary's Baby* (1968) and continued in *The Exorcist* and *The Omen* series of films. These works viewed American institutions such as the family, politics, and religion being vulnerable to assault by satanic forces. *The Devil and Daniel Webster* also contains ideas which would later occur in *The Texas Chain Saw Massacre* (1973), *Race with the Devil* (1975), and *The Hills Have Eyes* (1977) involving the revenge taken by losers in the American Dream on their more affluent counterparts. Also, unlike the original short story, *The Devil and Daniel Webster* does not contain a secure happy ending affirming the victory of wholesome American values over dark forces. If *The Omen* (1976) concludes with the Antichrist well on his way to the White House (an event unhappily dropped in the other two sequels), Dieterle's film ends with the comical (but still dangerous) Mr. Scratch getting ready to tempt another American victim, possibly one watching the film in the audience.

As Robert Singer has noted, *The Devil and Daniel Webster* is a film abundantly rich in its use of literary, historical, and cinematic traditions.[8] Benet's obvious model is the Faust legend. But Dieterle visually represents it according to familiar German expressionist traditions contained in productions such as *The Student of Prague* (1913, 1925) and F.W. Murnau's *Faust* (1926) in which he played a leading role.[9] As many critics have demonstrated, German expressionism also contributed to the distinctive character of American *film noir* as well as the 1930s Universal series of horror films.[10] Dieterle also expressed another debt to his former colleague Murnau by making Anne Shirley's Mary resemble not just conventional depictions of Faust's Marguerite but also Janet Gaynor's role as the Germanic "hausfrau" of *Sunrise* (1927). As Robin Wood has shown, *Sunrise* has close connections with the German expressionism of *Nosferatu* (1924). It also contains sexual tensions which also appear in the American horror film.[11] Simone Simon's Belle in *The Devil and Daniel Webster* is the spiritual heir to the vampish City Woman in *Sunrise* who seduces a simple farmer.[12] Unlike Irena in *The Cat People*, she is wholeheartedly on the side of the Devil. Belle also represents the European complement to Mr. Scratch's American folkloristic trickster figure.

The Devil and Daniel Webster is also firmly rooted in its historical context. As Singer comments, although set in the mid-nineteenth century, it is an "adaptation of astute political perception of twentieth-century America in the midst of crisis; the Depression and imminent world war are manifest in the words and deeds of Benet's screen characters. The nation and its farmers, particularly in New England, have fallen on hard times. Whether owing money to the bank or the greedy loan shark of the town, Miser Stevens, or later to Jabez Stone, Benet's farmers remain patriotic and true believers in heroes like Webster. They attribute special powers of foresight and salvation to him as if he were a prophet from the Bible or (organically) a New Deal Democrat."[13]

The real life Webster never resembled Edward Arnold's idealistic cinematic portrayal of a man of the people. Singer believes that Webster's character is presented as being positive throughout the film. But Dieterle takes a more sophisticated approach by revealing Webster's dangerous character flaws which nearly result in disaster in the last third of the film. Although Andrew Sarris criticized James Craig's character of Jabez Stone as a weak figure during the re-release of a film he described as a "Faust without a Faust," Singer correctly understands Stone's weakness as an important element in the film's structure.[14] Unlike his god-fearing wife and mother, Stone's greed and weakness provides the ideal entry for Mr. Scratch's tempting proposition. Also Stone's character flaws have other associations in terms of the American cultural traditions employed by both Benet and Dieterle. Singer notices the Will Rogers pastoral tradition represented by *David Harum* (1934) as a key influence on the film. However, Dieterle's feelings towards this cinematic bucolic ideal within works such as *True Heart Susie* (1919), *Way Down East* (1920), *Tol'able David* (1921), *Judge Priest* (1934), *Steamboat Round the Bend* (1935), *Young Mr. Lincoln* (1939), *Tobacco Road* (1940), and *The Sun Shines Bright* (1952), reveals more of Billy Wilder's cynical urban European sophistication than anything else. Non-urban American audiences often enjoyed simplistic country values contained in the B-Westerns of Gene Autry, Roy Rogers, and Tex Ritter rather than those of the urban milieu. These films appeared at a time when the West was won and rural communities suffered from the Great Depression. Judy Canova's screen brand of hillbilly humor also found its natural audience in "the sticks" rather than the city. The same remains true today for the films and direct-to-video productions featuring Jim Varney as Ernest. Despite their antiquated simplistic values, these films found a ready audience amongst small-town audiences whose ideological values differed little from their nineteenth-century forefathers. Recognizing the unsophisticated nature of mid-Western values, Billy Wilder later hit back at conservative reactions to *Kiss Me Stupid* (1964) by suggesting that "small-town hicks were ripe for a sexual revolution." [15] By depicting Jabez Stone as a childlike, hick, ripe for temptation, Dieterle aligned himself with European emigre feelings about the naivety of an American character unaware of the darkness within its midst.

As the credits show, Dieterle regards the film as a collaborative process. Rather than depicting the usual hierarchical Hollywood credits beginning with stars, supporting actors, key technicians, leading to the final prominent display of producer and director, everyone appears listed on an equal basis. If Brecht later failed in making Fritz Lang's *Hangmen Also Die* (1943) fit in with his proletarian dramatic theories, Dieterle definitely regards his film as a collaborative worker project.[16] The credits also anticipate the film's conclusion when Jabez relinquishes avaricious, capitalist desires and joins his fellow farmers in a Grange Union. After the final credit, a caption fills the screen. It warns the audience that the film's message involves the present as well as the past. "But it could happen anywhere, anytime - to anybody. Yes, it could even happen to you."

The film then opens showing Mr. Scratch approaching and surveying the rural landscape. He takes out his notebook and finds the name of Jabez Stone, a native of Cross Corners, New Hampshire. The audience then sees the god-fearing Stone family of Jabez, Mary, and Ma (Jane Darwell), who suffer economic problems and worry about paying a debt owed to Miser Stevens (John Qualen). Non-payment would result in the loss of the Stone family farm. Jabez's fellow farmers arrive, discuss forming a Grange Association, and mention the passage of a new bankruptcy law bill going through Congress.

Mr. Scratch's presence is part of an American cultural tradition influencing the film. He is now an everyday figure in the American landscape out to trap unwary Americans. Walter Huston's trickster persona evokes Herman Melville's title character in *The Confidence Man* who appeals to the prejudices of normal Americans. By working on their inner feelings, he becomes all things to all men in his grand design to lead the young American nation towards the path of destruction. Whereas Satan's presence was once regarded as an external feature on the American landscape in the Puritan era, *The Devil and Daniel Webster* reveals him as an average, devious American.

Dieterle's film also represents a transition point between two traditions of demonic representation. In D.W. Griffith's *The Sorrows of Satan* (1926), Satan takes the form of a foreign prince portrayed by Adolphe Menjou well known for his sophisticated playboy roles during this period. His victim, played by Ricardo Cortez, faces the same sort of sexual temptation Jabez Stone faces a generation later. The Cortez character is torn between the homely charms of his demure, wholesome American sweetheart (Carol Dempster) and a sexually alluring, foreign *femme fatale* demonic agent (Lya De Putti). These two figures correspond to Mary and Belle in *The Devil and Daniel Webster*. Eight years after Dieterle's film, the Devil appears in the *film noir Alias Nick Beal* (1949). Set in the city landscape, Ray Milland portrays Old Nick like a self-assured, hardboiled, tough guy at home in the mean streets and fully aware of the self-destructive flaws existing in any ambitious person wanting to make it in the American Dream. *The Sorrows of Satan*, *The Devil and Daniel Webster*, and *Alias Nick Beal* contain ideological versions of that perennial Hollywood axiom, "It's better to be poor and moral than rich and corrupt," a philosophy articulated by Mary and Ma in Dieterle's film.

However, despite its whimsical nature, *The Devil and Daniel Webster* takes the satanic threat seriously. It exposes it as the dark side of an American Dream belonging to the very beginning of the nation and continuing into the present. Despite Thomas Jefferson's championship of the yeoman ideal against the corrupt, industrial nature of the Old World, Dieterle recognizes that twentieth century capitalism now demolishes this anachronistic vision still dominating the American con-

sciousness. *The Devil and Daniel Webster* also represents the beginning of
the American horror film's socio-economic focus on distinctions between winners and losers in the American Dream: *Psycho*, *The Texas
Chain Saw Massacre*, and *Race with the Devil*.

The Virgin Land mythology prominent in the American Western influences this film. This is not really surprising. Themes within the classical Hollywood cinema frequently represent cinematic variants of the
American cultural tradition which various directors use and embody
within their particular generic and narrative frameworks.[17] In the film,
Dieterle provides several visual images of the agrarian myth for audiences. But he demolishes its supposedly secure foundations. Economic
problems disrupt family harmony which pious remedies prove futile to
heal. In the opening scenes Jabez discovers a pig with a broken leg, the
very object he intended to take to Miser Stevens as payment for his loan.
Ma reads from "The Book of Job" commenting that she never liked the
character because he "took on too much," an obvious comment on Jabez's desires. Mary then reads from "The Book of Ruth" to soothe her
husband with a more comforting biblical text. But unlike Job, Jabez will
immediately fall into temptation taking the path of least resistance.
Steadfast religious beliefs of country folk and the supposedly redeeming
values of the Virgin Land ideology will not save him.[18]

Although *The Devil and Daniel Webster* is set in New Hampshire, it
consciously utilizes the myth of America as garden of the world which
often appears in both literature and Hollywood cinema. John Ford's *The
Man Who Shot Liberty Valance* (1962) consciously refers to that philosophy as well as revealing its dark underside to an audience who would
still prefer to "Print the legend." *The Devil and Daniel Webster* also represents a subversive undermining of that legend within the visually expressionistic forms of the horror film. As Henry Nash Smith shows, that
distinctive American myth of agrarian life dominated American consciousness in the nineteenth century and beyond. It also continued to influence popular thought a generation later as various cinematic
representations reveal.

"The master symbol of the garden embraced a cluster of metaphors
expressing fecundity, growth, increase of blissful labor in the earth, all
centering around the heroic figure of the idealized frontier farmer
armed with that supreme weapon, the sacred plow."[19]

When Mary later suggests selling corn to pay off Stevens, Jabez is initially reluctant due to the influence of this myth. "I'm a farmer. Seed is
not the way to pay debts (with). It's alive, more alive than anything."
When a neighbor later borrows seed from Jabez, Stone describes it as
"the best seed you'll find in all New Hampshire." A series of dissolves

follows illustrating the dominant metaphor of fertility: a sower in a field, rain falling, corn appearing, birds flying in the sky, chicken, colts, pigs, calves all feeding from their mothers, and finally, a huge cornfield. The last image lap dissolves to a pregnant Mary resting on her bed.

As Smith notes, the idealized figure of the yeoman farmer provided the concrete, imaginative focus for the abstract metaphor of the garden.[20] An 1832 speech of Charles J. Faulkner praising his constituents employed the Jeffersonian ideal of a society of small landowners tilling their soil.

> Sir, our native, substantial independent yeomanry, constitute our pride, efficiency and strength; they are our defence in war, our ornaments in peace; and no population, I will venture to affirm, upon the face of the globe, is more distinguished for an elevated love of freedom - for morality, virtue, frugality, and independence, than the Virginia peasantry west of the Blue Ridge.[21]

Such sentiments would appear absurd a century later in a society suffering from the effects of the Great Depression. Contemporary audiences knew the differences between reality and illusion, especially those viewing John Ford's *The Grapes of Wrath* (1940) which also featured an Academy Award performance by Jane Darwell. In Dieterle's film, danger signs are already historically present. Mr. Scratch will cause both agricultural depression and the reduction of formerly independent farmers to the status of waged laborers or 1840 "Oakies." Also Mr. Scratch encourages Jabez to supersede Miser Stevens by being a more efficient, upwardly mobile loan shark, and engaging in farm foreclosure policies anticipating those of the Reagan era.

Mr. Scratch also plots against American democratic ideals and family values. Set in 1840, *The Devil and Daniel Webster* introduces audiences to a rural family who hold beliefs very similar to those voiced by Indiana Representative George W. Julian in 1851.

"The life of a farmer is peculiarly favorable to virtue; and both individuals and communities are generally happy in proportion as they are virtuous. His manners are simple, and his nature unsophisticated. If not oppressed by other interests, he generally possesses an abundance without the drawback of luxury. His life does not impose excessive toil, and yet it discourages idleness. The farmer lives in rustic plenty, remote from the contagion of popular vices, and enjoys in their greatest fruition, the blessings of health and contentment...."[22]

But the film begins by revealing the gap between ideology and reality. In debt to Miser Stevens, Jabez is "oppressed by other interests" and does not enjoy a life of "rustic plenty." As Singer points out the film's period setting is relevant to both past and present.[23] Reading the past in terms of the present, Dieterle and Benet see Thomas Jefferson's 1787 warnings now affecting 1840 New Hampshire and beyond. Jefferson then stated that the United States would remain virtuous as long as it remained an agricultural nation. He feared that the development of cities would cause social tensions leading to class war and attacks on property. In 1836, Thomas R. Dew voiced this very same fear. Although Dieterle's depiction of Daniel Webster is far removed from the real-life original, his historical counterpart also articulated American conservative feelings concerning social tensions.[24] They appear in the later church service where the preacher realizes what Jabez's exploitation is doing to the small community and prays to God "who hath given us this good land for our heritage, (to) save us from *discord, confusion, and every evil way*." [italics mine]

Dieterle and Benet clearly see capitalist exploitation as a fundamental part of the national character despite the Jeffersonian yeoman ideals influencing the film's historical period. Although Mr. Scratch appears as a seducing figure, Dieterle's expressionist and *noir* techniques clearly depict Jabez desiring his own seduction. Like his demonic counterparts in *The Student of Prague* and *Alias Nick Beal*, Mr. Scratch appears in answer to his victim's subconscious desires. After a number of domestic accidents, Jabez walks into his barn cursing, "If that ain't enough to make a man sell his soul to the devil! And I would for two cents!" He has also cursed frequently inside his house to Ma's dismay. Jabez then walks into a shadowy area which covers his face in complete darkness. He pauses for a moment, looks around furtively, and mutters, "Guess nobody heard me." As he is about to go away, Jabez thrusts his hand into his pocket and discovers two cents. Dieterle then cuts to a close-up of the coins. Jabez squeezes them. This action causes the sudden appearance of Mr. Scratch who reveals to him the presence of pre-Revolutionary Hessian gold lost from a wagon train ambushed on its way to Saratoga. He makes Jabez sign a seven year contract guaranteeing economic success in exchange for his soul. Jabez initially expresses reluctance. But Mr. Scratch overcomes his objections by playing on parochial values and greedy desires. "I've known other people who've gone back on their word. But I didn't expect it at New Hampshire.... You can have money. All that money can buy." Mr. Scratch makes Jabez touch the money, an action paralleling the squeezing of the two cents which expressed the farmer's greedy desire. Mr. Scratch does not appear out of the blue to tempt a previously pious yeoman farmer but makes his victim follow his desires for wealth and social status to their logical conclusion.

Mr. Scratch appears at significant moments in the film. He not only causes events to happen but makes suggestive comments to others clearly knowing what really occupies their minds in the first place. He stimulates Jabez into being a successful capitalist. "Hard work is only for people who aren't lucky. You don't work for other people. You make them work for you." After bad weather destroys every crop save Jabez's, Mr. Scratch walks into the tavern to begin the economic slavery of ruined farmers. He tosses coins at them suggesting they go to work for Jabez. One farmer implicitly recognizes this as a return to old European feudal ideals the young American nation has supposedly rejected. "I never worked for anybody in my whole life except when I was a shaver and only for my old man." Scratch buys them with the Hessian coins he used to purchase Jabez's soul. These coins represent a legacy from pre-1776 America when it was a battleground for European powers. Mr. Scratch not only wishes to undermine the independent American character but to return the country to foreign values it supposedly rejected in 1776. As Thomas Paine discovered on his return to an America rejecting democratic Enlightenment for Federalist conservatism, old values involving greed and economic bondage return to Cross Corners. Despite demonic associations, Mr. Scratch is clearly at home inside an American tavern. He also appears banging a drum at the annual Independence Day celebration like any normal member of the community. Mr. Scratch clearly subverts American values from within, rather than from outside, the community. He has already trapped Miser Stevens into his scheme. But Jabez represents bigger game since he is clearly a fundamental part of the farming community whereas Stevens is always on the outside.

The film sees socially disruptive economic desires as more powerful than populist ideology, family values, and religion. When Jabez rushes inside with his cap of Hessian gold, neither Ma nor Mary express joy at his discovery. Contrary to his usual custom, Jabez begins greedily gobbling his food before Grace is spoken. When he puts the cap containing Hessian gold down, Ma sharply responds, "That cap doesn't belong on the table!" When Jabez later becomes apprehensive about the negative effects of wealth, Ma comments that it is "Better to spend it. That's all it's good for." She also blames demonic intervention rather than internal causes for her son's abrupt change of character. However, Jabez soon becomes a man of wealth and property while Ma and Mary decide to remain in their humble farm.

Jabez's dialogue with Ma concerning the effects of wealth follow the discovery of Mary's pregnancy. When the film lost footage after its commercial failure and became reduced into a supporting feature, the actual significance of Mary's pregnancy became lost to audiences. But the full version of *The Devil and Daniel Webster* reveals it as part of the demonic scheme. Although far from the premises of *Rosemary's Baby*, Dieterle reveals the Devil already involved in causing the pregnancy of a young American wife for his own ends. Earlier in the film, the audience sees Jabez looking out of his bedroom while Mary lies in bed. He sees Mr. Scratch outside who looks back at him as if prompting him towards some course of action before departing in the distance. Jabez then goes to Mary and begins sexual intercourse. The sequence ends with a close up of Mary, her expression resembling more rape victim than loving wife. Mr. Scratch clearly sets out to destroy the American family several decades before the emergence of the family horror film. At this point in time, he cannot use a female body to bring the Antichrist to earth as in *Rosemary's Baby* and *The Omen*. But he knowingly employs certain contemporary cultural ideological factors which explain the nature of a particular strategy he uses in 1840.

The Devil and Daniel Webster is set in the Jacksonian era. As well as a time of great economic and social fluctuation, this was also the period of a cult of motherhood which attempted to provide an antidote to the outside world. Mary Ryan describes this ideology which also indirectly influences the film.

"It was this collision between the peaceful home and a society bent on disaster that generated the idea of the mother civilization. In this opposition domestic femininity found its meaning and its social function. The truncated personality prescribed for woman was an antidote to a world gone mad with change, acquisitiveness, and individualism. Her conservatism would tame the economic ambitions of men. Her warmth would assuage the pain of failure; her gentleness would mollify the ruthlessness of the successful. The women of the West would secure 'home calm' for those 'restless rovers' prone to land speculation. Woman's maternal purity would instill morality and social probity in generations to come."[25]

Mr. Scratch has to undermine Mary's ideological role to control Jabez. The film's relationship between husband and wife appears to involve religious taboos seeing marriage as exclusively directed towards childbearing. According to Mary Ryan, the contemporary female role involved subduing male passions, not encouraging them. "Excessive intercourse was sheer profligacy, destructive to a man's health, offensive to bourgeois frugality, and detrimental to the national economy."[26] In her book, Ryan also cites one contemporary doctor who advised celibacy as a prudent routine following pregnancy and lactation.[27]

Belle's *femme fatale* presence immediately follows Mary's delivery. It comes at the most opportune moment in Jabez's domestic life. Unlike

Mary, Belle would not share the Jacksonian female perspective of the marital bed as a "place of secret assassination where no mercy is shown to the victim."[28] Dieterle employs appropriate visual techniques depicting Belle as a sexually supernatural *femme fatale* during her first appearance. Mysteriously taking the place of the plain maid Dorothy, Belle sits before a fire, her face demonically lit up by the flames coquettishly smiling at her new master knowing what he really wants.

Jabez's newfound wealth also gives him access to sexual freedom. Before Belle appears in the film, the audience sees Jabez drive into Cross Corner to pay off his debt to Miser Stevens and free himself from economic obligations. He sings two lines of a song titled "Nothing else to do." As Robin Wood points out, this song has significant overtones when it also appears a year later in *The Cat People*.[29] The lines, "Nothing else to do, Nothing else to do, I strayed, went a-courting 'Cos I'd nothing else to do," articulate the dangers of sin and sexuality which honest toil, surface cleanliness, and celibacy are designed to avoid. Belle obviously performs other tasks for Jabez which Mary can not do!

During the dance scene following Jabez's first encounter with Belle, Dieterle again employs lighting techniques expressing the demonic nature of her sexuality. She initially refuses Jabez's offer of a dance and turns instead to the more socially prominent Squire Slocum (Gene Lockhart). A succession of shots depict Belle sensually dancing away while Jabez attempts to reach her, his face lit up to express sexual desire. The dance becomes faster and faster making it resemble more a *Walpurgisnacht* gathering rather than a yeoman community celebration of the birth of Jabez's son. This scene also foreshadows the *noir* lighting later employed during the celebrated jazz sequence in Robert Siodmak's *Phantom Lady* when drummer Cliff (Elisha Cook Jr.) musically expresses his yearnings for *femme fatale* Ella Raines. Dieterle concludes the sequence by revealing Mr. Scratch playing the violin with increasing speed hastening both the dance and Jabez's lust. Mr. Scratch plays "Pop Goes the Weasel," an old nursery rhyme telling of the threat to virtue by alcoholism. When Jabez later leaves Mary in their bedroom after baby disturbs his sleep, Mr. Scratch eagerly awaits him downstairs and pulls him through the window like a familiar spirit taking its victim to a Witch's Sabbath. The next scene reveals Jabez seated next to Belle in a sleigh whipping the horses in frenzy, an action metaphorically embodying his sexual desires.

Belle becomes Jabez's mistress and acts more like an approving buddy than disapproving wife. When Mary and Ma attend the Sunday church service, Belle eagerly supplies cards and liquor for Jabez and his friends. Mary later tells Daniel Webster about the extent of her husband's abandonment of monogamy and religion. "I've seen him mock at the church bells, the bells that rang at our wedding." When Jabez's baby cries and disrupts the card game, Belle silences it by softly singing a lullaby. She not only takes over Mary's role as wife and mother but also aims at subtly influencing him towards the seductive pleasures of the demonic realm like his father. Belle later encourages Jabez's son into anti-social behavior such as lying to his mother and using his catapult against man and beast. She also takes him along for the European sport of fox-hunting while Mary and Ma labor in the field like good Jeffersonian yeoman family members.

Jabez soon moves out of his humble farm and builds a mansion reminiscent of Xanadu in *Citizen Kane*. He becomes more gentrified and European abandoning the Jeffersonian farmer ideal for the very values the third President feared. Jabez's mansion contains chandeliers, liveried footmen, plus carpets, and Georgian chairs. Jabez now embodies selfish American characteristics involving affluence and class which Webster criticizes. "They think their state is the country and the way they live is their country and they're willing to split the country for it." Jabez's mansion also contrasts with Webster's Marshfield residence. When Mary visits Webster she sees him in the field with fellow laborers continuing the yeoman farmer tradition celebrated by Jefferson and George W. Julian. Unlike Jabez, Webster works besides his laborers with no sense of European class distinctions. Within Jabez's mansion Belle exercises pretentious civilizing restraints on her lover teaching him to say "people" rather than the rural expression "folks." Jabez's musical tastes also change. During a lavish party in honor of the local gentry, he refuses Mary's request for some homely music and insists the orchestra continuing playing genteel tunes. "That's music they play for rich people." While Mary wears a homely Victorian dress covering arms, neck, and shoulders, Belle wears a revealing gown displaying her neck, shoulders and arms as she undermines her rival's status. "You know that you're in my house." As well as having demonic associations, Belle's character embodies imagery resembling that Puritan *femme fatale* John Bunyan described as Madame Bubble in *The Pilgrim's Progress*.

"She makes variance betwixt rulers and subjects, betwixt parents and children, 'twixt neighbor and neighbor, 'twixt a man and his wife, 'twixt a man and himself, 'twixt the flesh and the heart. She is 'a gentlewoman', her clothes were 'very pleasant', she loves banquets and feasts, and she always speaks 'smoothly with a smile at the end of the sentence'."

Bunyan, significantly, concludes his description of Madame Bubble by describing her as "a witch." [30]

The party hosted by the gentrified Jabez occurs towards the end of his seven year contract with Mr. Scratch. Contrary to his expectations, he finds himself shunned by high society. Instead, a group of ragged, downwardly mobile individuals with worn and strange faces gaze at him outside his window. Singer recognizes their status. "They are poor and look like refugees in their own country. These were the same type of people, who in a superimposed and slightly out-of-focus close up of a mocking Scratch, walked over the ruined fields of wheat."[31] They are losers in the American Dream. Belle welcomes them inside. These mysterious figures may also belong to Belle's mysterious home "over the mountains" as well as embodying significant features within the American cultural tradition employed in the film.

In his **Letters From An American Farmer**, Crevecoeur believed that the process of westward expansion would create three main divisions within American society namely, a remote fringe of backwoods settlements, a central region of comfortable farms, and an Eastern area of growing wealth, cities, and social stratification. Henry Nash Smith points out that "Crevecoeur believed that both the beginning and the end of the process brought about undesirable social conditions. But the middle condition offered a unique opportunity for human virtue and happiness."[32]

Mr. Scratch wishes to destroy this middle condition. While Belle influences Jabez towards emulating Eastern class values, she also invites these impoverished rurals to the banquet. They obviously represent a proletariat who have failed in the agrarian ideal and invade Jabez's party as agents of the Devil to avenge themselves upon those who succeed in the American Dream. J. Fenimore Cooper's depiction of the Bush family in **The Prairie** resembles these uninvited guests. He depicts the Bush clan as little better than "semi-barbarous." Henry Nash Smith also notes Jefferson also used this term to describe American settlers only a few degrees removed from the social level of pastoral Indians.[33] These figures also anticipate later rural losers in the American Dream seen in John Hancock's *Let's Scare Jessica to Death* (1971), Tobe Hooper's *The Texas Chain Saw Massacre* (1973), Jack Starrett's *Race With the Devil* (1975), and Wes Craven's *The Hills Have Eyes* (1977). *Race With the Devil* actually concludes by revealing that virtually all the rural population of Texas are agents of the Devil.

When Jabez realizes that Mr. Scratch will soon claim his soul he rushes to enlist the aid of the film's nominal hero Daniel Webster. However, despite the heroic quasi-Roosevelt associations existing in Edward Arnold's performance,[34] Dieterle's view of Webster is much more cynical than the version which appeared in Benet's original short story.

When the audience first sees Webster, he sits at a table attempting to compose the Farm Rights Bill. As he struggles with writing a Bill appealing "to honest hardworking men, every man who follows his own plough, artisan, mechanic, laborer, who by honest means seek to gain an honest living," Webster also warns his constituents to beware of wolves in sheep's clothing. However, like Jabez, Webster also struggles with himself. He appears left of frame while Mr. Scratch's shadow occurs on the right in imagery clearly reminiscent of German horror film expressionism and American *film noir*. Scratch whispers, "If you write this, you'll never be President." By refusing temptation Webster wins the battle, but only for the moment. Mr. Scratch always emerges to take advantage of Webster's personal flaws, particularly the historical character's alcoholism.

By showing Webster's frequent fondness for New Bedford rum, *The Devil and Daniel Webster* draws upon contemporary gossip and newspaper cartoons criticizing the politician's fondness for strong drink. When Webster arrives in New Hampshire, Mr. Scratch appears at a horseshoe game, attempts to warn him about visiting Cross Corners and again offers help for a future Presidential campaign. Webster replies, "I'd rather see you on the side of the opposition." Mr. Scratch wittingly responds, "I'm there too." Later horror films such as *Rosemary's Baby* and *The Omen* (1976) reveal demonic involvement in White House politics. The Kennedys appear in the dream sequence in *Rosemary's Baby* while *The Omen* concludes with young Damien already on his way to the White House.

When Webster reaches Cross Corners, young Martin Van Buren Alden, son of the town's only Democrat, gazes at him. He looks in vain for the horns and tails his father told him Webster possesses. The politician's reply mocks what will later become a serious theme in later versions of the horror genre. "I only wear them while I'm in Washington. But if you come down there, I'll be glad to show them to you." Although Webster speaks humorously, his opening appearance revealed him almost tempted by Mr. Scratch's offer to help him reach Presidential office. Mr. Scratch then plans Webster's public humiliation. He hands New Bedford rum to another man to give to Webster. The politician comments, "Here's a man who knows what's good for Daniel Webster. Bedford rum, a breath of the Promised Land." This comment ironically foreshadows Webster's second participation in New Bedford Rum at a later point in the film, one which threatens to send him to Hell, not the Promised Land! Dieterle then inserts a close-up of Mr. Scratch ironically grinning at his victim's pompous self-assurance. Mr. Scratch then prompts the waiting audience to call for a speech by Webster knowing that his victim is now too intoxicated to deliver one. Although Jabez saves Webster from humiliation, Webster's fondness for New Bedford Rum nearly causes him to fail in his role of defense attorney before the jury of the damned later in the film.

After resisting Mr. Scratch's suggestion to extend his contract if his son becomes part of the deal, Jabez appeals for Webster's help. As both men wait for Mr. Scratch, Webster becomes confident that he can save a fellow American from what he regards as an enemy alien. However, he soon finds that his opponent is really an American citizen and not an external threat to the Constitution as the following exchange reveals.

> WEBSTER: Man is not a piece of property. Mr. Stone is an American citizen and an American citizen can not be forced into the service of a foreign prince.
>
> MR. SCRATCH: Who are you calling a foreigner?
>
> WEBSTER: I've never heard you claim American citizenship.
>
> MR. SCRATCH: Who has a better claim? When the first wrong was done to the first Indian I was there. When the first slaver put out for the Congo I was on her deck. Am I not spoken of still in every church in New England? 'Tis true the North claims me for a Southerner and the South for a Northerner, but I am neither. I am merely an honest American like yourself - and of the best descent - for, to tell the truth Mr. Webster, my name is older in this country than yours.

Mr. Scratch delivers a history lesson to both Webster and the audience, a lesson having uncomfortable associations despite the film's supernatural premise. It is the type of lesson which would later result in the blacklisting of any American college professor or high school teacher in the late 40s onwards. Dieterle's devastating attack on American values in *The Devil and Daniel Webster* is actually far more subversive than his involvement in *Blockade*, a fact his McCarthyite persecutors curiously overlooked.

When Webster demands a jury trial to free Stone from his contract, Dieterle again employs significant lighting techniques reminiscent of the horror genre. The trial's location is Jabez's own barn, the very place where he first signed his contract with Mr. Scratch. An over-confident Webster believes any American jury will easily defeat Mr. Scratch. "If twelve New Hampshire men are not a match for the Devil then we'd better give the country back to the Indians!" However, Mr. Scratch confronts Webster with a jury representing the dark side of the American Dream composed of figures such as Captain Kidd, Simon Girty, Walter

Butler, Thomas Morton, and Benedict Arnold. Presiding over the trial is Judge Hathorne, the bloodiest of all the Salem witchcraft judges. He was also the paternal ancestor of novelist Nathaniel Hawthorne. Hathorne provided a stimulus to the novelist's inherited ancestral guilt which led to those dark tormented tales of Puritan oppression. By casting H.B. Warner in this role, Dieterle probably employed the type of European exile humor leading Billy Wilder to employ the same actor as a discarded Hollywood "waxwork" legacy in *Sunset Boulevard* (1950). Warner's most well known performance was as Christ in Cecil D. De-Mille's *King of Kings* (1924). Like fellow exile Paul Tillich, Dieterle evidently believed that God was dead and subversively cast an actor who played his only begotten Son in a demonic role![35]

Attempting to plead Jabez's case before a biased jury, Webster nearly collapses. While initially expecting Mr. Scratch's arrival, the politician becomes over-confident and indulges himself in New Bedford Rum. When Webster later shows the after-effects during a crucial moment in the trial when it appears his alcoholism will result in his client's defeat, the jury of the damned whisper that he, as well as Jabez, would make another worthy American addition to Mr. Scratch's domain. However, Webster rallies round and delivers a patriotic speech reawakening those lost sensibilities within the individual consciousness of each jury member.

"He is your brother. You are Americans. You can't be on his side, the side of the oppressor. Let him keep his soul, the soul which belongs to him, his family, his son and his country. Don't let this country go to the Devil. God bless the United States of America where men are free."

At this optimistic stage of Hollywood cinema, Webster wins and the jury support his claim. A faint smile of relief appears on the damned features of Judge Hathorne as he dismisses the case. Although Webster then unceremoniously boots Mr. Scratch outside, the latter's defeat is far less definitive than the way Benet depicted it in his original short story. Dieterle understands that Satan has lost a battle. But he also realizes that this demonic American citizen will still conduct further campaigns in a continuing war for American souls.

The Devil and Daniel Webster moves towards a supposedly affirmative ending. A fire burns down Jabez's European mansion leaving him reunited with his family and fellow farmers. Jabez even decides to join the Grange and become a good union man. However, although the Stones hold a celebration in honor of Webster, Ma finds that a pie she has prepared specially for the politician has mysteriously vanished. The next shot shows Mr. Scratch munching it. However, although Ma has baked another pie to serve to Webster and the assembled community, the film reserves the last scene exclusively for Mr. Scratch. He gets off a fence, walks towards the camera, looks through his notebook for a new victim, looks around, focusses his eye on the cinema audience and points his finger at them. The film ends with an iris-in to Mr. Scratch planning his next demonic strategy. Less than ten years following the film's release, America would again become a divided nation in a way neither Benet nor Dieterle could foresee.

In 1943, Stephen Vincent Benet died of a heart attack which perhaps saved him from facing post-war charges of "premature anti-Fascism." Although never blacklisted, William Dieterle faced McCarthyite suspicions concerning his politics and financial aid for European refugees such as Brecht. Despite directing two later accomplished films containing expressionist romantic elements such as *Love Letters* (1945) and *Portrait of Jennie* (1949), Dieterle's Hollywood career never regained the heights it achieved in the thirties and early forties. He returned to Europe in 1958. However, in 1950 Dieterle attempted to film an independent production of Jack London's last novel **The Little Lady of the Big House** (1916). Although London's misunderstood and neglected work is far removed from the world of *The Devil and Daniel Webster*, it also criticized the agrarian dream and the devastating psychological damage it inflicted on its devotees in contrast to the utopian Jeffersonian vision contained in the author's earlier book **The Valley of the Moon** (1914).[36]

Both stylistically and thematically, *The Devil and Daniel Webster* has many claims for inclusion within the horror genre. It is a stylistically rich work combining William Dieterle's knowledge of both German expressionism and his intuitive recognition of the beginning phase of American *film noir*. The film thus marks the final legacy of the German expressionist tradition which characterized American horror films during the 20s and 30s and the beginning of the *film noir* tradition influencing the Val Lewton RKO horror film cycle as well as the later film *Alias Nick Beal*. It also represented a collaboration with the liberal concerns of a Pulitzer prize-winning writer the director must have regarded as a kindred spirit in a troubling historical and political climate. Despite Mr. Scratch's huckster demeanor, he is as much a major threat to the young American democracy as his counterpart in Herman Melville's **The Confidence Man** who preys on American innocence. *The Devil and Daniel Webster* presents Satan as an American citizen operating within national boundaries, not invading it from outside. Although Jabez escapes, his descendants will not be as lucky as economically dispossessed country cousins in *Let's Scare Jessica to Death*, *The Texas Chainsaw Massacre*, *Race With the Devil*, *Eaten Alive* (1976), *The Hills Have Eyes*, *The Texas Chainsaw Massacre, 2* (1985), *American Gothic* (1987), and *Leatherface* (1991) all show. Dieterle's film thus operates both as a classical horror film as well as an early example of the genre's socio-economic concerns. It combines the visually rich traditions of the classical Hollywood studio system into an accomplished work which will anticipate not only the creative RK0 Val Lewton productions of the 40s but also those themes contributing to the development of the American horror film in future decades.

Notes.

1. See John Wakeman, Ed. *World Film Directors. Volume I. 1890-1945* (New York, H.W. Wilson Company, 1987), 249.

2. For the relevance of this journal founded by Thomas Mann's son, Klaus, in 1941, which provided a literary forum for European refugees see Anthony Heilbut, *Exiled in Paradise: German Refugee Artists and Intellectuals in America, from the 1930s to the Present* (New York: The Viking Press, 1983, 268-273. William Dieterle also contributed to one issue. For relevant information on Benet see Charles A. Fenton, *Stephen Vincent Benet: The Life and Times of an American Man of Letters, 1898-1943* (New Haven. Conn.: Yale University Press, 1968; Parry Stroud, *Stephen Vincent Benet* (New York: Twayne Publishers, 1962).

3. Heilbut, 269.

4. See Thomas Schatz, *Hollywood Genres: Formulas, Filmmaking, and The Studio System* (New York: Random House, 1981), 111-121.

5. For the relationship of *Citizen Kane* to the horror film, especially the opening scenes of *Son of Frankenstein* (1939) see Tony Williams, *Hearths of Darkness: The Family in the American Horror Film* (Cranbury, N.J.: Fairleigh Dickinson University Press, 1996), 25, 43.

6. See Andre Bazin, "On the politique des auteurs," *Cahiers du Cinema: The 1950s* (Cambridge, Massachusetts: Harvard University Press, 1985), 248-259.

7. Charles Derry has also termed this group of American horror films as "the horror of personality" tradition. See *Dark Dreams: A Psychological History of the Modern American Horror Film* (London: Thomas Yoseloff, 1977).

8. See Robert Singer, "One Against All: The New England Past and Present Responsibilities in *The Devil and Daniel Webster*," *Literature/Film Quarterly* 22.4 (1994): 265-271.

9. For Dieterle's relationship to questions involving the problematic issue of the German origins of film noir, see Thomas Elsaesser, "A German Ancestry to Film Noir? Film History and its Imaginary," **Iris**, 21 (1996): 135-136.

10. See *Film Noir: An Encyclopedic Reference to the American Style.* **Third Edition**. Eds. Alain Silver and Elizabeth Ward (New York: The Overlook Press, 1992); *Film Noir Reader*. Eds. Alain Silver and James Ursini (New York: Limelight Editions, 1996); *Film Noir Reader 2.* Eds. Alain Silver and James Ursini (New York: Limelight Editions, 1999).

11. See Robin Wood, "The Dark Mirror: Murnau's *Nosferatu*," *The American Nightmare: Essays on the Horror Film*. Eds. Robin Wood and Richard Lippe (Toronto: Festival of Festivals, 1979), 43-49; *Sexual Politics and Narrative Film: Hollywood and Beyond* (New York: Columbia University Press, 1998), 31-44.

12. "The City Woman provides the strongest link in *Sunrise* to *Nosferatu*: once the connection is made, the close structural parallels become obvious." See Wood, *Sexual Politics*, 42.

13. Singer, 266-267.

14. Andrew Sarris, "*The Devil and Daniel Webster*," *Village Voice*April 12, 1988) quoted by Singer, 267.

15. Heilbut, 254. For Billy Wilder's characteristic European wit see also Ed Sikov, *On Sunset Boulevard: The Life and Times of Billy Wilder* (New York: Hyperion, 1998). I also write from experience of the fact that the Saturday night big events on the local PBS television station in Southern Illinois comprises nearly forty year-old repeats of *The Lawrence Welk Show*!

16. For Brecht's disappointing experiences on this film, see Heilbut, 184-185. Although Dieterle was neither Jewish nor a refugee, having arrived in America during 1930, he identified with them. In 1939, Dieterle faced criticism by congressman Martin Dies who believed *Blockade* and *Juarez* contained communist propaganda. Both Dieterle and his wife, Charlotte, actively supported their fellow unemployed artist by setting up the European Film Fund. They also helped bring to Hollywood the last batch of refugee writers to leave Marseilles and Lisbon in 1940 and 1941. Both Lang and Dieterle subsidized Brecht's last years in Europe. However, Dieterle's late 30s visit to the Soviet Union, his unfulfilled Karl Marx bio-pic project, and his role in bringing Brecht, Helene Weigel, and Hans Eisler to Hollywood led to the confiscation of his passport in the early 50s and subsequent "grey-listing." For relevant information see William R. Meyer, *Warner Brothers Directors* (New York: Arlington House, 1978), 126- 133; Wakeman, 245-251; Heilbut, 109, 111, 182, 184; Liam O'Leary, "William Dieterle," *International Directory of Films and Filmmakers 2* (Detroit: St. James Press, 1992), 254- 257; Michael Barson, "William Dieterle," *The Illustrated Who's Who of Hollywood Directors. Volume 1* (New York: Farrar, Straus, and Giroux, 1995), 114-117. In 1941, Dieterle contributed an article to a New York Institute of Social Research academic journal on the European crisis. See William Dieterle, "Hollywood and the European Crisis," *Studies in Philosophy and Social Science*, 9.1-3 (1941): 96-103. Although primarily dealing with the economic effects Hollywood faced through loss of European markets, the article does contain some significant sentences which reveal certain insights. Noting Hollywood reactions to the outbreak of World War 2, Dieterle remarked, "When the war broke out last September, no place on earth could have given less serious reflection to the war's potentialities than did Hollywood. The town's bitter hatred of Hitler and all he represented was one of the few genuine things about it." (96) After applauding the frosty reception given to Leni Riefenstahl on her Hollywood visit and stress-

ing that "films made for the American audience will no longer fit the psychology of a people embittered and saddened by the terrible hell they have been through" (99), Dieterle concluded that the industry should recognize its responsibility to American audiences and workers rather than mourn over lost overseas markets. "Besides, it is time for Hollywood to begin recognizing its responsibility to the millions of workers who, either directly or indirectly, depend upon it for a living." (102)

17. See Robin Wood, "Ideology, Genre, Auteur," *Film Comment* 13.1 (1977): 46-51; Tony Williams, *Hearths of Darkness*, 13-30.

18. For the problematic nature of the nineteenth century myth of the virgin land see Henry Nash Smith, *Virgin Land: The American West as Symbol and Myth* (Cambridge, Massachusets: Harvard University Press, 1970).

19. Henry Nash Smith, 123.

20. Op. cit. 126.

21. Op. cit. 134.

22. Op. cit. 171.

23. Singer, 266-67.

24. The real Daniel Webster belonged to the Whig party. He was never a "man of the people" or Jacksonian Democrat. See Sydney Nathans, *Daniel Webster and Jacksonian Democracy* (Baltimore: Johns Hopkins University Press, 1973), 141, also cited by Singer.

25. Mary Ryan, *Womanhood in America*, (New York: New Viewpoints, 1975), 146.

26. Op. cit. 158-159.

27. Op. cit. 163-164.

28. Quoted by Mary Ryan, 160-161.

29. Robin Wood, *Personal Views: Explorations in Film* (London: Gordon Fraser, 1976), 215.

30. See here Paul Boyar and Stephen Nissbaum, *Salem Possessed* (Cambridge, Massachusetts: Harvard University Press, 1974), 213-214.

31. Singer, 270.

32. Smith, 127.

33. Smith, 291, n.29.

34. See Singer, 269-270.

35. For Paul Tillich's radical thought and his sophisticated observations concerning American intellectual deficiencies see Heilbut, 67n, 75, 77, 84, 198.

36. See Tony Williams, *Jack London: The Movies* (Los Angeles: David Rejl, 1992), 170; "London's Last Frontier: The Big House as Culture of Consumption," *Jack London Journal* 2 (1995): 156-174.

Above, Paul Lavond (Lionel Barrymore) disguised as "Madame Mandilip" interacts with his daughter Lorraine (Maureen O'Sullivan), in *The Devil-Doll*.

Violence, Women, and Disability in Tod Browning's *Freaks* and *The Devil-Doll*

Martin F. Norden and Madeleine Cahill

Filmmakers who have populated their films with disabled characters have occasionally endowed them with violent behavior, and it should come as no surprise to learn that the vast majority of such characters have been coded as male. Indeed, the early history of disability depictions in the movies can be characterized in terms of a conspicuous gender-based dichotomy: male characters were often designed as castrated Captain Ahab types who destroy all in their wake in the name of revenge, while female characters were infantilized as docile, sexless, godly young things usually rewarded for their enduring purity with a miracle cure.

These so-termed "Obsessive Avengers" and "Sweet Innocents" anchored the ends of the disability stereotype spectrum for decades,[1] but Tod Browning, a filmmaker who frequently linked men, violence, and disability in his movies during the 1920s, disrupted the pattern with the release of two horror films the following decade: *Freaks* (1932) and *The Devil-Doll* (1936). In *Freaks*, disabled women participate in the slaying of a man and the crippling of a woman who had attempted to murder one of their friends. In *The Devil-Doll*, a disabled woman tries to stab an accomplice, then threatens him with a vial of explosive fluid, and finally blows up a laboratory after her plans to shrink the world's population go terribly awry. Browning's decision to inscribe disabled women as violent to place them on the opposite end of the stereotype spectrum, in effect, was virtually without precedent in the movies and violated one of mainstream society's most deeply held beliefs about women with disabilities.[2] This essay investigates the circumstances surrounding the making of these anomalous movies and Browning's strategies for representing the women and their actions.

Freaks and *The Devil-Doll* owe their existence at least in part to the eagerness of Metro-Goldwyn-Mayer, one of the most powerful studios in Hollywood, to cash in on the horror-film genre then captivating the country. In 1931, one of the smaller players in the studio system, Univer-

151

sal, scored a major box-office hit with its adaptation of Mary Shelley's *Frankenstein*. Earning more than seventeen times its production costs during its first run alone, *Frankenstein* sent the other Hollywood movie companies scurrying to develop their own competitive horror movies. In the case of MGM, production head Irving Thalberg turned to Tod Browning, one of his premiere directors, and allegedly said, "I want something that out-horrors *Frankenstein*."[3] Browning, whose earlier work included such horror films as *London After Midnight* (1927) and *Dracula* (1931), responded by creating *Freaks*, which remains one of the most notorious disability-related films ever made, and the lesser-known but still disturbing *The Devil-Doll*.

Freaks tells the story of a traveling circus currently encamped in a remote part of France. Hans (Harry Earles), a nattily dressed midget, is engaged to another shortstatured performer named Frieda (played by Harry Earles's real-life sister, Daisy) but develops an immense fascination with an able-bodied trapeze artist named Cleopatra (Olga Baclanova). He is little more than a joke to her until she learns that he stands to inherit a fortune. With the help of her new paramour, Hercules the circus strongman (Henry Victor), Cleopatra plans to marry Hans and then fatally poison him. The other disabled performers, including several women with microcephaly, two sisters conjoined at the hip, and a woman with no arms, catch wind of the plan, and, after Hans recovers from the poisoning, they do not hesitate to exact a cold-blooded revenge. In a nightmarish sequence replete with thunder and lightning, the title characters literally slither through the mud before slaying Hercules and mutilating Cleopatra to such an extent that she becomes a "freak," too: a grotesque "chicken woman."

The idea for *Freaks* initially came from Harry Earles, the shortstatured actor who played Hans and with whom Browning had worked previously. He suggested Browning read "Spurs," a short story by Tod Robbins published in a 1923 issue of *Munsey's Magazine*. Browning, who as a teenager had fulfilled many a schoolchild's dream by running away and joining a circus, was immediately intrigued by the tale: a circus dwarf named Jacques Courbé turns vindictive after able-bodied co-workers try to bilk him out of an inheritance.[4] Using "Spurs" as their starting point, Browning and his screenwriters (a legion that eventually included Willis Goldbeck, Leon Gordon, Elliott Clawson, Edgar Allan Woolf, Al Boasberg, and Charles MacArthur) set to work crafting the narrative details of their film.

Browning then took a major step beyond his horror film colleagues at the other studios by assembling a group of developmentally and physically disabled sideshow performers from around the world to appear in his film as themselves. For example, two recruits were Frances O'Connor, an armless woman known professionally as "The Living Venus de Milo," and Minnie Woolsey, whose body is believed to have been affected by a rare disorder that causes premature aging and who was billed as "Koo Koo, the Bird Girl from Mars." Though *Freaks* shares some general similarities with other horror films of the period, most notably, its revenge theme, the plurality of "Others" coded as aberrant if not outright abhorrent, and exotic/foreign settings, Browning's use of actual disabled performers constituted a major difference. Audiences viewing films such as Universal's *Frankenstein, Dracula,* and *Bride of Frankenstein* (1935), Paramount's *Dr. Jekyll and Mr. Hyde* (1932), RKO's *King Kong* (1933), and Warner's *Mystery of the Wax Museum* (1933), could reassure themselves that the freakish beings who appeared on the screen were played by heavily obscured able-bodied actors and/or rendered by special-effects technology. No such assurances were possible with *Freaks*, however, and the MGM publicity department, far from retreating on this point, repeatedly underscored the performers' "authen-

Below, the assembled "freaks" posed for a group shot with Tod Browning (center).

tic" quality in its promotional campaign. For example, its advertisements proclaimed that *Freaks* starred "humans and half-humans" and
that the film itself was "a mystery drama [set] behind the scenes in a
sideshow with strange and grotesque freaks and monstrosities playing
principal roles."[5]

MGM's production and marketing strategies backfired mightily;
Freaks was a disaster at the box office and a heavy blow to the studio's
reputation. Indeed, the film drew many highly negative reviews,
prompted civic groups across the country to renew calls for movie censorship, and was banned outright in the United Kingdom.[6] For reasons
that to this day remain unclear, however, MGM allowed Browning to
continue making movies. Irving Thalberg, the film's patron, went on
medical leave shortly after the *Freaks* debacle (his congenitally deformed
heart already weakened by rheumatic fever and the stresses of a high-
profile job, Thalberg suffered a heart attack late in 1932), and Browning
took advantage of the vicissitudes surrounding his boss's departure by
convincing other MGM authorities he could revert to his old box-office
form, especially in the horror genre.

After directing two other films, Browning returned to the Obsessive
Avenger theme with *The Devil-Doll*. His principal screenwriters bore im-
peccable horror film credentials: Garrett Fort, one of the *Frankenstein* scenarists; and Guy Endore, who had developed a reputation for horror
writing as a result of his work on 1935's *Mark of the Vampire, Mad Love*,
and *The Raven*.[7] Using Abraham Merritt's 1933 novel **Burn Witch Burn!**
as their basis, Browning, Fort, and Endore developed a script they called
"The Witch of Timbuctoo," a name that also served as the film's working title. MGM added numerous uncredited writers to the project at
various stages, however, and the written-by-committee movie that eventually resulted, retitled *The Devil-Doll*, told the story of Paul Lavond (Lionel Barrymore), a Parisian banker wrongly convicted of embezzlement
and murder. He escapes from Devil's Island with an elderly scientist
named Marcel (Henry B. Walthall), who prior to his incarceration had
been experimenting with a method of reducing humans to doll size and
commanding them to do his will. The two link up with Marcel's crutch-
using wife, Malita (Rafaela Ottiano), a saucer-eyed woman who has
maintained the laboratory in her husband's absence. Intrigued by the
possibilities of creating tiny humans with no will of their own, Lavond
moves to Paris with Malita to continue their work after Marcel dies of a
heart attack, and they set up a toy store there as the front for their experiments. Using the guise of an old woman named "Madame Mandilip," Lavond orders the "dolls" to seek revenge on the bankers who
framed him.

Though his actions and subsequent guilt make the ablebodied Lavond the primary avenging figure of *The Devil-Doll*, the orthopedically and morally impaired Malita offers him stiff competition. Malita, described by a *Variety* reviewer as "the scientist's wacky widow . . . with a white streak in her hair and hobbling on a crutch,"[8] shares a distinct quality with many other disabled characters in literature, theater, and the movies: she bears a disability that quickly takes on negative symbolic overtones. It does not take the audience long to learn she and her husband are insane, but Browning pushed her characterization one step further; she is not only crazy, but malevolent as well. She plans to avenge Marcel's death by maniacally insisting on carrying out their plans to shrink the entire world's population, with or without Lavond's cooperation. When Lavond refuses to put up with her obsession, she decides to shrink him to doll-size, too, and orders one of the dolls to stab him with a tiny poisoned stiletto. As she whispers to the miniaturized assassin: "We've served his purpose, Radin—now he'll serve ours, reduced to your size. I'll control him as easily as I control you." Lavond eludes Radin and then says to her, "Why, you poor insane wretch! I should destroy you with all the rest of this horror!" He starts wrecking the lab, and in response Malita threatens to throw a vial of explosive fluid at him. Lavond tries to stop her but she indeed throws the bottle and blows up the lab. In the tradition of such gothic literary figures as Edward and Bertha Rochester of *Jane Eyre* and Max de Winter and Mrs. Danvers of *Rebecca*, Lavond escapes the inferno but Malita does not. Lavond seals his morality in a gesture that recalls Edward Rochester; he calls out to the woman who would kill him, but he cannot save her from her own self-destructive compulsion.[9]

What are we to make of the violent disabled women who appear in *Freaks* and *The Devil-Doll*? What were the forces that led to their creation? And what do the films say about gender roles, disability, and violence?

Let's start by examining the place of these films within the context of Browning's earlier works. Browning had his greatest success as a filmmaker during the mid-to-late 1920s, and much of that success was related to the actor with whom he was frequently paired: Lon Chaney, the legendary "Man of a Thousand Faces." Browning developed a fondness for revenge-driven disability drama, and the protean Chaney offered him the perfect vehicle for expressing those ideas. Indeed, Browning, who had admired Chaney's work as a criminal who pretends to be disabled in *The Miracle Man* (1919) and a vengeful gangster with no legs in *The Penalty* (1920), had been slated to direct the actor in what would become one of the latter's most famous films, *The Hunchback of Notre Dame*

(1923). Alcohol-related problems forced Browning off that project, but he did go on to direct Chaney in such films as *The Unholy Three* (1925), *The Blackbird* (1926), *The Road to Mandalay* (1926), *The Unknown* (1927), and *West of Zanzibar* (1928), all of which featured disabled men (or men feigning disabled status) in revenge-minded situations.[10]

Chaney died of cancer in 1930, ending a collaboration that had shown no signs of declining. For example, Chaney had been Browning's choice to star in *Dracula*, the director's most famous film after *Freaks*. Chaney's death forced Browning to move his career in a new direction and prompted him to reassess the Obsessive Avenger image that he had spent years cultivating. Perhaps believing he could go no further with the Avenger in its lone-male characterization, and mindful of Irving Thalberg's call for a competitive horror movie, he decided that the 1930s were an auspicious time to create new variations.

Browning began this short-lived tradition with *Freaks,* a project that had been simmering on the back burner since the late 1920s. As we have seen, the film features an entire colony of Obsessive Avengers, male and female, who act as one when outsiders violate their moral code. Their sheer number is a major difference from Browning's other disability films (the earlier incarnation of the Obsessive Avenger had always spun his malevolent plans in solitude), and the director and his scriptwriters went to extreme lengths to create a sense of community among them, a quality conspicuously absent in the source material, "Spurs." Jacques Courbé "had no friends among the other freaks," wrote Robbins, "he loathed them,"[11] and during the wedding feast an otherwise perfect opportunity to reinforce the idea of community a major brawl erupts among them. The short story's vengeful male loner would ordinarily have fit in perfectly with Browning's preoccupations, but the director, perhaps believing that no single actor could fill Chaney's shoes, wanted something else for *Freaks.*

In the earlier films, the Chaney character typically begins as ablebodied, undergoes a traumatic incident, and then seeks revenge; in the case of *Freaks*, the females and males are already disabled at the start (the vast majority bear genetic disorders). Since so many of them have missing limbs, stunted growth, or microcephaly, the film seems to imply that individually they are "incomplete" (i.e., ineffective) but collectively they can form a whole quite capable of committing the most unspeakable atrocities.

The revenge scene in *Freaks* was the most conspicuous departure from the Robbins short story, both in terms of the number of assailants involved and the extent of their retribution. In "Spurs," only Courbé with the help of his trained dog exacts any retaliation and, though they do kill the Hercules character, they significantly do not slay or permanently disfigure the ablebodied woman who attempted to swindle him. Instead, she is enslaved and exhausted until she is reduced to a worn-out beast of burden: the antithesis of her formerly glamorous, purely decorative existence. Browning and his writers transferred Courbé's spiteful quality to an entire community of disabled performers, and, unlike Robbins' vengeful dwarf, the title characters resort to mutilation. (Indeed, Browning and his writers initially planned to have the "freaks" mutilate both Cleopatra and Hercules but dumped the idea of the latter's mutilation–castration, specifically–in the face of heavy censor opposition.) In a conspicuous departure from Browning's previous work, the director did not show his Obsessive Avengers receiving any form of punishment for their actions. Most critics have denounced the vengeful deeds as a significant miscalculation by Browning and his scenarists. John Brosnan represented the views of many when he wrote:

> This retaliation by the freaks, though partly justified, is a major flaw in the picture. Up to then Browning had effectively presented them as basically "normal" people, despite their physical handicaps... and much more likeable than the two physically perfect people. But by resorting finally to the popular image of circus freaks as being strange and sinister creatures he destroyed all his previous good work, laying himself open, at the same time, to the charge of exploitation though to be fair to Browning the idea for the story came from the midget, Harry Earles, himself.[12]

As for *The Devil-Doll*'s Malita, she bears more of a resemblance to the Chaney characters than do the disabled folk who populate *Freaks* in that she does pay for her obsessive behavior with her life. Though Lavond and Malita are jointly engaged in illegal and immoral activities, *The Devil-Doll* makes clear distinctions between the quality of their characters. Lavond's vengeance is bounded by a sense of rationality. The audience can understand his motivations; he wants to avenge himself on only the three people who caused direct harm to him and his family. Lavond's anger is actually shown to have a positive side: "Without my hatred, I never could have lived," he explains to Marcel as they escape from Devil's Island. Furthermore, Lavond is humanized by his love for his estranged daughter (she grew up believing him guilty of his crimes) and his blind mother, a wise and gentle woman who embodies Hollywood's "Saintly Sage" disability stereotype.[13] "I only wanted to vindicate my name . . . because of my family," he explains to Malita after quitting their devil-doll experiments. When she threatens to kill him, he tells her that "Death doesn't frighten me . . . but I still have something to do for my child."

Malita, on the other hand, is bound by no such rational motivations–a point illustrated by her desire to manipulate the fate not of three people but of the entire world. When a police officer comes to the toy store to question them, Malita wants to shrink him as well and must be reined in by Lavond. The implication is clearly that she is indiscriminate and ultimately insane. Ironically, though her participation in Lavond's scheme is less active than his own, it appears more morally suspect because of her lack of direct motivation for harming three men she has never met. Malita's delight in the strange results of their work (underscored with frequent close-ups of her wide, staring eyes and perpetually raised eyebrows) gives the appearance of criminal insanity. And, significantly, once Marcel has died, no loving connection to other people functions to humanize Malita or encourage audience identification with her.

Malita's rudimentary and fragmented character development is partly traceable to adaptation issues that arose during the film's production process. No such figure exists in the Abraham Merritt novel, but Malita does coincide with its main character, Madame Mandilip (who in the book is actually female, not a disguised male), in terms of her ability to create miniaturized beings who can be controlled by her will. The similarities end there, however; she neither physically resembles Mandilip (whom Merritt described as an elderly woman with a commanding presence, roughhewn but with surprisingly dainty hands and a mellifluous voice–qualities that do not readily apply to Malita) nor shares her overwhelming desire to command the dolls to wreak violence. Though she does order a doll to stab Lavond, she is far more interested, in the words of Bret Wood, in treating "them as playthings, ordering them to dance on a tabletop to the chimes of a music box."[14] Indeed, she and Marcel originally wanted to shrink people to doll-size for humanitarian reasons: to allow the world's dwindling supply of food and natural resources to go farther.

Malita evolved primarily from a character Browning, Fort, and Endore created in their "Witch of Timbuctoo" script but later abandoned: Nyleta, a black woman from the Belgian Congo who practices voodoo and witchcraft and who happens to be the mother of Ba-oola, the man who escapes with the Lavond character (named "Duval" in this draft of the screenplay) from Devil's Island. According to Wood, who conducted a thorough examination of The Devil-Doll's production history, "Baoola's mother, Nyleta, travels with Duval to Paris to help exact revenge on the three conspirators who contrived his downfall. Duval disguises himself as an old woman and opens a doll shop to cover his and Nyleta's operations. The two then abduct a small crew of gypsy-like criminals from a low-class dive and shrink them, arm them with tiny poison-tipped swords, and manipulate them through mind control."[15]

MGM was forced to make radical changes in the story, however, in response to censorship pressures from both Hollywood's internal regulatory agency–the Production Code Administration, then known colloquially as the "Breen office" after its current head, Joseph Breen–and its counterpart in Great Britain. In the 1930s, it was standard practice for movie studios to submit every script to the Breen office for approval prior to production. In the case of the "Witch of Timbuctoo" screenplay, Joseph Breen ordered many changes centering mostly on issues of morality and criminal activity unrelated to Malita. The British censors, however, had much stronger objections and made suggestions that would affect the film's entire narrative structure. Concerned that the actions of Nyleta and Ba-oola would incite black people in the British Empire, they demanded the removal of all black characters and all references to voodoo and witchcraft.

Since Great Britain represented an important market for MGM's films, the studio said it would oblige, thus sending the writers scrambling to revise their story. Following a suggestion by MGM story editor Samuel Marx, they turned the voodoo/witchcraft angle into a more traditional "mad scientist" one along the lines of *Frankenstein* and converted the black African mother and son Nyleta and Ba-oola into the white European wife and husband Malita and Marcel. Thus, the writers transformed Nyleta, characterized by Wood as a "threatening, exotic voodoo priestess whose black art is used for curses and vengeance"[16] and presumably the title character of the "Witch of Timbuctoo" script, into the minor figure of Malita. MGM forced Browning to accept the changes, but, in an echo of his previous work, he decided to make Malita disabled. In so doing, he put her on the same level with such infamous literary figures as Richard III, Captain Hook, Long John Silver, Captain Ahab, and his own many disabled male characters, in the sense that her physical disability comes to symbolize a moral disability. "Deformity of the body is a sure sign of deformity of the soul," wrote Joanmarie Kalter of one of the most deeply entrenched fears of people with disabilities,[17] and it finds ample expression not only in *The Devil-Doll* but in *Freaks* as well.

What messages related to violence, disability, and gender may be distilled from these films? It seems obvious to state that *The Devil-Doll* and *Freaks* helped weaken, if not outright shatter, the prevailing dichotomy of disabled male and female constructions in the movies: the male-in-scribed Obsessive Avenger and the female—inscribed Sweet Innocent. This development, however, hardly represented an improvement in depictions of characters with disabilities; disabled women, the films seem to say, are now to be feared as much as disabled men.

Despite their resemblance to the male Obsessive Avengers of earlier times, Browning's avenging females retain certain vestiges of stereotypes associated with women in general and women with disabilities in particular. One is the basic issue of infantilization, which is especially pronounced in *Freaks*. The disabled women (and, unusually, the men as well) of *Freaks* are initially portrayed as benign and childlike. An able-bodied woman who oversees them refers to them as children, for example, and one of the phrases that MGM used to characterize them in prerelease publicity was "strange children of the shadows."[18] In the case of *The Devil-Doll*, a woman whose name translates as "bad little one" obediently follows the directives of the men in her life like an unquestioning child; when she finally disobeys one of them, she dies moments thereafter in an explosion and fire. Audiences then and now could not help finding such characters unsettling, since these women, coded as infantilized "Others," were hardly expected to be violent.

Another distinction among female and male Obsessive Avengers concerns the reasons that they indeed become vengeful. Female Avengers, unlike their many male literary and filmic counterparts, become violent only for the sake of others. In other words, the male Obsessive Avengers typically seek revenge for wrongs (whether real or imagined) committed against *them*, while the female ones do so for wrongs committed against others.[19] The title characters of *Freaks* are in general an other-oriented, peaceable lot. As Mary Russo has pointed out, their community is a model of tolerance but only up to a point.[20] When an ablebodied person tries to exploit one of their own, their transformation from "children" to coldblooded killers and mutilators is swift, unexpected, and chilling. "Their code is a law unto themselves," a carny barker observes near the beginning of the film. "Offend one and you offend them all!" Malita, too, harbors the "other-oriented" trait frequently associated with women; she views her vengeful activities not so much as actions for her own sake but on behalf of her late husband. As she says to Lavond while threatening him with the explosive fluid, "You've had your vengeance. Now Marcel will have his!"

In addition, the female Avengers in both films are not major characters. Unlike the many Browning-Chaney collaborations of the 1920s, which featured the male Obsessive Avengers dominating almost every scene, *Freaks* and *The Devil-Doll* relegate their disabled figures to backseat status and focus instead on the able-bodied characters who wrong them: Cleopatra, Hercules, and Lavond.

Similarly, the women's obsessive and violent behaviors are not as consuming as the men's but are limited to several brief scenes. The censorship matters that plagued both films are clearly related to these narrative differences; topics that filmmakers could get away with in the 1920s were suddenly forbidden in the 1930s as a result of forces exerted by the Production Code Administration and other regulatory bodies. As we have already seen, *The Devil-Doll* underwent major changes to conform to censor demands, with its writers changing the ablebodied Nyleta into the disabled Malita and significantly reducing her prominence in the process. In the case of *Freaks*, the scenes of violence were greatly toned down for the censors. Several females may be glimpsed among the figures crawling through the mud in the final version of the film, but most of their violent acts ended up on the cutting-room floor. David Skal and Elias Savada, who conducted extensive research into the production of *Freaks*, noted that "the truncated version [of the film] jettisoned the horrifying details of the mud-dripping freaks swarming over the tree-pinned Olga Baclanova and pouring into a circus wagon to castrate her lover."[21]

Freaks and *The Devil-Doll* paradoxically both rupture and reinforce traditional views of female roles in films. While the disabled women of these films violate expectations of appearance and behavior established by decades of cinematic portrayals of Sweet Innocents, they simultaneously reinforce Hollywood's patterns of punishment of historically marginalized women: those women coded as unattractive, older women, women of color, poor women, and women unattached to men or children.[22]

As the prologue to *Freaks* points out, anything that deviates from the norm has traditionally been considered an omen of ill luck or a representation of evil.[23] Although the prologue purports to expose and challenge such superstitious thought, it does little to disguise the fact that Browning's film actually perpetuates this pattern in many ways. Browning's films create a distinction between "acceptable" women with disabilities (Lavond's blind mother and Hans's fiancée Frieda, who are models of maternal and feminine virtues) and "unacceptable" ones (Malita, many of the nameless "freaks," and ultimately Cleopatra) who are often used as spectacles of horror.

The women with disabilities in *Freaks* and *The Devil-Doll* are clearly categorized by appearance and behavior. Frieda, for example, is normalized both in relative appearance and in adherence to gender expectations. "Disabled" only in the sense of her small size, she is not shown to

Above, Cleopatra (Olga Baclanova) after her transformation into the "chicken woman."
Below, Johnny Eck leads the welcoming dinner chorus of "Gooble gobble...one of us."

be "malformed" in any physical or social way. Frieda and her able-bodied friend Venus are shown doing laundry and talking about their men—highly gender-coded and normalized activities that, in the world of Hollywood film, signal the audience that the characters conform to sex-role expectations. Frieda and Hans, in fact, form a parallel couple to Venus and Phroso (an able-bodied male circus performer) in terms of audience identification. Significantly, neither Frieda nor Hans is anywhere to be seen during the film's mutilation scene.

Cleopatra is much more active and powerful than either Frieda or Venus, and the narrative moment that crystalizes her evil is when she demonstrates her physical power by carrying Hans around on her shoulders at their wedding feast. While a groom carrying the bride across the threshold on their wedding night is regarded as the apogee of romance, the reversal of this heterosexual custom represents the nadir of Hans's humiliation. Though ostensibly challenging it, *Freaks* reinforces the cultural link between evil and disability/ugliness; the cruel woman who early in the film is a beautiful spectacle is made hideous by the end, journeying from her role as "peacock of the air" to that of a "chicken woman."

The contrasting disabled women in *The Devil-Doll* provide a similar duality in terms of reinforcing and rupturing genderrelated expectations. Lavond's mother is blind, but, having followed Freud's suggested path to feminine fulfillment by bearing a son, she is calm and loving. Her maternal nature continues to be evident in her protective relationships with both her son and her granddaughter. The character contrasts sharply with the decidedly unmaternal and therefore "unacceptable" Malita, all the way down to their physical representations in the movie; the quietly "faded" look of Lavond's mother bears little resemblance to Malita's generally stark appearance, epitomized by the stripes of white in her dark hair (a visual echo of the female monster's hair in *Bride of Frankenstein* the previous year).

The violence committed against Cleopatra resulting in her mutilation is worthy of further consideration, if only for its contradictory qualities that go beyond issues of gender.[24] Earlier in the film, during the infamous wedding feast sequence, Cleopatra watches in horror as the "freaks" stage a bizarre welcoming ceremony for her in which they chant "Gooble gobble, gooble gobble, we accept her, one of us." She is revolted at the thought and throws a proffered loving cup of wine at them. "Dirty, slimy freaks!" she says. "Make me one of you, will you?" The offended characters remember her words, of course, and during the storm-drenched revenge scene they literally do make her one of them. The film now represents her as newly infantilized; uttering nonverbal sounds in a fenced-off pen with sideshow gawkers looking down on her, she resembles a prelingual child in a playpen watched by adults. The implications of the violence against her, however, are far from clear; members of a traditionally disempowered minority use their collective force to disempower a majority member--to turn her into one of them, in effect--leading us to wonder if she is truly disempowered or empowered in a new way. Browning's ambiguity on this point only enhances the film's unsettling properties.

It is difficult to assess the impact of Browning's highly unusual movies. *Freaks* was a critical and financial disaster but since the 1960s has developed a cult-film following; *The Devil Doll*, though it turned a modest profit for MGM, is barely remembered today due to the studio's extensive interference that greatly vitiated its horror-genre aspects. A significant development arising from *Freaks* and *The Devil-Doll* was, without a doubt, Tod Browning's early retirement from the movies. His career ended shortly after these two films, and it is highly likely that their controversial (and heavily censored) imagery, mixed receptions, and mediocre-to-poor box-office performances helped put Browning, who had spent years cultivating the darker reaches of movie disability depictions, into retirement at age 57. Though 1939 marked his last film, his legacy, for good or ill, continues to be felt..

Notes

1. For discussions of these and other disability-related stereotypes, see Martin F. Norden, *The Cinema of Isolation: A History of Physical Disability in the Movies*, New Brunswick, New Jersey: Rutgers University Press, 1994. See also Norden's "The Uncanny Film Image of the Obsessive Avenger," *Paradoxa: Studies in World Literary Genres*, 1997, pp. 367-78.

2. We have discovered only two movies prior to *Freaks* that contained avenging disabled women. One is a 1908 onereel film called *The Sailor's Sweetheart*, in which a disabled woman strangles a man tormenting her daughter. The other is *Stella Maris*, a 1918 silent feature film that starred Mary Pickford in two roles. One character is Unity Blake, a woman with a malformed shoulder and hip who kills another woman and then herself to avenge the beatings of the title character, also played by Pickford. For discussions of these films, see Madeleine A. Cahill, "'A Bad Time of It in This World': The Construction of the 'Unattractive' Woman in American Film of the 1940's," Ph.D. dissertation, University of MassachusettsAmherst, pp. 41-51; and Norden, **Cinema**, pp. 28, 65-66.

3. Quoted in David Wheeler, ed., *No, but I Saw the Movie: The Best Short Stories Ever Made into Film*, New York: Penguin, 1989, p. 144.

4. *Munsey's* is a difficult magazine to access today, but fortunately "Spurs" has been reprinted in at least three anthologies: Peter Haining, ed., *The Ghouls*,

New York: Stein and Day, 1971; William Kittredge and Steven M. Krauzer, eds., **Stories into Film**, New York: Harper & Row, 1979; and Wheeler. Our references to "Spurs" come from the Wheeler edition.

5. *Freaks* pressbook, Billy Rose Theatre Collection, New York Public Library at Lincoln Center, New York City.

6. For a brief history of this film's censorship history, see Martin F. Norden, "*Freaks,*" in Kent Rasmussen, ed., **Ready Reference: Censorship**, Vol. 1, Pasadena, California: Salem Press, pp. 303-04.

7. Hollywood's legendary misfit, Erich von Stroheim, also received screen credit but little of his work found its way into the final film. See Bret Wood, "The Witch, the Devil, and the Code," *Film Comment*, NovemberDecember, 1992, pp. 52-56.

8. Review of *The Devil-Doll, Variety*, August 12, 1936, p. 18.

9. Hollywood produced like-titled movies based on **Rebecca** and **Jane Eyre** in 1940 and 1944, respectively.

10. Chaney also acted in many revenge-driven dramas directed by others. See Norden, **Cinema**, pp. 8499.

11. Tod Robbins, "Spurs" (Wheeler edition), p. 146.

12. John Brosnan, **The Horror People**, New York: St. Martin's Press, 1976, pp. 65-66.

13. A definition of this stereotype may be found in Norden, **Cinema**, pp. 13133.

14. Wood, p. 55.

15. Ibid, p. 53.

16. Ibid, p. 55.

17. Joanmarie Kalter, "The Disabled Get More TV Exposure, but There's Still Too Much Stereotyping," *TV Guide*, May 31, 1986, p. 42.

18. *Freaks* pressbook.

19. This important distinction is also true for the films' two silent-era predecessors, *The Sailor's Sweetheart* and *Stella Maris*, noted above.

20. Mary Russo, **The Female Grotesque: Risk, Excess and Modernity**, New York: Routledge, 1995, p. 91.

21. David J. Skal and Elias Savada, **Dark Carnival: The Secret World of Tod Browning, Hollywood's Master of the Macabre**, New York: Anchor, 1995, p. 174.

22. See Cahill for an extended study of the Hollywood representation of "unattractive" women.

23. Attached to most prints of *Freaks* in circulation today, this prologue was actually added after the film's initial run in an ill-considered effort to add a sociological spin to the film.

24. Indeed, Mary Russo has argued that Cleopatra's mutilation is the film's most important issue. See Russo, pp. 77-79.

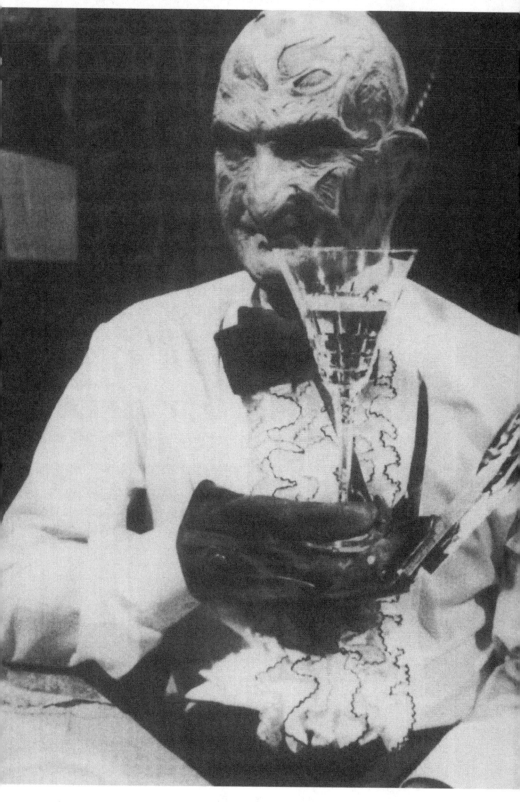

Above, the prototypical 80s monster, Freddy Krueger (Robrt Englund), dressed up and ready to party in *A Nightmare on Elm Street 5: The Dream Child*.

Monsters as (Uncanny) Metaphors: Freud, Lakoff, and the Representation of Monstrosity in Cinematic Horror

Steven Schneider

> Everything monstrous happening in the world has an ancient ancestry. The monster is intrinsic while our awareness of the monster has evolved.
>
> Frank Cawson, *The Monsters in the Mind* (161)*

> Monsters must be examined within the intricate matrix of relations (social, cultural, and literary-historical) which generate them. A mixed category, the monster resists any classification built on hierarchy. ...The monstrous is a genus too large to be encapsulated in any conceptual system.
>
> Jeffrey Cohen, "Monster Culture (Seven Theses)" (2-3)

> I have always supposed that the universal and the particular are compatible, that grounding in a particular historical and cultural matrix is inevitable and could not conceivably be in conflict with universal principles.
>
> Israel Scheffler, *Teachers of My Youth* (180)

Introduction: Horror Film Monsters

What, if anything, do the monsters of horror cinema have in common, besides the fact that they are not real? They may be human—just think of Norman Bates, Leatherface, or Hannibal Lechter—but they are not *real*, in the sense of experientially real. They may even be non-fictional—just think of *Henry: Portrait of a Serial Killer* (1990), a film about real-life mass murderer Henry Lee Lucas—but that still doesn't make them real (the Henry of the film is just an actor, Michael Rooker, pretending to be Henry Lee Lucas).[1]

So the monsters of horror cinema are depictions of monsters, representations of monsters. But what *else* are they, as a group? Perhaps noth-

* Parenthetical numbers refer to pages of books in the Works Cited list.

ing: after all, Dracula, Jaws, the Thing (both versions), Carrie, Chucky, Freddy Krueger, and the rest are a fairly diverse lot, to say the least. According to horror film expert Mark Jancovich, "Different groups will represent the monstrous in different ways and representations will develop historically" (9). In her 1995 book, *Skin Shows: Gothic Horror and the Technology of Monsters*, Judith Halberstam makes almost exactly the same claim: "The body that scares and appalls changes over time, as do the individual characteristics that add up to monstrosity, as do the preferred interpretations of monstrosity" (8). Can't we say of them this much at least, that their primary purpose is to horrify viewers? Sure, they don't always succeed—lots of times they fail—but isn't it the fact that they *try* that makes them *horror* film monsters? The dinosaurs of *Jurassic Park* (1993) may or may not be depictions of monsters, but *Jurassic Park* isn't a horror movie, and the dinosaurs aren't intended to horrify us. We may feel terror at the sight of a Tyrannosaurs Rex tearing some guy apart, but, to quote Stanley Cavell, "terror is of *violence*, of the violence I might do or that might be done me. I can be *terrified* of thunder, but not *horrified* by it" (418).

This is all, of course, to highlight the question, "What is horror?". And that is a very big question indeed. In a famous 1919 paper, Freud characterized the "uncanny" as that which "arouses dread and horror...certain things which lie within the class of what is frightening" (339). Now defining uncanniness in terms of horror obviously precludes us from defining horror in terms of uncanniness, on pain of circularity. Nor would our intuitions support any claim to the effect that these terms are synonymous (most dictionaries define "uncanny" somewhere along the lines of "eerie," "mysterious," or "seemingly supernatural"). But if we can at least find some independent reasons for thinking that psychoanalysis has the tools to explain the timeless appeal and efficacy of horror fiction, this will justify our use of Freud's theory of the uncanny to shed light on the nature of horror films, and, by extension, the nature of horror film monsters.

Such "independent reasons" are readily available. Though sneered at by the highbrow, largely ignored by mainstream academics, and censured by society's self-proclaimed moral guardians, it can hardly be denied that horror fiction (including cinema) serves a variety of psychological functions in society. The briefest review will suffice to make the point. Like tragedy, horror promotes emotional catharsis in audiences; like fantasy, it offers viewers an escape from the tedium of everyday life; like comedy, it provides a relatively safe (because relatively disguised/distorted) forum for the expression of socio-cultural fears. All of this is borne out by the fact that psychoanalysis has produced, by far, the most common and influential analyses of the horror film to date. Freud's hypothesis, that a sufficient condition of uncanny experiences is the return to consciousness of repressed infantile complexes, has been famously, albeit rather loosely, adopted/adapted by film theorist Robin Wood: "One might say that the true subject of the horror genre is all that our civilization represses or oppresses" (75). And note too, that the relationship between psychoanalysis and the horror film is mutually supportive. As Andrew Tudor points out, "the [horror] genre itself invokes psychoanalytic considerations, at times borrowing its imagery from the symbolic apparatus of dream interpretation as well as allowing fictional characters to advance pseudo-Freudian accounts of their own and others' motivations" (446).

As we shall see, not everyone is convinced that psychoanalysis has the resources to provide a satisfactory account of the horror genre. Besides which, it is possible to invoke psychoanalytic concepts in this context *without* focusing on Freud,[2] much less his (admittedly sketchy) theory of the uncanny.[3] To make matters even more complicated, partly as a result of its sketchiness Freud's theory of the uncanny can be applied to the horror genre in a number of different ways. But this multitude of alternatives need not intimidate us, at least not until they are all shown to be mutually exclusive. To the extent that the account of horror film monsters presented here is plausible (however one wishes to cash out the notion of "plausibility"), to that extent will the means used to arrive at this account be justified.

The thesis to be defended here, in four parts, is as follows: (1) paradigmatic horror narratives work by *reconfirming* for audiences infantile beliefs that were abandoned long ago, such as the belief in the ability of the dead to return to life; (2) horror film monsters are best understood as *metaphorical embodiments* of such narratives. As such, they are capable of reconfirming surmounted beliefs by their very presence; (3) these metaphorical embodiments are *conceptual*, not merely cinematographic, which is to say that they exist in the mind, not just on the screen; and (4) although the metaphorical nature of horror film monsters is psychologically *necessary*, their surface heterogeneity is historically and culturally *contingent*. Not only is it the case that "the monster is the reification, the embodiment in a symbol, of an unconscious content in the mind" (Cawson 1); it is also the case that "the monster...is an embodiment of a certain cultural moment—of a time, a feeling, and a place" (Cohen 2).

What makes horror film monsters at least *potentially* horrifying—what makes them monsters to begin with—is the fact that they metaphorically embody surmounted beliefs; to the extent that they *actually succeed* in horrifying viewers, however, it is because the manner in which they embody surmounted beliefs is invested with cultural relevance. James Iaccino, submitting the horror genre to what he calls (following Jung) "archetypal analysis," arrives at a similar conclusion: "As civilization progresses to higher stages of consciousness, newer interpretations of those age-old [horror] myths become necessary so that the links with humankind's archaic past can be appropriately maintained" (181). Iaccino thinks it "quite appropriate to refer to the new archetypes as *technomyths*, reflecting the technological advances that our society has attained" (181); our "cultural relevance" condition, in contrast, encompasses not merely the *technological*, but also the political, racial, religious, and sexual dimensions of society. And here, what gets reflected is often anything but an "advance."[4]

This same bias towards the present can be detected in an otherwise innocuous comment made by Barbara Creed: "The horror film is populated by female monsters, many of which seem to have evolved from images that haunted the dreams, myths and artistic practices of our forbears many centuries ago" (1). Point well taken, but why speak of changes in the face of the (here, female) monster in *evolutionary* terms? At the very least it is misleading to suggest that representations of monstrosity from ages past can be understood as "primitive" in comparison with those of today (cf. Iaccino's talk of civilization *progressing* to "higher stages of consciousness"). One might put the point as follows: although the face of the monstrous *varies* from time to time, and from place to place, there is no reason to believe that in doing so it becomes any more *horrific*. Placing a value-neutral "cultural relevance" condition on the efficacy of horror film monsters respects the fact that change does not always imply advancement.[5] A number of post-1960 horror films (e.g. *Targets* [1967], *Martin* [1971], *The Funhouse* [1981], *The Howling* [1981], *Frightmare* [1982], and *Popcorn* [1991]) have thematized the impotence of classic monsters when confronting today's supposedly more "sophisticated" audiences. But it is hard to believe that Freddy, Jason, Michael, or Pinhead would have been more horrifying to pre-1960 audiences than were Dracula, the Wolf Man, Frankenstein's Monster, or the Mummy.[6]

What follows is an attempt to show how a psychoanalytic explanation of monstrosity in terms of uncanniness may be compatible with a postmodernist explanation of monstrosity in terms of sociohistorical conditioning. Halberstam is mistaken when she claims that "monstrosity (and the fear it gives rise to) is historically conditioned *rather than* a psychological universal" (6: emphasis added); when it comes to horror film monsters, the domains of history and psychology are *not* mutually exclusive. By presenting (in broad outline, it must be admitted) a "two-tiered" theory of monstrosity, the goal is to blur—if not collapse—the sharp distinction that is usually made between *universalizing* accounts of the horror genre, those assuming "a social ontology wherein human agents are pre-constituted in key respects," and *particularistic* accounts, those assuming a social ontology "centered on active social agents who...use cultural artifacts as resources in rendering coherent their everyday lives" (Tudor 460).[7]

Freud[8]

> *(1) Paradigmatic horror narratives work by* reconfirming *for audiences infantile beliefs that were abandoned long ago.*

In 1906, the German psychologist Ernst Jentsch wrote a paper in which he hypothesized that the essential factor responsible for the production of uncanny feelings is intellectual uncertainty, those doubts and confusions which are liable to arise when we come across something completely unfamiliar in a foreign ("alien") environment. In his own paper on the subject, Freud concedes the *prima facie* plausibility of Jentsch's view, according to which feelings of uncanniness regarding objects and events in our immediate surroundings decrease as a function of our comfort level: the more we feel at home in our surroundings ("unhomely" is a more precise translation of the German word "unheimlich," from which the term "uncanny" was originally derived), the less likely we are to feel frightened there. But Freud's dissatisfaction with this view surfaces when he calls attention to the fact that clearly not *everything* instilling in us a sense of uncanniness is something we find alien or confusing. Attacking Jentsch on the grounds that intellectual uncertainty could not be a necessary condition of uncanny feelings, he urges his readers to resist the temptation "to conclude that what is uncanny is frightening precisely because it is not known and familiar" (341).

Freud proceeds by teasing out a secondary, and to some extent contradictory, meaning of the German word "heimlich": *concealed; kept from sight; withheld from others so that they cannot get to know of or about it.* This meaning serves to ground Freud's alternative explanation of uncanny phenomena, according to which "the uncanny is in reality nothing new or alien, but something which is familiar and old-established in the mind and which has become alienated from it only through the process of repression" (363). Or as he puts it a little later on: "[T]he *unheimlich* is what was once *heimlich*, familiar; the prefix '*un*' is the token of repression" (364). To support his radical thesis, Freud traces the most prominent uncanny themes back to infantile sources. Conceptual connections are established between, for example, womb phantasies and the terrify-

ing thought of being buried alive, the castration complex and the shocking sight of a severed limb, the instinctual compulsion to repeat and the
eerie recurrence of unexpected events.

It is often held that Freud identifies repressed infantile wishes as the
sole source of uncanny feelings. Thus, in his introduction to a casebook
on Gothic literature, Victor Sage claims that "the whole shape of [horror]
fiction for author and reader alike becomes, in Freud's view, a distorted
projection of desire for the womb" (23). Strictly speaking, however, "the
return of the repressed" constitutes only one class of uncanny phenomena. In his paper, Freud also identifies a *second* class of the uncanny,
constituted by surmounted beliefs which gain some measure of validation in either experienced or depicted reality. In response to something
which seems to confirm our long-since discarded (or so we thought) beliefs in the ability of the dead to return to life, the omnipotence of
thoughts, and the existence of a double, we get a feeling of uncanniness:
"we have *surmounted* these modes of thought; but we do not feel quite
sure of our new beliefs, and the old ones still exist within us, ready to
seize upon any confirmation" (370-71). Here, what has been relegated to
the unconscious is a *belief in the reality* of a particular ideational content,
rather than a particular ideational content *itself.*

Admittedly, "the reconfirmation of the surmounted" sounds less ele-
gant than "the return of the repressed"; nevertheless, the former too occupies a position of central importance in Freud's theory of the uncanny.
Tudor denies this, citing for support Freud's remark that only the class
of uncanny phenomena constituted by repressed infantile complexes is
guaranteed equal efficacy in fiction and reality.[9] But just because surmounted beliefs do not *necessarily* engender the same degree of uncanny
feeling when they are reconfirmed in fiction as opposed to reality, this
does not mean they *never* manage to do so. Quite the contrary. According to Freud, so long as a certain "conflict of judgment" condition on
this class of the uncanny is satisfied, the intensity of feeling evoked will
be the same—if not *greater*—in the depicted world. (We shall have more
to say about this "conflict of judgment" condition below.)

Freud does, however, view repressed infantile complexes as the more
fundamental class of uncanny phenomenon. Thus, "when we consider
that primitive beliefs are most intimately connected with infantile complexes, and are, in fact, based on them, we shall not be greatly
astonished to find that the distinction is often a hazy one" (372). In both
classes, uncanny feeling—as opposed to, say, mere intellectual recognition (of the ideational content, of the reconfirmed belief)—gets produced
the same way. Briefly, it is a tenet of psychoanalytic theory that anxiety
is the cause of repression. Therefore, with the unexpected return to con-

Above, **Funhouse**: Amy (Elizabeth Berridge) fends off a shower attack by her mon-
ster-masked little brother Joey (Shawn Carson) who is armed with a rubber knife.

sciousness of some previously repressed ideational content comes all of
the latent anxiety. And the same holds for the reconfirmation of primitive beliefs "intimately connected with...and...in fact, based on" that
same ideational content.[10]

Freud's qualification of "haziness" aside, the crucial points to keep in
mind here are (1) that a distinction between primitive beliefs and infantile complexes does exist, and (2) that despite the "intimate connection"
between them (the former are in some sense parasitic on the latter), this
distinction is still capable of being made. *Contra* Victor Sage, desire for
the womb does *not* shape the whole of horror fiction according to Freud.
And *contra* Robin Wood, the *true* subject of horror cinema may be less
"the struggle for recognition of all that our civilization represses or oppresses" than the struggle for validation of all that our civilization dis-
avows or denies.

> (2) *Horror film monsters are best understood as metaphorical
> embodiments of paradigmatic horror narratives, and as such,
> are capable of reconfirming surmounted beliefs by their very
> presence.*

In a recent article, Ivan Ward calls for a distinction between "the
narratives of [cinematic] horror and the images" (274). Following Freud,
one might begin to effect such a distinction by associating the most
disturbing *images* of horror cinema with the return to consciousness of
previously repressed ideational content, and the most frightening

narratives with the confirmation in depicted reality of previously surmounted beliefs. One perhaps surprising consequence of this approach is that the overwhelming majority of horror film monsters turn out to be not so much literal manifestations of paradigmatic uncanny images as metaphorical embodiments of paradigmatic uncanny narratives. Such a view diverges sharply from the one endorsed by a number of contemporary psychoanalytic-minded theorists, namely, the view that horror film monsters represent in various ways male fears of castration.[11]

On the "surmounted belief model" proposed here, the stars of classic reanimation tales--mummies, zombies, the Frankenstein monster--can be viewed as more or less distinct embodiments of our surmounted belief in the ability of the dead to return to life; a belief which, subject to certain conditions, gets reconfirmed by their very presence. Freud himself lends support in favor of this hypothesis: "many people experience the [uncanny] feeling in the highest degree in relation to...the return of the dead, and to spirits and ghosts" (364). Again, the stars of classic counterpart tales—doppelgangers, werewolves, murderous alter-egos (á la Mr. Hyde)—can be viewed as more or less distinct embodiments of our surmounted belief in the existence of a double (a psychological invention which provides infants with insurance against the threat of death and/or the destruction of the ego).[12]

In *The Omen* (1980), there is a memorable scene in which a large sheet of plate glass flies out from the back of a moving truck and decapitates someone, all as a result of demonic intervention. Although there is a minimum of gore, we are left with a disturbing image of the victim's head spinning end over end in mid-air. If what has been claimed here so far is correct, the effectiveness of this scene results primarily (though perhaps not solely) from its success in bringing back to consciousness the content of repressed infantile castration complexes (or their female equivalents[13]). The same holds true for all those scenes in which spectacle takes precedence over storyline. But in order to understand what makes Damien, the monstrous devil-child of *The Omen*, himself so disturbing, we need to ask which paradigmatic horror narrative (or narratives) he metaphorically embodies, and so which surmounted belief (or beliefs) his presence reconfirms for viewers. Considering Damien's uncanny ability to cause death in all manner of indirect ways, a preliminary answer would be that he metaphorically embodies a paradigmatic "psychic" narrative, thereby reconfirming our previously surmounted belief in the omnipotence of thought. Insofar as his birth signifies the return of Satan, however, he may *also* be said to metaphorically embody a paradigmatic reincarnation narrative, thereby reconfirming our pre-

viously surmounted belief in the ability of dead souls to return to life.
(Like many of his monstrous cohorts, Damien is a mixed metaphor.)

As was pointed out earlier, not *all* horror film monsters manage to
fulfill their primary purpose. Tudor, in presenting his case against universalizing accounts of horror cinema, stresses the fact that "precisely
the same representation of a monster can be found frightening, repulsive, hideous, pitiful, or laughable by audiences in different social circumstances and at different times." (456) Of course, the degree to which
a monster succeeds in horrifying viewers is, to a large extent, a matter of
age, personal history, and taste (or lack thereof). But there is a further
aspect of Freud's theory which may help to explain the fact that, although two (or more) monsters can metaphorically embody the *same*
surmounted belief, this by no means guarantees that both (or all) of
them will successfully engender feelings of uncanniness/horror.

Freud makes an important distinction in his paper between the *experienced* uncanny and the *depicted* uncanny. With respect to that class of uncanny phenomena stemming from repressed infantile complexes, it
makes little difference whether the return to consciousness takes place
in real life or in fiction. As was noted above, we are as apt to feel a sense
of horror reading about a dismemberment, for example, as we are actually witnessing one (although there can be little doubt that actually witnessing a dismemberment would be more *traumatizing* than merely
reading about one). With respect to that class of uncanny phenomena
proceeding from surmounted beliefs, however, the domain in which reconfirmation takes place makes a *huge* difference. In everyday life, a reconfirmation of that which has been surmounted almost always
produces uncanny feelings. In fiction, however, such feelings do not
arise unless there is a palpable "conflict of judgment" regarding the possibility of reconfirmation in reality. What we must believe, in spite of
our "better" (mature, conditioned, rational) judgment, is that the objects
or events being depicted really could exist or happen. But note: this is
not to say that what we must believe, in spite of our better judgment, is
that the objects (events) being depicted really *do* exist (really *are* happening).[14]

In reading works of fiction, "we adapt our judgment to the imaginary
reality imposed on us by the writer" (Freud 374). This applies to works
of film, as well. In the animistic worlds depicted in fantasy ("sword-and-
sorcery") cinema, for example, there is nothing uncanny or otherwise
horrifying about the reconfirmation of infantile beliefs in the omnipotence of thought and the prompt fulfillment of wishes; according to
Freud, this is because most of us are well aware of the fact that curses,
charms, magic spells, and the like are regular, everyday events in the

Fantasy Universe. Freud's "conflict of judgment" condition thus goes a long way towards explaining why, when we watch horror films starring Dracula, Frankenstein's monster, or the Wolf Man today, it often feels instead like we are watching R-rated fairy tales. Although the traditional/canonical monsters of horror cinema are just as *threatening* as they used to be, our overfamiliarity with the fictional worlds these monsters inhabit has rendered ineffective their efforts to horrify, since they no longer engender in us the requisite conflict of judgment. That is not to say that the *narratives* these monsters metaphorically embody have ceased serving as a source of uncanniness; rather, it is to say that the *manner in which* these narratives are metaphorically embodied has become outdated.[15]

Three recent trends in horror cinema can be viewed as attempts to sidestep, at least temporarily, this critical problem of audience overfamiliarity. One is the introduction of ever more bizarre, alien, and/or inchoate monsters (e.g. those in *Event Horizon* [1997], *Mimic* [1997], and *Phantoms* [1998]), monsters whose sheer novelty is supposed to overcome the conventionality of the fictional worlds they inhabit. A second is the creative merging of realistic serial killers with demonic, otherwordly forces, in films such as *Exorcist III* (1990), *The Frighteners* (1996), and *Fallen* (1998). Here, the writer/director "betrays us to the superstitiousness which we have ostensibly surmounted; he deceives us by promising to give us the sober truth, and then after all overstepping it" (Freud 374). And a third is the extreme self-reflexivity of "neo-stalkers" such as *Scream* (1996), *Halloween H^2O* (1998), and *Urban Legend* (1998). In these movies, survival depends not only on knowing the conventions of modern horror cinema, but on figuring out how to *use* that knowledge in order to break free of these conventions. Concomitant with the latter, of course, is a renewed opportunity for audiences to have a conflict of judgment.

Herein lies a Freudian answer to the question how horror film monsters are able to horrify, considering the fact that audiences are fully aware of their fictional status. Because a belief in the legitimate possibility of reconfirmation is enough to produce a conflict of judgment, a belief in the *actual existence* of horror film monsters (or the paradigmatic narratives they metaphorically embody) is not necessary to generate feelings of uncanniness/horror. Noel Carroll, in his provocative study, *The Philosophy of Horror; or Paradoxes of the Heart* (1990), fails to note this difference between actual and possible existence beliefs. Wisely rejecting the blanket assumption that "we are only moved emotionally where we believe that the object of our emotion exists," Carroll goes too far in the other direction, claiming (a) that "the thought of a fearsome

and disgusting character like Dracula is something that can be enter-
tained without believing that Dracula exists," and (b) that "thought contents we entertain without believing them can genuinely move us
emotionally" (80-81).

By itself, (a) is utterly harmless. But combined with (b), it is simply
mistaken. The mere *entertaining* in one's mind of a horror film monster is
insufficient to generate fear; at the very least, it renders the production of
such an emotional response either mysterious or irrational. Unless a belief in the possible existence of such a being (however fleeting this belief
may be), is *presupposed* by the activity of entertaining, there is nothing—
certainly nothing rational—for the fear to latch on to. We may agree with
Carroll's so-called "Thought-Theory of Emotional Responses to Fiction"
when it comes to the "return of the repressed" class of uncanny phenomena. But that is just because, what generates the uncanniness/horror here
is a return to consciousness of some particular ideational content and
nothing else . When it comes to the "reconfirmation of the surmounted"
class of uncanny phenomena, where most horror film monsters are to be
found, possession of a *possible* (not an *actual*) existence belief is required
for the necessary conflict of judgment to occur.

Let me diverge for a moment to respond to an objection raised by
Carroll against the bringing to bear of psychoanalytic considerations in
analyses of the horror genre. Near the end of his book, Carroll takes aim
at Wood's return of the repressed argument: "it is not clear to me that
monsters...much touch any infantile traumas or repressed wishes or
anxieties" (172). After citing as a "pertinent counterexample" the man-
and woman-eating cephalods from H.G. Wells' short story "The Sea
Raiders"monsters he claims are wholly *lacking* in latent psychic content,
Carroll concludes that "the psychoanalytic reduction of horrific creatures to objects of repression is not comprehensive for the genre; not all
horrific creatures portend psychic conflict or desire" (173). His own, *non*-
psychoanalytic characterization of horror film monsters invokes the
work of noted anthropologist Mary Douglas, who attributes feelings of
disgust and aversion to apparent transgressions or violations of cultural
categories: "given a monster in a horror story, the scholar can ask in
what ways it is categorically interstitial, contradictory (in Douglas'
sense), incomplete, or formless....[M]onsters...are unnatural relative to a
culture's conceptual scheme of nature. They do not fit the scheme; they
violate it" (34).[16]

Freud's central claim, that feelings of uncanniness result *either* from a
return of the repressed *or* from a reconfirmation of the surmounted, is
glossed by Carroll as follows: "To experience the uncanny...is to experi-

ence something that is known, but something the knowledge of which has been hidden or repressed" (175). Not bad for a start, but what about the experience of something the *belief* in which has been *abandoned* or *surmounted*? In light of what has been said thus far, it should be evident that by identifying repressed infantile complexes as the sole source of uncanniness/horror in psychoanalytic theory, Carroll is guilty of the same mistake as Victor Sage (and perhaps Robin Wood, as well). But Carroll goes on to make the additional mistake of throwing the baby out with the bathwater, taking the inadequacy of the return of the repressed argument as a reason to reject *all* psychoanalytic accounts of the horror genre (though he concedes that "psychoanalysis nevertheless may still have much to say about particular works, subgenres, and cycles within horror" [168]).

Because he ignores the "reconfirmation of the surmounted" class of uncanny phenomena, Carroll is tempted by an explanation of monstrosity which, at the end of the day, amounts to little more than an anthropologically-informed recapitulation of the Jentschian position so soundly defeated by Freud in his 1919 paper. According to Carroll, "monsters are not only physically threatening; they are cognitively threatening. They are threats to common knowledge. [M]onsters are in a certain sense challenges to the foundations of a culture's way of thinking" (34). This appeal to "cognitive threat" as the source of our simultaneous fascination and disgust with horrific monsters is reminiscent of Jentsch's appeal to "intellectual uncertainty" as the source of our feelings of uncanniness:

> Most people...incorporate the new and the unusual with mistrust, unease and even hostility... This can be explained to a great extent by the difficulty of establishing quickly and completely the conceptual connections that the object strives to make with the previous ideational sphere of the individual—in other words, the intellectual mastery of the new thing (8).

As a perhaps unsuspecting neo-Jentschian, Carroll's position is open to a revised version of Freud's original criticism: since clearly not *every* monster that successfully instills in us a sense of horror or uncanniness is "categorically interstitial, incomplete, or formless," cognitive threat could not be a necessary condition of uncanny feelings.

Even if we *accept* Carroll's highly counterintuitive claim, that horror film monsters must be "of either a supernatural or a sci-fi origin" (15), and so agree not to count against him the plethora of realist horror film monsters such as Norman Bates, Leatherface, and Jerry Blake (of *Stepfa-*

ther fame), cognitive threat-*qua*-categorical interstitiality *still* seems inessential. The entire class of psychic monsters (which includes Carrie, Patrick[17], and the eponymous "Scanners"), in fact, tells against the necessity of this condition, as the power of these monsters to horrify can be traced to external effects rather than internal properties.[18] Carroll's ulterior motive in analyzing the ontological status of horror film monsters is to distinguish the emotion of "art-horror" from that of (presumably, "art-") fear. This leads him to regard horror film monsters as both "threatening *and* impure. If the monster were *only* evaluated as potentially threatening, the emotion would [simply] be fear" (28: emphasis added). We shall leave it an open question whether Carroll's strategy works; for our purposes, it suffices to note (1) that his analysis most naturally fits the class of reincarnated monsters, whose members obviously transgress cultural categories in virtue of their "living dead" status; and (2) that his analysis only works for other classes/kinds of monsters if we apply the notion of categorical interstitiality with generous *ad hoc* breadth. Clearly, an alternative analysis is warranted.

That said, it is highly unlikely that every horror film monster, much less every monster in the whole of horror fiction, can be understood *solely* in terms of the "reconfirmation of the surmounted." Some of them—e.g. the Headless Horseman and the Beast With Five Fingers (a severed hand with a mind of its own)—may strike us as falling squarely within the "return of the repressed" category. And let us grant Carroll, at least for the sake of argument, that Wells' cephalods *are* frightening primarily because they are cognitively threatening. Even if we allow for a minority of monsters who correspond neither to repressed infantile complexes nor to surmounted infantile beliefs, however, would this be such a bad thing so far as our overall project is concerned? After all, one of the major criticisms levied against psychoanalytic theory in general, and its application to the horror genre in particular, is its propensity for self-confirmation.[19]

The account of horror film monsters presented here is not intended to serve as a strict, much less an "essential," definition; rather, it is intended to serve as an interpretive tool for the understanding and construction of cinematic representations of monstrosity. As such, it can withstand the pressure of a few *prima facie* counterexamples.[20] Near the end of his paper, Freud himself cautions that "we must be prepared to admit that there are other elements besides those which we have so far laid down as determining the production of uncanny feelings" (370). And if *Freud* can admit of "other elements," we certainly can too.

Lakoff

(3) Horror film monsters are conceptual, *not merely cinematographic, metaphors.*

It is one thing for metaphors to appear in a literary work; is it another thing—or perhaps no thing at all—for metaphors to appear in a *cinematic* work? Although not everyone agrees that the "metaphorical transformation of ideas exists in film" (Markgraf 46), Trevor Whittock, in an influential study, concludes that metaphor can come from the "role [of an image] in the thematic or narrative development of the film,...its place in social beliefs or customs, even its cultural and historical setting" (39). If horror film monsters really *are* metaphorical embodiments of paradigmatic uncanny narratives, and their role really *is* to reconfirm previously surmounted beliefs by their very presence, then what we need now is a theory of metaphor which can support and help to explicate this phenomenon.

George Lakoff has provided copious and convincing evidence for the view that "the locus of metaphors is not in language at all" (203), but in thought. According to Lakoff, metaphors function by facilitating an understanding of one conceptual domain in terms of another, usually more concrete, conceptual domain. Take the familiar LOVE IS A JOURNEY metaphor: here, entities from the "target domain" of love (e.g. lovers, their common goals, the love relationship) are understood in terms of entities from the "source domain" of traveling (travelers, destinations, the vehicle used to get there). This explains the ease with which we traffic in such metaphorical expressions as "their relationship is going nowhere," "they're stuck in the slow lane," and "she's got control of the wheel." The ontological correspondences constituting the LOVE IS A JOURNEY metaphor, and thousands of others, are *tightly structured,* insofar as target domain entities typically preserve the logical features of (and relations between) source domain entities. They are *conventional,* in that they function as relatively fixed parts of a culture's shared conceptual system. And they exist in a *hierarchical organization,* whereby "lower" mappings inherit correspondence features from "higher" mappings. To illustrate this last point, note that the understanding of, for instance, *difficulties* in terms of *impediments to travel* occurs not only in the PURPOSEFUL LIFE IS A JOURNEY metaphor (e.g. "From now on, it's going to be smooth sailing"), but also in the "lower-level" LOVE IS A JOURNEY metaphor (e.g. "Their relationship is rocky"), as well as in the "lower-level" CAREER IS A JOURNEY metaphor (e.g. "His rise to the top has hit a snag").

Three features of Lakoff's theory make it appealing in the present context. First, his emphasis on the conceptual, rather than linguistic, basis of metaphor satisfies our need for a theory which readily accommodates (or at least does not discriminate against) *cinematic* representations of monstrosity. Lakoff repeatedly stresses that, in his theory, "the language is secondary. The mapping is primary" (208). This is crucial, considering that in our theory, those narratives serving to reconfirm surmounted beliefs are "embodied" not in language, but by horror film monsters. In other words, the medium of our metaphor is primarily *visual*, rather than verbal.

Second, the conventional nature of conceptual metaphors goes a long way towards accounting for the seemingly ubiquitous presence of horror film monsters in our culture. Just as the Love is a Journey metaphor has become so much a feature of our unreflective thought and speech that we often fail to recognize particular instances of it *as* metaphor, fascination with—one might say affection for—the monsters of horror cinema has become so widespread that most of us have no need to stop and figure out just which uncanny narratives they metaphorically embody. Dracula, Freddy, Jason, and company are referred to in songs, star in cartoons, appear on postage stamps... some even have breakfast cereals named after them! For better or worse, the metaphorical nature of horror film monsters has facilitated their entrance into our collective consciousness.

Third, the systematic and hierarchical organization of conceptual metaphors helps to account for the intuitive plausibility of a "surmounted belief" horror film monster typology. The utility of arranging what looks at first to be a seemingly incommensurable mass of monsters in a system that is both theoretically acceptable and aesthetically satisfying has recently been remarked upon by Gregory Waller. In his introduction to a valuable collection of essays on the modern American horror film, Waller writes that "a fully developed typology of monsters would offer a valuable means of delineating the paradigmatic possibilities open to this genre and the sort of fears that will suitably trouble its audience" (9). Ironically, the reverse turns out to be the case. Starting with "the paradigmatic possibilities open to this genre and the sort of fears that will suitably trouble its audience," we discover a valuable means of delineating "a fully developed typology of monsters." In turn, however, this typology can serve to motivate additional insights into the means and ends of horror cinema. According to Lakoff, metaphorical mappings do not occur in isolation from one another.[21] Neither, as we shall see, do horror film monsters.

In light of our earlier discussion, and considering the three features of Lakoff's theory just mentioned, there is ample grounds for hypothesizing the existence of a SURMOUNTED BELIEFS ARE HORROR FILM MONSTERS conceptual metaphor, according to which entities from the relatively abstract source domain of surmounted beliefs are understood in terms of entities from the far more concrete target domain of horror film monsters. The former domain is "relatively abstract" because surmounted beliefs are propositional states with content that can only achieve literal reconfirmation *narratologically*: the surmounted belief that the dead are capable of returning to life (as opposed to, say, the belief that I am hungry) requires a whole *series* of events to take place before its truth can be (re-) confirmed. Freud would seem to concur: "apparent death and the return of the dead have been represented as uncanny *themes*" (369: emphasis added).

The latter domain, in contrast, is "far more concrete" for the obvious reason that horror film monsters are visual representations intended to engender a sense of horror/ uncanniness in viewers by their very presence. The claim here is that, as symbolic correlates of surmounted beliefs, horror film monsters can achieve (metaphorical) reconfirmation *pictorially* and therefore all at once. Given the requisite conflict of judgment (by no means an easy condition to satisfy), the very act of watching a horror film monster onscreen reconfirms for viewers whichever previously surmounted beliefs are associated with the paradigmatic narratives that monster embodies.

In keeping with Freud, we can effect an initial breakdown of the SURMOUNTED BELIEFS ARE HORROR FILM MONSTERS conceptual metaphor along the following lines:[22]

> I. surmounted Beliefs that the dead can return to life are **reincarnated** monsters
>
> II. surmounted Beliefs in the omnipotence of thought are **psychic** monsters
>
> III. surmounted Beliefs in the existence of a double are **dyadic** monsters

Each of these levels has at least one sub-level, whereby "lower" monsters inherit correspondence features from "higher" monsters. So, for example, beneath the SURMOUNTED Beliefs that the dead can return to life are reincarnated monsters level, we find the SURMOUNTED BELIEFS THAT DEAD *BODIES* CAN RETURN TO LIFE ARE *ZOMBIES* level (monsters here include the Mummy, Frankenstein's monster, the innumerable victims of Romero's *Living*

Table I: The SURMOUNTED BELIEFS ARE HORROR FILM MONSTERS conceptual metaphor

I. surmounted beliefs that the dead can return to life are **Reincarnated** Monsters

    A. surmounted beliefs that dead bodies can return to life are zombies

        1. **non-natural zombies**: *Dracula, The Mummy, The Golem*, Jason, *Night of the Living Dead*

        2. **medico-scientific zombies**: Frankenstein's monster, *The Crazies, Shivers, Rabid*

    B. surmounted beliefs that dead souls can return to life are **spirits**

        1. **disembodied souls**: ghosts, haunted houses (*The Haunting, Poltergeist, Amityville Horror*)

        2. **embodied souls**: demonic possessions (*The Exorcist, Fallen*), *Candyman*, Chuckie

II. surmounted beliefs in the omnipotence of thought are **Psychic** Monsters

    A. surmounted beliefs in the prompt fulfillment of wishes are **telekinetics**: Carrie, Freddy

    B. surmounted beliefs in mental transparency are **telepathics**: *Patrick, Scanners*, (vampires)

III. surmounted beliefs in the existence of a double are **Dyadic** Monsters

    A. surmounted beliefs in the existence of physical doubles are **replicas**

        1. surmounted beliefs in the existence of natural replicas are **doppelgangers**

            (a) twins: *Sisters, Dead Ringers, Raising Cain*

            (b) clones: *Invasion of the Body Snatchers*

            (c) chameleons: Carpenter's *The Thing, Phantoms*

        2. surmounted beliefs in the existence of non-natural replicas are **replicants**

            (a) robots: *The Stepford Wives, Westworld*

            (b) cyborgs: *Bladerunner, Terminator*

    B. surmounted beliefs in the existence of mental doubles are **psychos**

        1. **schizos** [same body, different consciousness]: Norman Bates, *Dressed To Kill*, (*Sisters*)

        2. **shape-shifters** [same body, physical transformation]: Jekyll-Hyde, werewolves, vamps

        3. **projections** [different body]: *The Brood*, (Frankenstein's monster)

        4. **serial killers** [same body, same consciousness]: Henry, Lechter,

Dead Trilogy, and Jason Vorhees), as well as the SURMOUNTED
BELIEFS THAT DEAD *SOULS* CAN RETURN TO LIFE ARE *SPIRITS*
level (monsters here include ghosts, haunted houses, and the
possessed). In turn, each of *these* levels has at least one sub-level of its
own. **Table I** on the previous page is an attempt at elucidating the
hierarchical organization of this metaphor (note that the terminological
choices are, to some extent, arbitrary, and that a number of more
particularistic taxonomies may very well be compatible with this one).
Perhaps as should have been expected, many of horror cinema's most
enduring monsters turn out to be mixed metaphors (recall our
discussion of Damien), insofar as their presence reconfirms *more than one*
surmounted belief.

Conclusion: the representation of monstrosity in cinematic horror

> *(4) Although the metaphorical nature of horror film monsters is
> psychologically necessary, their surface heterogeneity is
> historically and culturally contingent.*

Among the advantages of aligning our psychoanalytic explanation of
horror film monsters with Lakoff's conceptual theory of metaphor is
that we now have the resources to explain away the apparent
incompatibility between universalizing and particularistic accounts of
monstrosity. On the one hand, we know that the basic *types* of horror
film monsters—reincarnated monsters, psychic monsters, and dyadic
monsters—are psychologically necessary, in that the uncanny narratives
they metaphorically embody correspond to a specific, and limited, set of
infantile beliefs (namely, those which have been surmounted). What all
horror film monsters have in common, besides the fact that they are not
real, is that they all fall under the SURMOUNTED BELIEFS ARE
HORROR FILM MONSTERS conceptual metaphor. On the other hand,
due to the need for a conflict of judgment regarding the possibility of
reconfirmation in a depicted world, particular *tokens* of horror film
monsters (i.e. those at lower levels of the inheritance hierarchy) are
historically and culturally contingent. All horror film monsters
metaphorically *embody* surmounted beliefs, but not all of them manage
to *reconfirm* those beliefs by their very presence; that is why not all of
them manage to fulfill their primary (that is, their horrifying) purpose.

  In order to instill a conflict of judgment in viewers, the *manner in
which* horror film monsters metaphorically embody surmounted beliefs
must be periodically updated; investing monsters with cultural relevance serves to "keep us in the dark about the precise nature of the pre-
suppositions on which the world [depicted in the film] is based" (Freud

374).[24] And how else could we willingly suspend our disbelief? The distinction being made here, between (universal) monster types and (particular) monster tokens, is theoretically explicable in terms of Lakoff's distinction between (general) superordinate level mappings and (specific) basic level mappings:

> It should come as no surprise that the generalization is at
> the superordinate level, while the special cases are at the
> basic level. After all, the basic level is at the level of rich
> mental images and rich knowledge structure... A mapping
> at the superordinate level maximizes the possibilities for
> mapping rich conceptual structures in the source domain
> onto the target domain, since it permits many basic level
> instances, each of which is information rich (212).

We might say: mappings at the superordinate level of monster *types* maximize the possibilities for satisfying Freud's conflict of judgment condition on the depicted uncanny, since it permits many basic level instances of monster *tokens*, each of which is (potentially) culturally relevant.

Considering that analyses of the horror genre informed by psychoanalytic theory are typically assumed to be universalizing in nature, it may come as something of a surprise to find that Wood's "return of the repressed" argument comes in handy at just this point. One finds in Wood an invocation of the post-Freudian distinction between *basic* repression, which is universal, necessary, and inescapable, and *surplus* repression, which is culture-specific and contingent, varying in both degree and kind with respect to different societies.[25] And when Wood talks about horror film monsters in terms of a "return of the repressed," what he really has in mind is a "return of the *surplus* repressed": "in a society built on monogamy and family there will be an enormous surplus of repressed sexual energy, and...what is repressed must always strive to return" (80).

The problem with Wood's account is that, by not sticking to the fundamental suppositions of Freud's theory of the uncanny, he fails to explain why horror film monsters are capable of horrifying us. We may mistrust, despise, even *fear* the objects of surplus repression in our society, but it is not at all obvious that we are *horrified* by them. Indeed, Wood suggests the possibility of extending his theory to genres other than horror: "substitute for 'Monster' the term 'Indian', for example, and one has a formula for a large number of classical Westerns; substitute 'transgressive woman' and the formula encompasses numerous melodramas..." (79). But if we can so easily extend this "return of the repressed" argument, why should we believe that it captures anything distinctive about the cinematic representation of monstrosity?

Wood concedes that, as opposed to the Indian (and the transgressive woman), "the monster is, of course, much more Protean, changing from period to period as society's basic fears clothe the୲ ۱selves in fashionable or immediately accessible garments" (79). In order to characterize these "basic fears," however, we must turn to the SURMOUNTED BELIEFS ARE HORROR FILM MONSTERS conceptual metaphor; it is only at the *particularistic* level of "fashionable or immediately accessible garments" that we may wish to invoke (with Wood) the objects of surplus repression.[26] Alternatively, this is just the point at which we might fruitfully employ/extend one or more of the wholly *non*-psychoanalytic particularistic accounts of monstrosity provided by Carroll, Cohen, Halberstam, et. al.[27] Following Lakoff, cultural updates of traditional/canonical horror film monsters can be understood as *novel extensions* of the SURMOUNTED BELIEFS ARE HORROR FILM MONSTERS metaphor. Due to the fact that this metaphor is a fixed part of our conceptual system, new and imaginative mappings are capable of being understood immediately: our integration of the novel extension is "a consequence of the preexisting ontological correspondences of the metaphor" (Lakoff 210).

An example will serve to illustrate this point: Abel Ferrara's *The Addiction* (1996) is a horror film that updates the vampire mythos in order to explore and comment on a number of contemporary social issues. Although the bleakness and philosophical pretensions of this movie guaranteed that it would not draw all that well at the box office, a number of critics had great things to say about it: "this is the vampire movie we've been waiting for: a reactionary, urban-horror flick that truly has the ailing pulse of the time. AIDS and drug addiction are points of reference, but they're symptoms, not the cause" (Charity 70). In Freudian-Lakoffian terms, the vampire/blood-addicts in this film can be viewed as novel extensions (i.e. cultural updates) of the SURMOUNTED BELIEFS THAT THE DEAD CAN RETURN TO LIFE ARE REINCARNATED MONSTERS sub-level metaphor; as such, they are able to produce in many viewers that conflict of judgment necessary for a feeling of uncanniness.[28]

To sum up. One (empirical) problem facing any universalizing account of horror film monsters is how to account for the fact that such monsters often *fail* to horrify viewers, and so fail to fulfill their primary purpose. This is where particularistic accounts come in. But particularistic accounts have their own (conceptual) problem, namely, that of accounting for what it is that makes horror film monsters horrifying *by their very nature*. Call back the universalizing accounts. So it appears that these two kinds of account must somehow be rendered compatible, in order for a complete story to emerge. This paper is a first attempt at rendering just such a compatibility, by filtering certain key aspects of Freud's theory of the uncanny through the lenses of Lakoff's conceptual theory of metaphor.

Some final considerations. In answer to the question, "Why do we have the conventional metaphors that we have?", Lakoff postulates that a great number of them are grounded in real life: "correspondences in real experience form the basis for correspondences in the metaphorical cases, which go beyond real experience" (240). So if the account of horror film monsters presented here is correct, then the paradigmatic horror narratives such monsters metaphorically embody are likely to have a basis in reality. To make matters even worse, conceptual metaphors have the capacity to impose themselves on real life "through the creation of new correspondences in experience" (241). Now *that's* a horrifying thought.[29]

Notes

1. Noel Carroll would deny the latter two claims. In *The Philosophy of Horror; or Paradoxes of the Heart*, he defines monsters as "any being[s] not believed to exist now by contemporary science" (27). But cf. Cynthia Freeland: "In realist horror like *Henry*, the monster is a true-to-life rather than supernatural being. Henry is a monster" (130). Other horror films with non-fictional monsters include *The Honeymoon Killers* (1969), and *Deranged* (1976).

2. See, e.g., Barbara Creed for a Kristevan focus; James Iaccino for a Jungian focus; and Slavoj Zizek, "Grimaces of the Real, Or When the Phallus Appears," *October* 58 (1991) for a Lacanian focus.

3. Chief among the many examples to be found here are Carol Clover, *Men, Women, and Chainsaws: Gender in the Modern Horror Film* (New Jersey: Princeton UP, 1992); Harvey Greenberg, *The Movies on Your Mind* (New York: Saturday Review Press, 1975); Stephen Neale, *Genre* (England: BFI Publishing, 1980); and James Twitchell, *Dreadful Pleasures: An Anatomy of Modern Horror* (Oxford: OUP, 1985).

4. David Cronenberg is perhaps the most famous/infamous director to build a career on the taking of contemporary social anxieties to horrific extremes (Larry Cohen and George Romero are others). A quick tour through his *oeuvre* turns up films which explore—some would say exploit—sexual perversity (*Stereo* [1969], *Shivers* [1975], *Crash* [1996]), medico-scientific epidemics (*Shivers*, *Rabid* [1977]), mass-media manipulation (*Videodrome* [1982], *eXistenZ* [1999]), drug addiction (*Dead Ringers* [1988], *Naked Lunch* [1991]), cancerphobia (*The Brood* [1979], *The Dead Zone* [1983]), and, arguably, AIDS-phobia (*The Fly* [1986]).

5. It is worth quoting David Skal in some length here. In his book, *The Monster Show: A Cultural History of Horror*, Skal writes:

> Most histories of the horror genre begin with mythological and literary
> antecedents—horrors and monsters of antiquity find a nineteenth-century
> expression in popular fiction that is borrowed and "improved" upon by
> the mass media of the twentieth century... In short, the story is presented as
> a simplistic and self-referential chronicle of "progress." Progress is not the
> issue. Very little about the underlying structure of horror images really
> changes, though our cultural uses for them are as shape-changing as
> Dracula himself (23).

6. It is interesting to note that in at least half of the movies mentioned above—
   The Funhouse, Frightmare, and *Popcorn*—the classic monsters get to take a revenge of sorts on those who would disregard, scorn, or mock them.

7. Note: Tudor employs the distinction between universalizing and particularistic accounts when discussing various responses to the question, "What is the
   appeal of horror?", not when discussing various responses to the question,
   "What is a horror film monster?"

8. Some of the paragraphs in this section restate material from my 1997 article,
   "Uncanny Realism and the Decline of the Modern Horror Film."

9. Tudor 447.

10. I am grateful to Ivan Ward of the Freud Museum, London for help with this
    paragraph

11. See, for example, Neale 61, and Susan Lurie, "The Construction of the 'Cas-
    trated Woman' in Psychoanalysis and Cinema," *Discourse* 4 (1981-82).

12. It is a fairly complicated question, whether the double signifies a "return of
    the repressed" (through its connection with primary narcissism and repeti-
    tion-compulsion) or a "reconfirmation of the surmounted." Most likely, it sig-
    nifies both to some extent. In "The 'Uncanny'," however, Freud comes down
    in favor of the latter, with his remark that "the quality of uncanniness can
    only come from the fact of the 'double' being a creation dating back to a very
    early mental stage, long since surmounted" (358). And cf. Otto Rank, who, in
    The Double: A Psychoanalytic Study, attributes "the significance of the dou-
    ble [to] an embodiment of the soul—a notion represented in primitive belief
    and living on in our superstition" (82-83).

13. It may be wiser in this context to speak of "castration anxieties," a phrase that
    is gender-neutral, rather than "castration complexes," a phrase with phallo-
    centric implications. Cf. Elizabeth Lloyd Mayer: "castration anxiety, in men or
    in women, is anxiety over losing that genital which is actually possessed. The
    castration complex, on the other hand, has traditionally referred to the girl's
    fantasy of having had a penis that was lost. Such a definition of the castration
    complex implies an essentially phallocentric experience and resolution of fe-
    male castration concerns" (332).

14. This suggests an indirect means of testing the validity of Freud's theory: deter-
    mine whether or not those who have never surmounted their primitive be-
    liefs—people who must fail to experience a conflict of judgment with regards

to the reconfirmation of such beliefs—are immune to uncanny effects. In "Animism, Magic and the Omnipotence of Thoughts," Freud calls attention to the fact that "the omnipotence of thoughts...is seen to have unrestricted play in the emotional life of neurotic patients" (108). Question: Do neurotic patients experience a sense of uncanniness/horror when their beliefs in the omnipotence of thought, etc. are reconfirmed? Cf. the "frank incomprehension" expressed by Denis Nilsen (a serial killer who operated in London during the 1970s and 80s) "in response to the outrage felt by most people who know how he disposed of the bodies: 'I can never quite understand a traditional and largely superstitious fear of the dead and corpses,' he writes" (Masters 160). At the other extreme—but with the same effect—Freud claims that "anyone who has completely and finally rid himself of animistic beliefs will be insensible to this type of the uncanny" ("The 'Uncanny'" 371).

15. I discuss in some detail the ramifications of Freud's "conflict of judgment" condition on the horror genre in "Uncanny Realism and the Decline of the Modern Horror Film."

16. Mary Douglas, *Purity and Danger: An Analysis of Concepts of Pollution and Taboo* (New York: Praeger, 1966).

17. From the 1978 movie of the same name.

18. Carroll apparently agrees with this, although the alternative, psychoanalytic explanation he provides is closer to Wood's "return of the repressed" argument than the "reconfirmation of the surmounted" one offered here. Carroll writes: "the recent popularity of telekinetic nastiness in films and novels...might be explained as gratifying the infantile conviction in the unlimited power of repressed rage...while at the same time costuming this repressed fantasy in the drapery of horror" (172).

19. See Karl Popper, *Conjectures and Refutations: The Growth of Scientific Knowledge* (New York: Basic Books, 1962) for this criticism of psychoanalytic theory in general; and see Carroll 171-74; Tudor 450-51; and Mark Jancovich, *Horror* (London: BT Batsford, 1992), p. 12 for this criticism of psychoanalytic theory as applied to the horror genre.

20. In a sense, the account of horror film monsters presented here is intended to bootstrap its way from the theoretical/descriptive to the practical/prescriptive.

21. Lakoff 222.

22. It is unclear whether or not Freud thinks there are additional surmounted beliefs universal enough to qualify as potential sources of uncanniness. At one point in "The 'Uncanny'," there is mention of "secret injurious powers" (370), but this surmounted belief would appear to fall within the more general "omnipotence of thought" category. In any event, even if additional surmounted beliefs of the kind Freud has in mind could be found (within Freud's corpus or outside it), this would not pose an insuperable problem for the account of horror film monstrosity presented here.

23. Besides or instead of the hero of the film, it is often the viewer who is invited/compelled to be the double here: we are monsters to the extent that we identify (aesthetically, emotionally, intellectually) with the killer. See, e.g., *Peeping Tom* (1960), *The Driller Killer* (1979), *White of the Eye* (1987), *Henry: Portrait of a Serial Killer* (1990), and *Silence of the Lambs* (1991).

24. Cf. Schneider: "The monsters in such films [e.g. *Night of the Living Dead, The Hills Have Eyes, Sisters, Rabid,* and Carpenter's *The Thing*] embody the same surmounted beliefs as their all-too-familiar predecessors; because they embody these surmounted beliefs in novel ways, however, they manage to induce in viewers a conflict of judgment regarding the (im-)possibility of their existence" (125).

25. Wood invokes the views of Herbert Marcuse in this context.

26. Cf. Iaccino: "audiences will continue to direct their attention to the wide screen in hopes that the horror prototypes of tomorrow will continue to elaborate on those Jungian archetypes of past decades" (35).

27. See also in this context Andrew Tudor, *Monsters and Mad Scientists: A Cultural History of the Horror Movie* (Oxford: Basil Blackwell, 1989).

28. Perhaps Ferrara's vampires are not *all* that novel: cf. Bob Clark's *Deathdream* (1972), and George Romero's *Martin* (1978).

29. An earlier version of this paper was read at the 1998 Festival of Original Theatre and Film, held at the University of Toronto and sponsored by the University of Toronto Graduate Centre for Study of Drama. It later appeared in *Other Voices: the (e-)Journal of Cultural Criticism* 1.3, 1999 http://dept.english.upenn.edu/~ov/1.3. Thanks to Michael Arnzen, Vance Bell, Barry Grant, Judith Halberstam, Ivan Ward and an anonymous reader at *Other Voices* for helpful comments and suggestions.

Works Cited

Carroll, Noel. *The Philosophy of Horror; or, Paradoxes of the Heart*. New York: Routledge, 1990.

Cavell, Stanley. **The Claim of Reason**. New York: OUP, 1979.

Cawson, Frank. *The Monsters in the Mind: the Face of Evil in Myth, Literature, and Everyday Life*. England: Book Guild, 1995.

Charity, Tom. "Preview: *The Addiction*." *Time Out* (London edition) 16-23 April, 1997.

Cohen, Jeffrey. "Monster Culture (Seven Theses)" in *Monster Theory: Reading Culture*, ed. Jeffrey Cohen. Minneapolis: University of Minnesota Press, 1996.

Creed, Barbara. *The Monstrous Feminine: Film, Feminism, Psychoanalysis*. New York: Routledge, 1993.

Freeland, Cynthia. "Realist Horror" in *Philosophy and Film*, ed. Cynthia Freeland and Thomas Wartenberg. New York: Routledge, 1995.

Freud, Sigmund. "Animism, Magic, and the Omnipotence of Thoughts" (1913) in *Totem and Taboo: Some Points of Agreement between the Mental Lives of Savages and Neurotics*, trans. and ed. James Strachey. New York: W.W. Norton, 1989.

"The 'Uncanny'" (1919) in *The Penguin Freud Library Volume 14: Art and Literature*, trans. and ed. James Strachey. London: Penguin, 1990.

Halberstam, Judith. *Skin Shows: Gothic Horror and the Technology of Monsters*. Durham: Duke UP, 1995.

Iaccino, James. *Psychological Reflections in Cinematic Terror: Jungian Archetypes in Horror Films*. Connecticut: Praeger, 1994.

Jancovich, Mark. *American Horror from 1951 to the Present*. England: Keele UP, 1994.

Jentsch, Ernst. "On the Psychology of the Uncanny" (1906). Reprinted in *Angelaki* 2.1 (1997).

Lakoff, George. "The Conceptual Theory of Metaphor" in *Metaphor and Thought* (2nd edition), ed. Andrew Ortony. New York: Cambridge UP, 1993.

Markgraf, Sarah. "Review of *Metaphor and Film*." *Metaphor and Symbolic Activity* 7.1 (1992).

Masters, Brian. *Killing for Company: the Case of Denis Nilsen*. London: J. Cape, 1985.

Mayer, Elizabeth Lloyd. "'Everybody must be just like me': Observations on Female Castration Anxiety." *International Journal of Psychoanalysis* 66 (1985).

Rank, Otto. *The Double: A Psychoanalytic Study* (1925), trans. Harry Tucker, Jr. London: Carnac, 1989.

Sage, Victor (ed.) *The Gothick Novel: A Casebook*. Basingstoke: Macmillan, 1990.

Scheffler, Israel. *Teachers of My Youth: An American Jewish Experience*. Boston: Kluwer Academic, 1995.

Schneider, Steven. "Uncanny Realism and the Decline of the Modern Horror Film." *Paradoxa: Studies in World Literary Genres* 3.3-4 (1997).

Skal, David. *The Monster Show: A Cultural History of Horror*. New York: W.W. Norton, 1993.

Tudor, Andrew. "Why Horror? The Peculiar Pleasures of a Popular Genre." *Cultural Studies* 11.3 (1997).

Waller, Gregory. "Introduction." *American Horrors: Essays on the Modern Horror Film*, ed. Gregory Waller. Chicago: University of Illinois Press, 1987.

Ward, Ivan. "Adolescent Phantasies and the Horror Film." *British Journal of Psychotherapy* 13.2 (1996).

Whittock, Trevor. *Metaphor and Film*. New York: Cambridge UP, 1990.

Wood, Robin. *Hollywood from Vietnam to Reagan*. New York: Columbia UP, 1986.

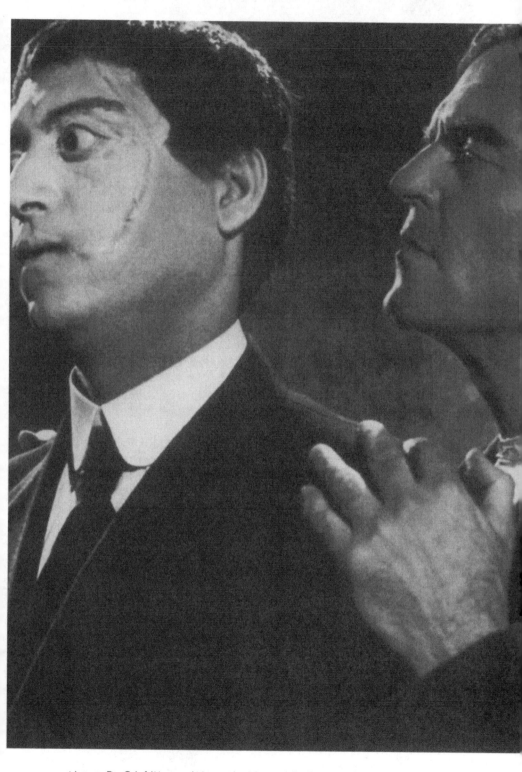

Above, Dr. Orlof (Howard Vernon) whispers into the ear of Morpho (Ricardo Valle), his zombie-llike assistant, who was turned into a ''bug-eyed 'sightless idiot''' by acting as a guinea pig for Orlof's experiments in *The Awful Dr. Orlof*.

The Anxiety of Influence: Georges Franju and the Medical Horror Shows of Jess Franco

Joan Hawkins

> "You're amazing, Doctor. And so _different_.."
>
> Nathalie to Dr. Moser, _Faceless_

For Europe's "low" horror directors, Georges Franju's _Eyes Without a Face_ (_Les Yeux sans Visage, The Horror Chamber of Dr. Faustus_, 1959) was an influential film. Its combination of traditional Sadeian motifs with what might be called the horror of postwar anatomical economy–too few faces to go around[1]–appealed to continental filmmakers who were trying to create a niche for themselves in a market heavily dominated by American and British horror. In addition, the film's invocation of death camp imagery seemed to lift a perhaps self-imposed political taboo. During the sixties and seventies Italian horror directors made a string of low budget SS sexploitation horror movies, frequently set in concentration camps. And the Nazi doctor–a figure of some anxiety in postwar Europe (just where exactly had all those sadistic physicians gone?)–showed up with increasing frequency in medico-horror tales.

In addition, the basic story of _Les Yeux sans Visage_–a father or other male relative kidnaps young women and surgically removes their faces in order to restore the face/beauty of his beloved daughter/sister/wife– became something of a stock tale in postwar European horror. Franju's movie was remade and reworked frequently, usually by directors who wanted to up the gore ratio. But at least one director–Spanish filmmaker Jess Franco–seemed to use _Les Yeux_'s story to push Eurohorror into a new, more overtly sexual arena, and in so doing, he changed the face of European horror.

Jésus (Jess) Franco is known primarily as the maker of what Mikita Brottman has called "cinéma vomitif,"[2] and, despite his second unit work on Orson Welles's _Chimes at Midnight_ (1965)[3] and his own later high budget work, he generally receives attention only in publications devoted to body genres and low culture. While the **BFI Companion to Horror** (1996) calls Franco (who has made over 160 feature films) "a hyperactive presence" on the post-1959 European film scene and devotes a full page to his work, for example, another BFI publication,*The Encyclopedia of European Cinema* (1995), does not give him an entry at all.[4]

To some extent, Franco's categorization as a "low" director is understandable. As Jim Morton points out, Franco often "makes his films quickly and seemingly with little regard to production values,"[5] and his graphic depictions of sex and violence link him to the category of "body genre" directors. Most of his films, as Jim Morton notes, are horror films "and several concern the exploits of women in prison... Because of their 'sexism' and 'bad taste,' his films are sometimes loathed by even staunch fans of weird films."[6]

While I've never seen Franco referred to as an "art" director, he does have a following of fans who appreciate his films as much for their paracinema aesthetics as for their affective emphasis on sex and gore. As Morton points out, his films have "a definite style and flavor,"[7] characterized by his "notorious" use of the zoom lens, his sometimes frantic dolly work, and what Cathal Tohill and Pete Tombs call an underlying jazz rhythm or beat.[8] At his best, Franco is an accomplished cinematographer. Orson Welles hired him to direct the second unit photography

Below, Edith Scob as the disfigured Christiane in **Les Yeux sans Visage**.

on *Chimes at Midnight,* and while some critics speculate that Welles's decision was influenced as much by the American director's vanity as it was by Franco's talent,[9] nobody underestimates the influence Welles had on the Spanish director.[10] Some of Franco's shot compositions are simply stunning. And his deep focus black and white work often screens like a low budget version of Welles/Toland's own.

At his worst, Franco can be sloppy. He makes his films quickly in order to give them a "different and spontaneous look;" and, as Tohill and Tombs point out, "sometimes it works, sometimes it doesn't" (88). The editing can be erratic. At times this leads to the syncopated jazz rhythm that critics praise in his work. At others, it simply leads to confusion, as narrative continuity is totally jettisoned for the sake of affect or economy. And for the uninitiated, the slow pace of Franco's early films can be maddening. As Tim Lucas–writing for *Video Watchdog*–notes, Franco can be "clumsy" and "numbingly dull."[11]

For many paracinephiles, though, any new Franco film is a big event.[12] Franco himself is considered one of paracinema's important auteurs. And his work is frequently discussed in auteurist terms. "If I've learned anything from watching 90 Franco films," Tim Lucas writes in one *Video Watchdog* article on the Spanish director, "it's that these movies cannot be watched in the same way one might view any comparable English-language releases. With the films of Richard Donner or John Badham (to use examples of Franco's own favorite contemporary American filmmakers), if you've seen one of their films, you've seen them all. With Franco's films it's different: <u>You can't see one *until* you've seen them all</u>. A degree of immersion is essential."[13] Franco is, he writes, "the Henry Jaglom of Horror–casting himself and his actor friends in anguished, blood-and-semen-scarred scenarios that tell you more about his inner life than you really want to know."[14] It isn't that these films are so exceptional in themselves, "indeed any one of them might seem just as disorienting or discouraging as any random selection to the Uninitiated–but rather that their maker's language at some indistinct moment begins to sink in, after one has seen a certain number of them, and this soft, persuasive language coalesces in some films more tangibly, more audibly, more obsessively, than in others."[15]

Here, as in Andrew Sarris's 1962 version of auteurist criticism, "the distinguishable personality of the director" is a "criterion of value." Part of the strength of Franco's work, Lucas argues, is that "over a group of films," he exhibits "certain recurrent characteristics of style, which serve as his signature." Indeed, Lucas argues, this is so much the case that it's impossible for a first-time viewer to watch one of Franco's films and "get it." The way his films look and move not only "have some relationship to the way...[Franco] thinks and feels,"[16] Lucas maintains, the way Franco thinks and feels is an essential component of the works themselves, constitutive of their idiosyncratic cinematic vocabulary. It's only through immersion in Franco's *complete* oeuvre–only through exposure to his total artistic and psychological development over time–that one can hope to understand the themes and language peculiar to the works.

The comparison Lucas draws between independent filmmaker Henry Jaglom and Jess Franco is an interesting one. Like Franco, Jaglom makes films for a specialized audience, and like Franco's horror movies, his arthouse flicks are an aquired taste. Jaglom specializes in Cassavetes-style productions, in which actors are encouraged to reveal a kind of inner truth in front of the camera. The films strive for a "spontaneous," improvised look, and they often deal with the way men and women view sex, love, family life, and friendship differently. Hence Lucas's comment about "blood-and-semen-scarred scenarios that tell you more about his [Jaglom's/Franco's] inner life than you really want to know."[17] The difference, of course, is that Franco doesn't push his actors to reveal themselves on camera the way Jaglom does; and, since he works in a genre with strict formulaic conventions, he is less interested in blurring the line between fiction and reality, more interested in simply telling a good story. To put it another way, Franco has fewer illusions than Jaglom has about fiction cinema's ability to get to the "truth."[18]

While Lucas compares Franco to Henry Jaglom, Tohill and Tombs situate him firmly in the Spanish tradition, likening him to compatriot auteurs like Luis Buñuel and Pedro Almodóvar. "There's something rigid and fossilized about the Spanish film industry," Tohill and Tombs write:

> Filmmakers like Almodóvar, Buñuel and Franco aren't exactly the norm inside Spain. They're outsiders and wild men, guys who have an unholy fascination with sex, excess, and the dreamlike potential of film. To these men, predictability means stagnation and death. Like Buñuel, Franco is a born rule breaker, a man driven to make his own brand of sex soaked cinema, a maverick trailblazer who personifies the untapped potential of film...Almodóvar, Buñuel and Franco are creative bedfellows. Each follows a different trajectory, but they all curve inexorably towards sex. Of the three, Franco has followed its steamy siren-call further and longer, he's taken his flesh-filled interest to the very limits of human imagination. (78-79).

While the rhetoric here is itself inflated and lionizing, the authors are right to link Franco to the other badboys of Spanish cinema. Like Buñuel, Franco brings a certain Surrealist sensibility to his work. And, like Almodóvar, Franco grew up in fascist Spain. That is, he came of filmmaking age in a political and social climate in which explicit depictions of sex and violence really were transgressive, revolutionary, often illegal.

Jess Franco began making horror films in the 1960s, sometimes called "los felices 60" (the happy 60s), a time of some liberalization in Spain. In 1962, Manuel Fraga was appointed as Minister of Information and Tourism. He was, as Tohill and Tombs note, "a cautious liberal" (63). In cooperation with another government minister, Cinema Supremo José Garcia Escudero, Fraga allowed the rigid censorship laws to relax a little. New laws were enacted to help Spanish producers, quota systems designed to help the Spanish film industry were put in place, and in 1967, a system of "special theaters" ("salas") modelled on the French ciné-clubs, allowed foreign films to be shown under "less rigid systems of control" (63).

This was "the Golden Age of Spanish cinema" under General Franco (Tohill and Tombs, 63). Genre films were popular and co-productions (copros) with other European countries gave Spanish directors a chance to work in the international arena, with American producers and directors as well as with European auteurs.[19] "Los felices 60" were, however, short-lived. At the end of the decade, social controls were tightened. The government was concerned by the rising number of cheap co-productions, and tried to limit them by imposing high minimum budgets. "This was combined with a general tightening up of the political situation, resulting in the removal of Fraga and an attempt to return to the 'good old days' of the 1950s. The immensely popular film clubs also came under close scrutiny" (Tohill and Tombs, 64).

But once a country's borders are opened, it's extremely difficult to close them again. In the 1970s, Spanish middle class audiences started going across the border to see forbidden films in France. "Special trips were arranged to Biarritz and Perpignan to see films like *Last Tango in Paris* or *Decameron* " (Tohill and Tombs, 64). French distributors were quick to seize on what seemed like a golden opportunity. Special "Spanish weeks"–in which films subtitled in Spanish would be shown to a largely Spanish audience–were arranged in the French border towns and advertised in the Spanish newspapers. As Tohill and Tombs describe it:

Every weekend during 1973 and through 1974, a regular convoy of battered Seat cars would descend on these border towns, and for years it was impossible to get a hotel room in Perpignan on a Friday or Saturday night. In 1973 five new cinemas opened there and *Last Tango in Paris*, a particularly hot item at the time, was seen by more than 150,000 viewers in the town's cinemas. With a population of 200,000 this is an astonishing figure. The cinemas would open their doors at ten in the morning and show films right up until midnight. Often keen Spaniards would catch three or four films in a weekend" (Tohill and Tombs, 64).[20]

Spanish horror was born out of financial necessity (Tohill and Tombs, 66). When the government tightened restrictions on cheap co-productions, the Spanish film industry needed to find films they could make cheaply and export (in order to recoup the costs of their bigger budget productions). Horror seemed the perfect choice. The films were popular and they sold well. Drawing on the formulae already established by England, Italy and the U.S., the Spanish film industry churned out a large number of Hammer take-offs, psycho killer flicks, and gothic supernatural thrillers. Most of the films were European and Euroamerican co-productions; some of them were filmed outside Spain. The government budgetary restrictions were met by simply making two versions of each movie–one for export and a milder, tamer version for domestic–and, in some cases, U.S and British–distribution.

Spain didn't have the same literary tradition of horror that England, Germany, the U.S. and even France had, and so it drew on different sources. Directors borrowed stories from other traditions and "nationalized" them with Spanish iconography. Drawing on the painting tradition of artists like Goya and Velázquez, the industry stamped the films with what Tohill and Tombs call "a Spanish flavor." The best Spanish horror films of the period–films like Amando de Ossorio's *Blind-Dead* series,Vicente Aranda's *La novia ensangretada* (*The Blood-Spattered Bride*, 1972), the films of Paul Naschy and Jess Franco–are "cruder" than their Anglo-american counterparts; "more violent and visceral, with a definite flavor of the grotesque. Audiences are more often led to identify with the monsters than their victims" (Tohill and Tombs 1994, 66). Some of the films–de Ossorio's "Blind Dead" films, for example–even have a Goya-esque look. The scenes are washed in browns and reds, a palette which beautifully captures the feeling of the medieval Church (the world from which the Blind Templars come).

The existence of these films is extraordinary, given the social and political climate of the time. Even the tame, domestic versions of Franco's films hint at illicit sexuality, lesbianism, and other activities officially designated as perversions by General Franco's government.[21] And de Ossorio's films link the Church to sadoerotic rites of torture and mutilation which, even when not shown onscreen, rival Sade's. The fact that the Templars were originally blinded and killed because of their excesses, the movies tell us, does little to mitigate the truly anticlerical, sacrilegious tone of the *Blind Dead* films. Furthermore, even with censorship editing, the films are often quite violent.

Horror cinema had special resonance in a society in which, as Marsha Kinder tells us, "the graphic depiction of violence is primarily associated with an anti-Francoist perspective." In many horror films–de Ossorio's being just one example–eroticized violence was used "to speak a political discourse, that is, to expose the legacy of brutality and torture that lay hidden behind the surface beauty of the Fascist and neo-Catholic aesthetics."[22] Even when horror films were not especially graphic, they served to make a strong political point. One of the most beautiful and emotionally moving art films of the period, Victor Erice's *El espíritu de la colmena* (*Spirit of the Beehive*, 1973), uses a child's response to James Whales's *Frankenstein* as a means of exploring political and social reality in the immediate post Civil War period. While not strictly speaking a horror film, Erice's masterpiece illustrates the way horror can be used to explore subversive cultural themes (John Hopewell, for example, sees the film as a demonstration of "the sadness and frustration attendant upon Franco's victory," clearly a forbidden topic under the dictatorship).[23] It is perhaps for that reason that *El espíritu de la colmena* is often mentioned in books treating the horror genre.

Spanish horror production began to decline after 1972. Government restrictions on the practice of making double versions of a film effectively undercut the industry's ability to export horror movies. And after General Franco's death in 1975, the industry no longer needed horror in order to finance mainstream production. But the lingering effect of horror's heyday is evident in the films of post-Franco Spain. Films like Almodóvar's *Matador* (1988)–which focuses on the relationship between love and death, eroticism and murder–explore the same troubling themes that horror does and perhaps demonstrate the degree to which eroticized horror became the very model of transgressive, revolutionary cinema for directors who grew up in fascist Spain. Interestingly, the images in the title sequence of *Matador*, Almodóvar tells us, come from films by Jess Franco.[24]

Franco's status in the U.S. Market

Franco's cultural significance and status in the U.S. is difficult to track. Until the 1986 publication of Phil Hardy's **Encyclopedia of Horror Movies**, nothing of significance had been written about Franco in English. Until the advent of home video, Franco's movies were largely unavailable to U.S. consumers. Never picked up for distribution by either exploitation entrepreneurs or late-night television, Franco's films remain largely unseen in the United States. Currently, he is best known to American horror fans as the director of *Count Dracula* (*El Condé Drácula*, 1971), a Spanish, German, Italian co-production starring Christopher Lee as a strangely lethargic count, *The Castle of Fu Manchu* (1968), another multinational production starring Christopher Lee, and *Deadly Sanctuary* (1970) an English-language French production based on the writings of the Marquis de Sade. Franco is also well-known as the director of *Succubus* (1968), the first mainstream horror film to receive an X-rating.

While the film titles mentioned above are available through companies like Facets Multimedia, which cater to a wide range of video collectors and movie buffs, most of Franco's movies are only available through paracinema and psychotronic video catalogues. Since different versions of Franco's films were often released simultaneously, publications like *Video Watchdog* try to keep track of which video releases contain the most complete (uncensored) footage, and which versions come closest to Franco's own vision of the movies. These are not always the most explicit versions available. Franco is one of the few European directors who has publicized the distribution practice of adding hard core inserts to body genre films. In an interview with Harvey Fenton and William Lustig, he describes seeing a "hardcore" version of a Christopher Lee movie in Paris:

> Christopher Lee... is one of the most proud men in the world, he would say things like "I don't want to kiss her on the mouth." And I saw a film of his, directed by Terence Fisher, with porno inserts...I saw that film and I laughed in my guts! I told Christopher immediately. I called him and said "I didn't know you had made a porno film!" And he went completely out of control, so I explained to him about the process and how the producers and distributors who had the rights for France and Germany and some other countries in Europe made these versions. And you know they are made with that awful quality also, because if you try to make a similar light or similar sets...
>
> No, it's just shit.[25]

The same thing had happened to his own films, he tells Fenton and Lustig. Producers added hard core sequences to *La Comtesse noire* (*The Black Countess*, 1973) to get what Franco called "a primitive porno film." "I have nothing against porno," he tells his interviewers, "but just that they do this normally very badly, because they are not real people of cinema."[26]

It is perhaps in response to the distribution practice of adding hardcore inserts to already completed films that Franco himself began making "erotic" versions of his own horror movies. *La Comtesse noire*, for example, was made three times—as a vampire film (*La Comtesse noire*), as a horrific sex film (*La Comtesse aux seins nus*, *The Barebreasted Countess*, 1973), and as what *Video Watchdog* calls a "non-supernatural hardcore picture" (*Les Avaleuses* [*The Swallowers*], 1973).[27] Even this practice, however, has not kept distributors from modifying Franco's horror titles to reach a wider "horrotica" audience.

What brings paracinephiles to Franco's work is a mixture of irritation at what *Video Watchdog* calls "the insultingly mild horror product tailored to fit the MPAA straightjacket" and curiosity about a director who has a kinky sex-horror reputation.[28] For many, as Tim Lucas writes, "Franco's defiantly uncommercial, acutely revealing taboo-breaking stance is like a breath of fresh scare, even when his movies are clumsy, which is (let's be honest) most of the time."[29] The implied connections between sex & death, blood and semen, cruelty and sexuality which haunt all of horror[30] are laid bare in Franco's work. In Franco's own version of *La Comtesse noire*, for example, the countess sucks the semen of her male victims rather than their blood; in a parody of *Deep Throat* (1972), she fellates them to death. Similarly, it is an excess of sexual passion rather than the loss of essential bodily fluids which destroys her female partners. In *The Awful Dr. Orlof* (*Gritos en la noche*, 1962), Franco's first reworking of Franju's *Les Yeux sans Visage*, the doctor caresses his victims'breasts before beginning his horrific operation to remove their faces; after surgery, he chains his victims—in sadoerotic bondage fashion—in the tower. Tohill and Tombs call *The Awful Dr. Orlof* (Franco's first feature length horror film) "a cinematic time bomb" and credit it with revolutionizing European horror. "Before *Orlof*," they write, "horror films had opted for the poetic approach, playing down the sexual element, only hinting at the dark recesses of the human psyche. With *Orlof* sex sizzled into the foreground, changing the face of Euro horror for the next twenty years."

But if Franco's films are taboo-breaking and sexy, they're also demanding in unexpected ways. Not only are they clumsy and thus "high in participation or completion by the audience" (in the way in which,

McLuhan tells us, all "cool" media are high in audience participation),[31] but they self-consciously create an aural dissonance which Laurie Anderson once humorously called "difficult listening."[32] That is, not only does the viewer have to work hard to "complete the picture," she has to listen through the music, which frequently serves as a counter-point to what is happening onscreen. If Dario Argento is the acknowledged master of the creative use of sound to "layer" meanings in his work, Franco is the forefunner who laid the groundwork for the creative–and often extreme–use of aural montage in horror. Furthermore, the film seems to challenge many of the assumptions traditionally made about the position of women in low genres and self-consciously (and self-reflexively) explores the connections between the worlds of high art and low culture.

The Awful Dr. Orlof

In many ways, The Awful Dr. Orlof[33] is more like a giallo—a graphically violent Italian thriller[34]—than like a horror flick. Oh, there are definite horror elements: the creepy Dr. Orlof stalking attractive women and kidnapping them, the laughably monstrous figure of Morpho, the amazing chateau with its winding candlelit passages, a beautifully-shot opening abduction scene, and a restrained operating room scene (the doctor makes an incision in a woman's chest), but the main driving force behind the narrative is the story of police inspector Edgar Tanner and his pretty fiancée Wanda. Which is not to say the film adheres to all the genre conventions of a police story. In fact, one of the interesting things about the film is the way in which it continually raises genre expectations and then disappoints them: the police inspector doesn't solve the mystery, his girlfriend does; Orlof is not killed or arrested at the end, just momentarily halted in his nefarious operations; a woman in the tower who might still be alive is forgotten, as the lovers walk away from the chateau. With the exception of Wanda and Tanner's survival, we never get quite the denouement we expect.

The film is set in 1912. The video box copy stresses the mad doctor theme: "Franco fave Howard Vernon is an obsessed surgeon trying to restore his daughter's fire-scarred face by abducting buxom young women and performing skin graft operations on them. Assisting him is his sadistic slave Morpho, a 'sightless idiot' (in creepy bug-eyed makeup), who occasionally BITES his victims(?) and keeps 'em chained up afterwards."[35] But the story which actually drives the narrative is, as I mentioned earlier, not the horror story; it's the story of the police investigation. When the film opens, five women have disappeared, all under identical circumstances. Long sequences show Inspector Tanner trying to make sense of conflicting eyewitness accounts of these abductions. The sheer amount of time spent on police business in the film, as well as the lengthy development of Tanner's relationship with his fiancée, tends to give *Orlof* a curious rhythm. Horror sequences frequently bottom out in farce or melodrama, so that the affect-level of terror or shock (or even suspense) is hard to maintain.

In addition, the film spends a lot of seemingly "dead" time investigating theatrical spectacle. There are extended sequences at both the Opera, where Wanda performs ballet, and the Cabaret, where Orlof looks for victims. While performance does not assume quite the central role here that it does in later Franco films, it still takes up more screen time than American audiences expect. So much screen time that we anticipate some important clue to derive from theatrical performance itself. While in later Franco films, nightclubs often become anarchic spaces where subversive dramas are enacted and bourgeois morals are travestied, in *Orlof* both the Cabaret and the Opera are connected to what Tim Lucas sees as Franco's aesthetic of "ennui." Places where people kill time, they represent the space in which "aberrant behavior begins."[36] It's interesting that at both the Opera and the Cabaret, characters are shown–dimly-lit–sitting alone in boxes; wrapped, it would seem, in their thoughts and obsessions. The threat here is not that Orlof, like Dr. Orlac in *Mad Love* (1935), responds to the performance of the woman he watches onstage, but rather that he doesn't. It's his inability to enjoy watching, to play the voyeur, that is immediately suspect. It's his inability to really enjoy looking at other women which makes us uneasy about the hours he spends staring at his comatose daughter.

Although *The Awful Dr. Orlof* is in many ways a curiously un-affective and tedious film, it also has a distinctly edgy feel. This derives largely from its use of music and sound to create dissonance and build tension. In fact, in *Orlof* Franco uses music in a way that's reminiscent of the dialectic potential which Eisenstein ascribed to sound. That is, he uses music as a form of "temporal counterpoint" which creates a sense of "collision" and enhances the dramatic potential of the film.[37] This is evident from the very first scene, in which the hard-driving (and very good) jazz score seems totally out of keeping with the 1912 "period piece" look of the film. And it continues throughout the movie as both the extradiegetic score and diegetic sound (echoes, reverberations) break in frequently as a marked juxtaposition to what's happening onscreen. Visually–canted framing, the occasional jump cut and some inserted shots (shots of cats and an owl watching, for example) create a similar sense of conflict; but in terms of pure affect, this is a film that seems to be largely sound-driven.

The score is not an easy-listening jazz score. This is bebop. The "background" music is characterized by unusual chord structures, accents on the upbeat, lengthened melodic line, and harmonic complexity and innovation. It's loud and it demands attention. This is the kind of jazz that makes non-jazz lovers nervous, the kind of music that creates an aural distraction. And it's a heavy presence in the film. While some scenes include only diegetic sound, a surprising number are introduced with the clash of cymbals or a long, frantic drum riff which seems as though it should come at the end of a piece, not introduce it. The music gives the impression that we are always coming in *in medias res*, joining a set that's already in progress. The demanding nature of the jazz score in *The Awful Dr. Orlof* helps to situate the film within the same kind of liminal space occupied by Franju's *Les Yeux sans Visage*. Invoking both the cerebral work/reception associated with high culture and the physical affect/response associated with low sex-horror, the film seems permanently poised between high and low genres, belonging to both of them simultaneously.

Thematically, the film plays pointedly with parallel story lines, contrasting images and twin motifs. Orlof's daughter Melissa, who spends all of her time lying motionless in what appears to be a little chapel, has a Janus-face. Half of her face, the half which remains hidden from the camera's and Orlof's view, is scarred; the half we see is lovely. Her visual twin in the film is Tanner's fiancée Wanda (played by the same actress). Since Melissa seems to spend all her time in a supine, trance-like state, Wanda almost functions as her emissary out in the world. Certainly, Wanda provides the emotional center to a film that desperately needs one. She's the only character whose fate we even remotely care about. It is Wanda's resemblance to Melissa that first catches Orlof's eye, and it is Orlof's fascination with Wanda's good looks that, in part, links him to Tanner.

The connection between Orlof and Tanner is less physical (they don't look like twins, as Wanda and Melissa do), but it's more stylistically emphasized than the connection between the two women. The film moves frequently between Orlof's pursuits and Tanner's, and the cuts between scenes are masked often by a graphic Orlof-Tanner match. Orlof puts his head in his hands; cut to Tanner putting his head in his hands. Orlof strokes Melissa's hair; cut to Tanner stroking Wanda's hair, etc. The men seem to mirror each other; they're paired or twinned in the way that criminals and crime fighters, monsters and exorcists, frequently are paired and twinned. And, as in most crime/horror stories, the pairing here makes a certain amount of sense. Orlof started his career, the narrative tells us, as a prison doctor. It was in this capacity that he met and fell in love with a female convict named Armée, and acquired the services of Morpho (incarcerated for raping and murdering his parents). Orlof helped Armée and Morpho to escape, and then began the experiments which turned Morpho into the bug-eyed "sightless idiot" we see throughout the film.

If Orlof is a monster figure, then, his monstrosity predates his obsessive need to repair his daughter's damaged face. And it's interesting that his mad science mania is linked in the film to the darker sides of law enforcement–incarceration, institutional medicine, experimentation on prisoners. The prison motif carries over into the chateau as well. If Dr. Génessier in Franju's *Les Yeux sans visage* embodies the modern clinical method (surgical mask, white coat, sterile environment), Orlof reminds one of a medieval torturer. He wears a day coat when he operates. Nothing in his operating room seems hygienic and, after surgery, he chains his victims–in sadoerotic bondage fashion–in the tower.

In some ways, then, he can be seen as the dark shadow figure, the primitive ancestral antecedent, to a modern detective like Tanner. While Tanner is initially linked to modern scientific method (he examines fingerprints, checks records, examines evidence), Orlof–like Dracula–seems permanently bound to barbaric rituals of the past. And Tanner must move from his well-lit (visually-speaking, "enlightened") office and enter the dimly lit, low-key underworld if he wants to fight Orlof. He begins frequenting the dive–literally, the cave–where Janot, the town

Below, Christopher Lee as the rapacious title figure in **El Condé Drácula**.

drunk, tells him about a mysterious chateau and a diamond necklace found at the site of an old boat launch. When a supposedly dead Morpho's fingerprints are found at one of the abduction scenes, Tanner even becomes a grave robber. He digs up Morpho's grave and finds an empty coffin.

Just as Franco emphasizes disturbing connections between the worlds of law-enforcement and horrific crime (in this film, the monster-criminal seems to emerge from and, in some ways to represent, the dark side of the legal/penal system), so, too, he underscores the parallel links between high art and popular culture. Scenes at the Opera segue into scenes at the Cabaret. And here the points of similarity–men in darkened boxes watching women perform onstage–are markedly clear. Performance sequences at both the Opera and the Cabaret are framed and shot in identical fashion. Furthermore, the two worlds are linked through the figure of Wanda. A professional ballerina, Wanda performs at the Opera. But determined to help Tanner solve his case, she also, unbeknownst to him, frequents the Cabaret after-hours. Dressed as a "shameless hussy" (English version) or "street girl" (French version)–another kind of gender performance–Wanda has absolutely no trouble passing as a club habitué. And the ease with which she migrates from the sacralized world of ballet opera to the eroticized popular milieu of the after-hours dance hall suggests that the difference between the two worlds is not so great as one might think.

There's a certain insistence on cultural transgressivity here, as high culture is emphatically paired with low culture. There's also a certain insistence on the way both high art and popular culture fetishize the female body, female performance. The dress Wanda is wearing the night that Orlof picks her up has the same heart-shaped bodice that her tutu has; and her pose, drinking cognac at the bar–upper body inclined slightly forward, head lifted, one leg stretched en arrière, slightly behind the other–resembles a dancer's attitude. Furthermore, she has come to the bar specifically in order to attract Orlof's gaze, and as she drinks her cognac she looks toward the balcony, searching for his face in the darkness–the same way that she had glanced earlier at the darkened Opera balcony, looking for Tanner.

Wanda is, as I mentioned earlier, the most interesting and emotionally compelling character in the film. What I find particularly interesting, though, is the way she is given command of the gaze. Unlike the fetishized female Hollywood character described by Laura Mulvey, who is always the object–never the subject–of an active (male) gaze, Wanda becomes the chief investigator on the Orlof case.[38] From the moment she first sees Orlof's eyes on her, she turns the tables and makes him the object of her active, inquiring, investigative gaze. She puts herself in danger, in the hope that he will invite her home. And when he does, she uses her time in the chateau to investigate Melissa's room and to search the tower. It is she who actually solves the case. And while she *almost* becomes Orlof's final victim, ultimately she is not punished for assuming the active male gaze and usurping police/patriarchal authority. She does not have to go through a protracted traumatizing battle at the end of the movie, the way final girls in slasher films do; and when Orlof is finally dispatched at the end, her role in solving the case is explicitly acknowledged by Tanner. "You're the best detective," he tells her. "My right hand from now on."

It's tempting to dismiss Tanner's final comments as another example of the patronizing "brave little woman" speech that screen detectives frequently make to their Girl Fridays. But here Tanner's speech serves to codify, or formally acknowledge, a kind of validation that the film has already shown. Throughout *Orlof*, much of the camera movement and many of the camera angles are motivated by Wanda's gaze. Certainly, her point of view drives most of the narrative in the second half of the film. If classical Hollywood Cinema can sometimes be seen, as Laura Mulvey argues, as being organized around the male gaze, here it is, at least occasionally, linked to an active female gaze. In a way, then, *Orlof* seems to foreshadow some of the remarkable Spanish arthouse films of the 1970s. Like Victor Erice's *El espíritu de la colmena* (1973) and Carlos Saura's *Cría cuervos* (1975), both of which use the gaze of a female child to destabilize the dominant militaristic male gaze, *The Awful Dr. Orlof* subtly challenges police hegemony and control through the measured use of a female's point of view.

Faceless

Faceless (*Les Prédateurs de la nuit*, 1988) is both a reworking of the *The Awful Dr. Orlof* and a sequel to it. Here Dr. Flamand (Helmut Berger), aided by his trusted wife and assistant Nathalie (Brigitte Lahaie), runs an exclusive cosmetic clinic in St. Cloud, France (a little town on the outskirts of Paris). In this clinic, he not only performs cosmetic surgery, but he rejuvenates wealthy female clients by injecting them with a serum made from the blood and bone marrow of kidnapped women. One of his middle-aged clients, dissatisfied with the results of her cosmetic surgery, surprises Dr. Flamand in a Paris parking garage one evening, and throws a vial of acid at him. The acid misses the doctor, but hits his sister, Ingrid (Christiane Jean), in the face. The rest of the film revolves around Flamand's attempts to restore his sister's beauty. To that end, he visits his old Professor, Dr. Orlof (Howard Vernon, the same actor who portrayed Orlof in the 1962 film). Orlof sends him to *his* old mentor, Karl Moser (Anton Diffring), a man who perfected his surgical methods in Dachau. It is Moser who finally performs the successful skin graft.

Interwoven with this story, is the story of the criminal investigation. Here, however, the hero is not a police officer, but a private detective, Sam Morgan (Chris Mitchum). Sam has been hired by a wealthy American, Mr. Hallen (Telly Savalas) to find his daughter, Barbara (Caroline Munro)–a professional model who has disappeared in Paris. Barbara has a cocaine habit and a propensity for what Sam calls "whoring around." But she was once Sam's lover and he's still crazy about her. Sentiment and Hallen's bank roll convince Sam he's the man for the job. In an interesting reversal of genre convention, though, Sam doesn't save the girl. When he finds Barbara in Flamand's clinic, he stupidly leaves the key he used to open her cell door dangling in the lock. Nathalie sees the open door and the dangling key, and imprisons them both in Barbara's cell. At Dr. Moser's urging, she walls them in with brick and mortar.[39] The film ends with the newly-restored Ingrid, Dr. Flamand, Nathalie and Dr. Moser drinking a champagne toast to the New Year, and Mr. Hallen (Telly Savalas) booking a plane reservation to Paris.

As I mentioned above, *Faceless* is heavily indebted to *The Awful Dr. Orlof* . Using the same basic plot and one of the same characters/actors, the film seems to both rework the story in 80's terms and to provide a kind of sequel. Flamand is, after all, Orlof's protegé; and repairing women's looks is his trade. But while *The Awful Dr. Orlof* seems–at this remove, anyway–curiously restrained, *Faceless* revels at times in special effects and excess. A woman is stabbed through the eye–an operation that is delineated with great precision and shown from almost every conceivable camera angle. A face donor's head is removed with a chainsaw. A male prostitute is stabbed in the neck. A nosy hospital worker is drilled through the forehead, with a powerdrill, as she cowers in a closet. One operating room scene shows Dr. Moser's failed attempt to remove the face of a still-living victim. Under the effects of sodium pentathol, the donor's skin is too elastic; it clumps and crumbles like cookie dough under Moser's fingers. A subsequent sequence shows a successful face-removal, this time from a pharmaceutically-paralyzed but fully conscious victim.

Here the famous face-lifting scene from *Les Yeux sans visage* is repeated almost shot for shot, but stretched out, elongated. Dr. Moser removes the face from the conscious victim on the table, displays it to the camera, and, then, in a supreme act of sadism, shows it to the woman to whom it once belonged. "See how beautiful she will be," he purrs. Then he hands the face to Dr. Flamand, who exhibits it again to the camera, before dipping it in some kind of solution and placing it over his sister's acid-scarred face. The effect is reminiscent of the shot-repetition Eisenstein uses in *Strike* and *Battleship Potemkin* to slow down time. But since the shot (displaying the face to the unflinching gaze of the camera) is duplicated using another actor, the sense of historical continuity, of one surgeon literally passing the results of his nefarious experimentation to another, is also highlighted. The scene plays like an *homage* to one of the central tropes of horror—what Robin Wood, in one famous essay has called the continual "return of the repressed."[40] Monsters may be temporarily laid to rest at the end of any given film, Wood notes, but the terror they represent always rises again. In Franco's films, as in *The Nightmare on Elm Street* series, every horror title contains the seeds of a sequel; closure is always illusory.

But despite the fact that *Faceless* shows more graphic violence than *The Awful Dr. Orlof* does and is, in some ways, more visually transgressive, it also strikes me as a more conservative, less edgy film than Franco's earlier work. Partly this is due to the crude quality of the makeup and special effects. Even *Video Watchdog*, which usually promotes graphic display over implied danger doesn't quite know what to make of the gore in this film. "The Watchdog was able to screen an uncut copy of *Faceless*, along with Malofilm's edited version," *Video Watchdog* reports in July/September 1990, "and while it's always better to see the unedited version of anything, I must say that the movie's special makeup effects are pretty crude, and the loss of some of them actually enhances the impact of certain scenes (particularly the first operating room mishap)."[40]

In addition, the choice of a pop music score and the overall glossy look of the film can be disappointing to fans hooked on Franco's jazz-beat. As *Video Watchdog* points out, *Faceless* is the first movie the ultra-prolific Franco had made with a complete production crew in nearly 20 years, and the result is a "slick, sick, All-Star production that unreels like a 'That's Entertainment' of Eurotrash."[41] But while *Video Watchdog* celebrates the film as one of Franco's best, I find the slickness a little off-putting; I miss the raw edges and bebop rhythm of the earlier low-budget work.

Still, the film exhibits the political and historical commentary of more "high-brow" art cinema. The allusions to Nazism, World War II and the Death Camps, which are implicit in *Les Yeux sans visage* are foregrounded here. Not only is Dr. Flamand played by Helmut Berger, a German actor, but Dachau and Auschwitz are explicitly mentioned as the laboratories where Moser's famed skin grafting technique origi-

nated. And the character of Karl Moser, the Nazi surgeon who appreciates fine wines, good art, and "unusual" women allows Franco to explore social and political contradictions more pointedly than he does in
his earlier films. "You French are a strange people," Moser tells Flamand
and Nathalie when they balk at the idea of operating on living flesh.
"You're really sentimental over trivial things. On the one hand you protect the baby seals. And, on the other, France, the country of human
rights, has become the third largest arms dealer in the world, behind
Russia and the United States. This industry of death earns your country,
a land of refuge, four billion dollars a year. A votre santé."

There's a certain irrefutable logic to Moser's position which allows
him, like the snake in the Garden of Eden, to persuade Flamand and
Nathalie to do what they had wanted to do all along. Actor Anton Diffring, who had played nefarious plastic surgeons in a number of Hammer films, brings just the right amount of seductive appeal to Moser;
and the fact that he does his own post-dubbing ensures that Moser's
character is one of the best-acted in the film. Lines are delivered with a
fluency and consistency of style that's refreshing after some of the
clumsy dubbing we see elsewhere in the movie. And Diffring plays his
role with a passion and a zest for life that's completely missing in the
other characters.

The choice of Helmut Berger for Flamand links *Faceless* to other films
about decadence, moral ambiguity, and the Third Reich. His previous
roles–in Visconti's *The Damned* (*La Caduta degli dei*, 1969) and Massimo
Dallamano's *The Evils of Dorian Gray* (*Il Dio chiamato Dorian*, *The Picture
of Dorian Gray*, 1970)–have created a star persona for Berger which exudes both seductive charm and moral instability, characteristics which
are perfect for Flamand. While this film does not insist on the connection
between homosexuality and fascism, as *The Damned* does, it does stress
the connection between medical moral depravity (Nazism) and sexual
perversion in Flamand's character. Here, we get more than a hint of incestuous longing, as Flamand watches his sister sexually humiliate Gordon (this film's equivalent of Morpho). In fact, the film suggests that the
only sexual pleasure Flamand might enjoy is the onanistic pleasure that
comes from watching. Lesbian love scenes between Nathalie and prospective skin graft donors are periodically staged for Flamand's–and the
film audience's–enjoyment (it's interesting that Flamand watches these
on the television monitors used to safeguard the patients'"stability" in
the clinic); and Nathalie, a kleptomaniac, tells Flamand that she would
steal less if he "loved" her more.

Certainly, here, as in both *The Damned* and *The Evils of Dorian Gray*,
we see Berger portraying what Peter Bondanella once described as a

"pathological case history bordering on the Grand Guignol."[42] And here, as in his earlier films, the depravity of Berger's character seems to extend to all facets of his life. Like Dr. Orlof, Flamand does not become monstrous *after* his sister's accident. The secret prison cells of his clinic contain not only potential skin donors, but women who are systematically drained of their blood and bone marrow in order to "feed" the clinic's regular clientele. Flamand, we are given to understand, always was something of an opportunist and a ghoul; a medical and corporate vampire. Ingrid's accident simply leads him into further excesses and abuses. And Berger–who plays Flamand as seductive but rather preternaturally subdued–captures, I think, the overall creepiness that constitutes the doctor's moral makeup.

If the film links medical procedures to death camp experiments, it also emphasizes an uncomfortable connection between the "skin jobs" at Dachau and the beauty industry, of which Flamand's clinic is a part. Not only does he cater to wealthy middle-aged women who wish to look young again, he repairs the faces of women who depend on their beauty for their livelihood. Barbara Hallen had come to the clinic for nose repair after excessive use of cocaine a year or so before the film opens. Melissa, a high-priced call girl, had similarly come to the clinic for face repairs, after her pimp-boyfriend Rashid had beaten her up. The fact that most of Flamand's potential skin donors are former clients gives the film something of a closed-world, hot-house feel. Flamand fingers the glamour photos in his files like a fashion designer choosing the models for his next runway show, before eventually selecting the famous face that will be right for his beloved sister. Once the choice is made, he knows exactly where to go to find the victim. And neither he nor Nathalie have any problem persuading the victim to come with them; the promise of drugs or sex is usually all that's required.

As in many Spanish horror films, the emphasis here is on the monsters'point of view, not the victim's. We rarely get a shot of the victim outside the mediating gaze of one of the monster figures.[43] Even camera movement and distance reflect the monsters'point of view–particularly that of Dr. Flamand and Ingrid–as the film moves from a relatively free, liquid camera style (in the credit sequence) to a claustrophobic and cramped series of long still takes and static shots. Most of the action takes place within the confines of the clinic–and confinement is indeed the main feeling which the shot composition and editing convey. Tight framing and the excessive use of closeups give the clinic scenes a cramped and oddly static feel. If Franco's early work is characterized by his notorious use of the zoom lens,*Faceless* tends rather to mimic fashion still photography, emphasizing glamour head and shoulder poses. Cutting tends to follow the classic shot-countershot Hollywood formation. And camera movement is subtle and slow. To some extent, it could be argued that the film plunges us into the same narrow cinematic space inhabited by its victims, but since we develop so little feeling for the victims I think we tend to read the claustrophobia more in terms of Flamand and Ingrid's own growing sense of confinement and desperation.

More provocative–although less easy to read–is the way that claustrophobia and claustrophobic filming attach to what the movie establishes as a distinct cinematic mode and (inter)national style. In fact, one of the most interesting aspects of the film is the way it more or less neatly divides into two genres or modes with two very different sets of aesthetic conventions.[44] There are the Euro-horror segments, which are dominated by actors from European cinema.[45] Here, the defining formal element seems to be the Antonioni-like claustrophobia and stylization mentioned earlier. The pacing is leisurely, even slow. Cuts are masked and emphasis appears to be on the mise-en-scène. Scenes are framed to convey a sense of confinement. Even the sex scenes are so tightly framed that it's hard to tell where exactly the players are. One memorable scene, which takes place in Ingrid's bedroom, is shot through a fish tank–heightening the sense that poor Ingrid is contained, not only because she is humiliated by the state of her face, but because she is the Flamands'domestic pet. Her sexual relationships–the few she's able to have–are carefully monitored by Flamand and Nathalie on the clinic's surveillance monitors. Furthermore, they seem to be shot with a long lens that compresses space, so that instead of appearing as acts of liberation, they function as still more examples of the claustrophobia that Ingrid increasingly feels. In the horror sequences, the only place where space regularly tends to open up and out (so that we get a sense of depth) is the Parisian club where Flamand and Nathalie cruise their former clients. But even these scenes, which do provide dynamic interludes in the European section, rely more on camera distance and mise-en-scène (strobe lights, dancing) than on camera movement or editing to achieve their effect.

Contrasting with this is the criminal investigation part of the film which is dominated by American actors Chris Mitchum (who bears a remarkable physical resemblance to his father, Robert) and Telly Savalas. The criminal investigation sequences rely heavily on what the film references as American "action" codes.[46] In his role as Sam Morgan, American private eye, Chris Mitchum pummels his way through Paris's high fashion industry, looking for clues about his girlfriend's disappearance. In these scenes, tightly framed, closeup shots of Mitchum's face and his opponent's body, alternate with high angle shots that have the curious visual effect of compressing the violence, holding it close to the ground. This compression tends to be shattered, though, as punches erupt up out of the center of the frame and push bodies out toward the edges. The signature move here is Morgan's fist jutting quickly upward and sideways, shattering the constraints and tight holds of fashion world thugs. The editing rhythm is fast-paced, full of quick cuts, and the framing gives a fairly accurate sense of space. While bodies and space are frequently fragmented, these (fragmenting) shots are almost always followed by an establishing or re-establishing shot, so that viewers generally know where the men are and have a sense of the amount of space (the surrounding space) they could conceivably occupy (where they could go).

Not only do these action sequences put the male body on display (providing a kind of male analogue to the punishing mechanisms of female fashion), they also shatter the constrained feel of the rest of the film. The scenes are beautiful to watch. The fights are well choreographed. The violence itself is stylized. Here, as in the action films that Yvonne Tasker analyzes, "suffering–torture, in particular–operates as both a narrative set of hurdles to be overcome, tests that the hero must survive, and as a set of aestheticized images to be lovingly dwelt on."[47] This contrasts with the clumsy gore shown in the horror sequences, whose function seems to be more one of gross-out comedy–the kind of images that leave you "laughing, screaming" in front of the television set.

It's tempting to read the action sequences metaphorically, as a celebration of the way European directors have increasingly used American movie conventions to break or challenge some of the constraints of European art cinema. Certainly the date of the film (1988) is right for such a move. The French cinéma du look films which–beginning with Jean-Jacques Beneix's *Diva* (1980)–rose to prominence in the 1980s,[48] as well as Pedro Almodóvar's films of the late 80s and early 90s–*Women on the Verge of a Nervous Breakdown* (*Mujeres al borde de un attaque de nervios*, 1988), *High Heels* (*Tacones lejanos*, 1991) and *Kika* (1993) often irritated critics precisely because they seemed to push continental cinema closer to a peculiarly Anglo-American, pop-culture, postmodern aesthetic.[49] So reading the action scenes as a kind of *homage* to American action films– and as a kind of jab at European critical response to the "new" European cinema–makes sense in terms of an increasingly Americanized, or American-fixated, continental film culture. And certainly Franco's own love of American film, which he tends to analyze in opposition to European art cinema, makes such a reading of the American action scenes feasible.[50]

But the film's diegetic construction of two different cinematic codes inevitably reinscribes binary oppositions into the text, and seems to undercut the central thematic thrust of the film. Like *Les Yeux sans Visage* and *The Awful Dr. Orlof, Faceless* seems to be about the disruption of polarized categories. Traditional binary oppositions between interior and exterior, Self and Other literally crumble as the skin of various women is cut, mangled, peeled away, sutured and resutured. And here, as in the slasher films that Carol J. Clover analyzes, fascination with both the opened body and with the destruction of the permeable membrane—which protects the corporeal inside from the outside world—is highlighted, as the camera closes in for a variety of gore shots.[51] But this fascination with the destruction of essential physical boundaries seems to exist at the level of plot–and skin–alone. Stylistically and generically, the film insists on maintaining the cinematic distinctions between action and horror, American and European, fluid and static (camera), open and closed (narrative), high and low (art/culture).[52]

While the American action sequences continually threaten to shatter the confines of the film text, they never really affect the (European, claustrophobic) clinic scenes. When Sam Morgan finds Barbara Hallen, he is simply locked in her cell with her. The two lovers are contained, walled-in together, to suffocate and die. Even the dual ending enforces the essential difference between American action codes and European art-horror codes. The film ends where an episode of *Kojak* might begin–with Telly Savalas standing in his office, making plans to take on a case. What's interesting here is the suggestion that the successful closure of a European art-horror film (the Flamands and Dr. Moser toasting the New Year) might open up into the beginning of an American action film sequel (Mr. Hallen, in his Kojak mode, coming in to save the day). But a real mixing up of codes, a real contamination of polarized genre conventions (in which elements of the horror film would bleed into the action film and vice versa), a real challenge to cinematic binaries seems outside *Faceless*'s scope. For that reason, the film seems less interesting and less truly subversive than *The Awful Dr.Orlof*, which really does destabilize traditional cinematic binaries and the hegemonic male gaze.

Cultural capital

Within dominant cultural codes, both *The Awful Dr. Orlof* and *Faceless* qualify as "bad art," as works that often look sloppy, that privilege affect over meaning and story, and that resist cohesion. But both works also enact an aesthetics shared by fans of low Eurohorror–a tendency towards excess, syncopated rhythms, and surreal frame compositions. They draw on what Pierre Bourdieu would call a "cultural accumulation"[53] that is shared by paracinephiles and Eurohorror afficionados, a "cultural accumulation" that accrues from both "high" and "low" culture. To really appreciate Franco's films, it helps to know something about—or at least like—jazz (which Bourdieu links to "aristocratic" culture, the cultural elite), the works of the Marquis de Sade, European art films, other horror movies, porn flicks (Brigitte LaHaie, one of the stars of *Faceless* made her name as an actress in adult movies), Nazi/SS exploitation films, American action movies, cop shows, and fascist history/ culture. In fact, without such cultural accumulation, it's difficult, as Tim Lucas points out, to "get" or even like the films.[54] There's simply not enough *affect* to help the viewer over the slow parts.

The idea that viewers have to learn to like Franco's style, have to learn how to watch his movies removes the director's work from the arena of what Theodor Adorno would call true "mass culture."[55] Here, as in Bourdieu's descriptions of mainstream elite culture, the viewer has to be educated into the system. The more Eurohorror experience one has, the more one is likely to be willing to immerse oneself in Franco's work, to put in the time that's necessary for a complete understanding of the director's "soft persuasive language."[56] And since the cultural codes that Franco draws upon derive from both a classical European education and from the "low" culture world of body genre movies, his films occupy a liminal cultural site much like the one occupied by Franju's *Les Yeux sans Visage* .Despite the raw visual quality of most of the films, they can still be situated at the intersection of high and mass culture, the place where traditional distinctions between high and mass culture become unhelpful, if not completely meaningless.

The fact that Franco's images are raw, too raw and grainy for most mainstream film buffs and too gory for many mainstream viewers, links them to a certain "classed" and politicized taste. Within Spain, it links them historically to an anti-fascist aesthetic, a subversive tradition of controlled resistance which has a certain cultural resonance inside contemporary American paracinema circles as well. American low horror fans turn to European cinema when their irritation at the "MPAA straightjacket"[57] begins to outweigh their impatience with a set of film codes they have to learn to decipher. As Lester Bangs puts it, "we got our own good tastes."[58] And those "good tastes" often encompass works which are difficult, which require cultural experience to properly decode. That is, the "good tastes" of low culture are every bit as complex, nuanced, and acculturated as is the elite taste for classical music, European art movies, and modern art.

Notes

1. As *Anxious Visions*, an art exhibit on the "real-life" inspiration for Surrealist painting, made abundantly clear, there is a medical crisis in the wake of every violent war—with too few limbs, faces, wheelchairs, drugs to go around. See Sidra Stich, *Anxious Viaions: Surrealist Art* (New York: Abbeville Press; Berkeley, Ca: University Art Museum, 1990) and David Skal, *The Monster Show: A Cultural History of Horror* (New York & London: W.W. Norton., 1993).

2. Films which purport to represent real bodies at the limits of pleasure and pain; films which are often "unambiguously delimited as gratuitous sadism for entertainment's sake." Mikita Brottman, *Offensive Films: Toward an Anthropology of Cinéma Vomitif* (Westport, Connecticut and London: Greenwood Press, 1997) 4.

3. Franco was the second unit director of photography for Welles'film.

4. Kim Newman, ed, *The BFI Companion to Horror* (London: Cassell and British Film Institute, 1996)121; Ginette Vincendeau, *The Encylcopedia of European Cinema* (also published by Cassell and the BFI) 159.

5. Jim Morton, "Film Personalities" in Jim Morton, guest editor, *Incredibly Strange Films; RE/Search #10*, V. Vale and Andrea Juno, editors(San Francisco: RE/Search Publications, 1986) 194.

6. *Ibid.*

7. *Ibid.*

8. Cathal Tohill and Pete Tombs, *Immoral Tales: European Sex and Horror Movies 1956-1984* (New York: St. Martin's Griffin, 1994) Subsequent citations will be given in the text.It should be noted that the ubiquitous references to jazz in relation to Franco's work derive at least in part from the fact that Franco started his artistic life as a musician and he still plays music (in fact he frequently composes and plays part of the jazz scores we hear on his film soundtracks). At least one mail order house,Video Search of Miami, markets CDs of Franco's music in addition to videos and laser discs of his movies. For more on Franco's thoughts on music, sex and just about everything else, see Harvey Fenton and William Lustig, "A Different Point of View: The Jess Franco Interview," *Flesh and Blood* 9 (London: 1997) 32-35.

9. One story has it that the Spanish producers for *Chimes at Midnight*, horrified by Welles'choice of second unit director of photography, dug out *Rififi en la ciudad* (*Rififi in the City*, 1963) in order to show Welles just how bad Franco's camera work could be.Unfortunately for the producers, Welles was charmed by *Rififi*'s obvious homage to *The Lady from Shanghai* (Welles, 1948). See Tohill and Tombs, 87.

10. See Tohill and Tombs, 87.

11. Tim Lucas, "Horrotica! The Sex Scream of Jess Franco," in Lucas, ed, *The Video Watchdog Book* (Cincinnati Ohio: Video Watchdog, 1992) 74.

13. Tim Lucas, "How to Read a Franco Film," *Video Watchdog* Number 1/1990, 23.

14. Lucas, "Horrotica!" 74.

15. Lucas, "How to Read a Franco Film," 19.

16. Andrew Sarris,"Notes on the Auteur Theory in 1962," in Gerald Mast, Marshall Cohen and Leo Braudy, *Film Theory and Criticism*, 4th edition (New York and Oxford: Oxford University Press, 1992) 586.

17. Jaglom's film, *Always* (1985), for example, is the director's look at marriage/divorce both onscreen and in real life. Written by, directed by and featuring Jaglom, the film co-stars his real-life ex-wife, Patricia Townsend. *Déja Vu* (1997) is a fictionalized retelling of the director's meeting and falling in love with his wife/collaborator Patricia Foyt. As Stephen Holden, writing for the New York Times puts it, "Henry Jaglom's autobiographical films, with their navel-gazing introspection, require a degree of patience that many moviegoers are loath to extend. But even the most self-indulgent Jaglom films loiter in psychic territory that more mainstream explorations of well-heeled angst often overlook." This seems like a fitting description not only of Franco's films, but of most low horror. See Stephen Holden, "How Puppy Love Can Teach New Tricks to Old Dogs," *New York Times* (Friday, April 24, 1998) B12. Jaglom's films, like Franco's, are difficult to find. Most of Jaglom's films are available for rental-by-mail from Facets Multimedia in Chicago; 1517 W. Fullerton Ave, Chicago, IL 60614; e-mail address: rentals@facets.org

18. It's also interesting that Jaglom, like Franco, had a curious relationship with Orson Welles. Welles agreed to act in one of Jaglom's early films and then continued to visit Jaglom in order to watch him work. Welles apparently was fascinated by Jaglom's attempts to move beyond acting/scripting–a process so different from Welles's own.

19. There was also a negative side to co-productions. As Virginia Higginbotham notes in her *Spanish Film Under Franco*, "while foreign funds put Spanish film professionals to work, they also raised production costs to levels entirely out of reach of Spanish directors. Actors who had been paid enormous salaries for small part in Italian and American films were no longer interested in working in low-paying Spanish productions. Most of the lead roles in copros were reserved for famous stars, while Spanish actors and actresses were left with minimal roles." Virginia Higginbotham, *Spanish Film Under Franco* (Austin: University of Texas Press, 1988) 15.

20. It should be noted here that during the 1970s, for many Spaniards the "weekend" didn't begin until Saturday afternoon.

21. As Marsha Kinder notes, "during the Francoist era, the depiction of violence was repressed, as was the depiction of sex, sacrilege, and politics." Marsha Kinder, *Blood Cinema: The Reconstruction of National Identity in Spain* (Berkeley, Los Angeles and London: University of California Press, 1993) 138.

22. *Ibid.*

23. John Hopewell, *Out of the Past: Spanish Cinema After Franco* (London: British Film Institute,1986) 209.

24. Frédéric Strauss, ed., *Almodóvar on Almodóvar*, Trans by Yves Baignères (London and Boston: Faber and Faber, 1994) 105. It's interesting that

Almodóvar refers to Jess Franco by one of the horror director's many anglicized pseudonyms, Jess Frank.Jess Franco himself sees a definite similarity between his own work and Almodóvar's. "I find Almodóvar very simpatico,"
he told Lucas Balbo in an interview. "He has the courage to show the public
who he really is...I like his earlier films better than *Matador*, because now I
think he's beginning to become too serious...I preferred him filming nuns
walking tigers in their gardens...and his first scatalogical film *Pepa, Luci, Bom y
otras chicas del monton (Pepa, Luci, Bom and Other Girls from the Masses)*. It's really excessive, but excessive in the best sense of the word." Lucas Balbo, "Un-
bearable Films and Terrible Headaches: A Conversation with Jess Franco,"
Video Watchdog No. 1/1990 39-40. For more on Franco's take on the Spanish
Film Industry, see Kevin Collins, "Interview with Jess Franco," *European Trash
Cinema* Special #1 (October 1996).

25. Harvey Fenton and William Lustig, "A Different Point of View: Jésus Franco
    Manera in Conversations with Harvey Fenton and William Lustig," *Flesh and
    Blood* Nine (1997) 34

26. *Ibid.*

27. Tim Lucas, ed, *The Video Watchdog Book* , 87

28. *Ibid.* 74

29. *Ibid.*

30. A lot has been written on the connections between sex and horror. See David
    Hogan, **Dark Romance: Sexuality in the Horror Film** (Jefferson, N.C: McFar-
    land, 1986), Gregory Waller, **The Living and the Undead: From Stoker's
    Dracula to Romero's Dawn of the Dead** (Urbana and Chicago: University of
    Illinois Press, 1986) 170-171. Christopher Craft, "'Kiss Me With Those Red
    Lips': Gender and Inversion in Bram Stoker's *Dracula*," *Representations* 8, (Fall,
    1984) 107-133, James **Twitchell, Dreadful Pleasures: An Anatomy of Modern
    Horror** (New York and Oxford: Oxford University Press,1985), and James
    Ursini and Alain Silver, **The Vampire Film: From Nosferatu to Interview with
    the Vampire**, Third Edition (New York: Limelight Editions 1997).

31. Marshall McLuhan, **Understanding Media: The Extensions of Man** (New
    York: McGraw-Hill, 1964), 23

32. Laurie Anderson, "Difficult Listening Hour," on Anderson, *Home of the Brave*,
    Elliott Abbott, Executive Producer (Talk Normal, distributed by Warner
    Brothers, 1986). The piece is not included on the audio recording.I don't mean
    to suggest here that Anderson specifically referred to Franco's work, but her
    comments on the demands which "difficult" music makes on the listener is
    very much in keeping with the kind of demands which Franco's soundtracks
    make on his viewers.

33. Something Weird Video sells the dubbed American version, which was re-
    leased by Sigma III in 1964. Video Search of Miami sells the "uncut French
    version" (which still appears to be missing some footage–there's a jump cut at
    the end, for example, which seems related more to missing film than to stylis-
    tic innovation). The French version includes two nude scenes missing from

the SWV edition. But Video Search's edition is much poorer visual quality than the SWV version; the lighting is poor and the whole tape seems to be washed with a curious green tint. The SWV edition is gorgeous. I should note that, according to Michael Weldon, these are the only two editions available from any of the companies which sell the film. See Michael Weldon, *The Psychotronic Video Guide* (New York: St. Martin's Griffin, 1996) 32.

34. Gialli are Italian thrillers, whose conventions are similar to films noirs. While they share many stylistic and thematic conventions with American thrilers, though, they are usually more explicitly violent and gory than American thrillers, and the plot isn't as tight.

35. Quoted from the box of Frank Henenlotter's Sexy Shocker release (Something Weird Video).

36. Lucas, "How to Read a Franco Film" 26.

37 See Sergei Eisenstein, "A Dialectic Approach to Film Form," in Mast, Cohen, Braudy, *Film Theory and Criticism*,143. For the discussion of "collision," see Eisenstein, "The Cinematographic Principle and the Ideogram," in Mast, Cohen, Braudy, *Film Theory and Criticism*, 133. Both essays were reprinted from Eisenstein, *Film Form.*

38. Laura Mulvey, "Visual Pleasure and Narrative Cinema," *Screen* 16 (1975) 6-18.

39. Like many European directors, Franco admires the work of Edgar Allan Poe. Sam and Barbara's fate in this film is reminiscent of the fate of Fortunato in "The Cask of Amontillado" of the premature burial theme which turns up so frequently in Poe's stories. Mr. Hallen's decision to book a flight to Paris almost has the status of a trick ending (as the friend watching the film with me said, "you think it's going to end like a Poe story, but then it ends like an O. Henry story instead"). Hallen hears a Christmas telephone message from Sam, saying that he's found Barbara and instructing Mr. Hallen to "call in the marines" if he doesn't hear from them in three days. Hallen does better than call in the marines. He makes plans to go to Paris himself.

40. Robin Wood, "Return of the Repressed," *Film Comment* , July-August 1978, 25-32.

41. Tim Lucas, "Face to Face with *Faceless* " in Lucas, *The Video Watchdog Book,* 195-196.

42. Peter Bondanella, *Italian Cinema from Neorealism to the Present* (New York: Continuum, 1983) 206

43. One of the few scenes shown entirely from a victim's point of view is the walling-in sequence; and here the point of view is Sam's. Female victims rarely control the gaze.

44. I am using "mode" here the way that David Bordwell does in "The Art Cinema as a Mode of Film Practice," to refer to a style of filmmaking which is characterized by certain formalistic (rather than plot) conventions and which encourages a specific reading strategy on the part of the viewer. See David

45. Helmut Berger, Anton Diffring, and Stephane Audran are familiar to fans of European art cinema. Howard Vernon and Lina Romay (Franco's wife) are familiar to fans of European horror. And Brigitte LaHaie is familiar to fans of European hardcore entertainment.

46. All of the things the French find distasteful about Americans are cited in these sequences–albeit with tongue firmly in cheek: the way we handled Vietnam, our annoying tendency to come in and start running things, our adolescent attitude toward sex, our reliance on violence to solve problems, our gum chewing.

47. Yvonne Tasker, "Dumb Movies for Dumb People: Masculinity, the Body and the Voice in Contemporary Action Cinema," in Steven Cohan and Ina Rae Hark, *Screening the Male: Exploring Masculinities in Hollywood Cinema* (London and New York: Routledge, 1993)230.

48. For more on the cinéma du look, see Guy Austin, *Contemporary French Cinema : An Introduction* (Manchester and New York: Manchester University Press, 1996; Dist in the U.S by St. Martin's Press); A. Goodwin, "Music Video in the (Post)Modern World," Screen 28:3, 36-55; and René Prédal, *Le Cinéma français depuis 1945* (Paris: Nathan, 1991).

49. Postmodernism remains a vexed term. The Anglo-American, pop culture, postmodern aesthetic I'm discussing here grew in part out of a Punk/80s New Wave aesthetic (reflected in films like *Blade Runner, Brazil, Diva, Liquid Sky, Repo Man, Star Struck ,Women on the Verge of a Nervous Breakdown,* and *Videodrome*). It's heavily indebted to themes, images, and formal—techniques drawn from advertising, comic books, music videos, science fiction, and TV dramas. If it has stylistic antecedents, they're to be found in the historical avant-garde schools of Surrealism and Dada. This branch of postmodernism is quite different from the coolly formal postmodernism of art directors like Peter Greenaway, Raoul Ruiz, and Lars von Trier which seems to have its roots in modernist aesthetics.
For more on pop postmodernism, see Jean Baudrillard, *America,* Trans. Chris Turner (London and New York: Verso, 1989) and *Cool Memories,* Trans Chris Turner (London and New York: Verso, 1990); Scott Bukatman, *Terminal Identity: the Virtual Subject in Postmodern Science Fiction* (Durham and London: Duke University Press, 1993); Jim Collins, *Architectures of Excess: Cultural Life in the Information Age* (New York: Routledge, 1995); Anne Friedberg, *Window Shopping: Cinema and the Postmodern* (Berkeley, Los Angeles, Oxford: University of California Press, 1993); Fredric Jameson, *Postmodernism or the Cultural Logic of Late Capitalism* (Durham: Duke University Press, 1991); Angela McRobbie, "Posmtodernism and Popular Culture," *ICA Documents* 4 (London: Institute of Contemporary Art, 1986) pp 54-58, and Christopher Sharrett, *Crisis Cinema: The Apocalyptic Idea in Postmodern Film,* PostModernPositions, Vol. 6 (Washington D.C: Maisonneuve Press, 1993). For more on the formalist postmodernism that I've linked to modern-

ism, see Ingeborg Hoesterey, ed, *Zeitgeist in Babel: The Postmodernist Controversy* (Bloomington and Indianapolis: Indiana University Press, 1991); and Andreas Huyssen, *After the Great Divide: Modernism.* For a discussion of the distinctions between the historic avant-garde and modernism, see Patrick Brantlinger and James Naremore, "Introduction: Six Artistic Cultures," in Brantlinger and Naremore, eds, *Modernity and Mass Culture* (Bloomington and Indianapolis: Indiana Univesity Press, 1991)1-23; and Juan Suárez, *Bike Boys, Drag Queens, and Superstars: Avant-garde, Mass Culture and Gay Identities in the 1960s Underground Cinema* (Bloomington: Indiana University Press, 1996).

50. In an interview with Kevin Collins, Franco describes the influences that made him want to make films. "I was eight. I was in school and I escaped from school to go to the cinema. But I didn't go to the cinema to see *Popeye* or something like that, no, no. I went to see Raoul Walsh films. My brother was two years younger than me and when I was ten and he was eight we made a list of the directors we loved. And we wanted to go see all of the films by them that we could. And, by chance, all of them were American directors and American films. Because in Europe there's a mistaken belief that a film is a way to talk about politics or social problems or philosophy–and I don't think so. I think a film is a complete thing and when a film ends I think it is important enough, you know to be just a show..." Kevin Collins, "Interview with Jess Franco," *European Trash Cinema Special #1* (1996) 6. Of course, when Franco talks about the depiction of sex in the cinema, his take on the superiority of American movies shifts dramatically (they don't show enough, he says).

51. See Carol J. Clover, *Men, Women and Chainsaws: Gender in the Modern Horror Film* (Princeton: Princeton University Press, 1992).

52. There is a blurring of the boundaries between high art and low culture within the European segment, though. Here, art cinema stars like Stephane Audran play opposite porn stars like Brigitte LaHaie.

53. Pierre Bourdieu, *Distinction: A Social Critique of Taste*, Trans. Richard Nice (Cambridge, MA: Harvard University Press, 1984) 25

54. Lucas, "How to Read a Franco Film," 19

55. Adorno argues that true "mass culture" is one which arises spontaneously from the masses themselves, not one which they have to learn to appreciate. For Adorno, most of what passes as "mass culture" is really just the product of a "culture industry" which has as its goal the inculcation and enforcement of certain hegemonic codes. See Theodor Adorno, "The Culture Industry Recosidered," Trans. Anson G. Rabinbach, *New German Critique* (Fall 1975), 12-19.

56. Lucas, "How to Read a Franco Film," 19.

57. Tim Lucas, ed, *The Video Watchdog Book,* 74

58. Lester Bangs, *Psychotic Reactions and Carburetor Dung* (New York: Vintage Books, 1988) 122-3.

Above, Alice (Lisa Wilcox) falls into Krueger's wonderland where she plans to save her child and break Freddy's hold on her in *A Nightmare on Elm Street 5: The Dream Child*.

Seducing the Subject: Freddy Krueger, Popular Culture and the *Nightmare on Elm Street* Films

Ian Conrich

The *A Nightmare on Elm Street* films have been an extremely successful series. A 1991 press release from the American producers, New Line, reported that the first five of the seven films had taken over $400 million from the domestic and foreign box office, video cassette sales, television and merchandising. *Variety* has recorded the productions as among the most profitable of horror films in terms of film rentals at theatres in the US and Canada. The first film in the series, *A Nightmare on Elm Street* (1984), directed by Wes Craven, has receipts of $9,337,942. *A Nightmare on Elm Street Part 2: Freddy's Revenge* (1985), directed by Jack Sholder, has receipts of $13,500,000, while receipts of $21,345,000 have been recorded for *A Nightmare on Elm Street Part 3: The Dream Warriors* (1987), directed by Chuck Russell. *A Nightmare on Elm Street Part 4: The Dream Master* (1988), directed by Renny Harlin, recorded receipts of $22,000,000. *A Nightmare on Elm Street Part 5: The Dream Child* (1989), directed by Stephen Hopkins, took $10,000,000 and *Freddy's Dead: The Final Nightmare* (1991), directed by Rachel Talalay, took $17,700,000. *Wes Craven's New Nightmare* (Part 7) was released in 1994.[1]

These figures reflect, on one level, the cultural impact of the *Nightmare* films. The marketing of Freddy Krueger and the merchandising associated with the series established the films, particularly in the late 1980s, as a popular culture phenomenon. It is, however, not so much the success of the films that is surprising, but the fact that they featured a child killer as their protagonist. The *Nightmare* films depict the activities of Freddy Krueger, a child molester and murderer, who, having escaped conviction on a technicality, was burnt to death in his boiler room by Elm Street's vengeful parents. Years later he returns, initially through the dreams of the teenage children of the parents who destroyed him, later through the dreams of all children living in the Elm Street area. Here, as the teenagers are tormented and killed, Freddy ruptures the boundaries between the imaginary and the real.

In this examination of the *Nightmare* series it will be suggested that the films have been largely successful through their ability to maintain a seduction of the subject, that is of the spectator and consumer. This has predominantly been achieved through Freddy, the cultural object, who seduces the subject through a combination of his power and personality and a supporting series of clever images and stimulating visuals. This seduction continues with the associated merchandising, where popular culture allows for the successful release of Freddy from the fictional world of the film into a consumer society reality.[2]

Freddy Krueger has a very recognisable identity: a red and green, horizontally striped jumper, a razors-for-fingers glove, a fedora hat and, in the words of Robert Englund, the actor who plays him, "a Cagney swagger and a cool-clown style"[3] His appearances are frequently marked by a maniacal laugh and the screeching of his razor-blade fingers on metal. In contrast, the other characters in the films possess weak identities and while Freddy is the "fixed" element in the *Nightmare* series, his various victims are easily interchangeable. Freddy's identity is so strong that it can absorb the images of his victims. In *Nightmare 2*, Jesse, possessed by Freddy's spirit, ceases to be the Jesse that his friends and parents know and slowly begins to display parts of Freddy's identity. Jesse's hand transforms into Freddy's razors-for-fingers gloved hand, and, while kissing his girlfriend, he sprouts an enormous Freddy tongue. Eventually, a complete Freddy emerges from within Jesse's stomach, leaving Jesse's empty body to fall to the ground. In *Nightmare 5*, Freddy's victims are presented as sperm-shaped expulsions that erupt from his body when he is destroyed in the film's conclusion. Similarly, *Nightmare 4* presents the trapped victims as little outlines of human forms frantically pushing at the surface of Freddy's torso from inside; the faces of recent victims screaming in pain, pressed against the membrane that traps them within Freddy's body.

Capable of transforming into almost anything, anytime, anywhere, Freddy possesses a tremendous power to surprise and entertain. As Henry Jenkins has observed,

> We face the challenge of Freddy's shape-shifting as he moves between different cultural categories - male and female, adult and child, animate and inanimate, takes control over domestic technologies, assumes identities from mass culture, mutates and disintegrates before our eyes, only to be reconfigured and re-embodied again.[4]

In *Nightmare 5*, he is both a diving board that attempts to curl itself around a diver, and a motorbike which penetrates and physically

merges with the body of its passenger. In an earlier film, *Nightmare 3*, he
becomes a giant snake that attempts to swallow a girl whole, and appears as an attractive nurse that seduces a boy.

Possessing the ability to destroy the individuals through their
dreams, Freddy functions as the personification of the ultimate nightmare. Frequently attacking his victims through their weaknesses, his
methods are astounding and ingenious. In *Nightmare 4*, a teenager with
an abhorrence for cockroaches is herself dramatically transformed in a
Kafkaesque fashion into a cockroach, which Freddy then crushes with
his foot. A girl who observes a strict diet is force-fed to death by Freddy
in *Nightmare 5*, while in *Nightmare 3* an ex-drug addict is lethally injected
through ten needles emerging from Freddy's fingers.

These elaborate special effects are of such importance to the films that
they are awarded lengthy end credits. Their technicians are grouped
into teams of "operators" that have an average of six members, with the
spectacles each given an individual descriptive title, such as "Dan's Mechanical Suit/Freddy Bike" and "Womb with a View/Fetal Canal" in
Nightmare 5. The special effects dominate the series to such an extent
that frequently spectators describing a *Nightmare* film will only mention
the spectacular moments: the human puppet in *Nightmare 3* or the explosion of the deaf boy's head in *Nightmare 6*. Jeffrey Sconce has described these repeated moments as "episodes of intense visual
excitement," suggesting that they are one reason why the *Nightmare*

Below, Freddy stretches out of shape during a tussle with Maggie (Lisa Zane) in
Freddy's Dead The Final Nightmare aka **Nightmare 6**.

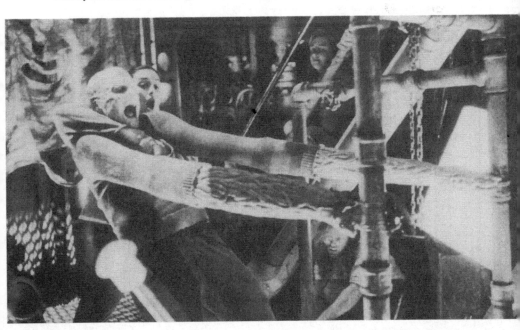

films have proved so popular with a youth audience.[5] Recent "kid culture" has been attracted to the spectacle as entertainment, where a rapid succession of perceptual information subverts the importance of the plot - a kind of visual stimulation manifested in many highly addictive video games.

The special effects employed in the films are spectacles that function around the appearance and performance of Freddy. As the dominant image, in narratives dependent on an episodic structure, Freddy's appearance signals the next series of outrageous and spectacular effects. As David Edelstein writes in the *Village Voice*, "The dreams are big production numbers and Freddy presides over them like a nightclub master-of ceremonies"[6] Other popular horror figures in contemporary films have tended to be faceless and devoid of personality. Monstrous characters such as Jason Voorhees of the *Friday the 13th* series, Leatherface of *The Texas Chainsaw Massacre* films and *Halloween's* Michael Myers are deadly but mechanical and silent, with the films structured upon a series of repetitive and predictable killings.

By contrast, Freddy is the confident performer, the host, the showman and the comic. He is ostentatious, "courteous," even courtly and is constantly cracking jokes. In *Nightmare 3*, when Nancy demands that Freddy release Joey, Freddy declares, "Your wish is my command!" and walks backwards away from Joey, his arms outstretched and his hat held in his right hand. Here he looks like an Elizabethan gentleman, his manner both accommodating and full of pomp. In *Nightmare 4* one sequence has a girl dreaming that she is on the beach of an exotic island, when Freddy appears through an exploding sand castle. Having made his grand entrance, Freddy walks towards his new victim, smiles and puts on a pair of sunglasses. His arrival is spectacular, his manner smooth - so smooth that he even gets to rap the song "Are You Ready for Freddy?" with "The Fat Boys" over the film's end credits. As Henry Jenkins writes: "Freddy moves through the film's ever-more-incoherent spaces as a kind of performer, delivering one-liners"[7]

Steve Seidman and Frank Krutnik have argued that comedians like Harpo Marx and Charlie Chaplin are "tricksters" or "shape-shifters," capable of transforming themselves into inanimate objects and of adopting the traits of others.[8] Krutnik writes that a comedian also functions not as a "localized" character but as a performer who is

> marked within the text as having a privileged status compared to other characters/actors: he is less functionally integrated and has a relatively disruptive function in relation to the fictional world and its codes of behavior and action.[9]

Above, a hapless Kristen Parker (Patricia Arquette) trapped in nasty nightmare in **A Nightmare on Elm Street 3: Dream Warriors**.

Freddy is the comic who can move freely from one place to another. Residing in a world constructed through dreams, he can emerge in the environment of his choice: the beach of an exotic island in *Nightmare 4* or, in *Nightmare 5*, an asylum for the insane, which was the venue for both his mother's rape and his conception. With an established identity, Freddy's deviation from the fiction is easily accepted. When he appears as the new cook, complete with chef's hat, preparing to serve food to a dieting girl in *Nightmare 5*, we are at first unaware that the cook is in fact Freddy. It is only when we are able to see his face that his attire is rendered comically false. His impersonation of the chef is a perversely ironic comment on the status of the dieting girl.

Like the comedian, Freddy also functions disruptively in relation to the fictional world, by manipulating, destroying or even completely altering its structure. In being, however, a dream "master," capable of recreating the fictional world in his own image, Freddy's status here is much stronger than that of other comedians. He is clearly able to disrupt the fictional world in a manner that other comedians cannot. Part of the comedian's disruptive function is a refusal to act "straight" against the acting of the other characters in the film. In the *Nightmare* series no one other than Freddy appears to act out of character; everyone else consistently delivers both stable and "sincere" performances. Nor can any of the films' characters be perceived to accept or appreciate Freddy's humor. He is, as Kim Newman writes, a "walking joke who kills his victims with a James-Bondish wisecrack"[10] A notable example occurs in

Nightmare 4, where Freddy appears as a surgeon in the operating theatre in which Dan is lying. "Krueger!" Dan exclaims, realising the surgeon's identity. "Well it ain't Dr Seuss!" Freddy replies.

Freddy as a comedian does not perform for the appreciation of the characters within the films. Instead, he entertains and "acknowledges" the subject watching the performance. Intervening between the overt fiction and the spectator, a space is established that is closer to the space of a theatre audience than that of a film audience. Umberto Eco noted that Walt Disney, in building Disneyland, achieved his personal dream of breaking down the wall of the second dimension and creating not a movie but total theatre.[11] It is this dream that is shared by the *Nightmare* films.

In an attempt to realize this vision, *Nightmare 6* presents a sequence in 3-D, which endeavours to efface the space that separates the viewer from the screen. This sequence occurs in the last fifteen minutes of the film, when Freddy eventually dies. Viewers were provided with special glasses through which at the appropriate time they could gain access to the space behind the screen. In the film, Doc hands a pair of 3-D glasses to Maggie, informing her that they have to be worn in order to defeat Freddy. Maggie puts on her glasses which dissolve into her face; this is the cue for the spectators to put on their own glasses. The film communicates directly here with the viewers, telling them what action they should take in order to continue a relation with the film's presentation. Failure to wear the glasses prevents spectators from being able to convert their space into an extension of the screen space. Not to wear the glasses would also imply a failure to defeat Freddy. For he is defeated not just by the characters on screen but also by the viewers who comply with the film's command and wear the glasses.

This attempt to efface the division between illusion and reality is continually explored throughout the *Nightmare* series. In *Nightmare 6* a boy who is interested in playing computer games is seduced by a psychedelic light show and is literally drawn into the television from which it is being emitted. Inside the television, he becomes a figure in a computer game, which Freddy is playing and controlling. Similarly, in *Nightmare 4* Alice is literally drawn into the space of the film she is watching. At the screening of a film, *Lost Burning Youth*, the black and white image suddenly transforms into an image of the cafeteria in which Alice works. In the film, a strong gale blows outside the cafeteria at the same time as a strong gale blows through the cinema auditorium. Finally, unable to hold herself down, Alice is sucked into the film. The audience in the theatre, unaffected by the gale, stands up and applauds. Now inside the screen, Alice observes the audience through the windows of the cafeteria that she had been viewing from her seat in the auditorium.

Unlike the previous films in the series, the seventh, *Wes Craven's New Nightmare*, is more concerned with narrative than spectacle, and has the most sustained interest in dissolving illusion and reality. The characters in this film, who are the film-makers involved in the production of the *Nightmare* series, are being destroyed by the Freddy that they have created. Freddy has been able to emerge from the fictional space of cinema into the "real" space of the diegesis, the supposed reality of the film-makers, in which the crew and actors of the series play themselves: Wes Craven appears as Wes Craven the director, Heather Langenkamp appears as Langenkamp the actress, and Robert Englund is himself, the actor who has played Freddy in the films.

The *Nightmare* films, acutely aware of their relationship with the audience, offer increasingly provocative images and situations. They attempt to establish a surface that will seduce the subject into the space of illusion, in which Freddy Krueger is the foregrounded image and principal attraction.

An example of this is the merchandising of products associated with the films. One of the more extraordinary of these products was a lifesize replica of Freddy Krueger's glove. This was marketed as a children's toy and was available from department stores and toy shops. The American advertising for the glove declared in large letters that "You Too Can Become the Bastard Son of a Thousand Maniacs," while in slightly smaller letters around an image of the glove were placed the statements "Soft Plastic Blades!" and "It's Play-Safe!," under which was written "Caution: do not use this glove in any violent manner." It is remarkable that the weapon used by a child killer in a series of violent horror films should be marketed as a plaything for children. What is produced here is a simulacrum of the glove used by Freddy in the films, with the metal razor blades replaced by plastic copies. The disturbing reality of this is contextualized by Sheila Johnston, commenting on an event that took place in Hadonville, New Jersey on 31 October 1988:

> A bright sunny morning for the children's Halloween parade. Here among the usual ghoulies, ghosties and long-leggedy beasties, were a good half dozen eight-year olds fitted out in approximations of the Freddy uniform: felt hats, red-and-green striped sweaters, variously simulated third degree facial burns, and the famous razor-fingered glove, which they waved merrily at the proud moms clustered round the gate.[12]

It is here that an extremely ironic situation develops. For the parents in *Nightmare 1* had supposedly incinerated Freddy Krueger for molesting and killing their children. In our reality, however, in the space that exists outside the film, parents actively encourage the presence of Freddy Krueger within their society. Whereas Freddy was destroyed for molesting children in the film, mothers are now content to see their children celebrating his character.

It would appear that Freddy had been released from the imaginary space of the film, "possessing" the subject that exists outside the screen in which he had been contained. The child who dresses as Freddy has been seduced by the object. As with Jesse in *Nightmare 2*, the weaker identity of the subject is lost as it is replaced by the strong identity of Freddy. At the Halloween parade in Hadonfield, New Jersey, the children temporarily appeared to be more Freddy than child.

This seduction has been facilitated by the products associated with the *Nightmare* films. As Sheila Johnston notes, Alison Emilio of New Line announced in 1988 that they had been thinking of launching a range of "Freddy-Chic" clothing.[13] This seemed never to materialize. However lifesize inflatable dolls and cardboard cut-outs were produced in order for the consumer to enjoy a closer union with Freddy. The object is here allowed to finally triumph over the subject, with the subject desiring either to resemble Freddy, or to acquire products that recreate parts of Freddy's identity.

Below, more hijinks from **Freddy's Dead The Final Nightmare** aka **Nightmare 6**: Carlos (Ricky Dean Logan) acquires a hearing problem in the dream world.

A similar phenomenon occurs with respect to Freddy's fandom. According to Douglas Thompson in 1989, Freddy Krueger's fan club had more members than U2's.[14] In 1988, *Rolling Stone* observed that Freddy "is perhaps as familiar a pop icon as any rock star of the day." Indeed Freddy has had a record with his own dance called "Do the Freddy" and has appeared occasionally as a presenter on the cable television rock station MTV.[15] He has also been "honored" by a number of hardcore porn films which imitate the form of the series: *A Nightmare on Porn Street* (1988), *Nightmare on Sex Street* (1991) and *Nightmare on Dyke Street* (1992).

Of further interest was Freddy's appearance in five editions of the British newspaper the *Daily Star*, in September 1992. At a time when other newspapers carried headlines of conflict in the former Yugoslavia, on Monday 8 September the *Daily Star* carried a half-page image of Freddy Krueger on its front page. Issued with the paper were a pair of 3-D glasses, enabling the viewer to gain a closer relation with special images of Freddy presented on the paper's centre pages. Emphasising obvious aspects of Freddy, such as his glove, they were a relatively successful attempt at deconstructing the two-dimensional image, presenting Freddy as an object that could supposedly "leap" out of the paper.

Despite this example, it is clear that Freddy is mainly marketed by appealing to young children. It is difficult, however, to understand fully how these children could be attracted to a figure who existed in films that were R-rated in America and given adult certificates in Britain.[16] One possibility is that children first accessed the films through the merchandising. The products would have assisted in Freddy's seduction of the subject and encouraged the child to develop an active interest in the films.

Phone lines were established which children could dial and hear Freddy tell horrific stories. A children's story book of *Nightmare 1*, complete with graphic color photographs, was published in the US, while bubblegum cards, yo-yos and watches with Freddy's face on the dial established him as an object that was omnipresent within the children's environment. Even an eighteen-inch talking Freddy doll was made available in 1989. The model, which in Britain was marketed by the respectable toy company Matchbox, was surprisingly for ages three and up. A well-crafted doll that bore a strong resemblance to Freddy, it had movable arms and legs and, if the cord on its back was pulled, could communicate a variety of messages: "Pleasant dreams," "Welcome to Elm Street," "Watch out, Freddy's back," and the frightening suggestion "Let's be friends."

One of the board games made available, the US "*A Nightmare on Elm Street* - The Freddy Game," produced by Cardinal in 1989 for ages eight and up, presented a situation in which the players move around Freddy's house, a cardboard construction in strong, bright colors.[17] Progress around the board is made by players selecting a counter which appears in the form of a character, who is clearly defined as suffering from a specific fear. If the player elects to be "Grandpa" then the personal weakness is "Empty Grave," while "Cheerleader's fear is "Freezing," Nice Guy's is "Fire" and Mom's is "Rodents." The game includes a "You Are Freddy!" card, which requires recipients to collect "Razor Fingers" and permits them to destroy other players and even win the game. The instructions explain that "In this game, one of the players will be "possessed" by Freddy Krueger...but which one! - it could be you!."

A child's desire to become Freddy could be explained by Gary Heba's suggestion that there exists in horror films "an ideological kinship of "otherness" between youth and the monster."[18] Elders have regarded youths as threatening and disruptive as a result of their pre-adult interests and appearance. Young people are consequently able to identify with the monstrous as "it, too, stands outside and apart from the members of dominant culture."[19] Freddy, a monster with attitude and limitless power, makes subversion appear exciting.

While planning the launch of a *Nightmare* computer game, the films' producers conducted market research into whether children would prefer to be the Elm Street kids or Freddy Krueger. Most of those questioned replied that they would prefer to be Freddy. These children do not want to defeat Freddy but instead desire to protect and support his existence. For them, it is the children in the films who need to be destroyed and not their killer.

Spin-offs from the *Nightmare* films were the number one selling merchandise of 1987, leading New Line's Alison Emilio to declare that Freddy was the "Mickey Mouse of horror"[20] Like Mickey Mouse, Freddy is instantly recognisable to children. As the Heather Langenkamp "character" in *Nightmare 7* tells a nurse: "Every kid knows who Freddy is. He is like Santa Claus." The image of Freddy has been softened to such a degree that his appearance ceases to terrify some children. For instance, an eight-year-old girl in America dying of leukemia had a final wish to meet Freddy before she died. This was met with Robert Englund, the actor who plays Freddy, appearing in his "costume" at her bedside. The young girl was not interested in meeting the actor who played Freddy, nor was she interested in meeting a more traditional children's idol. Instead, she, a dying girl, desired to meet Freddy Krueger himself, the killer of children. More important, it had to be the real Freddy, not a replica. When she met Robert Englund, in the original make up and costume, it was as if Freddy had completely crossed over from the space of illusion into reality.

In the conclusion of *Nightmare 5* Alice's unborn son, Jacob, tells his mother, "Mummy, meet my friend," with Freddy, in turn, telling Jacob, "I'm your real friend, Jacob. Just like a daddy." This is crucial, for Freddy arguably acts as a surrogate "father" for the many children drawn to the films. He is there for the children as a close friend who is funny, powerful and fascinating and who will always be present to play with them. At the start of *Nightmare 3*, Alice arrives at Freddy's house. Sitting on the pavement outside is a little girl drawing. As Alice bends down towards the picture, the little girl turns around and declares "Freddy's home!." Here, Freddy functions like a father who has returned home from work, a father whose arrival is eagerly awaited by the children. As the "father," Freddy also always provides the children with good "advice." In *Nightmare 1*, he informs the frantic Nancy, who is racing through her school, that there is "no running in the corridors." While in *Nightmare 5*, he tells a boy obsessed with comics, "Told you comic books were bad for you!," in *Nightmare 4*, he writes "Learning is fun" on a girl's test paper. He becomes a form of counsel and guidance and a protector of the children. The counsellor, however, is perverted, for Freddy attacks the children who receive his advice.

Below, young Dylan (Miko Hughes) in *Wes Craven's Final Nightmare* aka *Nightmare 7*.

The theme of paternity is present throughout the *Nightmare* series, with the later films in particular focusing on the paternal identity of Freddy. Jacob in *Nightmare 5* and Dylan in *Nightmare 7* are fatherless children. Both lost their fathers in road accidents caused by Freddy, which left him in loco parentis. In his "stepfather" role, Freddy exploits his union with the child in order to gain entry to the "real" world. The child is captivated by Freddy and encouraged to share in his power and knowledge. Jacob in *Nightmare 5* tells Freddy: "Let's go! I want to learn from you," while Dylan, in *Nightmare 7*, appears in Langenkamp's dream wearing Freddy's glove. Similarly, in *Nightmare 6*, Spencer, who is trapped in a computer game, has to combat a computer figure of a father. As the figure repeats the line "Be like me!," Freddy, who controls the game, declares, "Father knows best!" In the film's conclusion, Maggie discovers that she is Freddy's daughter. Enticing her with the offer of unlimited power, Freddy invites her to try on his glove. It is an invitation that has been willingly accepted by children in our own reality. They have allowed themselves to be "possessed," not only by Freddy but by consumerism itself.

Notes

I would like to thank Sarah Davy, Peter Kramer and David Woods for their invaluable comments and suggestions.

1. *A Nightmare on Elm Street* figure from *Variety* MIFED issue (15 October 1990), p.M140, all other figures from *Variety* Cannes film market issue (10 May 1993), pp.C76, C86.

2. See the following books by Jean Baudrillard for a discussion of the object, the subject and seduction: *The Ecstasy of Communication* (New York: Semiotext(e), 1988), *Fatal Strategies* (London: Pluto, 1990) and *Revenge of the Crystal* (London: Pluto, 1990). In *Fatal Strategies*, Baudrillard writes: In our philosophy of desire, the subject retains an absolute privilege, since it is the subject that desires. But everything is inverted if one passes on to the thought of seduction. There, it's no longer the subject which desires, it's the object which seduces. Everything comes from the object and everything returns to it, just as everything started with seduction, not with desire. The immemorial privilege of the subject is overthrown. For the subject is fragile and can only desire, whereas the object gets on very well even when desire is absent; the object seduces through the absence of desire; it plays on the other with the effect of desire, provoking or annuling it, exalting and deceiving it. (pp. 111-12)

3. Sheila Johnston, "Clawing in the cash," *Independent*, 10 November 1988, p.19.

4. Henry Jenkins, "Killing time on Elm Street: Freddy Krueger and the post-classical horror film," unpublished conference paper, University of East Anglia (1991), p.6.

5. Jeffrey Sconce, "Spectacles of death: identification, reflexivity, and contemporary horror," in Jim Collins, Hilary Radner and Ava Preacher Collins (eds), *Film Theory Goes to the Movies* (London: Routledge,1993), pp.113-14.

6. David Edelstein, "Drilling for fresh nerves," *Village Voice* 20 November 1984, p.58.

7. Jenkins, "Killing time," p.7.

8. Steve Seidman, *Comedian Comedy: A Tradition in Hollywood Film* (UMI Research Press, 1981) passim; Frank Krutnik, "The clown-prints of comedy," **Screen** 25, 4-5 (July-October 1984), pp.50-9.

9. Krutnik, "The clown-prints of comedy," p.51.

10. Kim Newman, "*A Nightmare on Elm Street 4: The Dream Master*," *Monthly Film Bulletin* 664 (May 1989), p.146.

11. Umberto Eco, *Travels in Hyperreality* (London: Picador, 1987), p.45.

12. Johnston, "Clawing in the cash," p.19.

13. Ibid.

14. Douglas Thompson, "Freddy - the man of your dreams," *You* magazine, *Mail on Sunday*, 2 April 1989, p.28.

15. "Fab Freddy," *Rolling Stone*, 6 October 1988, p.92.

16. *Nightmares 1-6* received an 18 certificate (film suitable only for persons of 18 years and over) for their theatrical release in the UK; *Nightmare 7* received a 15 certificate (film suitable only for persons of 15 years and over). *Nightmares 1-7* received an 18 classification for their release on video cassette in the UK. In one of the many self-reflexive moments in *Nightmare 7*, a nurse severely criticises Heather Langenkamp for supposedly allowing her young son to watch the *Nightmare* films.

17. Another game was the US "*A Nightmare on Elm Street* -The Game," produced by Victory Games in 1987, for ages 8 to adult. The game begins in the "Nightmare Zone"; other areas are "The House" and "Boiler Room." The instructions state that "You are asleep, adrift in the land where Freddy roams, and you have to wake up...you try to move your pawn through a maze to the Awake side of the board...if you are crafty enough, you can use Freddy's moves to attack other players who are getting too far ahead of you".

18. Gary Heba, "Everyday nightmares: the rhetoric of social horror in the *Nightmare on Elm Street* series," *Journal of Popular Film and Television* 23, 3 (Fall 1995), p.108.

19. Ibid.

20. Johnston, "Clawing in the cash," p.19.

Above, Seth Brundle (Jeff Goldblum) about to be teleported in **The Fly**.

What Rough Beast? Insect Politics and *The Fly*

Linda Brookover and Alain Silver

The opening six bars of the score for David Cronenberg's *The Fly* (1986) are reminiscent of a Puccini opera, appropriately enough, since this horror/sci-fi film is actually a love story of operatic dimensions masquerading as a monster flick. The remainder of the soundtrack by Howard Shore develops through evocations of Bernard Herrmann–from *The Day the Earth Stood Still* to Hitchcock–and other sci-fi undertones within its sometimes muffled and purposely strained sounds. And Shore's score is merely one aspect of the unusual sub-text of Cronenberg's remake (of the 1958 original directed by Kurt Neumann). Starring Jeff Goldblum as geeky genius scientist/ soulful monster and Geena Davis as his perky "Spider Woman," *The Fly* is Greek Tragedy, high opera, classic horror film and sci-fi love story rolled into one. Despite its visceral impact, it deals with delicate and complex emotional themes. But while the myth of scientific innovations gone wrong is present in the full cycle of horror film from the first *Frankenstein* adaptations to Cronenberg's earlier *The Brood* (1979), those protagonists are destroyed by their own creations, monsters they made and lost control of. Brundle's invention turns him into the monster.

On the surface *The Fly* is pure sci-fi. "Technology gone wrong" is a theme elicited subtly in the dialogue and grotesquely in the metamorphosis of Seth Brundle into quasi-human ("Brundle-Fly") and ultimately quasi-machine ("Teleporter-Fly"). With a gore factor that, for many, renders the picture unpalatable but also indelible, *The Fly* is referenced in at least eight films since its release. The 1987 Oscar awarded to Chris Walas (who directed the inferior sequel) for Best Make-up is a testament to its skillful depiction of a man who becomes an insect. Oozing skin and acid vomit aside, the scariest aspect of this truly adult horror movie is the theme of predator and prey in male-female relationships. There are many pointed lines from *The Fly*, its well-known tag line ("Be afraid. Be very afraid") aside. But perhaps the most interesting remark refers to insect politics. "Have you ever heard of insect politics? Insects don't have politics. They're very brutal, no compassion, no compromise. We can't trust the insect. I'd like to become the first insect politician."

237

Veronica "Ronnie" Quaife (Davis), reporter for *Particle* Magazine, discovers Seth Brundle (Goldblum) while on assignment at a cocktail party for the scientific community. Brundle unabashedly answers Veronica's opening interview question with "I'm working on something that will change the world and human life as we know it." Brundle lures her to his laboratory/apartment with his desperate boastfulness, that even colors the overstated promise of *cappuccino* made on his own Faema coffee machine: "Not the dilettante plastic kitchen model, a real restaurant espresso machine, the one with the eagle on top." As prologue to his demonstration, seated at an upright piano, Brundle plays an elaborate musical introduction before he unveils two telepods, which Veronica glibly remarks look like "designer telephone booths." To demonstrate their purpose, he asks for a personal item "something uniquely you." Dressed in dark leather, Veronica wears no jewelry, so she slips off a stocking, black to be sure. Brundle twitches with nervous sexual energy, while she is intrigued more by his wordy geekiness than any real expectation of seeing the next world-class scientific discovery. Skepticism turns to amazement when his "phone booths" disintegrate her stocking, send it out as an electrical signal, and rematerialize it identically.

Of course, Brundle never really intended for Ronnie to write about this; but she refuses to quash a story. Her editor, Stathis Borans (John Getz), doesn't see anything worth printing. Undaunted by his skepticism, she accepts Brundle's desperate proposal that she hold off on revealing his work in exchange for an exclusive on the whole story. So Ronnie returns to Brundle's warehouse home-laboratory for another demonstration, this time with a video camera and some steaks.

Journalist and scientist enter into the "realm of the flesh," which is the next step in their relationship and in the teleportation experiments. Brundle explains that teleportation to that point is only successful with inanimate objects: "I must not know enough about the flesh, I'm gonna have to learn." What he says foreshadows the imminent sexual relationship with Veronica. As the film progresses and as scientist places himself as a subject under the microscope, it will come to mean something much more, as *The Fly* examines what it is to be human. As a professional woman of the 80's paired with a social throwback, Veronica is definitely in charge. It is she who initiates their liaison and claims the upper position. While still in bed, Seth rolls over onto a misplaced computer part, which Veronica removes in a gesture that says his separation from the machine and his voyage into the realm of the flesh has begun. Of course, this off-handed wound in his back and the way it is made also anticipate Brundle's ultimate fate.

Inspired by their lovemaking and post-coital dinner, Brundle makes a breakthrough in the teleportation of half a cooked steak from one capsule to another. The meat arrives intact, though not tasting quite right. About the control steak, and alluding as well to their first physical encounter, Veronica remarks that it needed a "little finesse perhaps." Predator and prey, it is she who encourages Brundle in his scientific endeavors and triggers his fateful trip in the teleportation device. As in any good tragedy, jealously and *hubris* play major roles.

As the romance and the experiments continue, Brundle grows less monomaniacal and Ronnie lets her emotional guard drop. Veronica's relationship to Borans, her ex-boyfriend/editor, is fully revealed when she returns home to find he has let himself in to her apartment for a shower, which perhaps he needed because he had slimed himself with his own personal brand of egocentrism. The backstory on Borans is that he was Veronica's college professor and mentor. On the surface, he is entirely as self-absorbed as Brundle but without his genius or naive charm. As the third figure in a love triangle, the genre typing on Borans seems fixed from the first. But in one of Cronenberg's subtlest twists, the depth of

Below, the body language of Veronica "Ronnie" Quaife (Geena Davis) is unmistakeable as she speaks with her ex-boyfriend and editor Stathis Borans (John Getz).

Borans' hidden devotion to Veronica will be revealed when he goes to Brundle's disgusting donut-strewn warehouse laboratory to rescue her. Long before this, Cronenberg sets the full range of the tragic circumstances in motion with Veronica's display of disgust for the intruding Borans. Her demand for the return of the key (which he ignores) affirms that she has fallen for the quirky Seth. Over the course of the film, Borans has an emotional metamorphosis that parallels Brundle's physical transformations. He becomes a full-blown stalker when he follows Veronica into a men's store where she buys a leather jacket for Seth and humiliates himself in front of strangers. In buying clothes for Seth, who emulating Einstein had shown her a closet full of identical pants and sports jackets, Veronica is buying a suit of armor for her new knight, a thick, protective skin like her own, a sign that she is ready to wrap him in her sticky web. This realization prompts Borans into an unattractive desperate outburst, further proof of his true feelings for Veronica. He falls to the floor in mock worship saying "You're a goddess. Thank you for making my most paranoid fantasies come true," and then more desperately "Ronnie, you've got to talk to me!"

Undeterred by Borans' affirmations, Ronnie goes back to the lab, where the real horror show begins. When Brundle attempts teleportation using a baboon with Veronica's VCR aimed at the receiving teleportation chamber, there is a sickening thud and smear of bloody flesh on its glass door. In the receiver pod is a pitiful writhing creature who has been genetically turned inside-out but is still capable of screeching eerily at the precocious inventor and his journalist accomplice. The next time we see a baboon, the teleportation is a success; but instead of celebrating, Veronica is compelled to leave abruptly and conclude some unfinished business with Borans. He has sent her a mock-up cover of *Particle Magazine* which features Brundle and reveals that he is in partnership with her in producing a huge scientific discovery. When she goes to Stathis' office to confront him for horning in on the Brundle story, he implores her to keep him informed as a colleague and then adds "I don't want you to disappear from my life" which for the snide Stathis is his version of "I can't live without you." He then asks if they could have "casual stress-relieving sex."

Simultaneous attraction and repulsion and Cronenberg's finesse at producing variations in the script and staging underlie the sub-theme of *The Fly*. From old boyfriends to new ones who change into life-sized insects with big sad eyes, this conceit defines the nature of love in the context of the film. The central irony, the uncontrollable element which brings down the male egos in *The Fly*, is bad timing. Alone in the lab, Brundle has consumed the victory champagne and speculates wildly about Veronica's relationship with Stathis. Reacting to his feelings of jealousy, he impulsively decides to "go through" by himself. He succeeds with only a minor snafu. Before the pod door closed, a fly happened in and accompanied him from one chamber to another. Bad timing: "And what rough beast, its hour come at last, slouches towards Bethlehem to be born?" For in the process of teleportation Brundle has become genetically mingled with the insect. Unbeknownst to him or to Veronica, the metamorphosis has begun. Its first manifestation is his heightened physicality: from an insatiable sexual appetite to a new strength and agility greater than any gymnast's. As Veronica watches Seth's gymnastic routine in amazement, she is sure that something is amiss but still puzzled as to what it might be. Could it have anything to do with the very stiff hairs which she trims from the wound on Brundle's back?

Like any good journalistic researcher, she sends these cuttings to be analyzed. Before the results are in, over the next few days, Brundle becomes manic in his speech and begins to display an outlandish hunger for sugar and sweets. The relationship which quickly progressed to a full-blown love affair deteriorates just as quickly. The human Brundle, who buys Veronica a heart locket and dreams of going away together

Below, "You're changing Seth, everything about you is changing. You look bad, you smell bad, and you have these weird hairs growing out of your back."

when his work is done, is displaced by Brundle/Fly. When Veronica is not able to keep up with him, Brundle suggests then insists that she "go through," which he believes will energize her as it has him. Afraid, repulsed yet still fascinated, she refuses the invitation to join him in his new state. Angered because she will not take a "deep penetrating dive beyond the plasma pool," Brundle storms off to find someone who will.

In addition to personality changes, Brundle begins to change physically. At one point ,Veronica says to him, "You're changing Seth, everything about you is changing. You look bad, you smell bad, and you have these weird hairs growing out of your back." In the argument which ensues, Veronica admits that the hairs that she had analyzed were not human, possibly of an insect origin. Seth reviews his lab notes and discovers the truth about what is happening to him. As any scientist would be, he is intrigued by the implications of genetic mutation. He ob-

Below, Brundle (Jeff Goldblum) examines his deteriorating complexion in the medicine cabinet that will shortly become his museum of discarded body parts.

serves objectively, though with a mixture of sadness and excitement, as the hideous transformations occur. He says, "I won't be just another tumorous bore talking about his lymph nodes." On a subsequent visit, Veronica remarks to Seth that he has gotten worse. He replies eerily,"No, I've gotten better. I seem to have been stricken by a disease with a purpose. I know what it wants. It wants to turn me into something else; most people would give anything to be turned into something else." In this stage of his metamorphosis, Goldblum's idiosyncratic performance recalls the creepy, sibilant inflections of Peter Lorre. On another of Ronie's later visits, he remarks on his natural history museum of Brundle, which consists of a collection of fallen body parts, including his penis, housed in his medicine cabinet. In his last moments in a semi-recognizable human form, Seth tells Veronica, "I'm an insect who dreamed I was a man and loved it. I'll hurt you if you stay." It is clear that Brundle-Fly heeds the only law in the insect world: kill or be eaten.

Out of desperation, Veronica readmits Borans to her life. She confides in him after the discovery that she is pregnant. The expression on his face is genuinely surprised for a few seconds until it changes to horror when she tells the child has been fathered by a man who is undergoing a rapid genetic mutation which may have already begun at the time of conception. Despite this, or perhaps because of it, Borans stands by Veronica. She pays a final visit to Brundle ostensibly to tell him about the baby, or rather, the abortion that she plans to have. She is so repulsed by him that she insists on finding a doctor to do a midnight abortion. Stathis is by her side willing to rescue her from this story assignment turned nightmare. In one of the most hideous scenes in the film, we see Veronica on the operating table, Stathis at her side as the gynecologist (a cameo by director Cronenberg) assists her in the delivery of an enormous larva. As it turns out, this *was* a nightmare; but most of the scenes that follow are even more disturbing: Brundle-Fly, coming in through a skylight in the real Doctor's office just in time to intervene on behalf of his offspring. "Why do you want to kill Brundle? ...Please have the baby," he begs sweetly and, with his superinsect strength, carries his mate away. Is it the survival instinct of the insect or the last shred of his desire to be human that motivates Brundle-Fly?

In the final sequence, Borans is compelled to be hero. First his hand, then his foot are disintegrated by the fly's acid vomit, but he manages to save Veronica by firing his shotgun at the cables connecting the pods. Borans' heroics are gratifying and confusing, not to mention hideous. Stathis may be the unlikely hero, but Veronica's heart belongs to the grotesque creature who still begs "help me be human." When the computer monitor indicates that the genetic splicing sequence is in readiness, Brundle explains that "we'll be the ultimate family, a family of three in one body." But after Ronnie is dragged into the third teleportation device, Stathis arrives in time to shoot the cable to her telepod leaving only the mechanism itself to fuse with Brundle.

At the end, Brundle-Fly's mutation is accelerating so rapidly that one can actually see his skin split in half to make way for the new improved version, in which he has a pronounced proboscis and enlarged eyes on the side of his head. He emerges from the teleportation device dragging his hideously rearranged body parts. The monster is able only to peer at his victims pitifully and shake his head sadly. He makes an anguished

Below, although armed with a shotgun, Borans (John Getz) grapples ineffectually with Brundle-Fly.

groaning sound and then pulls the barrel of the gun which Veronica is holding to his head in an eloquent request to be killed rather than remain a giant insect/machine. Brundle becomes the first insect politician in his last moment before he is felled by his lover in her act of mercy on him.

Cronenberg's scripting and staging throughout The Fly, completely refocuses the narrative line of the original. There the none-too-subtle effect of an oversized fly's head on a human body makes the 1958 "Fly" more purely a monster in a standard horror/sci-fi story that quickly loses human interest. By emphasizing the human rather than technological aspects of inventive genius gone wrong, Cronenberg roots his story in the tradition of psychological horror echoing Stevenson's *Jekyll and Hyde*. Brundle's transformation is the eerie result of well-intentioned experimentation and of the pride which goes before the fall. Like Jekyll, like Dr. Hal Raglan (Oliver Reed) in Cronenberg's own *The Brood*, who perished at the hands of the little monsters his arrogant psychiatry had helped to create, Brundle has a tragic dimension. Thus even after he has been subsumed into the monster, that dimension compels whatever human instinct remains in Brundle to choose death. Since pride was his undoing and jealousy the catalyst for his fatal mischance, Brundle's fate is classic. Like Icarus, he falls from overreaching, although, curiously, wings are one appendage the movie fly never acquired. Brundle's *hubris* in trumpeting himself as the inventor of a machine that could change the world inevitably compels the she-still-loves-him-but-has-to-kill-him conclusion. Perhaps it is not authentic grand opera or Greek tragedy but, as horror/sci-fi films go, a most reasonable facsimile thereof.

Above, Max Renn (James Woods) on the brink of communion with the "new flesh" in **Videodrome**.

Demon Daddies: Gender, Ecstasy and Terror in the Possession Film

Tanya Krzywinska

For many cultures, both past and present, possession is a route to direct communion with the gods. Within the context of the horror film possession conventionally represents the fear of a loss of control. From the writhing body of the possessed nun in Christensen's *Häxan* (1922) to the techno-possessions of the cyber-world in science fiction/horror hybrids—the demonic invasion of the body has provided filmmakers with a potent metaphor to explore the terrors and ecstasies of irrationality. This article will map the generic contortions of the possession film and examine the shifting uses and meanings of demonic possession within these films. Despite the changing meanings of possession in film one aspect continues to persist: possession films tend to cohere around a fundamental fear of the primal father. My contention is that the possession film, from *Häxan* (1922) to *Fallen* (1998), is not as some horror genre critics maintain, a "feminine" genre; but instead it is ruled by an awesome dread of a primal masculine anarchic force which is figured as the demonic.

A common feature of recent work on the horror genre has been to eschew psychoanalytic concepts, which critics such as Judith Halberstam and Steven Shaviro claim perpetuate ideologically driven ideas of gender and spectatorship.[1] I have some sympathy with the attempt to shift the debates around the horror film into new arenas that do not constrain the analysis of horror to conservative forces such as the Oedipus complex. It is, however, the case that the possession film is, as I will show, strongly aligned to what Freud termed the "primal father".[2] As much as the irrational nature of possession might appear to inhabit a world of chaos, it nevertheless has a very specific pattern, which centres on an imagined force of primordial masculine energy that disrupts the social order. This presents a challenge to the conventional gender alignment of rationality to the masculine and irrationality to the feminine. While the possessing agent has remained solidly masculine, there has been a recent and significant shift in the gender of the possessee from women to

247

men. The invasive presence of the demonic masculine often works to put into question the gendered status of the male protagonists, and therefore the demonic can be seen as symptomatic of the precarious nature of masculine identity. This precariousness is often projected onto the hysterical possessed bodies of women, which serve as a means of defending against the uncomfortable recognition that masculine identity is unstable. This essay seeks to explore how the possession film seductively promises a transgressive liberation from order, and also to show that it is informed by gender-based anxieties.

Possessed Nuns: The Demonological Discourse

The first film to make use of the idea of demonic possession was *Häxan* made in Denmark in 1922. Although the film is mainly about witchcraft what is of interest here is the scene in which a nun is possessed by the devil. The devil incites her to perpetrate acts that are against her wishes: the desecration of the host and the theft of a statue of the infant Christ. We may take pleasure in watching her dance and poke her tongue out at the Mother superior, but her possession causes her great anguish and is linked to the repressive values of medieval convent-life. It may be inferred that the devil is working with the unconscious desires that the nun has kept in abeyance. A similar technique is used by the demon Pazuzu in *The Exorcist* (William Friedkin, 1973, US). Central to *Häxan's* libertarian message is that possession results from an unnatural sexual continence that is demanded of the young nuns. The film therefore follows a broadly Freudian line in linking possession to hysteria. The basis of this idea is that repressed sexual desires are dynamic and, rather than lying dormant, actively find ways of being fulfilled in exaggerated and extreme ways. It is common to many possession films to see demonic possession as the product of sexual repression. Given that in the modern world we are less ready to believe in the existence of supernatural forces, many filmmakers make use of psychoanalysis (in a rather simplified form) to explain the phenomenon. The devil is often not conceived of as real entity, as it was in medieval and renaissance cultures, but instead becomes a metaphor for what Freud has called the "return of the repressed" (which is frequently sexual in nature but can also be murderous and violent).[3]

The idea of repressed young nuns divesting themselves of their pious habits certainly has a historical basis, as is evident in documented accounts of convents being inhabited by the devil.[4] The theme has the advantage of offering a convenient metaphor for filmmakers touting a libertarian message. But, perhaps its primary lure is the indulgence of prurient, and delicious, curiosities about the imagined secret life of se-

Above, dreaming while possessed: Vanessa Redgrave as the tormented Mother Superior in *The Devils.*

questered, sex-starved nuns. In the nun-ploitation film, demonic posses-sion is often only a means to an end, the aim of which is to reveal a gamut of perverse fantasies involving lesbianism, sado-masochistic investments in the practices of exorcism, and the mayhem of excessive licentiousness. The watchword of the possessed nun film is transgression: of sanctity, order and puritanical religious discipline. Demonically driven transgression, whether it be supernatural or produced by the pressure-cooker of the split human psyche, is the tempting promise offered by possession as it is figured in the nun-ploitation context.

It was during the 1970s that the possessed nun emerged as a staple of European exploitation film. *The Devils* (Ken Russell, 1971, UK), *The Demons* (Jess Franco, 1972, Sp), *Story of a Cloistered Nun* (Domenico Paolello, 1973, It/Fr/Ger), *Flavia the Heretic* (Gianfranco Mingozzi, 1974, It), *Behind Convent Walls* (Walerian Borowoczyk, 1977, It), *Love Letters of a Portuguese Nun* (Jess Franco, 1976, Sp) and *Killer Nun* (Guilio Berruti, 1978, It) all make use of the figure of the sexually repressed nun to create an enhanced sense of religious and sexual transgression. Previously the possessed nun theme was used sporadically and because of the strange rigors of censorship appeared mainly in high art genres, as in Prokoviev's opera *The Fiery Angel* (c. 1928). The theme was also taken up in Powell and Pressburger's *Black Narcissus* (1947, UK).[5] Although this is a melodrama it carries many of the features of the later nun-ploitation films. The devil does not appear directly in the film, but the possession is effected in a nuanced way, mostly through the pervasive magic of the location of the nun's school. Set on the borders of India and Nepal, the nun's school was formerly a palace that housed a hareem of a local prince. The sensuous magic of the place invades the nuns' sense of religious purpose and prompts them to remember the desires of their past lives. One nun in particular is prompted to a fit of jealous rivalry over a local British man and she becomes a desire-anarchist who disrupts the order. Her skin turns a lurid green and she attempts to kill the Mother Superior. This has prompted reviewers to link the make-up used for the possession scene to that used in *The Exorcist*. The film subtly links possession to sexual repression and thwarted desires, which, as I have said, are common to the possessed nun theme and also present in *The Exorcist*. *Black Narcissus* figures possession in an allegorical and indirect way, whereas, in the 1970s the demonic possession of nuns becomes far more literal and sensationalist.

The Devils is perhaps the best-known possessed nun film and it set in motion the European nunploitation cycle. Made by *enfant-terrible* Ken Russell, the film is based on Aldous Huxley's loosely historical **The Devils Of Loudun** (1952). Rather than a supernatural phenomenon, Russell locates possession in terms of political expediency. He follows the view that, like witchcraft, possession was a tool used by the 17th century Church to maintain its power.[6] The historical dimension lends the

film a certain credibility that many of the subsequent Italian nun-ploitation movies do not have. But, as with the nun-ploitation films, Russell
makes full use of the sensationalist values of possessed nuns. His salacious "mucky-school boy" approach to history is, nevertheless, couched
within an engagement with the aesthetic and political use of possession.
Thereby the film explores the intrinsic, and often elided, links between
possession and the pleasures of dramatic spectacle. This strategy is characteristic of Russell's mix of high and low cultures. With all the flagrant
accoutrements of writhing nudity and sadistic operations on the body of
the nuns perpetrated by the presiding doctors and priestly exorcist, the
possession of the nuns of Loudun is played for maximum grotesque impact. More than this, the film dovetails possession with the political use
of spectacle. As occurred in the medieval and renaissance periods, the
possession of the nuns becomes a public entertainment. It is important
here to say that the possession of Sister Jeanne and the other nuns is
faked. Sister Jeanne claims that she has been possessed by Urbain
Grandier—a priest with whom she is sexually infatuated. This is seized
upon by a group of men who are in the pay of the Duc de Richelieu and
they use her accusations to be rid of Grandier, who endangers their control over the city of Loudun. Later the nuns of the order are threatened
with death if they do not feign a convincing case of possession—and
they comply with gusto. For those not caught up directly in this deadly
game, these events provide a grotesque form of diverting entertainment.
For example, when Sister Jeanne is interrogated by Father Barré and her
body is examined by the quack doctors for signs of possession and sexual activity, a masked audience is present. Later, when the nuns enact
their demonic possession, the King comes to visit them and treats the
whole affair as a theatrical masque. The King tricks Barré into believing
that he has with him a vial of Christ's blood, this temporarily ceases the
mayhem and reveals to the audience (but not the town) that the whole
affair as a fake. Russell therefore directly refers to the spectacular, if sadistic, pleasures of possession as masquerade. What many critics have
not said about the film is that possession is used here as a double political expedient. It enables de Richelieu to be rid of Grandier, and the spectacle diverts the people of Loudun's attention away from the grinding
power plays at work, which will ultimately wrest control of the town
away from them. As with the ritual pomp of kingship and religion—
both King and Cardinals are lavishly costumed in the film—possession
is yet another means by which politics are aestheticized. Russell impli-
cates the viewer in the diverting pleasures of spectacle. We, like the people of Loudun, are possessed by the dazzle of artifice. But we are further
invited to see what these pleasures are covering over.[7] This is done by

accentuating the visceral and grotesque effects on the material of the body, and is achieved with a certain relish that is calculated to disturb. It is this that has prompted critics to see the film as "meretricious," as if the focus on the visceral detracts any serious consideration of the issues it raises.[8] I would, by contrast, suggest that the film goes to the heart of the transgressive appeal of possession by revealing the role it implicitly has in many other films. Possession offers itself as a grotesque and salacious pleasure for the spectator. The possessed body is ruled by recalcitrant desires, which are generally held in abeyance if the social order is to function. It can consequently be said that the transgression, effected by possession, functions as a psychic and social safety-valve which preserves the status quo by constraining the abject and the anarchic to the diverting confines of vicarious spectacle.

In *The Devils* possession is used as a political expedient to divert the people of Loudun's attention away from the power struggles in play and to effect the downfall of the libertarian upstart Grandier. But it is also the case that hysteria and sexual repression are implicated, as in *Häxan*. Grandier says that "secluded women, they give themselves to God, but something cries out to be given to man." Corroborating Grandier's view, Sister Jeanne's retributive action is borne of her unfulfilled sexual desires for Grandier. These desires are apparent in the graphic fantasy sequences in which she has sex with Grandier, who is cast in the role of Christ. Within the logic of her holy order this is indeed a form of demonic possession but the film makes it clear that Sister Jeanne is a hysteric, and a dangerous one. This accords with the libertarian message inherent in many of the possessed nun movies. The underlying idea is that possession results from the repression of the nuns' "natural" sexual desires. As with many of the subsequent nun-ploitation films *The Devils* follows Wilhelm Reich's psychoanalytically informed idea that a lack of sexual fulfilment produces a hysterical or psychotic person—whose unconscious desires will be magnified and acted out in a grotesque, perverse and excessive way.[9] This was a fitting message with which to counter the anti-permissive crusaders of the 70s. Most of the nunploitation films, but *Häxan*, *The Devils* and *Flavia the Heretic* in particular, suggest that the rigid discipline of Christian orthodoxy produces aberrant forms of sexual desire. This is because it demands an abasement of the body and the purging of sexual desire. Within this logic sexual longings—and covert means of assuaging them—are considered to be demonically driven. As Nietzsche has said "Christianity gave Eros poison to drink—he did not die, but degenerated into vice."[10] Foucault too follows this line of thought and it carries a certain resonance within the libertarian discourse that informs the understanding of possession and hysteria in the nun-ploitation film.

Possession in the nun-ploitation film therefore offers transgressive pleasures, but it is also, ironically, shown that this transgression is actually produced by the logic of medievalist Christian ideals in which bodily desires are the playground of Satan. These films centre possession around the hysterical female body: the exorcists are all men and they are frequently "fathers" (of the priestly kind) with all the symbolic connotations of patriarchy. This suggests that the anarchy of possession can be read as a challenge to their hegemonic rule. But, this is limited, demanding that we ignore the frequent closure produced by the death of a nun or the defeat of the invading demon. Flavia, for example, is flayed alive and Sister Jeanne is no longer of use after the death of Grandier when she is left to her "perverse" fantasies. For the exorcists and good fathers possession offers a challenge to prove their power and devotion as well as allowing them to indulge in all manners of sadistic and sexual behaviors in the name of God the father. Over the bodies and desires of cloistered women these men play out fantasies of defeating the "bad" demonic father in the name of the "good" heavenly father.

The Spectator's Pact with Pazuzu: *The Exorcist*

The Exorcist is almost certainly the most famous possession film in cinema. Its figuring of possession has subsequently shaped many representations of the phenomena. The story centres on the possession of an adolescent girl. While it may appear that the film hinges on the display of the abject female body, I contend that she is in fact simply a body over which the good and bad father do battle. This is a struggle between the forces of good and evil, and is mapped through the conflicting forces of rational scepticism and irrational faith. The dramatic structure of the film leans on Father Karras's crisis of faith. In many horror films, such as *Night of the Demon* (Jacques Tourneur, 1958, UK), the audience's identification is channelled through the central protagonist. This figure is often sceptical about the veracity of the supernatural. Through the supernatural events of the film the audience and the hero are channelled into believing its (diegetic) truth. By contrast, *The Exorcist* makes it very clear to the viewer from the outset that the demon is real. So we, unlike Karras, the doctors and Regan's mother, know that the demon is not the product of Regan's unconscious mind. It is then Karras, in particular, and not the audience, who must be brought to a place of faith. As such the film is only partially interested Regan's psychic state but is more focused on the priest's psychic conflicts, which manifest through his struggle with the demon Pazuzu.

Above, Jason Miller as Father Karras in **The Exorcist**.

Pazuzu makes use of the central characters' unconscious desires: Regan and her mother's Oedipal tensions as well as Karras's loss of faith and guilt caused by the death of his mother.[11] The first to die at the hands of Pazuzu is Burke, Chris MacNeil's lover (McNeil is Regan's mother). Pazuzu also works with Chris MacNeil's desire that Regan should remain a child. By prompting Regan to speak of sexuality, Pazuzu taps into MacNeil's fears of losing her daughter's innocent love. The figure of the mother is also important to Father Karras. He only begins to believe in the existence of the demon once Pazuzu speaks about his mother, setting into play his unconscious Oedipal crisis. Karras' conflict with the demon is framed by Oedipal tensions and betrays a further aspect of the Oedipal through the battle between the good father and the bad father. The fantasy that Karras is playing out is a classical Freudian scenario in which the son desires to kill the bad father to rescue the mother.

Freud's term for the bad father is the "primal" father and he maintains that buried deep within the masculine psyche is a fear of the primal father who prevents his sons from achieving power and access to the bodies of the women. In "Moses and Monotheism" he says:

> The strong male was lord and father of the entire horde and
> unrestricted in his power, which he exercised with violence.
> All the females were his propertywives and daughters of his
> own horde and some, perhaps, robbed from other hordes.
> The lot of his sons was a hard one: if they roused their
> father's jealousy they were killed or castrated or driven out.
> The expelled brothers united to overpower their father, and,
> as was the custom in those days, devoured him raw.[12]

I am wary of the idea that the primal father is either a pre-historical fact or hardwired into the evolutionary processes of the human brain. Instead it seems more likely that the fantasy of the primal father is a construct of the social imagination, which works with the power relation between father and son, and is subject to cultural differences and historical change. The primal father is then a fantasy, and as it crop-ups regularly in film and other narrative modes, it would seem to be a collective fantasy. Just because it is a product mainly of the imagination does not mean it can be dismissed: it has real effects on people and is instrumental to the reiteration of conventional gender roles. Films often act as a screen on to which this fantasy is played out. Thereby the fantasy exceeds the individual and is reiteratively cloned, which further entrenches it within the cultural imagination. The battle with the primal father is evident in many popular films in which the young male hero has to do battle with an older and more cunning oppressor or villain. Often this is enacted by the villain's abduction of the hero's female love interest. We might be sceptical of the essentialist reading of the primal father, but the value of "Moses and Monotheism" is that in it Freud identifies an aspect of the configuration of masculinity that continues to inform the horror film.

What is clear from the quote from "Moses and Monotheism" is that the primal father has a demonic aspect. It is this that is reiterated in the possession film and is important in the consideration of the origin and function of the demon in *The Exorcist*. Through the struggle for the souls of Regan and his mother, Karras is able to indulge and satisfy his Oedipal hatred for the bad father (who keeps all the women to himself). Ironically the presence of the bad father as demon also allows Karras to re-establish his failed religious faith. Therefore, unlike Barbara Creed, I would argue that the abject status of Regan's body is not simply the reflection of a male fear of the leaky female body.[13] Instead Regan's pitiful abject status is simply a further spur to Karras's determination to save her from the clutches of the demon and thus fuels a classic male fantasy of rescuing the beleaguered child or woman. I would also reject the notion that the demon is gendered female. Creed maintains that we should read Pazuzu as female and that Pazuzu is a symptom of Regan's Oedipal relation with her mother.[14] By contrast, I would claim Pazuzu is male, as his snake phallus implies, and importantly that he uses the unconscious material of those with whom he comes into contact. Regan does not use possession as a means to power, as Creed implies. Instead it is the demon that exaggerates and brings to the surface Regan's desires, which is why she uses her mother's swear words and reflects her sexual frustrations. In some ways I am sympathetic to Creed's desire to render Pazuzu as a figure of the anarchic feminine, but this seems to be a wish reading that elides the masculine dynamic which structures the film. Pazuzu is not the monstrous feminine, but the monstrous masculine. As his ancient pagan Babylonian roots testify, Pazuzu is the castrating bad, archaic father who disrupts the civilized world of rationality and order. And Regan is his manipulated victim and not his creator.

It may appear that I have sewn myself into the constraints of seeing Regan's possession as purely the product of the male imaginary. While this might be so, it is also useful to point out a further related dynamic that circulates around the figure of the primal father. Illusionist cinema depends on its ability to put scepticism in abeyance. Conventionally speaking, rationality and scepticism are gendered male. This is a common feature of the horror film: women are often portrayed as closer to the supernatural than men. Examples include: *The Haunting* (Robert Wise, 1963, US), *Don't Look Now* (Nicolas Roeg, 1973, UK), *Poltergeist* (Tobe Hooper, 1982, US), *Hellraiser* (Clive Barker, 1984, UK) and *The Craft* (Andrew Fleming, 1996, US). However the main goal of the genre is to reach across the boundary between the screen and the viewer—or between subject and object—and elicit a powerful response.[15] In its goal to terrify, the horror film regularly forces the viewer into identification with the victim of an aggressive attack. This might be perpetrated by *Nightmare's* Freddie, a zombie, or a demon from hell, or an attack that comes from within the body as in *Shivers* (Cronenberg, 1975, Can), as well as in the werewolf and possession films. As such the horror film is not as partial to the sadistic or voyeuristic channelling of the gaze as it is often thought. It asks us, both men and women, to inhabit the "feeling" position—and this mobilizes a set of masochistic fantasies. We feel pity and terror but we are also put into the position of passive subjugation. I would therefore extend Steven Shaviro's argument, that passivity—which implies a temporary dissolution of identity—is a key pleasure of the Zombie film, the possession film and indeed the horror genre in general.[16] I would claim that through our identification with the possessed Regan, *The Exorcist* works with the pleasures of the annihilation of the contours of the self. That this might be experienced as pleasurable and not as simply terrifying is reliant on the retention of the idea that what we are watching is a fictional cinematic construct. But, at the same time, this can be set aside so that we are able to derive a sense of something in excess of the mundane quality of everyday life. We therefore enter into a complicit pact with the text. It would appear that the dissolution of the self that is partially entered into militates against masculine, rational control. The irrational and the rational thereby work together in the horror film. The frisson of "letting go," believing in the unbelievable and acquiescing to a demonic masculine power has to be framed by—and work with—a rational safety net. As such the horror film allows the viewer to "have their cake and eat it too." This spectatorial dynamic is embedded in the content of *The Exorcist*. Karras is a sceptical and macho boxing priest, but nevertheless, he gives his body to Pazuzu, in the final scene of the film. By offering himself up to the annihilating force of Pazuzu, Karras regains his faith and power. He sacrifices himself to irrationality, but restores the rational order. To achieve faith, he must give himself up to something beyond the human, and in so doing his life is given rational purpose. In being consumed by the demon, and becoming one with it, he therefore partakes of the power of the primal father by entering into a masochistic relation with him. This reflects the pact that the spectator has with the horror film. We must give up rationality to partake of the masochistic pleasures offered by a film and its demons, but we do so within the frame of rationality, and ultimately we walk away from the film with an added sense of our own psychic and physical boundaries. Possession, as it is figured in *The Exorcist*, is therefore restorative and redemptive—something that David Lynch's possessions never become.

"What the Fuck is Your Name?": Art, *Ate*, and David Lynch's Demon-Daddies

Although Lynch's films may be considered to be non-generic "art" movies, I would contend that they are heavily informed by the horror genre. It is particularly the central use of possession which allows me to talk of *Fire Walk with Me* (1992, US) and *Lost Highway* (1997, US) as horror films. In these films it is men rather than women who are possessed. But as with the other films discussed above the irrational and the demonic is closely related to the primal father. Lynch's films are characteristically located in a world in which the stability of reality is constantly under threat, and meaning too is mutable rather than closed into one-to-one correspondences. Accordingly, the films' approach to concepts of good and evil are rather more diffuse than those found in the classical horror film. Borrowing from such films as *The Exorcist*, Lynch uses possession to explore the fragility of identity. The demons here, however, are neither extrinsic or intrinsic. Their othered force pervades and splits the psyche, often entailing the merging of separate characters or the acting out of unconscious collective fantasies (which as I have indicated above are not hardwired into the psyche, but act *as if* they are). The effect of this destabilising demonic force permeates throughout the form, texture and characters of the films, and is reflected in the lack of closure of many of their narrative enigmas. The impact of this instability consequently extends to the spectator.

Both Leland Palmer in *Fire Walk With Me* (and in *Twin Peaks*) and Fred Madison in *Lost Highway* appear to have made un-remembered pacts with the devil. As with Harry Angel in *Angel Heart* (Parker, 1987, US), this pact is associated with the perpetration of a primal crime. For Leland this means the serial rape and murder of his daughter, Laura Palmer. For Fred it is the brutal murder of his wife Renée. Both acts are carried out under the aegis of a demonic male figure. Leland has most obviously stepped into the role of the primal father through his transgression of the Oedipal pact and as such suffers the tragic anguish of his blood-guilt. Fred's crime is all together more complex. Unlike Leland, who is condemned to remember his act, Fred does not remember killing Renée. He has only seen the killing on video tape and continues to believe in his own innocence. He is also implicated in a further killing, that of sleazy gang-land boss Mr Eddy. This death is aided by the unnamed man and bears all the marks of a sacrificial murder of the bad father, who according to Freud has sexual dominion over all the women in his tribal "horde." Mr Eddy is often linked to pornography: he offers Pete a "porno" video tape, is present at the screening of hardcore films and just before his death he is shown a series of hardcore video clips. It would therefore seem that Mr Eddy too had a pact with the unnamed man (a kind of post-modern Mephistopheles) and his time is now up and is killed by his "son" successor, Fred. The sacrifice of Mr Eddy is laden with mythic and cinematic intertextual resonances, which seem to haunt the scene and load it with a collective mythic meaning. Mr Eddy is akin to a Frazerean "divine victim"[17] and he is killed with a knife connoting the castratory knife belonging to the primal father with which the son is threatened. As with the murder of Colonel Kurtz in *Apocalypse Now* (Francis Ford Coppola, 1979, US) by Captain Willard, Mr Eddy is killed by his double/son Fred. As such both Leland and Fred are possessed by the psychic dynamic of the murderous and irrational of the primal father. This precedes and exceeds their conscious sense of self-identity and they are therefore caught up in a channelling force that is greater than themselves. The trope of demonic possession is used in these films to evoke the psychic and social forces that determine who they are. As in Greek Tragedy there is no redemption or release from these extraneous forces and the idea that we are self-determined is unnervingly revealed to be an illusion.

Demonic possession is often used in the horror genre to uncover our fears of a lack of self-determination and the fragility of the body. In ancient and classical Greece the act of forgetting or of doing something that was counter to character was said to be motivated by *Ate*. *Ate* was cast out of the pantheon of the gods and condemned to cause the clouding of rationality. ER Dodds, a historian of Greek religion, makes the case that *Ate* resulted from the conflict between individuality and social conformity (and as such is close to psychoanalytic understanding of psychic conflict).[18] This is the very stuff of the Lynchian psycho-drama, as outlined above, which explores the disturbing place in which the ego is not in control of a person's actions. In *Fire Walk With Me* both Laura and Leland suffer a failure of the rational. Laura knows, but does not know, that Bob, who comes to her bed at night, is in fact her father. Leland too, is unable to contain his incestuous and ultimately murderous desires. In *Lost Highway* Pete and Fred, like Bob and Leland, slide in and out of each other's characters (further reminding me of Turner and Chas in *Performance* [Cammell, 1970, UK]). They are blind to the perpetration of some primal crime that has brought them into the demonic world of the unnamed man. All these characters are stunned by the machinations of something that appears to be the force of the primal father, which exceeds rationality and disrupts the integrity of the subject. For them, unlike Regan, there is no good father, or good god, who does battle with the forces of evil. Their demons cannot be exorcised. Accordingly there is no single solution or closure, nor any hope for redemption: which is why Leland weeps and Fred does not know who the fuck he is.

Techno-Possessions: *Videodrome* and *Event Horizon*

The possessed man has become a more regular feature of recent films, and in particular in SF/horror hybrids. The trend seems to have been kicked off by David Cronenberg's *Videodrome* (1982, Can) and the film has spawned a host of male heroes and anti-heroes possessed by different types of technology. In addition there is also a horde of demonically possessed computer based technologies. The latter trope seems to have come to light through the psychotic consciousness of computers such as HAL in *2001: A Space Odyssey* (Stanley Kubrick, 1968, US) and *Demon Seed* (Donald Cammell, 1977, US). Why is it that for men to be possessed the demon is required to be technologically embodied? Is it that computer technology is super-rational and therefore places the human male in a subservient role? Is it that possession has become a means by which the obsessive desires of the mad scientist can be set in a new context? Or is it simply that by technologising the demon, fears about being penetrated, with all its sexual connotations, are being worked through in a disguised way?

In *Videodrome* Max Renn is quite literally consumed by infernal desires relating to sex and death. The film uses S/M iconography to make this apparent. Max believes he is being fed videodrome tapes that operate as a kind of software re-programming of the brain. This produces hallucinations and, alongside the convoluted conspiracy-element of the film, destabilizes his hold on reality. Max is in essence possessed by the videodrome technology. Cronenberg uses possession as a means of attacking the conservative view that the media directly impacts on people's behaviors, an argument that is often deployed to support media censorship. Cronenberg therefore materializes this view by making the media itself a demonic possessing force that sweeps away rational will and socially oriented behaviors, following the trajectory of the pleasure principle. Possession is also used to dissolve conventional boundaries, and Max becomes literally a "desiring machine." So why was it expedient to make Max a man, rather than the traditional possessed hysterical woman?

Using a male body as the subject of the techno-possession Cronenberg heightens the sense (which I believe is meant to be read ironically) that anyone, and not just easily influenced "women and servants," can be affected by the media. If a woman had been used in the role the possession would have taken on a more ambiguous meaning. It would be more open to being read as the product of feminine hysteria (a common alignment in the horror and other genres and one that is deployed in many possession films). Through the use of a man and technology as demon, the possession film can be recycled with a marketable generic difference. Further, and this is important to my overall argument, it allows the mobilisation of the fear of the primal father to be covertly explored and it is this that gives the film its shocking, resonant power. By becoming possessed, Max is assigned with what Carol Clover has called, an "open" body and at one point he develops a vagina-like gash in stomach into which is a placed one of the videodrome tapes which will determine his behavior.[19] This, as Clover and others have argued, taps into a fear of the feminisation of the male body and is connoted through the act of penetration. But what Clover does not explore is how this anxiety is referred back to the fear of the primal father. It is also the case that the use of technology (which is generally regarded as gender neutral) as the penetrating agent tends to obscure the homosexual implications of the act of being penetrated. Beneath this lies the fear of being fucked and feminized (which may be taken as literal or as a metaphor for castration) by the primal father—who is here embodied as an ever-present castrating father who omnisciently sees unconscious desires. That the primal father is technologically rendered means that the trope is reiterated in a contemporary context, but further aligns the extrinsic and powerful other-ness of the media, with all its feared effects on morality, to the primal father. Max's identity, including his gender, is in peril—and to regain his male hero status he must do battle with the primal father. At first Max believes that a man, Brian O'Blivion, is the puppeteer behind the videodrome technology. There is in fact no one man behind it. This is because it is the product of a collective fantasy of the primal father. In other words videodrome is a power greater than an individual man, but which can see and uses—like Pazuzu in *The Exorcist* and the demons of *Event Horizon*—the unconscious desires of its beleaguered puppet sons who struggle to retain their sense of gender and identity.

The other example of possession in the SF/Horror hybrid I want to look at here is *Event Horizon*. The film takes us into the realms of HP Lovecraft's cosmic evil and the bodily tortures of *Hellraiser* (Clive Barker, 1987, UK). Dr Weir is a scientist who becomes possessed by an evil force. Unlike Max Renn in *Videodrome*, Dr Weir becomes fully identified with the intruding primal forces that feed off discord, pain and suffering. These forces have been released by Weir's invention of a gateway that allows the rules of the space-time continuum to be interfered with and Einstein's theory of relativity to be transgressed. Carried on a space-ship, it literally made the craft disappear for a time and then reappear with all its crew dead. Weir and a second crew are sent in to investigate what happened. As Weir's brain-child we could infer that the gateway technology carries with it his unconscious desires which appear to be taken up by the possessing force. The gateway opens onto a Lovecraftean dimension of living chaos. While at first this force is not embodied, it nevertheless, like Pazuzu in *The Exorcist*, makes direct use of unconscious material to create anguish, terror and death. The space-ship, which has in effect been to Hell and back, becomes a medieval torture chamber enhanced by its gothic arches that are covered in a coating of human gore. It resembles medieval depictions of the terrible horrors of the inferno and shifts the terrible house of the horror film into space. After a series of uncanny happenings chaos takes up residence in the mind and body of Weir. Discipline and punishment are viscerally carved into his skin, and he physically resembles Frank, as demon, from *Hellraiser*. The possessed Weir rules over the ship as the embodiment of the sadistic and castrating primal father and his bloody carnival of pain constitutes a terrible primal scene in which all bodies are simply canvases onto which agony is etched. This is a place where boundaries of morality, time, space, inside and outside are transgressed. The demonic force, which fuses with Weir's unconscious mind, demands the ultimate sacrifice. It decrees that eyes should be torn from their sockets, and thereby provides a clue to its subtextual Oedipal origins. The eye and the gaze are instruments of power. As Freud argues it, the guilty Oedipus tears out how own eyes in an analogue of castration and claims in "The Uncanny" that the violation of the eye is a metaphor for castration.[20] In the coda of *Event Horizon* two of the crew escape from the ship and are woken on their homeward journey by two masked men, one of whom is Weir. This is only a dream, but suggests that the chaos demon occupies the under-world of sleep and by extension the unconscious. It is also clear that the formerly protean chaos has found its preferred form—the corrupted and scarred body of the primal father.

The techno-possession film, such as *Videodrome, Event Horizon, Lawnmower Man* (Brett Leonard, 1992, US) and *Strange Days* (Kathryn Bigelow, 1995, US), in general, draws strongly on medieval demonology. Technology itself becomes demonic, as in *Demon Seed*, or opens a doorway for the demonic, as in *Event Horizon*. In these cases the possessing technology violently or seductively (often in tandem) intersects and interferes with rationality, gender and identity, and it does so in the guise of the violating primal father. This seems to betray a conservative message not to "interfere" with basic, god-given, ground rules (such as producing Artificial Intelligences, or breaking the rules of relativity). Scientific and technological curiosity, as in medieval cautions against playing with magic, provokes supernatural retribution mirroring the rule of *hubris* and *nemesis* in Greek Tragedy. By translating the invention of technology into the realms of the supernatural and the unconscious a further magical sleight of hand is achieved. Technology is divested of its political and economic origins and becomes "demonic," as also occurred in *Videodrome*. As such these films map technology through unconscious psychic investments—which through the deployment of the mythic primal father are taken as archetypal.

Masculinities, Family and Chaos: *Fallen*

What all the films discussed here have in common is that the agent of possession is figured as the primal father. Whatever shape the possession takes the demonic intruder is rendered as hyper-masculine and it would therefore be a mistake to term the possession film as a "feminine" form. Increasingly it would seem the demonic is figured as a now unacceptable form of masculinity that is unremittingly phallic in nature (a recent example would be Angelov in *Practical Magic* [Griffin Dunne, 1998, US]). The battle between the good and bad father has then become a stage on which the definition of masculinity is played out within an Oedipal context, and this is most markedly the case in *Fallen* (Gregory Hoblit, 1998, US).

In contrast to *The Exorcist*, *Fallen* is not a film about spiritual crisis, but instead is centred on a very contemporary crisis in the definition of masculinity. It is further hinged around the notion that the hyper-masculinity characterized by the primal father is a type of contaminating disease that corrupts morality and humanity. In the film the demon Azazel possesses people through the medium of physical contact and his identity is disguised by the fact that he moves through people at a rapid rate (they are in a sense his mode of transport as well as being his prosthetic tools). His method of movement makes a clear link between the open body of possession and the body that is open to viruses. Thereby the demonic primal father, as a collective, powerful and transcendent entity, is linked to contagion and corruption. Like Pazuzu, Azazel has a Sumerian origin and therefore precedes Christianity, but he is more mobile, and thereby less containable, than Pazuzu. Azazel figures himself into the role of serial killer. As in Fincher's *Seven* (1995, US), he leaves cryptic messages for his main pursuer, Detective Hobbes (Denzil Washington). Hobbes was instrumental in the electrocution of Azazel's previous host (and with whom Azazel is most closely identified). Once Hobbes realizes the demon is "real" he seeks to destroy it with godly righteousness, and will sacrifice himself to protect a child (his nephew). As with Karras, Hobbes is strongly motivated by guilt. Azazel has killed his "new-man," gentle, single-parent brother and therefore orphaned his nephew. Azazel is anathema to the caring Hobbes and his brother. Everyone he possesses swaggers down the street, using blasphemous words and indulging in various acts of murder and cruelty. Azazel also sings the Rolling Stones' song "Time is on My Side" which evokes the Stones macho-phallic "cock" rock.[21]

The hyper-masculine Azazel is figured as the bad father whose pestilential presence infects the bodies of the innocent. The main target of his cruelties are the good, caring black all-male family (Hobbes, his brother

Above, homicide detective John Hobbes (Denzel Washington) fleeing with his nephew Sam (Michael Pagan) in **Fallen**.

and his son). This revises the model of all-women families in horror films such as *Carrie* (Brian De Palma, 1976, US) and *The Exorcist* where it is implied that the absence of a father acts as a catalyst for supernatural trouble. Hobbes is a good father figure—he works hard, has a sense of duty and has divested himself of the "archaic" masculinity embodied by Azazel (primarily embodied by the white "cocky" prisoner and serial-killer Edgar Reece). As such the film centres around the idea that masculinity, to use the cliché, is a site of struggle in which the values of traditional white masculinity, with all its anti-social individuality, is at odds with the new caring family-oriented masculinity. It is this archaic masculinity that returns in the film, in demonic form, to disrupt order. Therefore the film, like many recent Hollywood films, is structured around the conflict between demonized hyper-masculinity and the new family-friendly masculinity.

Conclusion

In contrast to the possession of women in the earlier films, in *Fire Walk With Me* and *Event Horizon* it is the white male body that becomes the culturally determined home for the demonic. The possessing demon is the supreme corrupter, breaking the Oedipal Law in *Fire Walk With Me*, contaminating and disrupting the good family in *Fallen*, corrupting hyper-space in *Event Horizon*. These films work according to the anti-laws of the bad, demonic, father. What is common to the films is the context of a crisis in the meaning of masculine identity. This prompts psychic splitting either intrinsically, within the self, or extrinsically, in the clear divisions between good and bad characters. It is therefore possible to argue that the amoral hyper-masculine, often in the guise of a super-computer or Artificial Intelligence, has joined the dangerous seductive female as the new bogey. The recycling of the traditional idea of the devil as "bad-boy" has been re-vivified with the current crisis in the definition of masculine identity, prompted perhaps by post-feminist warrior-women heroines and the implicit fear of hyper-powerful computers. As Freud has said, in times of crisis there is a return to supernatural thinking. The crisis in the definition of masculinity then takes on, at the level of the imagination, an over-blown hysterical and contagious dimension equal to the retributive forces of the biblical apocalypse and Greek blood-guilt. As such through the fear of the primal father the male possession films figure the crisis in the definition of masculinity as the end of the world.

Notes

1. "Psychoanalysis, with its emphasis on and investments in the normal, quickly reveals itself as inadequate to the task of unravelling the power of horror" Judith Halberstam, *Skin Shows* (Durham/London: Duke University Press, 1995): 9. "I offer a theory of cinematic fascination that is a radical alternative

to the psychoanalytic paradigm." Steven Shaviro, *The Cinematic Body* (Minneapolis: University of Minnesota Press, 1993): 24.

2. The term refers to Freud's idea that in the pre-history of the human race men lived in small tribes, which were ruled by a powerful patriarch (the primal father). The patriarch's sons are jealous of his dominion over the tribe and they subsequently kill and eat him. The sons then feel guilty about this and instate laws against murder and incest. This is the blueprint for the Oedipus complex. The small boy desires to have the sole love and attention of his mother, but the father-figure intervenes in this and as a result the boy-child wishes him dead. According to Freud this process is later repressed. The boy fears that the father figure may know his secret thoughts and as a result kill or castrate him. After a short period the boy recognizes that he cannot achieve his goals and gives up his feelings for his mother in favor of identification with father-figure. In this article I am using Freud's concept of the primal father to argue that in the possession film, the archaic feared, castrating father returns as a possessing demon to disrupt the rational order. "Totem and Taboo" (1913) and "Moses and Monotheism" (1939) in Sigmund Freud, *The Origins of Religion* (Harmondsworth: Penguin, 1990).

3. Freud's paper entitled "A Seventeenth Century Demonological Neurosis" addresses possession in similar terms, but as the possessee is male, Freud makes the case that the possession is produced by the man's psychic conflict about his father. This will prove to be important to my overall argument and will be discussed in more detail later. "A Seventeenth Century Demonological Neurosis" (1922) in Sigmund Freud, *Art and Literature* (Harmondsworth: Penguin, 1990).

4. Documents related to the demonic possession of nuns in the 17th century were often made by Priests and court officials. Aldous Huxley's *The Devils of Loudun* (London: Chatto and Windus, 1952) and L'estrange Ewens' *Witchcraft and Demonianism* (London: Fredrick Muller, 1970) [originally published in 1933] reprint extracts from such documents.

5. Knowing of Ken Russell's love of Powell and Pressburger's films, it seems plausible to infer that *Black Narcissus* influenced Russell's decision to make *The Devils* (which in turn kick started the European cycle of nun-ploitation films).

6. H.R. Roper, "The European Witch-Craze" in Max Marwick (ed.), *Witchcraft and Sorcery* (Harmondsworth: Penguin, 1970): 126.

7. Because most critics have concentrated on Russell as mucky school boy (which he certainly is in part) they have tended to neglect the fact that the film accords with Brecht's, and other left-wing German intellectuals, concerns about the aestheticisation of politics that characterized Nazism.

8. Kim Newman, *Nightmare Movies* (London: Bloomsbury, 1988): 42.

9. Wilhelm Reich, *The Function of the Orgasm* (Souvenir Press, 1983).

10. Friedrich Nietzsche, *Beyond Good and Evil* (Harmondsworth: Penguin, 1973): 87 (Aphorism no. 168).

11. Here I disagree with Barbara Creed as she maintains that the mother-daughter relation is the *cause* of Regan's possession. I see it in terms of the tensions of the mother-daughter relation which Pazuzu uses as a tool to create discord and pain. Barbara Creed, *The Monstrous Feminine*. (London/NY: Routledge: 1993): 39.

12. Freud, "Moses and Monotheism': 324/5.

13. "What is different about *The Exorcist* is its graphic association of the monstrous with the feminine body'. Creed, 1993: 37.

14. Creed, 1993: 39.

15. In recent so called post-modern Slasher's, such as *Scream* (Wes Craven, 1996, US) and *Scream 2* (Wes Craven, 1998 , US), the use of inter-textual references and overt references to previous films is an effort to force this dissolution. In other words, by stating that all the previous films are *just* films, a space is opened up (temporarily) in which we can believe that what we are currently watching is "real'.

16. "Looking is an obsessive passivity, a violent forcing, that yet cannot be reduced to a situation of being manipulated, enslaved, subjugated and controlled." Shaviro, 1993: 50.

17. Frazer, writing in the early 1900s, claims that many early cultures depended on a magical system of kingship and sacrifice to ensure that a social group flourished. The king represented a god and the land, when he became sick he must be killed by his successor to ensure the continued fertility of the land. J.G. Frazer, *The Golden Bough: A new abridgement*. (Oxford/NY: Oxford University Press: 1994): 228-253. A previous abridgement was published in 1922.

18. E.R. Dodds, *The Greeks and The Irrational*. (Berkeley/ Los Angeles: University of California Press, 1951): 47-49.

19. Carol J Clover, *Men Women and Chainsaws* (London: BFI, 1992) : 197.

20. A study of dreams, phantasies and myths has taught us that anxiety about one's eyes, the fear of going blind, is often enough a substitute for the dread of being castrated. The self-blinding of the mythical criminal, Oedipus, was simply a mitigated form of the punishment of castration - the only punishment that was adequate for him by *lex talionis*." Sigmund Freud, "The Uncanny" (1919) in *Art and Literature* (London; Penguin, 1990): 356.

21. The film also uses the Rolling Stones song "Sympathy from the Devil" at the end of the film, which also appeared at the end of *Interview with A Vampire* (Neil Jordan, 1994, US) and was used to indicate the renewed strength of the "mad bad and dangerous to know" vampire Lestat. Lestat displays all the attributes of self-centred red-in-tooth-and-claw masculinity (which is perhaps his attraction) against Louis' gentle, caring, "new-man" ethics.

Above, Hichcock's new wife (Barbara Steele) and his assistant (Montgomery Glenn).

Women on the Verge of a Gothic Breakdown: Sex, Drugs and Corpses in *The Horrible Dr. Hichcock*

Glenn Erickson

Midnight in a fog-shrouded cemetery. An old man labors over a half-dug grave. From the shadows there appears a mysterious top-hatted stranger, who abruptly clubs the gravedigger senseless. Then he pries open the unburied coffin, revealing the pallid blue face of a female cadaver within....

So far, so good. We're in familiar territory, with familiar questions about this intruder's purpose. Does he need the cadaver for medical research? Doctors forced to turn criminal are often quite sympathetic in horror films. Is he a mad scientist seeking to create a living monster from dead tissue? No shock there— that's a revelation that wouldn't cause the average school kid to blink twice. But this ghoul has another agenda entirely. He leans purposefully over the opened coffin, runs his fingers over the face of the deceased, and begins to fondle and caress its presumably rigor-mortised torso. Ugh! Even Riccardo Freda fades out on that one!

The outrageous central concern of *The Horrible Dr. Hichcock* never has been considered appropriate material for any film openly advertised and exhibited to the public, horror or otherwise. That a film about the frustrated passions of a necrophiliac could even be released in 1962 is a censorial mystery in its own right— or, perhaps a testament to the way horror films were officially ignored on every cultural level back then[1]. Did the censors not know what was going on? Did they bother to even watch the film?

Of all Italian Horror from the classic era 1957-66, *Horrible* has perhaps the strangest reputation. Horror films unwilling to base their themes in conventionally conservative fantasies have always found difficulty reaching a mass audience. Outside of cult horror circles, films with conceptually challenging ideas such as *The Stranglers of Bombay* and *Peeping Tom*, can still be difficult to discuss, forty years after their release.

269

Also retaining its power to disturb, the unconventionally aberrant *Horrible* is well worth examining, from its peculiar place in the ranks of Italian Horror, to its bizarre, yet completely reasonable take on sexual relationships.

London, 1885. Dr. Bernard Hichcock (stern-visaged British actor Robert Flemyng) is leading a double life. At the clinic, his new anaesthetic makes him a surgical miracle man, while at home he indulges nightly in secret macabre love games with his devoted wife Margaretha.

Below, Dr. Hichcock (Robert Flemyng, right) and his assistant (Montgomery Glenn).

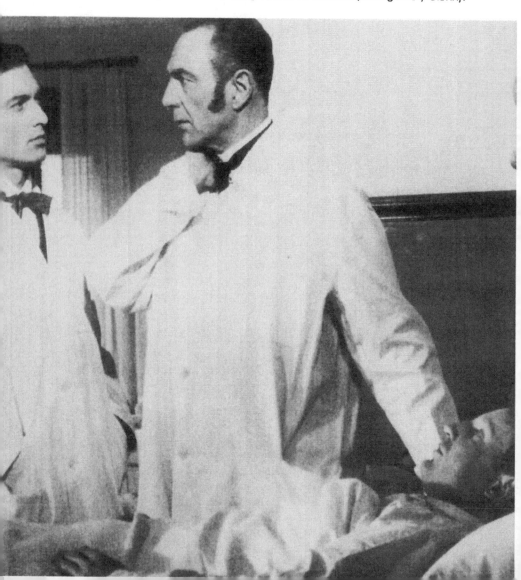

In a room draped in funereal black, Hichcock uses his anaesthetic to narcotize her into a deathlike state that arouses his passion to delirious levels of intensity. On one overzealous night, he injects her with a lethal overdose, and she convulses to death before his horrified eyes... Twelve years later the Doctor returns from Italy with his new wife Cynthia. No sooner have they arrived when the nocturnal hauntings begin: mysterious footsteps, creaking door handles, a skull under her pillow. Sinister housekeeper Marta guards forbidden rooms, Bernard becomes suddenly distant— all the better to conceal from Cynthia the fact that Hichcock has returned to his old habits.

The central focus of *Horrible* is the spectacle of the insane Bernard Hichcock as he wrestles with, and then embraces, his own demons. He's a perverse hero, one who dares to overstep, undeterred from unspeakable goals. These he pursues with unrepentant delight, largely uncriticized by any moralizing imposed by the filmmakers: In no way is this the sort of "responsible" film that proffers sordid content while pretending to condemn it. Also atypical is the presentation of the actual "corpse-molesting" partly from Hichcock's point of view, with the audience identification techniques commonly associated with Alfred Hitchcock. Unlike the fleeting glimpses of necrophiliac tableau presented in Edgar G. Ulmer's *The Black Cat* and Roger Corman's *The Tomb of Ligeia*, here the viewer is allowed an identification with the hero's perverted behavior, an obsession treated as if it were the pinnacle of erotic stimulation. Roman Vlad's swooning violin score signals the onset of Hichcock's unnatural cravings, and shafts of hallucinatory scarlet light erupt whenever he comes close to consummating his "unnatural lust."

Italian horror in the early 1960's had a unique set of commercial compromises, aesthetic characteristics that are clearly evident in *Horrible*. Precise camerawork and atmospheric visuals are stressed, but, more often than not, the actors seem to have been left to fend for themselves. The experienced Flemyng expands his character with a broad range of neurotic behaviors, but the young Barbara Steele tends to rely on mechanical hand-wringing to express her nervous state. In one baffling instance, Steele stares vacantly at the camera for a couple of seconds, as if she thought she were performing a run-through and not a final take. Both Ms. Steele and actress Harriet White are on record as having little memory of being given much direction from Italian Horror directors Riccardo Freda, Mario Bava, or Antonio Margheriti, who habitually filmed under crushing time constraints just to get scenes shot at all. Writer Ernesto Gastaldi, in his interview with Tim Lucas in *Video Watchdog*[2], explained that Freda was so concerned about the tight shooting schedule he simply eliminated pages of dialogue scenes that established motivations for the characters. The result of this combination of psychological incoherence and visual delight is that viewers, with little character exposition to aid them, must look to subtext to decipher *Horrible's* disturbing meanings.

It was not uncommon in commercial Italian films to see English-sounding pseudonyms substituted for the real names of the Italian actors and artists. They were apparently more than willing to hide behind ersatz English identities. It was an industry perception that Italian audiences considered domestic films inferior to American and English product.

Director Riccardo Freda first used his "Robert Hampton" alias on *Caltiki, il mostro immortale* (with second-string English actor John Merivale for its lead), a ploy which may have helped that film get its American release through Allied Artists. For *Horrible*, anglicized names were used throughout:

> Producers *Luigi* Carpentieri & Er*manno* Donati = Louis Mann
>
> Director of Photography Rafaelle Masciocchi = Donald Green
>
> Screenwriter Ernesto Gastaldi = Julyan Perry (often Julian Berry)
>
> Decorator Franco Fumigalli = Frank Smokecocks
>
> Actress Maria Teresa Vianello = Teresa Fitzgerald
>
> Actor Silvano Tranquili = Montgomery Glenn

Multiple titles were employed to court multiple markets. The original Italian release *L'orribile segreto dal Dott. Hichcock* became two variant versions in export: *The Terror of Dr. Hichcock* (England), and *The Horrible Dr. Hichcock* (U.S.).[3] The two latter versions are available in the U.S.A. on home video; the American print is about a dozen minutes shorter, and marginally tamer, than the English.[4]

The absence of explicit nudity, violence, and gore spared the export versions of *Horrible* from suffering the huge censor cuts that gutted many later European productions. With the deletion of all of Mario Bava's sado-masochistic scenes from *La frusta e il corpo*, its American remnant *What!* is reduced to an hour of atmospheric, but meaningless, corridor-wandering by Dahlia Lavi. For Yank viewers, a major part of the frustration/fascination of Italian horror is watching *Castle of Blood* or *Nightmare Castle* and trying to imagine what additional forbidden con-

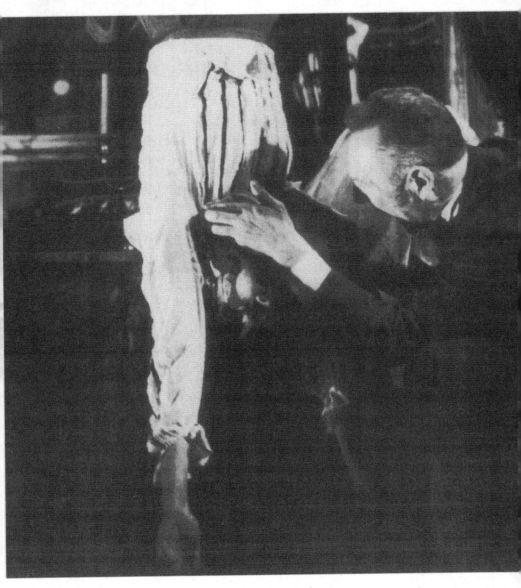

Above, Hichcock at work

tent comprised their original versions *Danse macabre* (5 minutes longer) or *Amanti d'oltretomba* (32 minutes longer!). Fortunately, most of *Horrible* actually seems to be intact.

Or is it? Unless one can see a rare quality print that retains its original lush photographic presence, *Horrible's* appeal is greatly diminished.[5] Assaying the pale, pan & scanned video cassette versions that have survived the years amounts to an act of faith in the accolades of critics who saw the original on theater screens.

Actually, contemporary criticism still comprises some of the best writing on *The Horrible Dr. Hichcock*. Raymond Durgnat's response went beyond his admiration for the hypnotizingly exciting Barbara Steele to focus on Freda's direction in the funeral scene, where sunlight shining through misty raindrops produces a painfully beautiful rainbow effect (here is where we can assume Durgnat saw a pristine copy of the film). Durgnat points out how death and beauty are effortlessly joined in one simple image, an equation he applies equally to Ms. Steele's screen persona. Fusing the concepts of desire and death, she herself has become a sort of morbid fetish-object.[6]

The Horrible Dr. Hichcock also attracted the attention of surrealist critics, who see the title character as a pioneer, a hero "on the trail of the marvelous" in territory untouched by moral conventions.[7] The surrealists love *Horrible* for its lack of concern for conventional cinematic "realism." They especially love movies that blur the filmic distinctions between "real" and "dream" content (*Peter Ibbetson*), or, better yet, make them undetectable (*Belle de Jour*). The "liabilities" of a narrative that often makes no sense and where simple day and night are sometimes indistinguishable[8] are plus factors; for surrealists, delirious, illogical dislocation is an end unto itself. The white-tiled surgery that suddenly and unaccountably glows bright red, and the "unholy lust" that distorts Hichcock's face into a horror-mask, are poetic effects totally without narrative rationalization.

In its initial review the *Monthly Film Bulletin* was amused by *Terror's* play with familiar Alfred Hitchcock film conventions, which for them, along with the humorous anglicized names, indicated a lively sense of humor at work. From *Rebecca* comes the basic "haunted bride" plot, complete with first wife's portrait and conspiratorial housekeeper. The poisoned glass of milk is a direct quote from *Suspicion*. The rainy funeral may immediately remind the viewer of a scene in *Foreign Correspondent*. Most telling is the very *Vertigo*-like color wash stylization that heightens Hichcock's delirium.

A comparison of the obsessive romantic/sexual agendas in *The Horrible Dr. Hichcock* and *Vertigo* suggests a more serious thematic relationship between the films than the *MFB's* "camp parody" conclusion would admit[9]. The obsessive manias of Scotty Ferguson and Bernard Hichcock bear sexual and political similarities that would seem to beg further investigation. Even a cursory analysis reveals that Freda's lowly horror film goes far beyond simply imitating the master of suspense, to propose a radical sexual theory of its own.

Bernard Hichcock's outrageous sexual manipulation of wives Margaretha and Cynthia, like Scotty Ferguson's obsession, is an expression of the masculine drive for an unattainable sexual ideal. This selfish and destructive mania is easily recognizable, even in contemporary American culture. There is at present a booming trade for mail-order brides from poor developing countries, chattel for men presumably seeking cooperative women uncomplicated by "liberal" American ideas. Is that not equally as chilling as Hichcock's scheme? Many of these men presumably seek compliant sex partners who can be dominated completely— is that not Hichcock's goal? Hitchcock's desire is for the perfect love object, not a companion. And his personal solution carries a certain logic. Would not a corpse for a lover be the perfect non-complaining, totally compliant partner?— an object, a victim, a scapegoat, a passive receiver of affection and abuse, one incapable of spoiling the selfishness of the sexual act with an agenda of its own? It's an ugly concept, but a completely believable one.

The thematic underpinnings of *Horrible* point to a reading of the film as a bizarre but accurate assessment of sexual alienation. The strange irony is that Hichcock's relationship with his first wife Margaretha is, up to a point, "conventionally conservative"— i.e., the male has the active desires, and the female's role is to be willing to indulge them. One doesn't have to be a Victorian to understand the sexual politics at work. Their private game in the secret black velvet "love room" also makes logical cultural sense. With the advent of anaesthesia, Victorian childbirth became the exclusive business of male doctors. Because the ideal Victorian female was supposed to be sheltered from such unpleasantness, it was assumed she would welcome the opportunity to not even be a conscious participant in the event. Under those conditions it would seem to follow that women consenting to sleep through the animalistic, painful, and messy experience of childbirthing, might also opt out of having to be present for the messy, animalistic and often humiliating sex experience as well. After all, this was a society where women were supposed to want sex not for themselves but only as a way of pleasing their husband/masters. The brief glimpse we are given of the doomed Margaretha shows her an avid participant in her hubby's "funeral" game, radiant in the knowledge that she and she alone can help him reach his sexual ideal. Cannot women identify with her unconditional surrender to the will of her mate? When does compliant devotion become sexual slavery?

Margaretha's return from the grave introduces a second relationship-based dynamic, a bald lift from *Rebecca* but distilled here to its essence. As competitors for Bernard's affections, Cynthia and Margaretha seem to function even more obviously as possessions of matrimony, as objects and not women. Before, Margaretha surely considered her domestic relationship a viable one: he fulfilled her needs, she his. Now, transformed by the serum (and/or a premature burial) into an insane hag, she has become a Dorian Gray-like personification of the sick truth of her marriage. The only communication between these two women is Margaretha's vicious gloating over the fact that Bernard has chosen her over Cynthia. Only one of them is a knowing partner in her husband's game, but neither is anything more than a sexual pawn in an equation that values only Bernard's needs and desires. How can honesty be achieved between beings with alien sexual agendas, conditioned from childhood to entice and possess the other through deception? No matter how much either wife may share in his obsession, neither satisfies Bernard's "forbidden desires', which are finding expression elsewhere— on the job, in

Below, assembled for a funeral, in the rain, of course.

the neighborhood cemetery.... *those pesky perverted men, anyway!*— always pursuing sensation, and not relationships!

In her doglike consent to "the game" Margaretha will never know her husband's desires for the tyranny they truly are. Cynthia's one unwilling experience in "the game', apparently with insufficient serum to render her completely unconscious, creates a macabre situation which rather nastily compares loveless matrimonial sex, to surgery without anaesthesia! The real horror in the film lies in the crimson spectacle of the helpless Barbara Steele experiencing the full extent of her husband's secret rapture— visualized when his horrifying face, engorged and distorted, materializes demonlike from behind the black lace of her fourposter canopy. That terrifyingly unexplainable bloated apparition, in universal terms, represents the menacing sexual stranger that, to a woman in doubt, any male can suddenly resemble.

Notes:

1. Contrast that indifference with the furor that caused the cancellation of the release of *Snuff* in the middle '70's, sight unseen, because of publicity implying that real snuff murders took place in the film. Ever since *Night of the Living Dead* (1968), American reviewers have been quick to seek out new horror films to condemn.

2. Lucas, Tim, "What Are Those Strange Drops of Blood in the Scripts of Ernesto Gastaldi?," *Video Watchdog* #39, 1997, 34-36.

3. Hardy, Phil, editor, *The Encyclopedia of Horror Movies*, Harper & Row, New York, 1986,ISBN 0 06 096146 5, x,149. Hardy also refers to *The Terrible Secret of Dr. Hichcock* and *Raptus* (which writer Ernesto Gastaldi identified to Tim Lucas as a working title) as being variant titles.

4. The actual differences between *Terror*, and *Horrible*: The English *Terror* begins with a full title sequence against black. The melodramatic title music is at one point amusingly interrupted by one of Ms. Steele's bloodcurdling screams, heard over pitch black. The film then begins with the graveyard scene. *Horrible* uses the graveyard scene as a precredit sequence, and truncates the English titles, substituting an ugly replacement for the main title card. *Horrible* has at least one extra off-camera line overdubbed: "Yes, but you must admit the doctor is a bit strange himself, isn't he!" is added to Margaretha's burial scene, just before Jezebel the cat is clearly thrown on her coffin. In *Horrible* fades have been imposed on most scenes, retaining most of *Terror*'s dialog but dropping entrances and exits and in general spoiling the pace and atmosphere of the whole show. Freda originally cut pointedly from Bernard holding his syringe aloft in the clinic to him identically holding his sex-game syringe later at home; *Horrible* ruins the moment by inserting an unnecessarily literal shot of a homeward-bound carriage in between. When Bernard dashes into the rainstorm in pursuit of the piano-playing phantom, *Horrible* omits a nice sequence of him returning to the house and confusing a

lightning-lit white curtain for the spectre, before finding the unconscious Cynthia in the garden. At the conclusion, the young intern's long climb into Hichcock's window is shortened by almost a minute. No key sex scenes are actually missing, but most are abbreviated with the addition of the early fadeouts: in the graveyard, in the Funeral Game Room, and in the morgue, Hichcock's attentions to various corpses linger a bit longer in *Terror*. Contrary to expectation, there is neither nudity nor graphic footage in the longer English cut.

5. A recipe: Take one Italian production of any quality. Ineptly dub it into English.Make blearily colored, grainy 35mm prints. Chop these up with clumsy splices to remove offending nudity or gore. Dupe these prints again for television, cropping off their original widescreen compositions. Let these 16mm copies fade on a shelf for twenty years while local television stations censor them even further. Then hastily transfer the result to fuzzy video, distorting their already tortured soundtracks. Finally, screen the video to your associates while trying to explain its artful worthiness! For American fans unable to see museum showings of rare prints, the world of Italian Horror is a cinema that, oftentimes, "isn't there."

6. Durgnat, Raymond, *Films and Feelings*, The M.I.T. Press, Cambridge, Massachusetts, 1967, 53, 147-148.

7. Matthews, J. H., *Surrealism and Film*, The University of Michigan Press, Ann Arbor Michigan, 1971 ISBN 0 472 64135 2, 23-28, 149. Here *The Horrible Dr. Hichcock* keeps company with the likes of *King Kong* and the works of Luis Buñuel.

8. A typical example: On the night of Cynthia's arrival, housekeeper Marta says she will remove her insane sister from the house "tomorrow." The very next evening, Marta says she sent her sister away *yesterday*.

9. After seeing the spectacle of Robert Flemyng's Bernard Hichcock in the throes of his obsession, the nervous anguish and blind mania of James Stewart's Scotty Ferguson seem perverted in a disturbingly similar way.

Credits:

    Barbara Steele

    Robert Flemyng in

    THE HORRIBLE DR. HICHCOCK

Produced by:Louis Mann, for Panda

in Technicolor®

with: Montgomery Glenn

Teresa Fitzgerald

Harriet White

Original Story and Screenplay by: Julyan Perry

Director of Photography: Donald Green

Directed by: Robert Hampton

76 minutes. Filmed in "Panoramic" (anamorphic)

THE TERROR OF DR. HICHCOCK includes the following listings after Harriet White:

(also with:)

Spencer Williams

Al Christianson

Evar Simpsom

Nat Harley

Asst. Director: John M. Farquhar

Production Manager Charles Law

Camera: Anthony Taylor

Makeup: Bud Steiner

Hairstyles: Annette Winter

Sound Engineer: Jackson McGregor

Set Designer: Joseph Goodman

Decorator: Frank Smokecocks

Costume Design: Inoa Stanley

Editor: Donna Christie

Music by: Roman Vlad

86 minutes.

His Secret was a Coffin named Desire!
The Candle of his Lust burnt brightest in the Shadow of the Grave!

Above, Candyman (Tony Todd) claims the mind and body of Helen Lyle (Virginia Madsen) in **Candyman**.

"How much did you pay for this place?" Fear, Entitlement, and Urban Space in Bernard Rose's *Candyman*

Aviva Briefel and Sianne Ngai

Is it a privilege to be haunted, or afraid? Is fear somehow endowed with the status of an inalienable right or property, conferring dignity or legitimacy to the individuals who experience it? Can fear or the control of fear thus be used as a cachet, or as a means of justifying and confirming predetermined claims to cultural power? In restricting the representation of fear or anxiety to figures we immediately recognize as privileged, the last two decades of horror and slasher films suggest that being frightened is paradoxically a sign of empowerment. Victims in these films are consistently white, suburban residents engaged in the middle-class routines of moving to a single-family home, celebrating holidays, or going on vacation. The characters who seem to have the most claim to being afraid are thus themselves owners or future inheritors of property, as if the entitlements of material ownership automatically extend to the psychological or affective realm. Our thesis is that because all horror or Gothic narratives derive from this point of private proprietorship, one that produces anxieties about proprietorship in general, these narratives subsequently establish anxiety as a form of emotional property. Fear or anxiety constitutes "property" on several levels of meaning: as something inherent/inherited, as a lawful claim or title, as well as a concrete possession. The genre of the horror film presents owning a house in particular as a form of proprietorship which automatically entitles the buyer to the experience of fear, as if fear itself were a commodity included with the total package—just as sophisticated alarm systems and security guards have become standard components of the purchase of an upscale home or condominium.

In Sean Cunningham's *Friday the Thirteenth* (1980) and Wes Craven's *Nightmare on Elm Street* (1985), for example, two landmark films in this genre, the fear-provoking figures of Jason Vorhees and Freddy Krueger emerge foremost in the context of a territorial struggle between those who own property and the cooks, janitors, and caretakers whose right to

live on the property is predicated on their labor. Freddy is a maintenance man who lives in the basement of the suburban high school attended by his victims; Jason is the son of Camp Crystal Lake's cook.
Significantly, we learn that both figures were themselves subjected to
experiences of fear and violence similar to the ones they later impose on
their victims; Freddy is attacked and set on fire by a mob of angry parents, who accuse him of abusing their children, whereas Jason's cries for
help while drowning are ignored by the summer camp's middle-class
counselors. The originating experience of fear felt by these economically
marginalized figures, figures who moreover stand in a peripheral relation to the property they maintain and inhabit, is thus repressed and
supplanted by the fears of the property owners, who then occupy the
subject position of the haunted. It is with this secondary, derivative fear
that the horror film begins, while the fear of the haunter is relegated to a
historical past which is never visually represented. The contrast between
the respective relations of the haunted and haunter to the property at
stake raises the question of proprietary rights centrally positioned in the
horror film. If home ownership as the starting point for horror narratives automatically entitles homeowners to fear, then it would seem to
also exclude non-property owners from their own experiences of anxiety. The struggle we see in the horror film is not only a struggle over
property, but a struggle over who has the right to be afraid.

Why this transfer of fear as emotional property or entitlement from
one social group to another? It may be no coincidence that the emergence of the horror film is often viewed by critics in relation to Reagan-
ism, particularly since the release of Cunningham's trend-setting film
occurred in the same year as the former movie actor's election. As Douglas Kellner writes:

> horror films...have presented, often in symbolic/allegorical
> form, both universal fears and the deepest anxieties and
> hostilities of contemporary U.S. society. A subtext of these
> films is the confusion and fright of the population in the
> face of economic crisis; accelerating social and cultural
> change; a near epidemic of cancer, industrial diseases, and
> AIDS; political turmoil; and fear of nuclear annihilation.
> The wide range and popularity of post-1960s Hollywood
> horror films suggests that something is profoundly wrong
> with U.S. society and a probing of these films may help
> reveal something about the sources of contemporary
> fears.[1]

While Kellner implies that these films focus their attention on the
increasingly changing sociopolitical topography of a new age, it seems

that their concern is actually with spaces resistant to change; namely, white, middle-class environments, as foregrounded in *Nightmare on Elm Street*'s nostalgic depiction of suburbia with a soft-focus lens. Among the social and cultural shifts to which Kellner vaguely alludes, the changing demographics of the American middle class at this period may have been a particular source of anxiety motivating the horror film's characteristic presentation of its victims as a homogenous, unchanging group. Despite the detrimental cuts in social programs effected during the Reagan-Bush era that reinforced racial and economic inequalities, the multicultural reality of American society in this period—and the upward mobility of a few minority groups, specifically—threatened the traditional topography of "middle-classness" by diversifying its spaces. In particular, as William Julius Wilson notes, "the exodus of black middle-class professionals from the inner city [in the 1970s and 1980s] has been increasingly accompanied by a movement of stable working-class blacks to higher-income neighborhoods in other parts of the city and to the suburbs."[2]

Anxiety about the racial diversification of suburban communities may explain the horror film's investment in depicting the haunted as a stable control group, comprised almost exclusively of white individuals who are virtually interchangeable in every narrative in which they appear. In both *Nightmare* and *Friday the Thirteenth*, the white middle-class affili-ation of the victims is so strongly pronounced they are barely individu-ated, existing merely as a set of "neighborhood" types: the jock, the prankster, and the preppy prude. In contrast, aside from their common working-class origins, the haunters or fear-provoking figures vary in ap-pearance from film to film, markedly distinguished by props ranging from hockey masks to steel claws, and in their methods of killing. Whereas the horror genre standardizes the constituency of the victim group, the subject position of the haunter fluctuates. In this manner, the white middle class's ability to maintain itself as a cohesive, autonomous group from film to film ultimately suggests a fantasy of its resilience to the changes embodied in the many vicissitudes of the haunter, who functions as an emblematic representation of change itself. The horror film is thus primarily a survival narrative of a homogenous class of property owners.

As such, the genre not only indexes white middle-class anxiety over the racial diversification of suburban enclaves due to trends in upward mobility, but also anxiety related to an obverse yet concurrent phenome-non: the displacement and subsequent dispersion of lower-income indi-viduals from contained inner-city neighborhoods following Reagan's drastic cuts in public housing funds:

> The housing crisis for the poor reached a new level of severity under policies of deliberate cruelty during the Reagan and Bush administrations. From 1977 to 1980, during the Carter administration, the federal government added an average of 290,000 new families each year to the list of those receiving housing assistance. However, after ousting Carter from the White House in 1980, Reagan slashed federal housing allocations from $30 billion in fiscal year 1981 to barely $8 billion in 1986. The number of available housing units dropped sharply in virtually every city.[3]

While this legislation obviously worked to further disempower people at low-income levels, the elimination of sufficient housing raises the troubling question of *where* these newly displaced individuals would go. The horror film's insistence on preserving the intactness of its middle-class control group of victims may also bear witness to an irrational fear of infiltration from those evicted from subsidized housing.

Released in 1992, the year officially ending the Reagan-Bush regime, Bernard Rose's *Candyman* marks an interesting deviation within the genre by introducing African Americans, figures most obviously excluded from the restricted suburban landscapes of prototypical films such as *Nightmare* and *Friday the Thirteenth*, as both killers and victims. The setting, moreover, conspicuously shifts from a middle-class enclave to the Cabrini-Green housing projects in Chicago. This shift dramatizes *Candyman*'s distance from earlier films by directly acknowledging a type of social fear that seems furthest removed from the concerns of the traditional horror film: the everyday reality of urban violence in low-income neighborhoods.

The plot centers around the anthropological research of two graduate students at the University of Illinois: Helen Lyle, a blonde woman, and her partner Bernadette, who is black. Helen and Bernadette are in the process of researching and ultimately debunking urban legends for a collaborative thesis. The film begins with Helen interviewing a white teenager about Candyman, a bogeyman who can be invoked by the ritual of saying his name five times in front of a mirror. In the teenager's kitsch narrative, transmitted by a "friend of a friend who knew someone," a baby-sitter invites her boyfriend to the house and dares him to perform the incantation. The boyfriend pronounces the name four times before going downstairs. Alone, the baby-sitter stares at her reflection in the mirror and utters the final "Candyman." An indistinguishable figure flashes behind her, followed by a shot of the living-room ceiling from

the boyfriend's perspective, punctured by a hook and seeping with
blood. Later, Helen and Bernadette jokingly replay the teenager's version of the story by beginning the incantation, which only Helen com-
pletes. Nothing seems to happen.

The baby-sitter's story later appears confirmed by Archie Walsh, a
British professor played by the director, who provides a historicized
version of the Candyman myth. Walsh recounts the following family romance:

Candyman was the son of a slave. His father had amassed a considerable fortune from designing a device for the mass-producing of shoes after the Civil War. Candyman had been sent to all the best schools and
had grown up in polite society. He had a prodigious talent as an artist,
and was much sought after when it came to the documenting of one's
wealth and position in society in a portrait. It was in this latter capacity
that he was commissioned by a wealthy landowner to capture his
daughter's virginal beauty. Well, of course, they fell deeply in love, and
she became pregnant. Poor Candyman! The father executed a terrible revenge. He paid a pack of brutal hooligans to do the deed. They chased
Candyman through the town to Cabrini-Green, where they proceeded
to saw off his right hand with a rusty blade. And no one came to his aid.
But this was just the beginning of his ordeal. Nearby there was an api-
ary: dozens of hives filled with hungry bees. They smashed the hives
and stole the honeycomb and smeared it over his prone naked body.
Candyman was stung to death by the bees. They burnt his body on a giant pyre and scattered his ashes over Cabrini-Green.

The third version of the urban legend is given to Helen by a black
janitor, who attributes the death of a woman living at Cabrini-Green to
an eponymous Candyman.

Intrigued by these stories, Helen persuades the hesitant Bernadette to
accompany her on a visit to the scene of the crime, on the premise that
field research will greatly enhance their project. Helen eventually returns to Cabrini-Green alone and asks Jake, a young boy, to show her
where Candyman lives. The reluctant child takes her to a public bathroom in which she is cornered by a gang from the projects, led by a tall
black man holding a hook. With the proclamation, "I hear you looking
for Candyman, bitch. Well, you found him," he hits her face with the
hook and knocks her unconscious. After identifying the gang leader
who calls himself "Candyman" in a line-up, Helen is informed that the
police have finally succeeded in catching the perpetuator of the recent
crimes at Cabrini-Green.

Myth uncannily intrudes into contemporary reality when Helen then encounters the fantastical Candyman (played by Tony Todd) in an empty parking garage, where he tells her, "I came for you." Overcome by this encounter, she loses consciousness and unexplainedly wakes up in the projects, where she is arrested for the abduction and suspected murder of a single mother's baby. In the events that follow, she also emerges as the prime suspect for the gruesome murders of Bernadette and a psychiatrist at the hospital where she is committed. After escaping she returns, again unexplainedly, to Cabrini-Green where she discovers Candyman in a Gothic lair hidden within its structure. He asks her to become his bride in exchange for the missing baby's life, a promise that entails the sacrifice of her own. Ultimately, Helen discovers that she is a reincarnation of the landowner's daughter from the legend told by the professor. Somewhat arbitrarily carrying a hook, she heroically rescues the baby from a burning heap of garbage reminiscent of the pyre in the professor's story, in which she and Candyman are annihilated. The film concludes with her husband, Trevor, who in a state of mourning utters the name "Helen" five times in front of a bathroom mirror. Holding a hook in her hand, she slaughters him, to the horror of the young teenage girl who discovers him.

Rose's decision to concentrate terror at the site of a high-rise housing project populated by working-class African Americans rather than the conventional suburban locale could be described as a sensationalist maneuver; particularly since Cabrini-Green had been the subject of national attention since its inception in 1955. Helen's perusal of microfiche newspaper articles on the recent elevation of crimes at this site points to the film's awareness of the controversy surrounding Cabrini-Green. As one urban sociologist notes, "The press, radio, and television have not hesitated to remind Cabrini Green [sic] residents that the place they call home is a slum. The mass media has shaped the image of the Cabrini Green neighborhood as much as the residents themselves."[4] This widespread notoriety reached its peak in the early 1980s, when Chicago public housing became synonymous with the violence perpetuated within its boundaries. Although the Henry Horner projects and the Robert Taylor Homes were also singled out by the media as extremely dangerous sites, Cabrini-Green ultimately gained the most prominent reputation after the eleven murders and thirty-seven gun injuries reported in the first two months of 1981. Likewise, in 1992 it once again attracted national attention with the shooting of a seven-year-old boy by an unknown sniper in one of the buildings.[5] The unconventional use of a well-known urban setting in Candyman is particularly striking as films

within the horror/slasher genre traditionally feature anonymous locations:

> The stalker film is almost always positioned in a
> middle-class American community, which fosters a degree
> of likeness to that of the viewing audience or, at least, to
> their American ideal. But this setting is never identified as
> an existing geographical location: the destinations are
> fictional: "Camp Crystal Lake," "Haddonfield, Illinois," or
> merely unspecified. This generality gives them the ability
> to represent a place that is simultaneously everywhere and
> nowhere, but yet distinctly American.[6]

While in its setting and engagement with contemporary social issues
Candyman seems to align itself with the genre of the "ghetto film," it
would be more accurately described as a slasher film that takes place
within the ghetto. Unlike pioneer films such as John Singleton's *Boyz N
the Hood* (1991) and Allan and Albert Hughes's *Menace II Society* (1993),
which represent drive-by shootings as the central threat to inner-city
residents, *Candyman* substitutes the omnipresent gun for a hook. The
three weapons in the film, Helen's hook, the hook carried by the gang
leader Candyman, and the hook bloodily integrated into the arm of the
Tony Todd Candyman, point to its participation in the slasher film's
standard use of archaic objects. As Carol Clover writes, "In the hands of
the killer, at least, guns have no place in slasher films. In some basic
sense, the emotional terrain of the slasher film is pretechnological. The
preferred weapons of the killer are knives, hammers, axes, ice picks,
hypodermic needles, red hot pokers, pitchforks, and the like."[7] In
addition, *Candyman* conspicuously veers away from the social realism of
the "ghetto film" and its characteristic emphasis on the
overcrowdedness and noisiness of a public housing setting. When
Bernadette and Helen are discussing their plans to research this place
first-hand, we are made to believe that it will fit the conventional
representation. Bernadette worriedly tells Helen, "I won't even drive
past there. I heard a kid got shot there the other day," to which she
replies, "Every day." When the film actually takes us to Cabrini-Green,
however, we see only a few tough-looking teenagers who mildly
threaten the women before they disappear. In place of the expected
images of guns and gangs, the film depicts the Cabrini-Green projects as
a void haunted by a single man with a hook.

In substituting the threat of the many for a singular killer, *Candyman*
indicates its overarching allegiance to the 1980s horror film, despite its
referencing of the social. In this genre a terror such as Freddy Krueger
can permeate the collective unconscious of a group of suburban teenag-

ers through their dreams. *Candyman* deviates from this model, however, by claiming that such myths can no longer naturally and effortlessly intrude into a community. By making its protagonist a pragmatic anthropologist, it implies that myths can be consciously sought and uncovered as well as unconsciously dreamt. Whereas the teenagers in *Nightmare* involuntarily fantasize about a figure guiltily repressed by their parents, Rose's heroine actively pursues the legend through interviews, recordings of oral histories, and newspaper articles. Similarly, while monsters like Freddy and Jason do not allow their victims the option of requesting their presence, the invocation of Candyman is a complicated ritual involving volition on the part of the caller. Candyman is thus trapped in the same subservient position as the ex-slave's son for hire in the profes-

Below, residents of Cabrini Green walk through a cemetery led by Anne-Marie Mc-Coy (Vanessa Williams, right) and young Jake (DeJuan Guy).

sor's postbellum narrative, at the beck and call of consumers in a service economy.

Immediately following Helen's assault by the gang leader Candyman, there is a confused interchange between herself and Jake. After having identified her assailant, she tries to allay Jake's fears that Candyman will retaliate against him for having shown her his hideout.

JAKE: Candyman will get me.

HELEN: Candyman isn't real. He's just a story, you know, like Dracula or Frankenstein. A bad man took his name so he could scare us, but now he's locked up, everything's going to be okay.

JAKE: *(perplexed)* Candyman ain't real?

HELEN: No.

Helen misunderstands Jake's anxiety, assuming that he is referring to the legendary Candyman she has so far only encountered in the white teenager's and British professor's stories, instead of the gang leader. By positioning Candyman as the successor in a lineage of European monsters (Dracula and Frankenstein), Helen reveals her own desire to establish him as a part of the project's literary canon as well. This scene points to how she has created her own hybrid mythology by combining narratives from both popular culture and academia. Bernadette unconsciously seems to comment on Helen's tendency to read the events at Cabrini-Green in relation to these white mythologies when she says, "Helen, this is sick. This isn't one of your fairy tales. A woman got killed here."

The miscommunication between Jake and Helen suggests that she in fact believes or has some investment in believing that the inhabitants of Cabrini-Green are deceived by the fantasy she initially sought to repudiate. En route to their first visit to the projects, Helen condescendingly rebukes Bernadette for her reluctance to proceed with her plan of using Cabrini-Green as the site for their field research. Glancing at Bernadette while she fumbles with her mace and pepper spray, Helen comments sarcastically, "What's with the arsenal, Bernadette? We're only going eight blocks." Bernadette responds: "You're the one who got us dressed up like cops."

HELEN: I said dress conservatively.

BERNADETTE: No, we look like cops.

Dressing "conservatively," for Helen, implies dressing inconspicuously; an attempt to signal neutrality or sameness. However, Bernadette's rebuttal calls attention to the fact that this vestmental code could be received suspiciously by a different community of readers, as a marker of intrusive authority rather than anonymity. By responding defensively, Helen refuses to acknowledge the possibility that her status as an intruder into this community cannot be altered, in spite of efforts to downplay signs of social difference:

HELEN: Why are you trying to scare me?

BERNADETTE: I'm not trying to scare you, Helen. I just want you to think. The gangs hold this whole neighborhood hostage.

HELEN: (*angry, stops car*) Okay, let's just turn around then. Let's just go back, and we can write a nice, little boring thesis regurgitating all the usual crap about urban legends. We've got a real shot here, Bernadette. An entire community starts attributing the daily horrors of their lives to a mythical figure. Now, if Trevor and Archie were in on this, do you think they'd chicken out?

BERNADETTE: In a second.

HELEN: Exactly.

"An entire community starts attributing the daily horrors of their lives to a mythical figure." With her assessment of the Cabrini-Green inhabitants' relation to the figure called Candyman, Helen implies that she understands the origins of their social reality better than they do. For her, they are naively translating reality into the fictional. What Helen fails to consider in making this assumption is the possibility that in order to position herself as an educator, she may actually *need* to believe that they believe in the legend. From the privileged standpoint of an outside authority, Helen constructs herself as a missionary of social truth, as if in expiation of white liberal guilt. This stance is evinced in the defensiveness of her response to the idea that she is in fact responsible for Bernadette's death and the disappearance of the baby from Cabrini-Green. Alluding to an unspecified and repressed part of her consciousness, she insists, "That's not possible. I'm not capable of that. No matter what's going wrong, I know one thing—that no part of me, *no matter how hidden*, is capable of that." Her use of the abstract pronoun *that* increases the extent of her responsibility to encompass not only the two individual victims involved, but the ills of modern society as a whole.

Helen's assertive expedition into the high-rise projects recalls an event highlighted by the media in 1981, when mayor of Chicago Jane Byrne moved into Cabrini-Green to help restore order following a particularly violent period in the project's history. As Alex Kotlowitz recounts, "Along with a contingent of police and bodyguards, she stayed for three weeks....But that single act by Byrne, more than any murder or plea for help, highlighted the isolation and alienation of these poor, mostly black inner-city islands. It was as if the mayor, with her entourage of police, advisers, and reporters, had deigned to visit some distant and perilous Third World country—except that Cabrini-Green sat barely eight blocks from the mayor's Gold Coast apartment."[8] Byrne's conciliatory gesture is all the more ironic in light of the fact that under her administration, the Housing Department's Home Acquisition Program was reduced by $2.8 million in 1982. During her term in office, Byrne also destroyed 16,177 residential units in black and Latino neighborhoods, while building only 12,811. Not surprisingly, in 1983 the Chicago Coalition for the Homeless estimated that the number of homeless people in the city was between 12,000 and 25,000.[9]

Helen's conversation with Bernadette en route to the projects reveals that her own house is also eight blocks from Cabrini-Green. She repeatedly alludes to the fact that this proximity is only geographical, while a world of social difference separates her condominium from the projects. At the same time, however, Helen can only establish this difference by using her own dwelling as a map to read the other space. Her major discovery in researching the history of Cabrini-Green is that her own building was originally intended as public housing, but was transformed into overpriced condos due to the lack of a structural barrier separating it from the wealthy Gold Coast.

HELEN: My apartment was built as a housing project.

BERNADETTE: (*in disbelief*) No.

HELEN: Yeah. Now take a look at this. (*Walks over to the window and draws curtains.*) Once it was finished, the city soon realized there was no barrier between here and the Gold Coast.

BERNADETTE: Unlike over there where you've got the highway and the El train to keep the ghetto cut off.

HELEN: Exactly. So they made some minor alterations. They covered the cinder block in plaster, and they sold the lot off as condos.

BERNADETTE: How much did you pay for this place?

HELEN: Don't ask. *(Walking to bathroom.)* Now, wait till you see this; here's the proof. *(Detaching the bathroom mirror.)* The killer, or killers, they don't know which, smashed their way through the back of this cabinet. See, there's no wall there. There's only a medicine chest separating us from the other apartment.

Helen turns her Lincoln Village apartment into a template for Cabrini-Green, using the gap between the adjoining condos as an explanation of to how the murders at the projects took place. This analogy supports the hypothesis she propounds as a means of debunking the myth she believes the inhabitants of the projects believe. The spectral housing project Helen imagines concealed within her own building posits Cabrini-Green as a Gothic house-within-a-house; cinder blocks hidden under a layer of white plaster. As the architectural ghost of Helen's domestic space, Cabrini-Green thus embodies a set of buried economic and social relations underlying the structure of Lincoln Village.

Though Helen's discovery of her building's invisible substructure is compelling, her hypothesis is flawed. Her theory about the lower-class origins of her building is undermined by the fact that Chicago's projects were mostly based on commercial designs for upper middle-class housing:

The Cabrini-Green apartment slabs, which ranged from ten to nineteen stories high, resembled high-rise factories with exposed concrete frames filled in with glass and brick. They followed the architectural style pioneered by Mies van der Rohe, who had built his first concrete-frame commercial apartment building in Chicago in 1949. Public agencies were probably attracted to this kind of architecture for the same reason that many real-estate developers are partial to modernist design: repetitive, stripped-down, and undecorated buildings can be decorated quickly and inexpensively.

However, it's one thing to build apartment towers for the upper-middle class–as Mies usually did–and quite another to embrace them as solutions for housing the poor. The well-off have doormen, janitors, repairmen, baby-sitters, and gardeners; the poor have no hired help. Without restricted access, the lobbies and corridors are vandalized; without proper maintenance, broken elevators do not get fixed, staircases become garbage dumps, and broken windows remain unreplaced; without baby-sitters, single mothers are stranded in their apartments, and adolescents roam, unsupervised, sixteen floors below.[10]

While Helen is correct, then, in assessing that her building is in some sense a template of Cabrini-Green, she disregards the economic factors differentiating these structures despite their architectural similarity.

As Bernadette notes, the highway is one of the urban landmarks maintaining the division between racially and economically segregated neighborhoods. This image of the highway is a predominant motif in the film, at once marking our entry into its narrative space with the opening credits, and connecting its various scenes. Nearly every time the film switches locales, the camera takes us over the highway, following its straight path to an implied destination. As a structure that at once separates and connects relationally, the highway functions as a line of repression separating two linguistic neighborhoods that cannot be crossed without producing a symptom.

This theory of divided neighborhoods may be useful in understanding the relationship Helen constructs between Lincoln Village and Cabrini-Green. Faced with the myth as a free-floating element, in search of a home and resembling a disembodied spirit looking for a new body to haunt, Helen extracts the ghost of a housing project from Lincoln Village, and relocates this spirit in the buildings at Cabrini-Green. Because the film presents the projects as an evacuated space, a hollow shell, it reinforces their image as just a body anticipating its inhabitation by a soul. Averaging seventy dwelling units per acre of residential land and housing over 10,000 people,[11] it seems strange that Cabrini-Green should be portrayed as an empty wasteland in Rose's film. Aside from the three or four young males gratuitously positioned around the building's entrance when Helen and Bernadette arrive, *Candyman*'s version of Cabrini-Green is strikingly deserted.

The ghost of the tenement in Lincoln Village for which Helen conveniently finds a home at Cabrini-Green is set loose like the homeless bees in the professor's narrative. Having stolen their original home, the hive or honeycomb, the mob hired by the landowner to punish Candyman release this mass into the city. The image occurs in the beginning of the film, in which a close-up shot of a swarm of bees is followed by their disoriented flight in the midst of Chicago's crowded skyline. Candyman's association with the bees seems to elucidate another function they adopt in the film. Like the ghost Helen uproots and relocates to Cabrini-Green, these bees appear as frustratedly seeking a new dwelling. The professor's description of the bees as "hungry," an unusual characterization of an insect that produces its own home in the form of food, indicates an unnatural and fundamental poverty connecting the bees to the inhabitants of the projects, who have also been deprived of adequate housing by institutionalized racism. The eviction and subsequent dis-

placement of the bees as implied by the film's leitmotif of these insects
in unnatural locations (suspended in swarms above skyscrapers, over-
flowing a toilet, and deep in the pitch-black interior of Cabrini-Green) is
accompanied by anger, as evinced in the ominous tone with which Candyman pronounces his voice-over. This anger recalls the biological fact
that bees attack humans only from fear, in an effort to protect the threatened hive.

In addition to imposing her belief in the conglomerated Candyman
myth onto the inhabitants of Cabrini-Green, Helen seems unaware or in
ignorance of the fact that this myth is one she has extracted from two
white sources: the academic's romanticized postbellum narrative and
the teenager's clichéd ghost story. Though Helen smirks (not surprisingly) after hearing the latter, she immediately assumes that the black
janitor is referring to the same Candyman as the one in the teenager's
narrative. Entering to clean Helen's office, the janitor overhears the end
of the tape-recorded interview in which the teenager repeats Candyman's name.

> JANITOR: Candyman, huh?
>
> HELEN: Yes, you've heard of him?
>
> JANITOR: Mm-hmm. You doing a study on him?
>
> HELEN: Yes, I am. What have you heard?
>
> JANITOR: Everybody scared of him once it get dark. He
> live over at Cabrini. My friend told me about him.
>
> HELEN: Cabrini-Green?
>
> JANITOR: Yeah, in the projects. I live on the South Side
> so I don't know too much about it, but my friend she
> know all about it. Her cousin live over at Cabrini. They
> say he killed a lady.
>
> HELEN: Can I talk to your friend?

Responding to Helen's eager request, the janitor asks her friend, who is
conveniently outside mopping the hallway, to come into the office.

> JANITOR: Tell her what you told me about the
> Candyman.
>
> JANITOR 2: Well, all I know is that there was some lady
> in a tub and she heard a noise.
>
> HELEN: Do you remember her name?

JANITOR 2: I think her name was Ruthie Jean, and she
heard this banging and smashing like someone was
trying to make a hole in the wall. So Ruthie called 911
and she said there's someone coming through the walls.

JANITOR: They thought the lady was crazy, right?

JANITOR 2: Mm-hmm. So she called 911 again and they
still didn't believe her. When they finally got there she
was dead.

HELEN: Was she shot?

JANITOR 2: No. She was killed with a hook. *(Makes
ripping noise).* You know?

JANITOR: It's true. *(Responding to Helen's expression.)*
Yeah, it is. I read it in the papers. Candyman killed her.

JANITOR 2: Yeah, but uh . . . I don't know nothing
'bout that.

Contrary to Helen's immediate conclusion from this conversation, the
janitors are discussing the Candyman who later emerges as Jake's gang
leader from Cabrini-Green, the same man identified by the police
detective as one of the project overlords.

In this manner, the three distinct Candyman scenarios (teenage horror story, academic fable, urban reality) converge in Helen's consciousness alone. This is somewhat obscured by the fact that Rose
reverses the sequence of shots conventionally used to determine a hy-
potactical relationship between the dreaming subject and the dream.
Hollywood films conventionally use a close-up of the dreamer's face
as a point of departure for the fantasy into which it dissolves. In this
case, however, the fantasy precedes its site of production and seems an
independent existence. The dream thus becomes disembodied
from the dreamer. *Candyman* begins with an image of bees eventually
absorbed into a close-up of Helen's face, as she listens to the tale told
by the teenager. While such a juxtaposition of shots would normally
imply that the first is producing and controlling the second, here it
seems that the second counter-intuitively releases the first. This reversal of causality between the projecting/narrating consciousness and
the projected/narrated image is used to divert us from the suspicion
that Candyman may actually be a hybrid creature spliced together
from the various stories housed in Helen's imagination. Solipsistically,
Helen believes that Candyman has come for *her*.

As a connective mechanism, her consciousness performs the same rhetorical function as the object in the film: the hook that hooks the various stories together. The disturbing implication of this parallel structure is that Helen's mind is in fact coeval with the weapon from the traditional white slasher film. The equation of white liberal consciousness with a metal hook is dramatized by the penultimate scene of *Candyman*, which could be described as the narcissistic fantasy of a woman imagining her own funeral. Helen sees herself mourned by the two communities she seeks to conflate: white middle-class academia and the entire population of Cabrini-Green. The funeral scene is framed and hence entirely contained by two identical close-up shots of Helen's face inside the closed coffin, as if to establish her point of view. To the surprise of the white mourners, a procession of inhabitants from the projects silently enters the cemetery, led by the single mother whose baby Helen supposedly rescued, and Jake, who gratefully drops Helen's hook into her grave. The sound of the hook clanging against the metal coffin is immediately followed by what seems to be a reaction shot of Helen's immobile face, concluding the sequence. This scene at once refers to and contrasts dramatically with the far from narcissistic moment at which Helen is struck by the Cabrini-Green Candyman's hook while sleuthing in the men's bathroom.

The funeral fantasy could be seen as an attempt to rectify the anticlimax of Helen's encounter with the reality she sought to mythologize. Through his humiliating blow to the face, the Cabrini-Green Candyman marks Helen's intrusion into a space to which she did not belong yet nevertheless tried to claim. A crucial turning point in the film's development, the mortifying experience of being knocked unconscious by the gang leader's hook thrusts Helen into the epicenter of the myth she previously attempted to repudiate. Here the film shifts from one narrative dimension to another; from its previous gestures at social realism to the supernatural. This is reinforced by the abrupt transition from the narrative's focus on the two graduate students' excited involvement in their research to the eerie calmness of Helen's solitary entry into the vortex of the Candyman myth. In a deserted parking lot, Helen produces the Tony Todd Candyman as a *deus ex machina* after her wounded face has healed, as if to extricate her from the reality she unexpectedly encountered at Cabrini-Green. By facilitating Helen's disavowal of this confrontation with the all too literal gang leader, the legendary Candyman enables her to insert herself at the center of the hybridized narrative from which he emerges. The hook as object instantiates the complete reversal of Helen's ideological stance; from skeptic to believer; from dream interpreter to dreamer; from debunker of myths to mythic heroine.

In its rudimentary engagement with contemporary social issues, *Candyman* seems to offer an oblique yet affirmative response to the question of whether privilege inheres in being haunted. As Judith Halberstam writes, "While the film on some level attempts to direct all kinds of social criticisms at urban planners, historians, and racist white homeowners, ultimately the horror stabilizes in the ghastly body of the black man whose monstrosity turns upon his desire for the white woman."[12] According to Halberstam's reading, the film's surface acknowledgment of relevant social problems masks its pervasive racism: "No amount of elaborate framing within this film can prevent it from confirming racist assumptions about black male aggression towards white female bodies." While this is true, what may even be more suppressed is the fact that *Candyman* is less a film about the implications of being haunted than about the superior privilege of transforming oneself into the haunter, now from the external standpoint of liberal empathy. If the traditional horror film ultimately posits fear as a cachet for its white middle-class victims, *Candyman*'s protagonist seems to want to reverse this dynamic by reclaiming the originating fear of the killer, as if to offer proof of her distance from the victim control group. In the passage from victim to victimizer, Helen's self-mythologization as a female Candyman is perhaps an attempt to rectify the originating supplantation of the Freddy/Jason figure's fear, by putting herself in his role.

Helen's insertion of herself within the myth she creates exposes the disparity of her sources. Like Frankenstein's monster, her fantasy is patched together from elements particular to each version of the story. The British professor's influence is detected in the presentation of Candyman as a noble yet suffering prince. Recalling the maimed hero of a Brontë novel, he is a tragic figure who intimidates while generating pity. Tall, handsome, eloquent, and clad in a fur-trimmed black cape, Helen's Candyman speaks in a Romanticist vernacular, demanding "one exquisite kiss" and seductively repeating the refrain, "Be my victim." This literary paradigm is most pronounced when Helen translates the Candyman legend into a domestic melodrama. In this version of the story, Helen wanders into Candyman's lair in a trancelike state. His chamber, entered through a series of tunnels, exists deep within the structure of Cabrini-Green, again recalling the house-behind-the-house motif of the Gothic genre. She hesitantly approaches Candyman's peacefully sleeping form to sentimentalized piano music. When he awakes and states, "Helen, you came to me," her eyelids flutter as the camera goes into a soft-focused shot of her face. As if in a swoon, Helen's body goes limp as Candyman pronounces, "Surrender to me now." Alternating between their two profiles, the camera spins dizzily, suggesting their engagement in a dance. Candyman then lifts Helen into his arms and carries her to a raised platform resembling both an altar and a bed.

In this scene, sexual seduction is conflated with the lure of self-mythologization. Helen is equally enticed by Candyman's physicality and by his promises of immortality through the transmission of a narrative: "Our names will be written on a thousand walls.Our crimes told and retold by our faithful believers." The equivalence established between mythic inscription and sexuality is emphasized by the juxtaposition of Candyman's erotic caresses with his prophetic statement, "We shall die together in front of their very eyes and give them something to be haunted by....Come with me and be immortal." With the implied consummation scene that follows, Helen and Candyman seem to be re-enacting every step of the professor's postbellum narrative. The scene thus appropriately closes with Helen reading the words, "IT WAS ALWAYS YOU HELEN," presumably scrawled on the wall by Candyman, and staring into the painted eyes of what appears to be her nineteenth-century counterpart: the woman impregnated by the son of an ex-slave. This marks a mirror stage in Helen's consciousness, a moment at which she clearly identifies with an image construed as a more complete and satisfying, *legendary* version of herself. The cathartic identification is enhanced by the camera's alternation between her real eyes and those of the ideal image.

For Helen to install herself within the postbellum myth legitimately, however, she cannot position herself as a desiring agent. By definition, myths cannot be autobiographical, as they are atemporal and transhistorical narratives. As the Ovidian tradition illustrates, myths about ordinary mortals require either their self-effacement or transformation. In their encounters with the gods, human beings only gain mythological status by turning into things: a tree, nightingale, flower, or, in Helen's case, a portrait. To reach this inanimate state, she must thus reconceptualize her role in the Gothic story by turning what initially seems to be sexual pleasure into the disgust and pain accompanying acts of martyrdom. She positions herself as partaking in a shameful, self-sacrificial bargain, in which she promises to "surrender" herself to Candyman in exchange for the missing baby's life.

HELEN: The child. We had a deal.

CANDYMAN: Surrender to me now, and he shall be unharmed. (*Helen appears to acquiesce by swooning into his arms.*)

CANDYMAN: We have a bargain.

This exchange of vows immediately before Candyman takes Helen to
the bed/altar suggests an unsanctified form of union, a marriage
ceremony without a presiding authority or priest. In the absence of the
mediating figure guaranteeing the social validity of their alliance, the
relation between Helen and Candyman is made to reflect the
illegitimacy of miscegenation in the original story. It shares the
ambiguity of an equivocal pregnancy, which the professor's story seems
to imply was the result of a rape. In this manner, Helen's conflicting
responses to Candyman could be read as a way for her both to access
the prohibited object of desire, as well as keep him as the racist
stereotype of a black rapist. While a handsome prince, Candyman
remains a threatening assaulter.

While Helen assimilates the professor's narrative into her private version of the Candyman myth by structuring it as a family Gothic, she also
draws from the teenager's kitsch narrative. The romantic imagery of the
former is abruptly dispelled by Helen's apparition as a Freddy Krueger
figure in Trevor's bathroom, after he performs the requisite incantation
by repeating her name in front of the mirror. Once she has gleefully disemboweled him with her hook, Helen's husband is discovered by his
teenage girlfriend, who screams uncontrollably while clutching a
kitchen knife. This almost comic scene pays its respects to the eighties
horror/slasher genre, in which terror almost always takes the form of
kitsch. Helen even utters a Freddy Kruegeresque one-liner when she
quips, "What's the matter, Trevor? Scared of something?" Likewise, referring to the genre's common sequencing of sex followed by graphic
violence, Helen orgasmically moans while ripping her hook through
Trevor's body. The openendedness of this concluding scene prepares us
to anticipate *Candyman II*,[13] establishing yet another alliance with the
slasher film tradition through its dependence on the sequel.

The closing credits of the film are accompanied by an image of Helen
as a martyred saint, complete with halo of fire around her head, painted
on the wall behind the altar at Cabrini-Green. The camera's slow zoom
onto the painted figure's face reverses the conventional dreamer/dream
shot sequence as evinced in the opening scenes. Once again, Helen's
face, this time in its mythical form, seems to claim the preceding events
as if they had been projected from her consciousness at the beginning. In
switching us back to the Gothic environment of family melodrama from
the teenage kitsch narrative, the film suggests that the legend produced
and controlled by Helen's consciousness is a merger of highbrow literary romance and the cult horror movie. This amalgamation of high and

low elements is reinforced by the manner in which the architecture of the nineteenth-century Gothic revival is internalized within a contemporary public housing project; even featuring "stained glass" comprised of graffiti written over windows.

In her full assumption of both the guilt and glory of the Candyman legends, Helen recalls Eve in **Paradise Lost**, who similarly proclaims herself the central protagonist of Milton's narrative by an admission of culpability that situates her as the only possible redeemer of the Fall: "All by me is lost,/Such favor I unworthy am vouchsafed,/By me the Promised Seed shall all restore."[14] Helen strategically deploys white liberal guilt to access the space of the other and install herself as both savior and culprit. As if unsatisfied with the marginal position allocated to the heroine in the professor's tale, she must assume both her role and that of Candyman, whose status as suffering hero earned *him* immortal fame. Substituting her own martyrdom for his, her maneuver recalls that of the heroine of Craven's *Nightmare*, who can only consider her victory against Freddy Krueger complete once she has positioned herself as ultimately responsible for his existence as well as his downfall. As Nancy informs Freddy at the end of the film, "I know you too well....I take back all the energy I gave you. You're nothing, you're shit." Similarly, in *Friday the Thirteenth,* Alice cannot emerge unscathed from the massacre at Camp Crystal Lake without having committed an equally gruesome act herself: decapitating the serial killer with an ax. As the sole figure able to defeat the horrific monster, Alice occupies the subject position Carol Clover describes as "Final Girl," while also constituting herself as both victim and perpetrator. Survival in the slasher film is thus already predicated on the haunted's identification with the haunter. Taking this necessary condition one step further, Helen colonizes the latter position completely. Upstaging Candyman's status in both the literary and the kitsch narratives, she edges out her competitor by appropriating his hook, his name, and his violence.

By using the Final Girl scenario as a vehicle for her initiation into the lineage of canonical haunters, Helen revises the position of the female heroine in the conventional slasher film. Referring to this teenage prototype, Clover writes:

> The one character of stature who does live to tell the tale is in fact the Final Girl. She is introduced at the beginning and is the only character to be developed in any psychological detail. We understand immediately from the attention paid it that hers is the main story line. She is intelligent, watchful, levelheaded; the first character to sense something amiss and the only one to deduce from

the accumulating evidence the pattern and extent of the
threat; the only one, in other words, whose perspective
approaches our own privileged understanding of the
situation. We register her horror as she stumbles on the
corpses of her friends. Her momentary paralysis in the face
of death duplicates those moments of the universal
nightmare experience—in which she is the undisputed
"I"—on which horror frankly trades. When she downs the
killer, we are triumphant. She is by any measure the
slasher film's hero. This is not to say that our attachment to
her is exclusive and unremitting, only that it adds up, and
that in the closing sequence (which can be quite
prolonged) it is very close to absolute.[15]

The "privileged understanding" available to the Final Girl as haunted is
compounded in *Candyman* by Helen's added privilege of having taken
over the role of haunter, as if to reclaim the property rights of the
haunter which had been suppressed in the conventional horror movie.
More than just living to tell the tale, she ultimately *is* the tale.

The imaginary relation Helen constructs between herself and the inhabitants of Cabrini-Green brings to mind the failed reciprocity in Hegel's master/slave dynamic, in which the master relies on the slave to
produce an image of his own identity. In claiming the new privilege of
being the haunter, through the liberal stance of empathetic identification
with the Other, as well as the prior privilege of being the haunted, Helen
bridges and subsumes both roles within her consciousness. So much is
at stake for her in trying to assume the slave's position that she literally
has to move into Cabrini-Green, the site where she has determined the
myth belongs, as if following the ghost she initially expelled from Lincoln Village. In her last visit to Cabrini-Green, this time without the me-
diation of the highway, she wears a polyester uniform stolen from a
nurse during her escape from the mental institution. This uniform connects her to the only person from the projects with whom she truly interacts; the single mother of the missing baby, who wears a similar
garment. In fantasy, Helen finally achieves the vestmental inconspi-
ciousness she sought on her first visit to the projects, this time successfully assimilating into the environment of Cabrini-Green and thereby
positioning herself as entitled to the property shared by its inhabitants.

Helen's desire to eradicate the social barrier that the highway represents marks her ultimate belief in what she had initially sought to dis-
prove: the supposed mythmaking of the residents of Cabrini-Green.
Revising the terms of Hegel's dialectic, Helen constructs a myth for the
slave that can now be believed by the master. Whereas in Hegel's original scenario the slave fully comprehends the master while remaining in-

comprehensible to him, Helen's imposition of the white Candyman legend onto the project's inhabitants eliminates the one aspect of power the
slave maintains. By revising her own belief system to correspond to
what she believed the Cabrini-Green inhabitants to believe, Helen sacrifices her privileged social position to participate in what she has turned
into the slave's myth. The master thus gains the territory of knowledge
or psychological property previously demarcated as the slave's. Occu-
pying the stance of the former, Helen's production of myth allows her to
claim an understanding of the slave far superior to his understanding of
the master or himself.

In its attempt to surpass the horror film's standard collapse of the barrier between the imaginary and the real, *Candyman* tries to eliminate social distinctions as well. While the film purports to subvert binary
oppositions, its agenda appears less to undermine the difference between white middle-class mythologies and those of the economically
disempowered than to force the former onto the latter, subsuming the
marginal into the category of the privileged term. This suggests that the
horror film ultimately may be an inadequate vehicle for addressing the
issues *Candyman* wants to address, despite Rose's innovative attempt to
revive the genre for the 1990s, accommodating the post-Reagan/Bush
era's greater investment in social awareness. Perhaps to succeed in this
politically conscious endeavor, the horror film would have to accept its
own annihilation, since, as *Candyman* demonstrates, belief in social reality murders myth. This paradox is already incorporated within the film
in the form of a newspaper headline read by Helen during her preliminary research of the murders at Cabrini-Green. "What Killed Ruthie
Jean? Life in the Projects." In response to the formulaic question asked
by all horror films, *What* killed X?, Helen ignores the answer already
provided by the headline to create her own answer. Like its heroine,
Rose's film must begin dreaming at the exact point at which reality
strikes it in the face, losing itself in the madness of its hybrid mythology.

Notes

1. Douglas Kellner, "Poltergeists, Gender, and Class in the Age of Reagan and
   Bush," *The Hidden Foundation: Cinema and the Question of Class*, eds.
   David E. James and Rick Berg (Minneapolis: University of Minnesota Press,
   1996) 217.

2. William Julius Wilson, "The Truly Disadvantaged: The Hidden Agenda,"
   Readings in Urban Theory, eds. Susan Fainstein and Scott Campbell (Cambridge: Blackwell Publishers, 1996) 194.

3. Manning Marable, *Speaking Truth to Power: Essays on Race, Resistance,
   and Radicalism* (Boulder: Westview Press, 1996) 103.

4. Cited in Robert Halpern, *Rebuilding the Inner City: A History of Neighborhood Initiatives to Address Poverty in the United States* (New York: Columbia University Press, 1995) 79.

5. Witold Rybczynski, *City Life: Urban Expectations in a New World* (New York: Scribner, 1995) 166. As Rybczynski writes, "Television journalists drew parallels with violence-ridden Sarajevo. This sounds far-fetched, but I was struck by how much the bleak background the television reporters did indeed resemble a war zone The littered expanse of bare earth, the abandoned cars and broken windows, the battered apartment blocks with walls covered in graffiti and piles of garbage in the corridors."

6. Vera Dika, "The Stalker Film, 1978-81," *American Horrors: Essays on the Modern American Horror Film*, ed. Gregory A. Waller (Urbana: University of Illinois Press, 1987) 93.

7. Carol Clover, *Men, Women, and Chain Saws: Gender in the Modern Horror Film* (Princeton: Princeton University Press, 1992) 31.

8. Alex Kotlowitz, *There Are No Children Here: The Story of Two Boys Growing Up in the Other America* (New York: Anchor Books, 1992) 25.

9. Marable 53.

10. Rybczynski 165-66.

11. Rybczynski 164-65.

12. Judith Halberstam, *Skin Shows: Gothic Horror and the Technology of Monsters* (Durham: Duke University Press, 1995) 5.

13. Incidentally, *Candyman: Farewell to the Flesh* was directed by Bill Condon in 1995. In this sequel, Candyman (Tony Todd) returns to haunt the descendants of the landowner responsible for his murder during their Mardi Gras celebration in New Orleans.

14. John Milton, *Paradise Lost*, Book 12, *The Norton Anthology of English Literature*, fifth edition, volume 1 (New York: W.W. Norton & Company, 1986) 1590.

15. Clover 45.

Above, Theo (Claire Bloom) and Eleanor (Julie Harris) share a moment of terror in **The Haunting**.

The Haunting and the Power of Suggestion: Why Robert Wise's Film Continues to "Deliver the Goods" to Modern Audiences

Pam Keesey

> I've had any number of people over the years say to me, "You know, Mr. Wise, you made the scariest picture I've ever seen and you never showed anything. How'd you do it?" And it goes back to Val Lewton, by the powers of suggestion.
>
> Robert Wise in *Fearing the Dark: The Val Lewton Career*

When I first saw the preview for Jan de Bont's 1999 production of *The Haunting*, I was both skeptical and excited. Why, I thought, would anyone tamper with a film (directed by Robert Wise in 1963 and a film I still consider to be one of my favorites) as compelling as the original? At the same time, I was excited by the possibility that, in this more liberal day and age, many of the complexities of Shirley Jackson's novel would finally find their way to the big screen. And so, it was with mixed feelings that I anticipated the release of this high-tech, big-budget extravaganza.

Not surprisingly, although much to my dismay, I saw the film and was greatly disappointed. Then again, the film (according to its producers) was never intended to be a remake. With a cache of special effects technology in hand, executive producer Steven Spielberg felt the need "travel the road not taken by Wise" and "deliver the goods for modern audiences."[1]

Spielberg isn't alone in his belief that modern audiences are waiting for "the goods" to be delivered. Stephen King, although he admires the Wise film, has also commented on the lack of a monster: "Something is scratching at that ornate, paneled door," writes King, "something horrible...but it is a door Wise elects never to open." King acknowledges his disapproval of this method, the decision to "let the door bulge but...never open it," a tactic King refers to as "playing to tie rather than to win."[2]

Spielberg and de Bont do open the door and all manner of computer-generated ghosts and goblins come flying over the threshold. Unfortunately, the story also took the nearest exit and left us with a film that, more than anything, highlights the prowess of Wise's filmmaking and reinforces my belief that the key to supernatural storytelling—whether on-screen or on the page—is the power of suggestion.

The complexity of Robert Wise's filmmaking, his attention to detail and his incredible skill as a storyteller, editor, cinematographer and director, are exemplary. It is this complexity that raises Wise's films from the level of the works of a skilled craftsman—the director who worked his way up from the mail room, so to speak—to the oeuvres of a artisan of the highest level.

Wise was among the last of directors to be brought up through the studio system. He began his work in Hollywood as a film porter whose responsibility it was to carry prints up to the projection booth for the executives to watch and to check them afterward for damage. From there, Wise moved on first to sound editing, story editing and film editing before trying his hand at directing. At various stages in his career, Wise worked with a variety of directors, not the least of whom were Orson Welles and Garson Kanin. In addition to his work with some of the most notable directors in Hollywood history, Wise also excelled in the field. Altogether, his films have been nominated for 67 Academy Awards and 19 Oscars. Wise himself was nominated for seven Academy Awards, eventually winning four Oscars, two each for West Side Story and Sound of Music.

It was during the final stages of the production of West Side Story that Wise, inspired by a favorable review, picked up a copy of Shirley Jackson's The Haunting of Hill House. In an interview Wise recalled, "I was reading one of the very scary passages—hackles were going up and down my neck—when Nelson Gidding [the screenwriter]...burst through the door to ask me a question. I literally jumped about three feet out of my chair. I said, 'If it can do that to me sitting and reading, it ought to be something I want to make a picture out of.'"[3] And make a picture he did.

Jackson's novel reminded Wise of his early days with producer Val Lewton and Lewton's brand of psychological horror. Lewton was hired by RKO in 1942 to produce a series of low-budget psychological thrillers. He set the tone for his new series with Cat People (1942), followed by I Walked with a Zombie (1943) and The Leopard Man (1943). With these films, Lewton established a standard for "literate and subtle explorations into man's fear of the unknown."[4] Wise cut his directorial teeth on Lewton productions. His first opportunity to direct came when he was chosen to replace Gunther von Fritsch, the original director of *The Curse of the Cat People* half way through filming.

Wise had long wanted to make a film in honor of his mentor and Jackson's novel seemed the perfect vehicle. Lewton's distinct style and how it influenced those who worked with him is aptly described by Edmund G. Bansak in *Fearing the Dark: The Val Lewton Career*:

> Lewton trademarks—the reverence for the underdog, the focus upon humanist concerns, the alliance between danger and darkness, the depiction of fate as an unstoppable force, and, of course, the preoccupation with things unseen—permeate the postwar films of all three directors. In addition, other Lewton film characteristics, those of content (negative forces, doomed characters, ambiguity, paranoia, deception, predestination, nihilism, death) and of form (expressionistic interplay of light and dark, meticulous multilayered soundtracks, literate scripts, dynamic compositions, understated performances), seemed to have filtered into the respective works of Tourneur, Robson, and Wise.[5]

There is a lot of resonance between Lewton's work and Jackson's style of psychological suspense. Jack Sullivan in *The Penguin Encyclopedia of Horror and the Supernatural* writes:

> [T]he depiction of intense loneliness and mental disturbance in an ambiguously supernatural context became Jackson's trademark. Reversing M.R. James's dictum that a ghost story should leave a narrow "loophole" for a natural explanation, Jackson wrote stories of psychological anguish that leave a loophole for a supernatural explanation. The supernatural is a final dark corner in the desolate room where Jackson's isolated protagonists, usually women, find themselves.[6]

In *The Haunting of Hill House*, we see many qualities reminiscent of Lewton's characteristic style, not the least of which are the aforementioned "negative forces, doomed characters, ambiguity, paranoia, deception, predestination, nihilism, and death." Jackson, however, was rather more misanthropic than Lewton. There is no underdog in Jackson's novel, despite the use of Eleanor as a point of view character, and Jackson's characterizations focus more upon human frailties than humanistic concerns.

Taking advantage of the similarities in tone and atmosphere between Jackson and Lewton, Wise deliberately developed the characters in a more Lewtonesque style. Despite the differences in plot development and characterization, Wise managed to create a Lewton homage that was also faithful to Jackson's novel. Nelson Gidding, who wrote the screenplay for *The Haunting*, says of Wise, "He is a storyteller par excellence; one who translates into purely cinematic terms the stories of others that he makes his own."[7] Jackson was apparently pleased with the results, feeling that "the movie retained the original atmosphere of the book."[8]

Although Jackson's characters are all misfits, each very self-centered in his or her own way, Wise and Gidding choose to emphasize Eleanor's outcast qualities, giving her a sympathetic edge and thereby creating the "underdog" of Lewton fame. Theo, a lesbian in both the novel and the movie, is given more of an edge in the film, becoming a foil for Eleanor and further establishing Eleanor's status as a persecuted innocent. Luke becomes less brooding and more carefree, while Dr. Markway (Dr. Montague in the novel) is much less self-conscious about his outsider status within scholarly circles as a research scientist primarily interested in the paranormal.

The house, described in the novel as "diseased" and "not sane," remains essentially the same. Hill House, we are told, is not merely haunted. It is the haunt. In addition to its history of death, decay and suicide, Hill House is visually disorienting to the beholder. "It had an

Below, the assembled protagonists seem to be enveloped by the house.

unbelievably faulty design which left it chillingly wrong in all its dimensions," writes Jackson, "so that the walls seemed always in one direction a fraction longer than the eye could endure, and in another direction a fraction less than the barest possible length."[9]Wise (who was shooting the film in Panavision) called the president of Panavision in search of a wider-angle lens than was commercially available at the time. "We have developed a 30mm, but it's not ready for use yet," was the reply. "It's got a lot of distortion in it."[10] Wise immediately accepted it. The distortion resulting from this prototype lens helped to create the atmosphere of Hill House. In Wise's words, "I want[ed] the house to look almost alive." It is the awareness of this house as a living, breathing entity that establishes the atmosphere of the rest of the film.

The film opens with a long shot of Hill House. The house--actually a 700-year-old manor not far from Stratford-Upon-Avon, England--was, in Wise's words, "a pretty horrifying-looking thing,"[11] a look Wise accentuated with the use of infra-red film. "An evil old house, the kind some people called haunted," begins the voice-over, "is like an undiscovered country waiting to be explored." With these words and the discordant accompaniment of brass and cymbals, the viewer is introduced to the tainted history of Hill House and the disorientation begins.

Wise is a master filmmaker, and his unique and dynamic style is apparent from the beginning. From the victim's eye-view of the upset carriage that killed Hugh Craine's first wife, her hand falling lifeless across the screen, to the tumbling camerawork that gives us the vision of his second wife's final moments, to the visual descent of the spiral staircase after the companion's suicide, Wise establishes the camera itself as the primary tool in his cache of special effects.

The narrative voice of the opening montage, we discover, is Dr. Markway himself. Markway is discussing his desire to rent Hill House with Mrs. Sannerson and her lawyer. Once Mrs. Sannerson accedes to giving Mr. Markway his lease, we are shown a shot of Markway working on a shortlist of names, people who have "all been involved before, in one way or another, with the abnormal." With Markway's checkmark next to the name of Eleanor Lance, we are introduced to our point of view character for the rest of the film.

The argument between Eleanor, her sister and her brother-in-law is as jarring as the rather saccharine, carnivalesque music that accompanies the scene. It is only when Eleanor banishes the others from her "bedroom" and suddenly stops the music by removing the needle from the record that we realize that the music is not incidental. The music exists in stark contrast to the rather disconcerting family dynamics and to Eleanor's shift in tone from begging for the use of the car to her angry outburst at the entire family. This use of a multi-layered soundtrack—dialogue over music or multiple tracks of dialogue at any given moment—is very characteristic of Val Lewton and a technique Wise uses to great effect.

When Eleanor takes the car without permission, we are introduced to Eleanor's inner world—her fantasies, her hopes, her desires—and she is established as our narrative voice throughout the rest of the film. She is desperate, and we experience the first faint twinges of desperation on her behalf. She surprises us, however, with a rather aggressive action that belies her otherwise passive and desperate demeanor by gunning the engine after Mr. Dudley finally opens the gates and allows her entrance onto the grounds of Hill House. "You seem to be the one who's afraid," she says with a giggle.

Eleanor's first view of the house is as disconcerting to the viewer as it is to Eleanor. Several quick edits between differing angles of the house and Eleanor's face establish not only discontinuity for the viewer (are we looking at Eleanor or at the house?), but also for Eleanor. "It's staring at me," she says. And, by way of Wise's editing, we know that it is.

This sense that the house is watching Nell is reinforced by Wise's excellent camera work. As she bends to pick up her suitcase, she sees her own image reflected in the polished wood floor. As she follows Mrs. Dudley up the stairs, she is again startled by her own image, this time reflected in an unexpected mirror on the wall half-way up the stairs. Eleanor's reference to being "scared of your own shadow" is apt as it is Eleanor who lives in constant fear of her shadow self, the one who may or may not have chosen to let her mother die only two months earlier.

The repetition of eyes, faces, and reflections—subtle images worked into scenes by Wise reinforce the feeling that Eleanor, indeed everyone, is being watched. From the momentary flash of the fish's eye that cuts from the before dinner drinks to the dinner scene, to the plethora of faces that appear in Theo's room when she and Eleanor are hovering in fear from the noise in the hall (in the opening sequence, Wise superimposes a cherub's face over the stairway; Eleanor watches her and Theo's reflection in a mirror across from the bed; the door knob—in the shape of a cherub's face—being turned by some unseen source, the gargoyle on the wall), the imagery is constantly reinforcing the feeling that the house is watching every step, every movement, every breath.

Mrs. Dudley--a grand dame of the housekeeping tradition on par with the unforgettable Mrs. Danvers of *Rebecca*--ushers Eleanor into her room. "I'm like a small creature swallowed whole by a monster, and the monster feels my tiny movements inside," Eleanor intones as the camera swallows her in a sweeping shot beginning at the ceiling and looking

Above, Eleanor turns away as the others probe the secret beyond the door.

down at the awkward Eleanor encircling her as it moves down and across, sweeping back to shoot Eleanor from underneath. She has been swallowed, completely engulfed by the house. The use of overhead shots and the frequent use of them in scenes with Eleanor strengthen our perception of Eleanor as the object of the house's (and of the viewer's) gaze.

This connection between Eleanor and Hill House is further reinforced in a scene moments later when Eleanor and Theo are lost in the maze-like hallways of Hill House. Eleanor feels a presence, one Theo isn't aware of until, perhaps able to sense Eleanor's awareness by virtue of her ESP, Eleanor calls attention to it. "It wants you, Nell," says Theo, "The house is calling you." Every step of the way, Wise makes us aware of Eleanor's kinship with the house, even if the viewer isn't consciously aware of the careful manipulation of story, sound, and point of view shots to establish this kinship.

The viewer's identification with Eleanor is built through Wise's construction of Eleanor as the underdog of the film. It is clear from the moment Eleanor enters Theo's room for the first time that she is out of her league. Claire Bloom as Theodora, complete in fashions by Mary Quant, is a cut above the average, a stylish, worldly and accomplished woman in stark contrast to the shy, mousy, and sheltered Eleanor. This contrast is reinforced by Eleanor's often humorous but self-deprecating remarks such as "It's Theo who's wearing velvet, so I must be Eleanor in tweed."

Theo's hostility begins at the first signs of affinity between Dr. Markway and Eleanor. Markway's kind yet innocent words to Eleanor are met with sour looks and harsh tones from Theo. This hostility becomes more and more pronounced as the story develops. Is Theo jealous of Markway's attention to Eleanor? Does she want to be the center of attention, or does she resent the deflection of Eleanor's attention from her to Markway? Or is it a disdainful pity she belies as she witnesses Eleanor's growing devotion to a married man? Interesting questions to pose, and an interesting dynamic that helps to build discord between characters, although they are ultimately questions that go unanswered.

Eleanor's awkwardness, her self-doubt and her fear of her own abilities are beautifully demonstrated when Eleanor, having denied her connection to any paranormal or psychic behavior, resorts to a self-conscious and defensive outburst even after the others have moved on to another conversation. "That was the neighbors! They threw the rocks!" Eleanor blames the outburst on the stress caused by her mother's death two months earlier and Theo, her ESP in high gear, is immediately aware that Eleanor was relieved, not sorry, when her mother died—relieved but also extremely anxious and guilt-ridden.

Wise continues to build the tension between characters and for the viewer with his use of dissonance. The foursome, having finished dinner, are relaxing in the parlor. Luke and Theo are playing a "friendly" game of Gin when Luke's outburst startles Eleanor. Wise's use of the multilayered soundtrack in these scenes—all four characters speaking at once and in agitated tones of voice—builds the tension even further, leaving us somewhat startled at the silence following Eleanor's scream.

Wise's mastery of sound--a skill honed over years as a sound editor-- is at work throughout the whole of the film, but there are few scenes where it is more apparent than the scene which takes place the first night. A quiet has descended over Hill House. The sound—a not-gentle pounding—increases in volume and vigor, an unexplained noise reminiscent not only of Eleanor's mother's death, but also the death of Abigail Craine. The sound is moving, as though traversing the halls of the house in search of something—or someone. The feeling that the house—or something in the house—is searching for Eleanor is strengthened by the subtle turning of the doorknob—the face that looks at Eleanor and Theo as they cower in the four-poster bed—and the heavy panting followed by a maniacal laughter.

The fear that Eleanor and Theo feel turns quickly to a nervous giddiness when they realize it's all over and realize that Luke and Markway are completely unaware of the chaos that reigned only moments before their arrival. The laughter that erupts from both Eleanor's and Theo's throats mirrors the ghostly laughter that accompanies the terrific pounding at the door. Markway, aware of the oddity of the experience, becomes suspicious. Markway's cautious speculation "Wouldn't you say that something, somehow is trying to separate us?" is followed, as many other scenes have been, with a cutaway to Hill House itself.

The next morning, the house asserts its claim to Eleanor. Her delight in her awareness that finally something is happening to her is abruptly cut short by Luke's revelation of the mysterious message bearing Eleanor's name. Eleanor, recently aglow with the excitement of the events of the night before (an indication, Markway warns Eleanor, that she has "fallen under the spell of Hill House") is frightened. "It knows my name!" she cries. The message is our first indication that the house, perhaps, is falling under Eleanor's spell.

"Help Eleanor come home Eleanor" reads the message. The intimacy of the message and the intimacy of the moment is made tangible by the fact that the message appears on the wall in the hallway. Wise, aware of the power of the moment, has all four characters huddling in the narrow hallway to view the message, a message the viewer can only see parts of at a time. Eleanor's feeling of being threatened, being cornered by the house, is portrayed in the claustrophobic environment constructed on the set of Hill House.

Below, Theo (Claire Bloom), Luke (Russ Tamblyn) and Dr. Markway (Richard Johnson) hang back as Eleanor (Julie Harris) enters a room apprehensively.

Eleanor eventually enters into an intimate exchange with the Hill House by way of her imaginary dance with Hugh Crain, a brief dance that results in quiet humming, the rise of the wind and the slamming of the door. The house, "vile" and "hideous", both attracts and repels Eleanor. She is, after all, the "main attraction" and Eleanor is dizzy with the elation of being the center of attention. She has no one—and no place—of her own. The attention heaped upon her by the house, and by the others as a result, is the only attention she's ever known.

The house continues to reach out to Eleanor. That night, after a spat with Theo, Eleanor is awakened by a man's voice and a woman's laughter. A face forms in the pattern on the wall and Eleanor, very frightened, speaks up and asks Theo to take hold of her hand. Her grip becomes tighter and tighter, compelling Eleanor to warn "Theo, you're breaking my hand!" When Eleanor cries out, Theo is immediately awakened. That's when Eleanor, along with the viewer, realizes that somehow Eleanor has moved to the couch across the room and it was not Theo who was holding her hand. "Whose hand was I holding?" asks Eleanor, and once again there is a cutaway to the house itself.

Eleanor's isolation is reinforced by the arrival of Grace, Markway's wife. Displaced now that his attention is focused on his wife rather than on her, and threatened by displacement now that Mrs. Markway is sleeping in the nursery, the heart of Hill House, whose doors have mysteriously opened to allow her to enter. "She's taken my place," Eleanor fears. "I'm the one it really wants."

Anxious of what might take place, Markway moves everyone—except his wife, who is intent on staying in the nursery, and Luke who is to take turns with Markway in watching over her—to the parlor. Luke sneaks down to the nursery to get a nightcap when the door slams, trapping everyone inside. The door does indeed bulge and there is, without question, something on the other side. (In this case, it is a strong prop man leaning against a door made of many layers of varnished wood to give the impression that the door is elastic at the hands of some unseen force.12) But Wise resists the temptation to show us what it is on the other side. He deliberately chooses to not open the door.

By the time Eleanor's car collides with the tree, Wise, who has carefully constructed our experience at each and every turn, has us so tied up in Eleanor's experience of the house that we feel deeply that she has, at last, come home to Hill House. "Journeys end in lovers meeting."

This film, so filled with layers of imagery, meaningful exchanges, and depth of story, is so carefully constructed that the movie flows almost effortlessly from beginning to end. The monster of Hill House—is it the house? Hugh Craine? Abigail? Theo? Eleanor herself?—is never brought to light. The complex interplay of personality and experience, of light and sound, of circumstance and setting—these are the monsters of Hill House. It is a feeling of horror that the viewer carries away from this film, a heightened awareness of the feeling of being watched, of unexplained sounds, of faces in the patterns of the wall, all experiences we ourselves have had and fears each one of us has confronted at one time or another.

Spielberg, Self and de Bont, by determining the monster of Hill House in their remake, by naming the monster Hugh Craine and giving him the shape and form of a CGI ghost, lose the subtle complexity that makes Wise's version of *The Haunting* such a richly disturbing experience. In focusing so much attention on the technology of the effect and not the effect of the technology, Spielberg, Self and de Bont lost track of the essential core of the viewer's experience. Without the proper set up, the monster behind the door isn't really all that scary after all.

Perhaps the tide is changing. Perhaps the popularity of films such as *Blair Witch Project* and *The Sixth Sense* indicates a return to the psychology of fear rather than the complexity of the special effect in fantastic filmmaking. The remake of *The Haunting* and its failure to measure up to Wise's original reminds us that, despite the rapid development of special effects technology and the untapped potential of this new resource, special effects need to be a tool in the service of storytelling and not the story itself.

Notes

1. Jensen, Jeff. "A Shiver Runs Through It." *Entertainment Weekly*. July 23, 1999. p.22+.

2. King, Stephen. *Danse Macabre*. Everest House, 1981.

3. Leeman, Sergio. *Robert Wise on His Films: From Editing Room to Director's Chair*. Silman-James Press. 1995.

4. Bansak, Edumnd G. *Fearing the Dark: The Val Lewton Career*. MacFarland & Co., 1995.

5. Bansak.

6, Sullivan, Jack. *The Penguin Encyclopedia of Horror and the Supernatural*. Viking Press, 1986.

7. Leeman.

8. Friedman, Lenemaja. *Shirley Jackson*. Twayne Publishers, 1975.

9. Jackson, Shirley. *The Haunting of Hill House*. Penguin Books, 1959.

10. Leeman.

11. Leeman.

Above, Dr. Van Helsing (Anthony Hopkins) closely inspects his subject in **Bram Stoker's Dracula**.

Notes on Contributors

Aviva Briefel and **Sianne Ngai** are collaborating on a book on the development of the American horror film in the early nineties. Their essay in this volume originally appeared in *Camera Obscura*.

Linda Brookover has written on a variety of subjects for *oneWorld*, an on-line magazine which she co-edited; has created electonic learning aids for Disney and Tomy; and also works as a focus group moderator and educator. She has contributed essays to *Film Noir Reader*, *Film Noir Reader 2*, and *the Noir Style* and co-wrote the screenplay for the Showtime feature *Time at the Top*.

Madeleine Cahill is an Assistant Professor of Communication at Westfield State College in Westfield, Massachusetts. Her primary research interests are in the portrayals of marginalized women in Hollywood film.

Ian Conrich is a Lecturer in Media and Cultural Studies at Nottingham Trent University. He has contributed to *Sight and Sound*, and the *Journal of Popular British Cinema* and he is the author of *Yakov Protazanov's Aelita* (I.B. Tauris, forthcoming) and co-editor of *The Films of John Carpenter* (Flicks Books, forthcoming). He has written on horror and fantasy for the following recent publications: *The British Cinema Book* (BFI, 1997), *Liberal Directions: Basil Dearden and Postwar British Film Culture* (Flicks Books, 1997), *A Handbook to Gothic Literature* (Macmillan, 1998), *British Science Fiction Cinema* (Routledge, 1999) and *The Modern Fantastic: The Films of David Cronenberg* (Flicks Books, 1999).

Raymond Durgnat is currently Visiting Professor at the University of East London, Docklands, and sometime Head of History of Art at the St. Martin's School of Art. He has previously taught at Dartmouth College, the University of California at Los Angeles, Berkeley, and San Diego, Columbia College New York, and the Royal College of Art and has lectured on aesthetics in Italy, India, Finland, and New Zealand. His articles have appeared in *The London Times, The Independent, Film Comment, Cinema* (U.K.), and *Positif*. His books include *The Crazy Mirror, Eros in the Cinema, Jean Renoir, Buñuel, A Mirror for England, Sexual Alienation in the Cinema,* and (with Scott Simmon) *King Vidor, American*.

317

Glenn Erickson is the co-author of *The Making of 1941* (1980), on the production of which he also served as Coordinator of miniatures and other effects. He has also written program articles for *FILMEX*. He works primarily as a film and videotape editor whose credits include several independent features and was a long-time staff editor at MGM/UA.

Joan Hawkins is an Assistant Professor in the Department of Communication and Culture at Indiana University, Bloomington. Her articles have appeared in *Film Quarterly, The Hitchcock Annual, Scope*, and *Ons Erfdeel*. Her book, **Cutting Edge: Art Horror and the Horrific Avant-garde**, is forthcoming from University of Minnesota Press.

Pam Keesey has been a film enthusiast for as long as she can remember. She is the editor of three collections of short stories: **Daughters of Darkness; Dark Angels**; and **Women Who Run With the Werewolves**. Her most recent book is **Vamps: An Illustrated History of the Femme Fatale** [Cleis Press, 1996].

Tanya Krzywinska holds a PhD from University of North London and lectures in film at Brunel University in the UK. She has published work on horror and video-pornography, contributed extensively to *The Movie Book*, and is currently completing a book-length study of possession, witchcraft and voodoo in film to be published by Flicks Books in mid-2000. Her article is based on a chapter from this book.

Martin F. Norden is a Professor of Communication at the University of Massachusetts-Amherst. His articles have appeared in such journals as *Wide Angle, Film Criticism,* and *Paradoxa* and in numerous anthologies. He is the author of *The Cinema of Isolation: A History of Physical Disability in the Movies* (Rutgers, 1994) and maintains a home page at "http://wwwunix.oit.umass.edu/~norden."

Steven Schneider is working towards PhD degrees in Philosophy at Harvard University and in Cinema Studies at New York University's Tisch School of the Arts. His work on the horror genre appears in such journals as *Paradoxa, CineAction, Scope,* and *Post Script*. He has contributions forthcoming in **Violent Bodies: Extreme Film** (ed. Graeme Harper & Xavier Mendik, Creation Books) and **Drive-In Horrors** (ed. Gary Rhodes, McFarland & Co.). And he is the author of numerous entries on horror cinema in the *St. James Encyclopedia of Popular Culture* (1999). Currently, he is co-editing (with Richard Allen) a collection of essays on psychoanalysis and the horror film entitled **Freud's Worst Nightmares**.

Ad art from the classic period of American horror: Universal's **Dracula's Daughter** and RKO's **Cat People**.

Alain Silver wrote, co-wrote, or co-edited the other books listed in the front of this volume. Two of those books were derived from his graduate work at U.C.L.A.: his Master's thesis on Robert Aldrich and his doctoral dissertation on David Lean. Forthcoming from Hyperion is an interview book on feature film directors. Shorter pieces have appeared in *Film Comment, Movie, Literature/Film Quarterly, Wide Angle, Photon,* the *DGA Magazine,* the *Los Angeles Times,* and the on-line magazines *Images* and *oneWorld.* He has co-written two feature films (*Kiss Daddy Goodbye, Time at the Top*) and produced several others (*Beat, Palmer's Pick-up, Cyborg*[2]), as well as documentaries and music videos and over 50 soundtrack albums. More details are at "http://members.aol.com/alainsil."

James Ursini has previously co-authored with Alain Silver two studies of supernatural cinema: *More Things Than Are Dreamt Of* (1994) and *The Vampire Film* (3rd Edition, 1996). They also co-wrote many of the titles listed in the front of the book. He contributed articles to *Mediascene, Cinema* (U.S.), *Photon, Cinefantastique, Midnight Marquee,* and the *DGA Magazine.* He has produced Oral Histories and been a researcher for the American Film Institute and has also been associate producer and producer on feature films and documentaries for various school districts and public broadcasting. He has lectured on filmmaking at UCLA and other colleges and continues to work as an educator in Los Angeles.

Tony Williams is the co-author of *Italian Western: Opera of Violence* (1975), co-editor of *Vietnam War Films* (1994), and author of *Jack London: the Movies* (1992) and the forthcoming *Hearths of Darkness: the Family in the American Horror Film.* His essays have appeared in the anthologies *Making Television* (1990); *From Hanoi to Hollywood* and *Inventing Vietnam* (both 1991); *Fires Were Started: British Cinema and Thatcherism* and *Crisis Cinema* (both 1993); and *Re-viewing British Cinema, 1900-1992* (1994). He has also written articles for *CineAction, Film History, Jump Cut, Movie, Viet Nam Generation,* and *Wide Angle.* He is Associate Professor of Cinema Studies in the English department of Southern Illinois University at Carbondale.

Robin Wood, whose numerous books on motion pictures include seminal English-language *auteur* studies of Alfred Hitchcock, Howard Hawks, Ingmar Bergman, and Arthur Penn and most recently *Hollywood from Vietnam to Reagan,* is now writing fiction. He is a former Professor of Film Studies at Queen's College and York University and remains a founding member of the collective which edits the film journal *CineAction!*